NORRIS McWHIRTER'S
BOOK OF HISTORICAL RECORDS

NORRIS McWHIRTER'S
BOOK OF HISTORICAL RECORDS

The story of human achievement
in the last 2,000 years

Virgin

First published in Great Britain in 2000 by
Virgin Publishing Ltd
Thames Wharf Studios
Rainville Road
London W6 9HA

Distributed in the United States by
Sterling Publishing Co., Inc.
387 Park Avenue South
New York, NY 10016-8810

Distributed in Canada by
Sterling Publishing
c/o Canadian Manda Group
One Atlantic Avenue, Suite 105
Toronto
Ontario
Canada M6K 3E7

A catalogue record for this book is available from the British Library.

ISBN 1 85227 894 3

Picture research: Richard Philpott at Zooid Pictures Ltd
Text editing: Sue Harper, Charles Phillips
The author and publishers would like to thank Stanley Greenberg, Tessa McWhirter,
Peter J. Matthews, Trevor Morris, Joanna Norcross, Clare Richards and Christina
Rodenbeck for their valuable assistance in preparing this book for publication.

Design by Diane Meacham at Slatter-Anderson

Repro by Highlight Digital
Printed by Oriental Press, Dubai

As we look back over recent centuries of unprecedented and indeed accelerating progress, we must realize that while we can change our prospects for the future, we cannot truthfully rewrite the past. We can only learn its lessons if we have ready access to the facts. This volume is an updated, revised and expanded version of the *Book of Millennium Records*, published in October 1999. As with its predecessor, this is the fruit of more than 40 years of hunting in libraries, reading specialist periodicals and corresponding with experts.

The *Book of Historical Records* charts the unfolding of humankind's restless inventiveness in searching for better and newer ways to live over hundreds of millennia. In keeping with its title, this book treats records not simply as the extremes of this moment, but as progressive milestones or markers which chronicle how today's levels of attainment have been reached.

Each themed chapter covers a range of different topics that can be read either as individual articles or together. Taken as a whole, these stories add up to a comprehensive overview of the last two thousand years and beyond – and give some indication of what we can expect in the near future.

Whatever that future may hold for the next 35 generations who will span this third millennium, I trust that readers (whether at home or at school, today or in years to come) will find this compilation entertaining, informative and useful.

Norris McWhirter
Compiler

October 2000
Wiltshire, England

CONTENTS

CONTENTS

The pre-Christian era

	700–400,000BP	390–250,000BP	240–100,000BP	90–79,000BC
Everyday life, transport and sport	**680,000BP** *Homo erectus* migrates to Europe.	**250,000BP** *Homo sapiens* develops new tools such as borers and scrapers.	**120,000BP** Neanderthals dominate Europe. **100,000BP** *Home erectus* and *Homo sapiens* improve hunting skills.	**90,000BC** People light their caves with simple stone lamps fuelled with animal fat.
Architecture and the arts		**380,000BP** Oval huts built in France. **245,000BP** An English hand axe features the earliest known artistic design.	**100,000BC** The earliest known ornament is carved on a limestone fossil in Hungary.	
Science and medicine				
Politics, government and war			**Pre-100,000BP** Humans gather in small nomadic bands.	**90,000BC** Hunters co-operate to kill big game such as mammoths.
Language and writing	**620,000BP** First evidence of articulate language from the complexity of ritual markings on an Ethiopian skull.			

In the Amazon, chewed plants are used as a simple antidote to a snake bite. Many of the earliest medicines were natural remedies to help wounds heal.

The first stages of civilisation go back only 5000-6000 years, but *Homo sapiens* has existed for at least ten times as long. The achievements of our species have progressed with ever-increasing vigour. This book focuses on the period AD1 to 2000, but this timeline looks at some key developments before the present (BP) and before Christ (BC).

70–40,000BC	35–25,000BC	24–15,000BC	14–8500BC	8–7000BC
60,000BC Humans reach Australia. **45,000BC** Bows and arrows are pioneered in North Africa.	**30,000BC** Neanderthals mysteriously disappear from the face of the Earth.	**24,000BC** Bone sewing needles are used in France. **15,000BC** Humans cross the Bering Straits to America.	**10,000BC** Dogs are domesticated in Mesopotamia and Canaan. **8000BC** Potatoes are cultivated in Peru.	**7500BC** In Egypt and Southwest Asia, floodwater is used in agriculture. **7000BC** Pigs domesticated in eastern Asia.
45,000BC Aboriginals make Rock Art in Northern Territory. The pictures include animals with human features.	**29,000BC** Ceramics showing the figure of 'Venus' made in Dolní Vestonice, Czech Republic.	**15,000BC** The caves of Lascaux in France are painted with scenes of hunting and ceremony.	**11,000BC** Copper trinkets are hammered in Asia Minor. **8700BC** Earliest murals created in Turkey.	
60,000BC First herbal medicines for pain relief and poultices made in what is now northern Iraq.	**30,000BC** Paleolithic people in Europe are using tallies on bone, ivory and stone to count. Wolf bone from this period shows 55 cuts in groups of five.	**20,000BC** People in the Near East create lunar calendars using notches in bones.		
	Democracy is a political newcomer. In Athens, Pericles (c.490-429BC) was an early champion, but some countries were still waiting for it to arrive more than 2000 years later.		**8500BC** Humans begin to build permanent settlements in the Near East.	**7500BC** The inhabitants of Jericho fortify their village.
40,000BC Little is really known of the origins of language, but some scholars speculate that at this time there was still a 'world language'.		**15,000BC** The first known map – of the local region – is scratched onto a bone near what is now Mezhirich, Ukraine.		

The pre-Christian era

	6500–5500BC	5400–4900BC	4800–3600BC	3500–2100BC
Everyday life, transport and sport	**6500BC** Cattle are domesticated in Anatolia. **5000BC** Sails used on Persian Gulf.			**3500BC** Wheeled vehicles are used in Sumeria and Poland. **2700BC** Silkworms cultivated in China.
Architecture and the arts	**6500BC** Woven mats are made in what is now Jordan. *The step pyramid of Saqqara, Egypt, built in c.2950BC, is the oldest stone monument in existence.*			**3500BC** The potter's wheel is invented in Mesopotamia.
Science and medicine	**6000BC** Trepanning (drilling therapeutic holes in the skull) is practised around the Mediterranean.			**2680BC** The Sumerians are experimenting with alloys using carbon and sulphur, so laying the foundations of chemistry.
Politics, government and war		**5000BC** Catal Hüyük in Anatolia develops into a substantial 32-acre settlement.		**2371BC** Sargon I, king in Mesopotamia, establishes the world's first Empire. Sargon uses maps for the purpose of land taxation.
Language and writing	*This battle scene, carved on the walls of the Temple of pharaoh Ramses II in the 13th century BC, remains eloquent across hundreds of generations.*		**4500BC** The earliest written numerals are painted on pottery at Ban'po, near Xian in modern China.	**3500BC** The Egyptians invent writing material made from papyrus.

2000–1200BC	1100–650BC	600–400BC	350–250BC	200BC–AD1
2000BC Contraceptives are used in Egypt. **1250BC** Egyptians start a canal to link the Nile to the Red Sea.	**776BC** Earliest known Olympic Games are held in the Peloponnese. A truce is called among the city-states for the duration.	**c.563BC** Buddha is born. **420BC** Athenians send their children to school.	**335BC** Aristotle teaches logic at his Lyceum. **264BC** The first gladiator fight takes place in Rome.	**110BC** The Chinese use the collar harness, still the most efficient type.
1338BC 18-year-old Tutankhamen is buried along with a treasure trove of furniture, religious objects and funerary goods.	**850BC** The Illiad and the Odyssey are composed. **750BC** The Olmecs build pyramids in Mexico.	**520BC** Alcmalon of Croton dissects a corpse and locates the optic nerve. **400BC** First cataract operation by Susrata.	**304BC** The Colossus of Rhodes is erected.	**100BC** The Chinese standardise musical pitch. **100BC** Alexandros of Antioch carves the Venus de Milo.
1900BC First zoo, called the 'Park of Intelligence' built in China.		**430BC** Hippocrates develops a code of ethics for doctors.	**300BC** Euclid publishes Elements – a treatise on geometry that will be used for the next two millennia.	**c.87BC** A differentially-geared mechanical computer sinks in a ship in the Aegean.
1380BC The Hittites of Anatolia start to attack neighbouring territories. At first their iron weapons make them invincible.	**735BC** According to legend, Rome is founded. **675BC** Greek city-states introduce conscription.	**490BC** Greeks repel Persians at Marathon. **450BC** Roman law is codified in 12 tables.	**325BC** Alexander founds the biggest empire the world has yet seen, stretching from Greece to India.	**73BC** Spartacus leads the slaves of Rome in rebellion. **27BC** Octavius declares himself Emperor Augustus of Rome.
1650BC Phoenicians use a 22-letter alphabet similar to the modern European one.	**1100BC** The Chinese produce the first dictionary.	**430BC** Thucydides' reports from the frontline between Athens and Sparta make him the first war correspondent.	**290BC** The library at Alexandria – the first research institute – is built. It attracts scholars from all over the Greek-speaking world.	

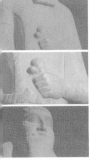
How it was in 1000BC

The period around 1000BC was one of great differences in cultural and technological achievement. In many parts of the world the Stone Age continued, but in Europe and Asia, the Bronze Age was already beginning to pass into the Iron Age.

The **Mycenaean Empire** of the eastern Mediterranean had fallen, and the city of Troy was destroyed in perhaps the 12th century BC, but Homer had not yet composed his epic poem *The Iliad* on the subject.

In the lands of the Bible, the hero Saul had died, and his kingdom was ruled by the most famous Israelite king, David, who was on the way to achieving his grand ambition to unify the 12 warring tribes of Israel. He established Jerusalem as his capital and placed on Mount Zion the Ark of the Covenant, the holiest object of the Israelites. In the following century, his son Solomon (*c.*1015–977BC) built the Temple in Jerusalem.

Outside Jerusalem, the Hebrews lived in small village communities, tending goats, and growing figs, olives and vines in the promised 'land of milk and honey'.

The change from bronze to iron as the metal of choice for artefacts meant that smiths could produce a harder metal, but the implications went far beyond that.

The most important was the cost of the metal. **Bronze** had always been expensive because its constituents, copper and tin, are rare. In Europe, Mediterranean

The Assyrian King Ashurnasipal II inaugurated his new capital of Nimrud with a state banquet for 60,000 guests. His palace was decorated with sculptures and alabaster murals celebrating his accomplishments in war and peace.

smiths brought tin from Cornwall or Brittany, and copper from the Carpathians or the Balkans.

During the Bronze Age, many tools and weapons were still made of wood or stone. Bronze objects tended to belong to chieftains and were often highly decorated.

Iron ore, by contrast, is found in many places. This made **iron** cheaper, so it could be afforded by the mass of the population. Wherever the secret of iron manufacture was known, ordinary farmers could use tough, metal tools to clear fields and produce more crops.

Partly as a result, there were developments in agriculture and lifestyle across Europe in around 1000BC. Many **new crops** were planted for the first time. Cereals such as **millet and rye were sown alongside the long-established staples of wheat and barley, while legume crops such as peas and beans became**

common together with oil-producing plants, such as flax and poppies.

Horses were being used for farming and for transport. A primitive type of glass was beginning to appear, though it remained rare and expensive.

Most settlements in Europe remained small **isolated farming communities** but fields became larger in size. Trade in metals, glass ingots, amber and jet was growing in importance.

Perhaps because of the growing population and improved farming techniques, the period saw a significant **increase in warfare** throughout Europe, the Middle East and Asia.

As a result, many settlements were fortified with **hill-forts and stockades**, some of which were complex, with several

By 1000BC, the casting of bronze vessels and other artefacts was a major Chinese industry. Animals were a favourite theme of Zhou dynasty artists, and this three-legged ornamental vase is a typically elegant example.

ramparts and ditches. The warriors had swords, spears and armour – such as helmets, cuirasses, greaves and shields. Horses were being ridden into battle for the first time.

The Middle East was particularly prone to warfare as peoples jostled against each other in the Tigris–Euphrates basin. The density of population led to the appearance of **early cities** which were among the wonders of the world.

In the Assyrian city of Nimrud, Ashurnasipal II (883–859BC) had a private zoo with lions, ostriches and monkeys. In Nineveh, the library of Ashurbanipal (669–640BC)was said to contain 22,000 clay tablets. Such wonders were sometimes built by slaves captured in wars. Whole nations could be enslaved after defeat and forced to work in the great cities of Assyria and Babylon.

The Assyrians of the upper Tigris were particularly adept at conquest. They controlled the iron ore deposits of Asia Minor and developed the technology to make advanced weapons and armour. The Assyrian cavalry was dreaded, and the army was expert at siege warfare.

The Assyrian empire was held together by a system of rigid authoritarian control. The king had supreme power but was heavily influenced by priests and astrologers who advised when he should go to war or make peace, and many other aspects of life.

Older civilizations were also experiencing change. In China, the **Zhou dynasty** (1071–221BC) was in a state of permanent unrest. The constantly feuding warlords were eventually to break up the kingdom.

Nonetheless, Zhou dynasty China led the way in many developments. Coinage and writing were developed, and large irrigation projects and road works were undertaken. This period later produced two of the greatest figures in Chinese history – **Confucius** (c.550BC) and the founder of Taoism, **Lao Tzu** (c.600BC).

Egypt was undergoing a troubled period. Ramses III (died c.1167BC) was the last powerful pharaoh of the New Kingdom. After his death power passed to the priests of Ammon and was later divided between the nobles. Egypt suffered from famine and repeated attacks by the 'Sea People' from the north and the Nubians from the south.

In Central America, the **Olmec** civilization (c.1150–400BC) around the Gulf of Mexico was at its height. The Olmecs carved gigantic basalt heads with curious helmets, weighing up to 40 or 50 tons, using only obsidian tools. The heads were placed at ceremonial sites made up of huge earthworks standing high above valleys.

The Olmecs appear to have had an animistic religion with a god who was half jaguar-half human infant. Representations of the figure are found in jade and on pottery. They also used a form of hieroglyphic writing and had an accurate calendar.

Western Europe was experiencing a period of religious change. Archaeologists have dubbed the period c.1300–800BC the **Urnfield period** – so named after the fact that people stopped burying their dead under mounds and began to cremate them and bury the ashes in urns placed in burial fields. The remains were often accompanied by elaborate grave goods such as ornaments, weapons and chariots. Available evidence suggests that this period was in fact the immediate ancestor of the Celtic Iron Age of middle Europe.

The Indo-European Aryans who had migrated into **northern India** c.1500BC had settled in the Ganges Valley and driven the native Dravidians further south.

The first of India's sacred writings were written down around 1000BC. The *Rig Veda* was a compilation of priestly hymns dedicated to the deities of creation, war and fire such as Indra, Krishna and Varuna. Vedic scriptures express a longing for union with the Sublime Truth, which later developed into Hinduism and gave birth to the practice of yoga.

The spiritual face of India was to be changed by the prince-turned-hermit, **Gautama Siddhartha, the Buddha** (c.563–c483BC), whose teachings became the basis of modern Buddhism.

This classical Olmec head found at La Venta, Tabasco, Central America, is more than 8ft *2.4m* tall. It is probably a portrait of of an important ruler. The name 'Olmec' means 'people from the land of rubber'. Little is known about Olmec history, but they established many of the cultural and technological foundations on which were built the later Central American civilizations of the Toltecs, Maya and Aztecs.

How it was in AD 1

At the dawn of the Christian era the dominant power in the western world was the **Roman Empire** under Emperor Augustus (r.27BC–AD14). Roman civilization and the *Pax Romana* ('Roman peace') held sway from England to

The Great Wall of China was built by the Chin emperor Shih Huang Ti beginning in 221BC and in his era stretched 1500miles *2400km*. It was extended in the centuries either side of AD1 by rulers of the Chinese Han dynasty, who added 25,000 turrets.

Armenia and from Germany to North Africa.

In the east, the Han Emperors in **China** (202BC–AD220) also presided over a long period of peace. The Han Empire ran from the Great Wall of China in the north and west to Korea and the north of Vietnam. A census in AD2 revealed a population of 57 million.

Both empires had developed administrative structures. Han **civil servants**' jobs included keeping records of laws enacted, and regulating irrigation and transport. The Han founded an imperial university to train officials in the principles of moderation and virtue taught by the sage Confucius (551–479BC).

The **Roman army**'s task was to protect the frontiers of the Empire and carry out engineering works. Augustus kept the army at a minimum of 150,000 men in 28 legions.

Similarly the **Han army**'s most important job was garrisoning the Great Wall. Both armies were conscripted and consisted of heavily armed foot soldiers. They were, however, vulnerable against horsemen.

Merchants thrived in the Roman Empire, crisscrossing northern Europe and the Mediterranean with trade routes. Cotton and wheat came from Egypt, lead and tin from Britain and slaves from any lands outside the empire that the Romans wished to subdue. Rome itself had 150 guilds of artisans, from bakers to silversmiths. Food and wine came from well-established farms outside the Imperial City.

Goods travelled westwards from China along the **Silk Road**, a 4000-mile *6400 km*-long caravan trail that ran all the way to the Levant. Silk, lacquerware and bronze goods were traded for horses, jade and furs. From the 5th century BC goods were transported internally by water. China's canal system was well developed by AD1.

There were vast discrepancies between the lifestyles of the wealthy and the poor. The Romans became famous for gluttonous **banquets** with Black Sea caviar which might cost more than a yoke of oxen. The 1st century author Petronius Arbiter describes a banquet which featured a wild boar stuffed with live thrushes.

Wealthy **Chinese** lived in wooden pagoda-style houses several storeys high. They wore silk robes and furs and their meals were served in lacquered bowls. As well as pork and chicken, they ate dogs, owls and quail and had many different spices to season their food.

The staple diet of the poor, on the other hand, widely throughout both empires, was a sort of **porridge** of cereal. Vegetables or beans might be added, if available.

In Rome, all but the very poor had **slaves** to fetch and carry, clean and labour. In the cities, often the slave was his master's clerk and might well be the only literate member of the household. These slaves could occasionally buy their freedom and set up in business themselves. In the country, slaves formed the backbone of the agricultural labour force.

The **amusements** on offer in the Roman Empire were often brutal crowd-pullers. Circuses and other entertainments took place on the festivals associated with the gods or dates of famous military victories of the past. The Circus Maximus

Under the Han rulers a thriving Chinese silk trade with Europe was established. The 'Silk Road' caravan trail ran from Shanghai to the Mediterranean. As well as silk, Chinese knowledge of papermaking and iron-smelting went west; and from c.AD50 Buddhism travelled from India to China and southeast Asia.

hippodrome in Rome was rebuilt in the 1st century BC to seat 150,000 spectators for the chariot racing, which was enormously popular. There were amphitheatres in most major cities, in which gladiators fought, sometimes to the death, prisoners were brought from the jails to murder each other and wild beasts released to fight.

Not all Roman amusements were so brutal. The Romans inherited the love of theatre from the Greeks. **Bath-houses** were also to be found in all the major towns throughout the empire – places where men could go for conversation, relaxation and exercise. Most bath-houses contained gymnasia.

Several more sophisticated arts had reached their apogee in China at this time. The emperors and other wealthy people designed and laid out elaborately landscaped **gardens** with canals and arched bridges in which to contemplate human harmony with nature. **Music** was divided into banquet and temple music and subtle, elaborate tunes were played on the bamboo mouth-organ and long zither.

It was during the Han dynasty that the Chinese invented **paper**. At about this time the first bibliographic catalogue was made of the vast Imperial library.

Roman **women** were excluded from many of the occupations of the men, and also often from domestic tasks – these were done by slaves. By Augustus' time, wealthier women had also gained a certain amount of control over their own property and the *sine manu* ('without authority') marriage bond meant that the woman remained part of her own family rather than coming under the control of her husband.

Among the poorer people, women worked, especially in shops, or bakeries, or on the land. In both empires women were barred from the civil service and were not recognized as having any public status. In China, however, they could practise as **doctors** or sorceresses.

Life outside the two great empires was generally poorer and more dangerous. The **German** and **Celtic** tribes outside Roman sway were devoted to fighting.

The Roman historian Tacitus (*c*.55–120) described the Germans going naked under short capes; in the battle fought between the Roman general Agricola and the Celts on the island of Anglesey, Wales, Tacitus described women darting like Furies (vengeful spirits) among the ranks of the Celtic warriors, whipping up their fighting spirit.

On the other hand, women in the warrior tribes probably were able to avail themselves of greater freedom than in the civilized empires. On the death of her husband Prasutagus in *c*.60, the British **Boudicca** became queen of the Iceni tribe and led an uprising against the Romans.

The tribes of central Asia between the empires of Rome and China – the **Scythians**, **Huns** and **Mongols** – were nomadic horsemen, herding cattle and yaks from pasture to pasture and living in yurts or animal-skin tents. Their life was necessarily a simple

The Colosseum in Rome witnessed games – including gladiator contests – for more than 300 years. When it opened in AD80 it was called the Flavian Amphitheatre in honour of the dynasty of that name (69–96) founded by Emperor Vespasian (9–79). It became known as the Colosseum (Lat. *colosseus* – gigantic) around the 8th century, not because of its own size but because a large statue of Emperor Nero (37–68) stood nearby.

one, as they only carried the bare necessities with them.

They changed little between the studies of Greek historian Herodotus (485–425BC) and the Roman Ammianus Marcellinus (AD330–395). Both described the tribes' warlike nature, their remaining on horseback all day and their barbaric burial rites entailing slaughter of wives, slaves and animals.

How it was in AD 1000

By *c.*AD1000 the peace established by the Roman Empire had been broken up. In the West – where the empire had ended in 476 with the deposition of the last Emperor, Romulus Augustus – the **Vikings** had control of the seas. In the East, where the Byzantine Empire had grown up, based on Byzantium (modern Istanbul), the forces of **Islam** were beating at the doors of Christendom.

Europe had fragmented into a large number of self-enclosed feudal states. It is in this sense that the term 'Dark Ages' which is often applied to Europe from *c.*AD500 to *c.*AD1000 is appropriate. After the great affairs of the Roman age, people's horizons had shrunk to their immediate communities.

In China, by contrast, the **Song dynasty** produced a great flowering of the arts and of civilization. It was under this dynasty that printing was discovered, with wooden or earthenware

The first Chinese porcelain was made under the Song Emperors (960–1279), a time of great cultural achievement. The grace and simplicity of this delicate Song-era cup suggests it is the product of an accomplished and sensitive civilization.

moveable type. It was also the golden age of Chinese watercolour painting – delicate studies of mountains and rivers imbued with the Zen Buddhist sense of identity with nature. Poetry flourished, too, and painters added quotations in brushed ideograms to their scrolls.

Japanese society had become settled by the Heian period (794–1195). It was strongly feudal. Buddhism and its associated arts had been introduced from China and lacquerware and scroll paintings were produced.

The soil of both China and Japan was intensively cultivated, with scarcely a patch of ground unused and the hillsides covered with terraces. The largest part of the population were **peasant farmers** working by hand – or possibly with oxen – on tiny holdings.

By far the greatest force in the world at the time was **Islam**. The militant Islamic faith was born in Arabia in 711 and spread west through North Africa and Spain, and east through Persia to the borders of India. The Abbasid dynasty of caliphs or deputies (750–1258) was by AD1000 beginning to split up into susbstantially independent caliphates, the most important being those of Cordoba in Spain, Cairo in Egypt and Baghdad (in present-day Iraq).

Islamic centres of learning and the arts at this period were unrivalled. At Baghdad a university had been founded early in the 9th century and the Muslims had access to the philosophy and

science of both the Hellenistic and Oriental civilizations. The philosopher and physician **Avicenna** (980–1037) wrote at least 200 books on subjects ranging from astronomy to Aristotle. In Cordoba, the library at the mosque numbered some 500,000 books.

Because their religion forbade the representation of the human form, the craftsmen of the Islamic faith became superlative **decorative artists**: calligraphy of the flowing Arabic script was exquisite, with elaborate flourishes and stylized plant-forms; Arab music, played on the lute and varieties of reed instruments, shared the same subtle decorative nature.

The eastern empire of **Byzantium** was much beleaguered by Muslims, Russians and Bulgars. The bounds of the Byzantine empire were very elastic, and more than once the only unassailable part was the core city of Byzantium itself.

In AD1000, however, the empire was enjoying a respite under Basil II (*r.*976–1025). Basil's sister married the Russian Grand-Duke Vladimir and from this dates the conversion of Russia to the eastern – or **Orthodox** – form of Christianity that had developed in the Byzantine Empire. Nonetheless, Basil fought a continuous war against the Bulgars to the west throughout his reign.

Byzantium stood at one of the world's crossroads on the Bosphorus: merchants and travellers passed through from all parts of the east and Europe and the empire itself was a racial melting-pot of Greeks, Serbs, Slavs and many others. They were united by Orthodox Christianity, which had mingled Christian belief with the intellectual subtlety of the Greek inheritance. According to contemporary accounts, bakers, bath attendants and market traders would conduct heated discussions on the nature of the body of Christ or the power of good and evil.

Byzantine art was devoted to producing religious icons – decorated with gold and jewels – and to the architectural design of basilica such as Ayía Sophia at Thessaloníki and the monasteries on Mount Athos in Greece.

Education was freely available at the time and the university of Constantinople was re-opened in the mid-10th century. The city provided public baths, pleasure gardens and the Hippodrome, where chariot-races and circus acts could be watched by 60,000 spectators.

Western Europe also had pockets of high civilization – the great **Celtic monasteries** in Ireland and Scotland, the **Romanesque churches** of France (Tournus, Dijon) and Italy (Ancona), and the **Cathedrals** of Durham and Ely in England.

The Church flooded the lives of people with colour. **Illuminated manuscripts** were produced in the monastery scriptoria, full of quaint birds and beasts and richly decorated margins; stained-glass windows cast glowing colours on the worshippers; and the church provided mystery plays and the pageantry of Christmas and Easter, at once the

holidays and spiritual nourishment of the people.

The great **monastic orders** flourished: the Benedictines had been founded *c.*529, the Carthusians were established in 1084 and the Cistercians in 1098. The monasteries provided medical care and poor relief as well as being centres of education and intellectual life, keeping historical records and studying agriculture.

These centres were under constant threat from **Viking** pirates who sacked isolated monastic communities off the coast of Ireland and Scotland. The Vikings were fearless sailors from Scandinavia who reached Newfoundland and Greenland in their longships.

Their religion was a warrior's religion: those who died in battle were carried to Odin's hall of **Valhalla**, where they feasted and fought as they had on Earth and burials were often spectacular cremations on blazing ships. Their home villages on the Scandinavian coast consisted of wooden houses with small farms, which the women managed when the men left on raiding parties.

Iron ore was dug from bogs and forged into weapons, farm tools and nails for boat-building. The Vikings amused themselves with dice and board games similar to draughts and listened to long **sagas** of heroic deeds recited by *skalds* (bards).

Another isolated pocket of Christianity resistant to the power of Islam was in **Ethiopia**, converted in the 4th century, but almost wholly unknown to the rest of the Christian world. Huge churches were built and monasteries cut out of solid

rock, and sacred music preserved ancient chants from the first centuries of Christianity.

Other civilizations flourished in Africa at the time about which little is known. In Zimbabwe, the Shona peoples built a complex of palace, fortress and burial-ground at **Great Zimbabwe** (meaning House of Stone), near present-day Victoria. The Monomatapa empire, of which Zimbabwe was the heart, was based on trade in gold with the Muslims of the east coast and further north.

In Central and South America AD1000 was a time of transition. The **Mayan civilization** centred on the Yucatan Peninsula of Central America was losing its strength as the expansionist energy of the Mexican Aztecs and Toltecs rose.

Both Aztec and Toltec civilizations used pictographic or hieroglyphic writing and were skilled architects. Their religious rituals were elaborate, governed by the astronomic calendar, and involved human sacrifice.

The **Incas** of Peru were just emerging at this time to form the great empire that would stretch down the west side of South America to Chile. They, too, were great builders – their interlocking stone blocks were earthquake-proof. They used knotted strings (*quipu*) in place of writing for their records.

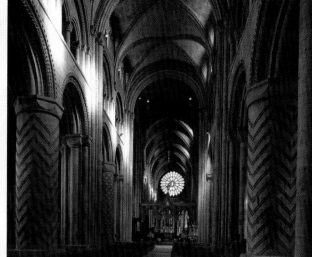

Monks driven from their monastery on the island of Lindisfarne by Viking attacks came to Northumbria, eventually settling at Durham in the late 10th century. The Norman King William I (*c.*1027–87) ordered the construction of Durham's stone Cathedral, which began *c.*1094.

How it is in AD 2000

In 2000 many people's daily lives and work are only remotely connected with the realities of survival. Our food may be shipped from the other side of the world, our clothing made in factories.

Yet certain societies still live by **hunting or gathering** fruit and nuts for their subsistence. Some Australian Aborigines, the bushmen and pygmies of Africa and some tribes of Amazon Indians are living a life that has not much changed in millennia.

It is likely that they will not survive for long: the hunting-gathering lifestyle needs a relatively large amount of space per individual. The world's rising population means that the untouched areas of the Earth are increasingly encroached on.

The **growth in population** may be the single most important factor in the life of the planet. World population is now about 22 times what it was in AD1000 but the rate of growth was exponential –

The lightning speed of the communications revolution has left many adults floundering. Children are often far more confident in the use of the latest technology – such as this battery-operated 'laptop' computer or the Internet – than their parents.

Almost half – 43 per cent – of the world's population lives in our increasingly crowded cities. In developed countries, urban centres are brought to a standstill with traffic and choked with pollution. The world's largest city is Tokyo in Japan.

that is, the graph of growth became increasingly steep. The population reached 5 billion in 1987 and with the present rate of increase may double by 2050.

Population pressures perhaps contribute to the patterns of human aggression in the late 20th century. In many areas of the world, **ethnic groups** are fighting not only to achieve a hegemony over others, but to exterminate them altogether. In the 1980s thousands of Kurds were killed in Iraq and thousands more made homeless. In Rwanda, Africa, in the 1990s the Hutu tribe attempted to wipe out the Tutsi minority.

Yet there has been no war between the major nations of the world for more than 50 years and the 20th century has seen the formation of **international organizations** promoting peace-keeping and co-operation. The United Nations, with a membership of 185 nations, operates a peace-keeping force and can supply emergency assistance in disaster situations or for aiding development; the Organisation of African Unity provides a forum for African

countries to meet and assist or regulate each other.

The increase in population is greater in less developed countries, which means that, despite higher infant mortality, their population is relatively young. In developed countries a lower birth rate – allied to greater life expectancy for older people due to access to hygiene and modern medicine – means that the population is getting older all the time.

Contraception is available through most of the world and is used by about 50 per cent of couples. This is linked to the increasing ability of women to take an active part in society: in most countries, women now have the right to the same education as men and an equal participation in political life.

This has led to changes in **family life** and structures,

FROM THE SECOND TO THE THIRD MILLENNIUM AD

This table focusses on how human records and society have changed in the last ten centuries.

	AD 1000	AD 2000
World's population	c.275 million	c.6158 million
Number of sovereign countries	8	192
Largest city (population)	c.1.1 million: Rome, Italy	27.37 million: Greater Tokyo, Japan
Mountaineering altitude record	c.20,000ft 6080m Tibetan passes (Kang-ti-suu)	29,028ft 8,848m Mount Everest (first conquered on 29 May 1953)
Human speed record	c.35mph 56km/h, sledging and horse riding	24,790.8mph 39,897km/h Cdrs. Cernan and Young and Col. Stafford, USAF in Apollo 10 mission on 26 May 1969.
Deepest penetration into space	Perhaps c.165ft 50m, black powder (huo phao) rockets, China c.AD1000	3670 million miles 5910 million km, US Pioneer 10 rocket, launched 2 March 1972 from Cape Canaveral, Florida, left the Solar System in 1986.
Deepest ocean descent	c.100ft 30.5m, breath-held pearl diving	35,813ft 10,916m, US Navy bathyscaphe Trieste (Dr Jacques Piccard and Lt Donald Walsh USN), Mariana Trench, Pacific, 23 January 1960.
Tallest structure	480.9ft 146.5m, Great Pyramid of Cheops, Giza, Egypt	2120.6ft 646.38m, Warszawa Radio mast, Plock, Poland, completed July 1970, collapsed in 1991.
Longest bridge span	c.250ft 76m, Lantshang river iron chain bridge, China, of 65AD	6351ft 1.99km, Akashi-Kaikyo Honshu-Shikoku road link, Japan, 1988.
Longest tunnel	3.5 miles 5.6km, Lake Fucinus drain tunnel, near Rome, c.AD 40–50	105 miles 168.9km, Delaware Aqueduct (water supply), New York, USA, 1937–1944.
Largest ship	c.430ft 131m long, Ptolemy IV's Tesserakonter, built at Alexandria, Egypt.	1504ft 458.45m long Jahre Viking, (564,763 deadweight tons) tanker.
Greatest explosive	Black (later gun) powder (huo phao) in China	57 megatonne (also estimated at 62 to 90 Mt), USSR H bomb test, Novaya Zemlya, 30 October 1961.
Longest long jump	>23ft 7.00m Chionis, Ancient Olympics (prob. using dumb-bell weights) c.650BC	29ft 4in 8.95m, Mike Powell (US), Tokyo, 30 August 1991.
Most distant visible object	Messier 33 Spiral in Triangulum (Mag. 5.79) (naked eye object) 2900 light years	Observable horizon now assessed to be at 14,000 million light years (optical and radio telescopes).
Number of known chemical elements	10	112 (including 19 transuranic elements).

especially in the developed world. Women may be equal wage-earners with their partners; children may be cared for by non-family members or sent to nurseries from an early age.

Another 20th-century development inconceivable to our ancestors is the **leisure** industry. In former centuries, rich young men might travel for amusement or education. In our century, the streamlining of employment into a

9am–to–5pm pattern has meant that everyone in the developed world has some leisure and is a potential consumer of tourism or countless other facilities.

But the single most significant advance in the developed world in the last 20 years of the millennium has been the growth in information technology. Sales of **personal**

computers top those of TVs in some countries. E-mail can be sent around the world from a computer and the Internet provides a vast mass of information worldwide. Satellites transmit TV broadcasts across the world and pocket-sized mobile phones number an amazing 450 million.

Once remote and seemingly inaccessible, by the end of the 20th century Mount Everest was within relatively easy reach of sportsmen and women using the latest climbing equipment. The world's highest peak is regularly scaled by around 750 mountaineers each year.

Life on Earth in 3000

Seen from the vastness of space, humankind's floating home appears small and fragile. Conditions on Earth may radically alter in the next 1000 years – the constitution of the atmosphere and the average surface temperature could change owing to the generation of greenhouse gases and the effects that these have on global warming.

Two major factors governing global conditions – the Earth's distance from the Sun and its rate of revolution on its axis – will not alter appreciably over the next millennium. Although they are subject to change, it is at a rate so slow that for them a thousand years is but a blink in time.

The – less predictable – future impact of human pollution is a matter of much anxiety. The **greenhouse effect** is caused by rising amounts of atmospheric carbon dioxide that trap more and more of the Sun's heat on Earth. It could raise surface temperatures to such an extent that polar ice melts, lifting sea levels and causing flooding and changes in weather patterns.

The hole in the **ozone layer** over parts of the Antarctic continent – discovered by scientists in the 1980s and blamed partly on pollution – could increase in size and allow dangerous amounts of the Sun's ultraviolet radiation into the atmosphere. This would cause damage to plants and skin cancers in humans.

The enormous gap in **quality of life** between affluent and poor is another global problem with consequences for both pollution and energy consumption. In Beijing there are reportedly more than 8 million bicycles in use. If economic prosperity enabled this army of cyclists to obtain scooters, let alone cars, the fumes generated would be harmful or even lethal.

Every year, the average Texan uses 564 million BTU (British thermal unit – the amount of energy needed to raise 1lb *0.45kg* of water by 1° Fahrenheit). It is doubtful whether the planet could sustain this level of energy consumption worldwide.

In the last three decades of the 2nd millennium, ecology became a matter of political concern – and the prospect of effective intervention to reduce pollution was accordingly greater. In any case, the increase in pollution may be balanced by the inevitable **depletion of fossil fuels**. It seems likely that the consumption of energy on a late 20th-century scale will not be possible in the next millennium as non-renewable deposits of oil, gas and coal are gradually used up.

Alternative methods of energy production are available – using the tides, the wind and methane gas, for example – but could not keep pace with current levels of demand.

Various materials, such as **plastics** and many clothing fabrics that are derived from petroleum will also become unavailable. Just as 'smart' plastic cards and computers become the very basis of our lives, we could conceivably run out of the materials with which to manufacture them.

Many argue vehemently that the greatest threat to the future survival of humankind is **overpopulation**. The world's population has been increasing since 7500BC, gently at first but exponentially in the last three centuries. In 1998 it rose to almost 6 billion. The US Bureau of Census estimates that by 2025 it will have grown to 7.9 billion, while in 2050 it will be 9.3 billion. United Nations projections, though tentative, have indicated that a century later in 2150, the figure should stabilize at about 11.6 billion.

This means there would be a density of 170 people where there are 100 people today. If no other factors are taken into account, the **population density** in 3000 might mean that once space had been set aside for housing, roads and other necessities there would be no room to grow food.

Developments in medicine and science promise great things. The completion *c.*2005 of the **Human Genome Project** that is mapping the human gene pool should produce knowledge that will transform doctors' ability to treat hereditary diseases.

Advances in surgery already allow the transplant of human organs and the implant of artificial ones. Techniques of **genetic engineering** may allow organs from animals such as pigs to be genetically 'labelled' as human and then used for transplants without risk of rejection; the animals could be bred as donors.

But such treatments will be so selective and expensive that their impact in global terms is unlikely to be great. Similarly while fertility treatments such as IVF (in vitro fertilization) are of immense importance for individuals they are available only to a tiny minority of the world's population.

When British scientists successfully cloned a sheep – Dolly – in 1997, it opened the prospect of the **cloning of human beings** in the near future. Ethical concerns over both animal and human cloning were strong at the end of the 2nd millennium but these may shift or even dissolve. One possible medical use for the process is the production of a human clone for each individual that could be used to provide replacement organs in case of disease or accident.

No future forecast can take into account the **unknown** – an epidemic of a new disease, a catastrophic natural disaster or a major war. However, the effect of war on population levels is limited. The 54 million lives lost during World War II were made up within ten months by the naturally occurring surplus of births over deaths.

Diverse human societies may become more like each other. The power of advertising and the spread of international brands – combined with the fact that more people live in cities, and that cities are growing more similar – may lead to an increasingly **homogenous culture** across the globe.

For a sector of the population, the tendency to retreat into computer-generated **virtual reality** reflects a growing disinclination to engage with the real world. With rising stress and overcrowding, people could become more aggressive and intolerant. Wars may spring up from competition for food and basic resources.

The great fear of the mid-20th century – that of **global destruction** by way of nuclear holocaust – retreated in the early 1990s with the end of 45 years of Cold War between communist Eastern bloc states and Western capitalism. However, atomic fission and fusion cannot be uninvented, and nuclear

technology is being exploited, and nuclear tests carried out, by several countries.

When the Sun finally burns off all its hydrogen to become a 'red giant' star, all possibility of life on Earth will cease. Even though hydrogen is being consumed at 4 million tons per second, it will take more than 4 million millennia for this to happen. **Escape to another planetary system** need hardly be a priority in the foreseeable future.

The rapid growth of the world's largest cities looks set to continue in the 3rd millennium. The United Nations has estimated that the 1995 population of Tokyo (16.9 million), Mexico City (16.5 million) and Sao Paulo (16.5 million) will, by 2015, rise to 28.9, 19.1 and 20.3 million respectively.

POPULATION GROWTH

Country	1998 (millions)	2025 (millions)	2050 (millions)
Australia	18.6	22.2	22.8
Canada	30.7	38.0	40.5
China	1236.9	1407.7	1322.4
France	58.8	57.8	48.2
Germany	82.1	75.4	57.4
India	984.0	1415.3	1707.0
Japan	125.9	119.9	101.3
New Zealand	3.6	4.4	4.6
Pakistan	135.1	211.7	260.2
Russia	146.9	138.8	121.8
United Kingdom	59.0	60.0	54.1
USA	270.3	335.4	394.2
World	**5926.5**	**7922.3**	**9346.4**

EVERYDAY LIFE

- **Food and drink**

- **Lighting**

- **Agriculture**

- **Clothing**

- **Marriage and relationships**

- **Education and childcare**

- **Beliefs, rituals, religions**

- **Crime and punishment**

- **Money**

- **Banking and finance**

- **Business and trade**

An old woman holds a prayer wheel during a religious festival in Tibet. The prayer wheel is one of the artefacts of Buddhism. After the Christian and Muslim religions, Buddhism represents the third largest in the world, with adherents largely in India, Tibet, China, Sri Lanka, Myanmar and Japan.

Food and drink

BEFORE AD 1

Experiments with spits and the first stone pots

The earliest evidence that our ancestors could domesticate **fire** and use it for cooking comes from Dering-Yuryakh, Siberia (discovered 1984) and at Swartzkrans, Transvaal, southern Africa (discovered 1988). It is dated to *c*.1.5 million years BP. Rotary or spit-roasting probably began *c*.3600BC in Mesopotamia (modern Iraq/Iran). Pounded tubers, cereals, unshelled eggs and nuts in their own shells could be baked in embers. There is evidence of this use of **dry heat** in the open from 1.4 million years BP in Chesowanja, Kenya.

Sides of salmon are baked beside an alder fire in a re-creation of the village life of the Tillicum natives of North America on Blake Island, Washington State, USA. Archaeological evidence indicates that man first used fire for cooking some 1.5 million years BP.

In western Europe *c*.50,000BC people began to experiment with **toasting** on the end of a stick or **frying** in a hollow stone with fats. Boiling and stewing over open fires became possible with heat-resistant vessels. First, more deeply hollowed **stoneware** was invented, possibly *c*.35,000BC in south-western France. Poaching fish in milk or shelled eggs in water became feasible with the invention of **pottery** *c*.12,000BC, in southern Japan.

The earliest surviving **recipes** are those deciphered from an Assyrian cuneiform tablet of *c*.1700BC found in Iraq. There are 25; one was for a small, unidentified bird called a *tarru*, cooked with onion, garlic, milk and a condiment called *samidu*.

Closed containers or **ovens** – which first appeared *c*.7000BC in the Near and Middle East – made possible a number of more refined methods of cooking. Meat or vegetables could be **baked** in a controlled process, or **braised** or **steamed** in closed containers heated from beneath.

AD 1000

Cook books and stoves

The earliest **cook book** in English was the manuscript *Forme of Cury* (cookery), mainly on hashes and stews by the Master Cook to King Richard II (1377–99) in London. Blasius Villafranca (It) published in *c*.1548 *Methodus refrigerandi*, a description of his **wine**-cooling device in which saltpetre was dissolved.

In 1635 Henry Sibthorp registered a patent for a coal-fired iron **kitchen range**. The kitchen stove, at one time widely known as a Franklin, was introduced by Benjamin Franklin (US) (1706–90) in 1745.

The **pressure cooker** was invented by Denis Papin (Fr) (1647–1712) in London in 1679. It was first used in August 1682 for a dinner for the Royal Society. Called a 'digestive', the tight-fitting lid was fitted with a pressure-releasing safety valve.

The earliest production of **ice** by mechanical means in 1786 enabled the use of ice boxes to be extended both in season and geographically. These were often zinc-lined cabinets, insulated with heavy wooden casings.

Heat-resistant cooking pots enamelled with white porcelain were made by the Konigsbronn Foundry, of Württemberg, Germany in 1788.

On 27 February 1802 George Bodley (GB) (*c*.1770–1832) of Exeter, patented the first moveable **stove** 'for dressing victuals'. Also that year, in Austria, Zachaus Andreas Wunzler (1750–*c*.1830) introduced the first **gas cookers**. In 1824 Aetna Ironworks near Liverpool, England, made a gas-powered **grill** and in 1834 James Sharp (Eng) (1790–1870) of Northampton Gas Co. marketed his first gas cooking stoves.

Gas rings were introduced in 1867 (developed from the Bunsen burners of 1855) by John Wright & Co. Birmingham. But electricity was soon to rival gas. In 1879 St George Lane-Fox (Eng) (1816–96) registered a patent for cast iron radiant panels containing bare iron heating wires embedded in enamel. This device effectively paved the way for the **electric hob**.

The first **dishwasher**, the Cochran, was manually operated. Worked by a handle, it was constructed in 1886 by Mrs Josephine G. Cochran (US) of Shelbyville, Indiana, USA. The capacity was later increased to over 200 dishes, and it boasted a removable wire basket and a spray pump with rotating rollers. From 1892, it was run by steam. Mrs Cochran's motive in developing the machine was said not to be to minimize the work of her servants but rather to reduce the level of breakages suffered by her crockery and glassware.

By the late 19th and early 20th centuries, electric appliances multiplied. A hydro-electric-powered oven was installed in 1889 in the Hotel Bernina, Samaden, Switzerland and the earliest example of an electric **toaster** was advertised by the Crompton Co. in 1893 in Chelmsford, Essex, England.

Although the first patent in 1904 for an automatic **tea maker** from Birmingham, England used a wound alarm clock, a safety match and a spirit stove, it was never marketed. The Hawkins' 'Teasmade', using an electric clock and an immersion heater in the kettle did, however, find a niche in the market from 1932.

The Presto Company of Wisconsin, USA, manufactured the first **aluminium pressure cookers** in 1905.

The Hamilton Beach Manufacturing Co. of Washington, North Carolina, marketed the first electrically powered **food mixer**. The American company Universal marketed a mains-powered electric mixer in 1919.

In 1911 the 'Prometheus' **electric kettle** appeared. More sophisticated models with automatic cut-off were developed by William Russell (GB) (*b.*1920) and Peter Hobbs (GB) (*b.*1916) and first marketed in 1954.

In 1915 the Corning Glass Works, Corning, New York launched **Pyrex**, heat-proof oven glassware – initially, for use in US railroad kitchens.

In the same year, the Lorraine oven, with a **thermostat** to regulate the temperature in the oven, represented a breakthrough in controlled cooking. In 1923 the Davis Gas Stove Co's 'New World' gas cooker incorporated temperature control by means of an 'expanding rod' thermostat.

Powerful domestic **detergents** were seen as a great breakthrough in the kitchen. One such, Nikala (sulphated alkyl-naphthalene) was first synthesized in Germany in 1916. Lux soapflakes were developed by Unilever in Britain in 1921.

The Electrolux model of **refrigerator** with vapour compression was marketed in Sweden in 1924 from the 1922 patent of Carl Munters (Swe) (1897–1989) and Baltzer von Platen (Swe) (1898–1984).

Nils Gustav Dalén (Swe) (1869–1937) in 1924 introduced **multifuel cookers** and oven ranges. The highly insulated cast iron **Aga** ranges were designed to burn continuously fuelled by coal, gas, oil or wood.

Charles Strite (US) invented the Toastmaster in 1927. The **waste disposal unit** was devised in 1929 by J. Powers

The Kenwood Chef pioneer food processor boasted smooth lines as well as functions including can opening, mincing, slicing, shredding and liquidizing. It was developed in 1947 by Kenneth M. Wood (GB) (1916–97) of Woking, England.

(US) of the General Electric Co. and by Grundig of Germany. It was first marketed by GEC of Connecticut, USA, from 1935.

The earliest practical electrically powered **dishwasher** was marketed in the USA in 1932 and in 1940 the first automatic electric model appeared.

Earl S. Tupper (US) (1907–83) developed a range of high quality plastic kitchenware beginning in 1945. Frustrated by the take-up from retailers, he launched a new marketing technique with **Tupperware Parties** at which the housewife-hostess earned commission on sales.

Non-stick kitchenware (PTFE plastic) was discovered by Dr. Roy J. Plunkett (US) (1911–94) in 1938. Teflon coating was manufactured by Mark Grégoire (Fr) of Tefal Co. of Paris and marketed in May 1956 in Nice, France.

The Kelvinator, a soapless and waterless appliance to clean dishes by ultra-sound, was first demonstrated in 1962 in Seattle, Washington.

A demonstrator reveals the ins and outs of the first microwave oven, the Raydarange. Made by the Raytheon Co. of Massachusetts, USA, it was first marketed for restaurants in 1953. A domestic model followed in 1967.

Greenish-gold Chardonnay grapes in an Australian vineyard. Winemakers have transplanted grape varieties all over the world. The widely popular Chardonnay is a native of Burgundy in France. This variety is mixed with Pinot Noir grapes to make champagne.

THE STORY OF WINE

The fruit of the vine

Wine was probably discovered accidentally from exposed mixtures of berries, fruits or honey in warm air that either self-fermented or was catalyzed by airborne yeast. Wines were made using **wild grapes** from the ninth millennium BC using skin bags as fermentation vessels. In May 1996 some fermented grape juice was found in a stoppered pottery jar in Hajji Firuz Tepe, Iran, possibly dating from *c*.4000BC. In 1988 two bottles of wine believed to date from *c*.1300BC were found in a tomb at Xinyang, China.

Organized wine-making is believed to have begun in Egypt *c*.4000BC. By *c*.1600BC **Greece** had become the world's wine centre, exporting wine in amphorae (large pottery jars) holding up to 16.5 gallons *75 litres* to Italy *c*.650BC. Later, the trade was extended to Gaul.

The **Romans**, who developed vintages from *c*.130BC,

The English developed a taste for port wine in the late 17th century when Louis XIV embargoed the export of wines from France. Portuguese wine was fortified with brandy to help it to travel, and took its name from the town of Oporto. These barrels of port are stacked in an Oporto warehouse.

replaced amphorae with casks and barrels. They took winemaking all over the empire, even establishing a vineyard at Tortworth, Gloucestershire. In France, Bordeaux, Burgundy and the Loire Valley (by AD250) became established wine-making centres, as did Mosel and the Rhineland in Germany by AD300.

Brandy – distilled from wine and usually *c*.40 per cent alcohol – was first known *c*.AD50 in the vineyards of the Roman estate of Falernian. The name is derived from Dutch *brandwijn*, burnt wine.

Vermouth – a fortified aperitif wine, flavoured with herbs and quinine – was known in Roman Italy by AD100. Its name comes from German *Wermut*, wormwood, the toxic ingredient in early vermouth, now omitted.

Winemakers bred several different varieties of grape. By *c*.1350 the **Pinot Noir** grape had become famous in Burgundy from the Cistercian vineyard of Clos de Vougeot. Its dominance was challenged by the **Chenin Blanc** or Pineau de la Loire grape by 1500. Wine was exported to England, and the British invented the name **claret** *c*.1398, for red wine from the Bordeaux region.

The Spaniards took European vines to the New World. Vineyards were established in **Mexico** in 1525. **Chile** was reached by 1555. The flourishing **Californian wine industry** was founded by Franciscans at the Mission San Diego in 1769.

The French double-distilled brandy liqueur known as **Benedictine** is flavoured with more than 25 herbs and spices. It was devised 1510 by

the Benedictine monk, Dom Bernardo Vincelli, of Fécamp Abbey in France. The recipe was lost *c*.1790 but found again in 1863.

The invention of **champagne** is attributed to the Benedictine monk Dom Pierre Pérignon in 1688. Champagne is sparkling wine made by a second fermentation in the bottle, exclusively from the Champagne region of northeastern France.

Chartreuse – a green, yellow or white liqueur – was pioneered in 1605 by François Hannibal d'Estrées and passed on to the Carthusian monks of La Grande Chartreuse monastery near Grenoble in France. In 1762 Brother Jérôme Maubée interpreted the formula and the liqueur was put on sale in 1765.

The sweet Rhine Valley white wine named **Liebfraumilch** was first mentioned in 1833. The name is taken from the vineyard next to the Liebfrauen Kirche, Worms, of which the Virgin Mary (Liebfrau) was the patron.

From 1875 to 1887, disaster hit European vineyards. The root louse *Phylloxera vitifoliae*, introduced from the USA, almost destroyed the vineyards of France, Germany and Italy. They were saved by grafting the vines on to rootstocks native to the USA that proved immune to the disease.

Kir – a mixture of cassis or blackcurrant liqueur and dry white wine – is named after Canon Félix Kir (1876–1968), the Mayor of Dijon in Burgundy, who invented the drink as a pleasant way of dispensing with a glut of local white wines.

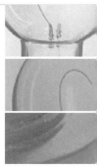

Lighting

BEFORE AD 1

Fire, candles and oil lamps

After nightfall, the only source of light for the earliest humans was **fire**. Around 30,000BC **lamps** of hollowed-out stone with floating wicks of vegetable fibre in animal fat were used.

Egyptian tomb paintings dating from *c.*2055BC show cone-shaped candles held in saucers, and candlesticks have been found in Crete from the Minoan civilization of the same era.

Lighthouses were at first just primitive flares but it is thought that the Pharos lighthouse at Alexandria, built *c.*280BC, was lit by some form of petroleum and the beam was focused using polished bronze mirrors. The lighthouse could be seen for 35 miles *56 kilometres*.

The first **street lighting** used oil lamps strung on rope. Evidence of this has been found in the Near East dating from *c.*AD370.

AD 1000

Gas and electricity light up

Marco Polo (It) (*c.*1254–1324) described 'firesticks' in China in AD1275, more than four centuries before Hennig Brand (Ger) (*b.c.*1630) discovered **phosphorus,** used for matches in the West, in the period 1669–75.

The streets of London saw their first lamp-posts bearing oil-lamps in the mid-17th century. **Coal gas** from the distillation of coal was first obtained in 1727 by the Rev.

Stephen Hales (1677–1761) in Teddington, Middlesex. In 1730, Carlisle Spedding (Eng) (1695–1755), colliery manager to the 1st Earl of Lonsdale in Whitehaven, Cumberland, lit his office with methane gas from the mines. His offer to **light the streets** of Whitehaven with 'damp air' was rejected by backward looking local magistrates.

Despite these setbacks, **gas street lighting** was eventually accepted. In 1804, Frederick Albert Winsor (Ger/GB) (1763–1830) lit the south side of Pall Mall in London. The first public utility **gasworks** were established in Manchester in 1817. Samuel Clegg (GB) (1781–1861), Chief Engineer of the Chartered Gas Light & Coke Co. patented the Gasometer in 1818.

Meanwhile, by the mid-18th century, experiments were being made with **electric lighting**. The incandescent electric lamp was devised in 1834 by James Bowman Lindsay (GB) in Dundee, Scotland. In the absence of an electricity supply, he used Voltaic cells and an evacuated glass tube.

In 1840, Warren de la Rue (GB) (1815–89) produced a **platinum filament** incandescent lamp in an evacuated horizontal tube and in 1841 experimental electric **arc lighting** was installed at Le Quai Conti and La Place de la Concorde, both in Paris, by L. J. Deleuil (Fr) (1794–1862) and Dr. Henri Archerau (Fr).

Experiments over the next years were directed towards

producing a long-life filament and an effective vacuum in bulbs. Joseph Wilson **Swan** (GB) (1828–1914) raced with the American Thomas **Edison** (1847–1931) to perfect and patent the electric lightbulb.

Swan and Stearn manufactured their **first incandescent lamp** in 1877 with a stick filament of carbon and platinum wires, and in 1879 Swan gave the first public demonstration. Meanwhile, the dynamic Thomas Edison had formed the Edison Electric Light Co. in 1878, although at that time he had not yet managed to manufacture a durable lamp.

During 1879 and 1880, both Swan and Edison were experimenting with filaments which would last satisfactorily and with methods of preventing the glass blackening. Swan patented a filament of parchmentized thread and in 1881 Gateshead Town Hall became the first public building in England to be lit by incandescent light.

The world's first **electric power station** was the Central Power Station at Pullman's Leather Mill, Godalming, Surrey, England, which produced a regular supply from 1881.

Meanwhile in the USA Edison had founded the Edison Electric Illuminating Co. and was devising a system of electric **power distribution** into urban

Domestic lamps powered by electricity rather than gas came on to the market at the end of the 19th century. This lamp was developed by inventor Thomas Edison (US).

Neon lights dominate city nightscapes. The lights contain neon gas, which is agitated when electricity passes through it and so glows in order to release the energy.

In 1885, Count Carl Auer von Welsbach (Aus) (1858–1929) invented the asbestos incandescent **gas mantle**, impregnated with 99% thorium oxide and 1% cerium oxide. This changed the uncertain flare of the gas to a steady white light. In 1901 Peter Cooper-Hewitt (US) (1861–1921) introduced the first low-pressure **mercury discharge lamp**, in effect a fluorescent tube. The light it shed was blue, which proved a distinct practical drawback for both domestic and municipal lighting.

William D. Coolidge (US) (1873–1975) in 1909 developed **tungsten filaments** that required only a third of the energy used by carbon lamps, so reducing the running costs below that of gas lighting.

In 1910 Georges Claude (Fr) (1870–1960) demonstrated two 115ft *35m* long red-glowing **neon tubes** at the Motor Show in Paris. Neon

areas. He installed a steam-driven dynamo at his power station in New York and procceded to establish an infrastructure of mains cables, circuits and switchboards. However, gas was still very much cheaper and the Swan bulbs available had an average life of only 50 days. At this time, therefore, domestic and public lighting was still almost exclusively using gas rather than electricity.

did not become commercial until 1922 and was used for highway lighting from 1933.

Fluorescent tubes were perfected in the USA by Westinghouse and GEC, and by 1938 they were available in a choice of seven colours.

Late 20th-century developments increased both the **efficiency** and **life** of bulbs and tubes. The Philips S-L Lamp had a life five times that of previous bulbs and used a quarter as much energy as its predecessors.

In 1990 Nelson Waterbury (US) was granted a US Patent for a **double filament bulb** which recycles some of the invisible infrared light into visible white light.

In 1992 a high-tech lightbulb with a 14-year average life was devised by Don Hollister and Don Pelazzo (US). It uses high frequency radio waves to illuminate a bulb filled mercury vapour.

Agriculture

BEFORE AD 1

The first crops

The first humans lived as hunter-gatherers: it is likely that the domestication of early cattle and sheep began at the same time as the deliberate **cultivation** of grains and fruits. Nomadic tribes herded their flocks with them while more settled ones cultivated crops.

Evidence of early cultivation is a hotly contested subject among archaeologists. Stone implements found in Papua New Guinea bear what

appear to be starch grain marks from cultivated **taro** and **yams** that may have been grown there c.28,000BC. Finds at Spirit Cave, Karst area, northern Vietnam indicate that **water chestnuts**, bottle gourds, species of **peas** and common bean may have been cultivated there between 11,000 and 7500BC.

These finds have been contested by experts, but evidence from **China** indicates that agriculture was practised in the provinces of Guangdong, Guangxi and Hebei between c.10,000 and 8000BC.

Crop **irrigation** using manmade canals was practised at Choya Mami, near Mandali, central Iraq, c.5500–4750BC. Subterranean **granaries** for storing crops were built at Ban-po, Shensi, China in c.4800BC. Ox-drawn seed drills are depicted on seals from Sumer (Iraq/Iran) c.2650BC.

The first **farm tools** were hand tools used for breaking the ground to sow or plant crops, and to hoe weeds. Heavier implements to plough or drill semi-mechanically were drawn by people or animals, such as oxen or, later, horses.

Greatly improved tilling of land was made possible c.3500BC by the introduction of the **ard**, a light plough of antler or hardwood which cuts a furrow but did not turn over the soil as a plough does.

The **plough** was first introduced in China but no Chinese illustration of a plough survives before c.AD50. The people of ancient Mesopotamia first used **oxen** to pull ploughs.

Two thousand years after the rotary fan was introduced, it is still used for threshing rice in China.

The earliest appearance of **iron ploughshares** was c.1975BC in Palestine. Cast iron ploughshares were introduced in China c.400BC, and the harnessing of horses with collars only came in there c.120BC. By c.50BC the **rotary fan** (*shan thui*) was in use to separate the grain from the chaff in China. Evidence of a **wheeled plough** from the same era has been found in Switzerland.

AD 1

Improved tools

In China c.AD1 iron-headed **rakes** (*chhü nu*), clodding **mauls** and multi-pronged **dray-hoes** (*thich tha*) were used in paddy fields. In Europe at the same time the Romans spread the use of the *rastrum*, or rake. Later, c.250,

the two-wheeled seed drill (*vellus* in Latin) is described in Roman Gaul, and scythes with barred handles were also in use.

A tined **harrow** (*chhiao*) was used in Kwangtung, China, c.310. This breaks soil up into a finer tilth for sowing.

The great Hanchia tax **granary** with a capacity of nine million bushels was built in south western China during the Thung dynasty c.AD900.

AD 1000

Open fields and the first agricultural machines

Hand **barrows** (*yin thang*) were invented by the Chinese and appeared in the Yangtze basin, China c.1350.

In Europe, during the Middle Ages, farming was carried out by **villeins**, who worked for the Lord of the Manor. Each villein had his own strip of land to grow food for himself and his family. The land was arranged in the '**open field**' system where each parish or manor had a number of large fields, divided into strips which were worked communally. Some fields were left fallow in rotation.

The great **monasteries** owned huge tracts of land and were often enthusiastic farmers. In England, the Cistercian abbeys of Yorkshire produced tons of **wool**, much of which was sold to Italy.

In the 14th century, the Black Death – an epidemic of bubonic plague – killed about a third of the population of England and other European countries, with a profound effect on the availability of agricultural labour.

THEY GAVE THEIR NAMES - HORTICULTURAL IMMORTALS

Species	Named after	Dates
Aubretia	Claude Aubriet (Fr)	1665–1742
Begonia	Michel Begòn (Fr)	1638–1710
Bougainvillia	Louis de Bougainville (Fr)	1729–1811
Cattleia	William Cattley (Eng)	1788–1835
Clarkia	William Clark (US)	1770–1838
Dahlia	Anders Dahl (Swe)	1751–89
Douglas Fir	David Douglas (Scot)	1798–1834
Forsythia	William Forsyth (Scot)	1737–1804
Freesia	F. H. T. Freese (Ger)	d.1876
Fuchsia	Leonard Fuchs (Ger)	1501–66
Greengage	Sir William Gage (Eng)	1656–1727
Gentian	Gentus, King of Illyria	*fl.*180–168BC
Gunnera	Bishop Johann Gunner (Nor)	1718–73
Lobelia	Mathias de L'Obel (Flem)	1538–1616
Macadamia (nuts)	John McAdam (US)	
Magnolia	Bernard Magnol (Ire/US)	1775–1816
Nicotiana (nicotine)	Jean Nicot (Fr)	1530–1600
Paeony	(Goddess) Paeonia (Gk)	–
Poinsettia	Joel Poinsette (US)	1779–1851
Sequoia (tree)	(Chief) Sequoyah (Cherokee)	c.1770–1843
Wisteria	Prof. Caspar Wister (US)	1761–1818
Zinnia	Johann Zinn (Ger)	1727–59

In 18th-century USA cotton was an important crop, picked and processed by slaves. Inventors set about developing machinery to speed up the work. In 1793 in Georgia, Eli Whitney (US) (1765–1825) devised the cotton 'gin' (short for engine) to separate the cotton fibres from the seed case or boll.

Farmers from traditional cultures have not forgotten the need to replenish the Earth's resources. Here an Aboriginal in Arnhem Land, Australia, keeps an eye on a fire deliberately started in order to enrich the soil.

In response to these conditions, scientific and technical advances were swiftly applied to agriculture. These improvements applied to both **mechanization** and the beginnings of scientific breeding. In 1700, spiked rollers to flatten and aerate the soil were employed in Essex, England.

In 1731 Jethro Tull (GB) (1674–1741) published *Horse Hoeing Husbandry*. He had invented his unpatented one horse **seed-drill** at Howlerry Farm near Wallingford, England in 1701, and developed his **seed box** and dropper unit at Prosperous Farm, near Hungerford. This meant that seed could be sown evenly without wastage and more quickly. Camillo Torello (It) had secured a Venetian patent for a similar device in 1566 but it is not known whether or not his machine had a rotating feeding mechanism.

Michael Menzies (GB) devised a flailing **thresher** – to separate grain from chaff – driven by a water wheel in 1732 and his fellow countryman Robert Ransome (1753–1830) introduced self-sharpening ploughs with interchangeable parts.

The production of cereals such as **corn** spread. In 1794 a chaff-cutter with a regulator for cutting straw was invented by James Cooke, and in 1799 Joseph Boyce took out the first patent for a **horse-drawn reaper** to replace lines of men and women working with scythes or sickles.

Franz Karl Achard (Swiss) (1753–1821) built the world's first **sugar beet** extraction factory at Kurem, Silesia in 1801. Andreas Marggraf (Ger) (1709–82) had first extracted sucrose from the beet (*Beta vulgaris*) in 1747.

In 1814 a **hay-making machine** was built by Robert Salmon (1763–1821) at Woburn, Bedfordshire and in 1826 a two-horse reaper designed by Rev. Patrick Bell (1799–1869) was built in Forfarshire, Scotland. An improved traction reaper (with cutter-bar action) was built by Cyrus McCormick (US) (1808–84) in 1831.

Steam-power was now beginning to be applied to agricultural machinery. A steam-powered **cable plough** was first demonstrated in 1833 by John Heathcoat MP (1783–1861) and Josiah Parkes (1793–1871) in Britain. E. C. Bellinger of South Carolina, USA, patented a cable system for steam-powered ploughing in the same year.

In 1836, the earliest known **combine harvester** (which would both reap and thresh) was reported from USA. This was not demonstrated until 1854 with a machine built in Chicago by Harris Moore and J. Hascall.

Intensive rearing was first applied to poultry. Steam-heated incubation was patented in 1843 by Napoleon Guerin of New York City. Poultry farmers first employed incubators to speed up the hatching process in the 1870s.

By this time, the American West was given over to large-scale **ranches**. These were so immense that fencing them was an enormous task in the absence of sufficient fencing timber. This problem was solved in 1867 by Lucien B. Smith of Ohio, who invented **barbed wire**; however, no example of his original creation exists. The familiar two-strand twisted version was patented by M. Kelly (US) in 1868.

Breaking up the soil after preliminary ploughing improved with the **disc-harrow**. William Crosskill called his invention – serrated discs on a central axis towed by three horses – a clod-crusher. The steel disc harrow was built in the USA in 1856.

Artificial **fertilizer** was first manufactured in 1843 by Sir John Bennet Lawes (Eng) (1814–1900) at Deptford Creek, London. His superphosphates were marketed at 4s 6d a bushel from 1 July.

The greater demand for milk in the new industrial cities meant **larger herds**. The first milking machine was invented by L. O. Colvin (US) and manufactured in Auburn, New York.

The first self-propelled combine harvester was unsuccessfully introduced by Daniel Best (US) (1838–1923) in 1888 but in 1889 the Charter Engine Co. of Chicago, Illinois changed the future of agriculture with the first **petrol-engined tractor**.

The 'pulsator' model of **milking machine**, imitating the sucking action of a calf on its mothers teats, was invented by Dr Alexander Shields (GB) in 1895.

Nitrogenous **fertilizers** were first promoted by Prof. Fritz Haber (Ger) (1868–1934) from Karlsruhe in 1909.

In 1928, John D. and Mack D. Rust of Texas, USA patented their spindle **cotton-picker** which, by 1969, had eliminated all but four per cent of hand-picking. This resulted in the mass migration of workers to the northern states.

In the 1920s **vitamin-enhanced feed** for poultry was first used and vaccines and **antibiotics** were introduced into animal husbandry in 1946. Animal breeding advanced as a result of **artificial insemination**, in which previously collected semen is injected into the female uterus, usually cows or pigs. The genetic characteristics of good animals can thus be stored frozen and used more widely.

In the 1930s, **droughts** in the plains of central North America led to the excessive erosion of the soil which created the 'dust bowl'. The land had been over-farmed and the fertility dropped sharply.

John Deere (US) (1804–86) patented his integrated mould board and **steel ploughshare** in Chicago in 1837. The steel would retain its cutting edge much longer than cast iron and the mould board helped to shape the furrow.

Manual work was again cut in the US with the **sugar-beet harvester**, invented in 1941

and in 1949 Frank Zybach of Colorado, USA, devised an automatic centre-pivot sprinkler able to irrigate an area of 133 acres *53 hectares*.

The first **axial threshing machine** was International Harvester's Axial Flow of 1975 and in 1980 Allis Chalmers Inc. marketed the first successful **round-baling machine**, meaning that bales could be stored in the fields without coming to any harm and thus changing the face of the countryside.

Gordon C. Hanna (US) in 1964 bred a variety of **tomato** which fruits and ripens synchronously so that mechanical harvesting became feasible: a crew of 12 could collect 12 tons per hour.

AD 2000

An uncertain future

Modern **electronics** are now being applied to agriculture, In 1980, computerized farming in the US supplied access to terminals for supplying soil analyses and advice on maximizing fertilizer dressings. In 1993, the first robot milking machine was introduced in Assen, Netherlands.

The advent of fertilizers made the 'Green Revolution' possible. Countries of the Third World which had been colonies of the Western countries had been subjected to **monocultures** of crops destined for export. Brazil, for example, relied wholly first on sugar from the 1580s to the 1690s and then on coffee, which dominated the economy until the 1940s. But monocultures, with their intensive use of fertilizers and pesticides ultimately sow the seeds of their own decline. The land, it emerged,

became progressively impoverished.

US agriculture, which comprised 72 per cent of the nation's activity in 1820, had fallen to 36 per cent by 1900, to 12 per cent in 1950 and 3.3 per cent in 1979.

In the UK, farmers started to **diversify** into other activities such as tourism and turning land into golf-courses. They also started to farm new breeds of animal to titillate public taste and bypass competition from, for example, New Zealand lamb and Danish bacon. In the 1990s, herds of ostriches, llamas and deer could be seen in the fields of Europe.

At the same time, many methods of **scientific agriculture**, originally embraced to improve yields, have produced a backlash. Synthetic fertilizers and pesticides leave more or less toxic residues in food and water, and some farmers and horticulturalists are turning to organic methods. Green manures are used and pests are controlled by companion planting or biological control.

The **battery system** of poultry farming was subjected to public enquiry on grounds of cruelty in the UK in 1998. Public concerns were also raised about the effect on the environment of **genetically modified crops**, such as soya, and the possible medical side-effects on the consumer of eating them.

Cloning – that is, the reproduction of life artificially – came to public knowledge in 1997, with the successful cloning of Dolly the sheep. It is also subject to intense ethical debate, but may have profound effects on the future of agriculture.

The future of farming? In hydroponic agriculture, plants are fed by nutrient-rich liquid rather than grown in soil. These hydroponically grown lettuces thrive in a giant greenhouse.

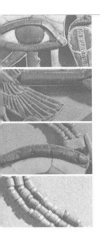

Clothing

BEFORE AD 1

Protection from the elements

The earliest peoples made **simple cloaks from animal hides** to keep the wind and rain off their bodies. The first shepherds doubtless admired the thick coats of their sheep and goats and experimented with plucking wool from the animals. **Wool** was first spun into a strand using spindles of bone or pottery *c.*3500BC.

Dye from the plant *Indigofera tinctoria* – indigo – has been found in Egyptian cloth dating from the Fifth Dynasty (*c.*2400BC). But indigo was certainly used earlier in the third millennium BC in Sumer (modern Iraq) and was originally derived from India. Tyrian purple is recorded from *c.*1500BC and describes the cloth dyed with extracts from the molluscs Purpura

These thick fire-fighting suits saved the lives of Royal Navy crewmen in World War II. Protective clothing made from fire-resistant asbestos was first developed in 1836.

*c.*1600–1400BC, records list flocks of thousands of sheep which provided wool for an extensive cloth industry.

AD 1

Togas for men – and for women, early bras

Men of the Roman civilization *c.*800BC–AD410 wore **togas**, loose garments made from a single piece of cloth and wrapped round the body, leaving the right arm free. The first proto-**bra**, a breast-supporting scarf called a strophium, was used by female gymnasts; other women used handkerchiefs. Evidence from Sicilian mosaics *c.*AD350 suggests that the strophium developed into a cloth binding the breasts.

AD 1000

Covering hands and feet

The earliest known use of knitting needles was in Egypt, *c.*AD1150. At around this time, men wore gauntlet gloves with large cuffs in battle or for hawking. Fingerless gloves were first recorded in 1386.

Until *c.*1550 **pockets** were small pouches, separate from the trousers; seam slits in trousers for pouches became a feature in 1585. At this time a '**wardrobe**' was a room in

which clothes were kept and the name was not applied to furniture until *c.*1794.

The hard-wearing cotton cloth named **denim** was first recorded *c.*1695. Its name is an abbreviation of *serge de Nîmes*, twilled cotton material made in the town of Nîmes in southern France.

In the 18th and early 19th centuries, the correct attire for men at public baths was a voluminous flannel **gown**. From *c.*1865, women wore loose ankle-length gowns for sea bathing.

Up to this time, the principal materials had been wool, cotton, linen and silk. But in the 19th century **new materials** were developed. In 1830, Messrs. Rattier et Guibal of Saint Denis, Paris, first wove **elastic rubber thread** as a warp into elastic.

Khaki was introduced on the North West Frontier of India in 1846 by Lt. Gen. Sir Harry Lumsden (1821–96) as a Lieutenant at Peshawar, near the Khyber Pass, Pakistan.

In 1876 the French actress Sarah Bernhardt converted the fashionable set to the idea of the **trouser suit** for women. In 1916, this smart outfit was adopted by the

In the 16th century pedestrians on city streets had to be wary of thieves. Both purses and 'pockets' were worn outside trousers, hanging from the belt – and were easily cut or snatched. These revellers were painted by a follower of Dutch artist Pieter Brueghel the Elder (*c.*1525–69).

and Murex from the Mediterranean coast between Tyre (modern Lebanon) and Haifa (northwest Israel).

During the Mycenaean civilization in ancient Crete

EARLIEST SURVIVING PHYSICAL EVIDENCE OF CLOTHING

This table underlines the fact that textiles and animal hides and furs only rarely survive, under freakishly favourable circumstances. It can provide no true indication of the antiquity of such forms of clothing or tailoring. Finds of bone-eyed needles dated to c.20,000BC suggest that suits of skins or furs were at least 7000 years earlier than any surviving examples.

Item	Location	Source	Period	Date
Belt and trousers	Laussel, France	bas-relief of hunter	Aurignacian (Stage II)	c.28,000 BC
Trousers	Sungir, Klyazma-Oka, Russia	grave goods	Gravettian	c.23,000 BC
Buttons and toggles	Grotte du Cavillon, Italy	burial of a male	Gravettian	c.20,000 BC
Knitted skirting	Lespugne, France	'Venus' statuette	Solutrian	c.18,000 BC
Fur trousered suit with snood	Mal'ta, Siberia, Russia	perforated statuette	late Palaeolithic	c.13,000 BC
Skin wind-proof suit with hood	Buret, Angara River, Russia	bone statuette	late Palaeolithic	c.13,000 BC
Buttoned garment	Montastrac, Dordogne, France	engraved bone	late Magdalenian	c.11,000 BC
Fur skirts	Cogull, Lerida, Spain	cave art	Mesolithic	c.8000 BC
Woven textiles	Catal Hüyük, Turkey (Level VIB)	in linen (flax) and in wool	Neolithic	6610–6540 BC
Woven linen pieces	Nahal Hemer, Judaean desert	cache	Neolithic	c.6500 BC
Cotton garments	Meyrgarh, Indus plain, Pakistan	garments	Neolithic	c.4500 BC
Silken garments	Hsi-yin-ts'un, southern Shansi, China	domesticated silkworm cocoons	Neolithic	c.3000 BC

Prussian State Railway as the uniform for all its train conductresses.

Sleeping suits or **pyjamas** for men originated in India and were widely adopted in Europe in the late 19th century, when jackets and trousers of wool or silk replaced the night-shirt. The name derives from the Persian *pae* (leg), and Hindustani *jamah* (clothing).

JEWELLERY

The earliest items of 'jewellery' were probably **attractive shells**, corals and pebble stones. **Mammoth ivory and animal teeth** were also used for decoration or as talismans and have been found in Eurasian graves as early as 30,000BC. A very elaborately carved bracelet made from mammoth bone and dating from 20,000BC has been found at Mezin in southern Russia.

By 5500BC stone and mineral beads were being made in Mesopotamia (the fertile plain that encompasses modern Iraq and parts of Iran and Syria). Among them was the hard black volcanic glass-like rock, obsidian.

In 1971 Dr Ivan Ivanov (Bul) excavated a cemetery dating from c.4200BC in Varna, Bulgaria. It contained stylized figurines with metallic earrings and beaten face masks of local gold, together with carnelian and obsidian beads.

Lapis lazuli was mined for gemstones from 4000BC in Mundiguk Province, Badakshan, Afghanistan. It was transported to Egypt from c.3000BC.

The earliest evidence of granulation – the long-lost art of fixing granules of gold onto a surface and then fusing them by firing with copper hydroxide – is from c.2500BC.

Sir Leonard Woolley (GB) (1880–1960) discovered burial pits at the site of Ur, a Sumerian city-state, in 1926. One figure, believed to be that of a queen, was covered with **beads** of agate, carnelian, chalcedony, gold, lapis lazuli and silver and wore a diadem of golden leaves and rosettes.

Royal status demands priceless jewels. This gold necklace inlaid with lapis lazuli and nephrite was found in the tomb of Egyptian boy king Tutankhamen (14th century BC). It depicts the eye of the sky god Horus, whose emblem was the hawk.

Early Egyptian attempts to make **glass beads** in the third millennium BC were probably an effort to substitute for rare stones in bead necklaces. 'True' jade or nephrite (a silicate of calcium and magnesium) was imported into China in c.2500BC from the Khotanese and Yarkend districts of central Asia.

Emeralds, green beryl, were first mined c.1700BC in Upper Egypt. The name is derived from the Greek *smaragdos*, a (green) stone. In 1969 a 7025-carat crystal was found in the Cruces Mine, near Gachala, Columbia. Emeralds were first synthesized in 1930.

By c.1400BC **costume jewellery** was established with the production of a blue glass paste imitating the appearance of lapis lazuli and known as 'Egyptian blue'.

Sapphires were first reported as gemstones c.800BC though the Greek name *sappheiros* was applied to the much earlier established lapis lazuli. Today, the term sapphire is applied generally to all translucent gem corundums except the ruby. Lone Star – at 9719.50 carats,

the largest ever asteria or 'star sapphire' – was cut in London in November 1989.

The 'power-dressed' Emperor Artaxerxes II (r.404–358BC) of Persia (modern Iran) wore, on state occasions, up to **12,000 talents of gold jewellery,** worth some $6.5 million in AD2000.

In June 1936 a Parthian tomb, dating from c.50BC–AD50, near Baghdad, Iraq, was accidentally unearthed during railway building, revealing a clay jar 7 inches *17cm* tall, containing a copper cylinder and an iron rod sealed with bitumen. The only feasible purpose of such a device was to contain acid and form a battery. Others have been discovered at the nearby Parthian city site of Ctesiphon. If wired up in series, such jars (which individually could yield $^1/_2$ volt for 18 days), might possibly have been used for **electro-plating**.

The word **diamond** is derived from the Greek *adamas*; invincible. It was first used by the Roman astrologer and poet, Marcus Manilius in AD16. But scholars believe that a reference to precious stones from the region of Bihar, northern India, c.300BC is to diamonds. In 1796 diamonds were first recognized as pure crystallized carbon.

Large stones were unrecorded before c.AD1000. Praised and coveted above all jewels, large diamonds have been at the centre of a number of celebrated intrigues. The 191-carat *Koh-i-Noor* (Mountain of Light) was taken from the Raja of Malwa by Sultan Ala-ed-Din in 1304. It was presented by the British East India Co. to Queen Victoria in 1862. It

was then recut to a 108-carat brilliant and incorporated in 1937 into the Imperial crown.

The 199.6-carat stone now known as the Orloff was reputedly stolen from a temple at Trichinopoly, India. It was purchased in Amsterdam in 1744 by Prince Grigory for presentation to Catherine the Great of Russia (1729–96) and became the centrepiece of the Romanov sceptre. Today it is in Russia's diamond treasury.

HATS

At horse racing meetings in England from c.1660 jockeys wore peaked velvet **caps** bearing the horse owner's colours. From c.1850, the caps were made of light silk.

Top hats were introduced by the London haberdasher John Hetherington in 1797. In 1849 the **bowler hat** was made by William and Thomas Bowler of Southwark Bridge Road, London for William Coke (later 2nd Earl of Leicester) of Holkham, Norfolk, to

The rock-sized Cullinan diamond was found at Mpumalanga, South Africa. Stones from the diamond adorn the crown worn by Queen Elizabeth II.

protect huntsmen and his estate workers from low branches. First called 'Cokes', the hats were known as 'Bowlers' after 1861.

In the USA, the name **Derby** for the bowler hat came into use in 1888. It was named after the 12th Earl of Derby (1752–1834), founder of the horse race held on Epsom Downs, Surrey, each June.

The **Homburg** was made fashionable by the Prince of Wales (1841–1910), later King Edward VII, who frequented the health resort of Homburg, in Germany.

In 1895 the **Stetson** – a soft, wide-brimmed slouch hat – was created by the American J. B. Stetson (1830–1906). The **Trilby** hat was worn after 1895. It was a narrow-brimmed, soft felt hat of the Homburg type, with an indented crown.

SHOES AND STOCKINGS

The **earliest form of footwear**, c.160,000 years ago was the monodermon, a leather or skin bag, gathered at the ankle and secured by threaded thongs. They were made with stone scrapers and borers; much earlier foot coverings, made with obsidian tools, must have existed in palaeolithic times, particularly when trekking began c.1.9 million years BP.

Before 3400BC in Egypt, shoes were made of papyrus. **Sandals** of reed on a cord warp were found in Egyptian graves dating from c.1580BC. Custom-made shoes were produced by Greek shoe-makers from c.550BC, and perhaps from c.650BC by the Etruscans. **Platform shoes**, raised with 3in *7.5cm* thick

soles (*kothornos*) – later termed 'buskins' – were allegedly invented by the dramatist Aeschylus (Gk) (c.525–455BC), for the theatre.

The earliest example of a **sock** comprising a Roman looped fabric was found in Dura-Europos, Syria, dating from before AD256. **Stockings**, also known as hose, are first seen in paintings c.750.

Tennis shoes with soft soles were used for court tennis in c.1520. For lawn tennis, shoes with India rubber soles were introduced in 1878.

Wellington boots made of leather were introduced in 1817, named after the first Duke of Wellington (GB) (1769–1852). They were made in rubber by the North British Rubber Co. Edinburgh, Scotland from 1867.

Trainers, soft spikeless rubber or composition shoes, first appeared in the 1940s. They took their name from their use in sports training.

MAN-MADE FIBRES

The first wholly synthetic fibre, **nylon**, was developed in the USA in 1937 by the chemist Wallace H. Carothers (1896–1937) at the Du Pont Co. **Terylene** – a polyester – was developed in Britain in 1941. By 1989, it made up more than half of the world's synthetic fibre production.

The man-made elastomeric (rubber-like elastic) fibre **Lycra®** was invented and

produced by Du Pont in 1958, originally as 'Fiber K'. It became known in North America as Spandex and as elastine in Europe. In 1968, it was adopted by the French Olympic ski team, and was first used in swimwear in 1974. In 1984 the fabric appeared in high-performance shorts for athletics and basketball.

Gore-Tex® is named after W. L. Gore & Associates, founded in 1958 by Bill and Vieve Gore (US) to explore the potential of PTFE (polytetrafluoroethylene) in making a fabric that is both waterproof and 'breathes' - that is, it does not trap the body's natural moisture within the garment but instead allows it to pass outwards into the air, reducing condensation and giving greater comfort.

Kevlar was created at Du Pont de Nemours by a team led by Stephanie Kwolek from 1964–69. It is a highly resistant polyparaphenylen-eterphthalamide fibre and is five times stronger by weight than steel. Kevlar was commercialized on a major scale from 1973 and has been widely used by police and the army for bullet-proof vests (see page 193).

Gore-Tex garments that allow sweat to pass out but do not let water in are now standard issue for many armed forces. In 2000, annual sales for the US company that manufactures Gore-Tex passed $1000 million.

Marriage and relationships

BEFORE AD 1

Roaming bands create the first settlements

Early humans evolved slowly over hundreds of millennia. During the 2.7 million years between the invention of stone tools in Africa and the dawn of agriculture (most probably in China *c.*10,000BC) humans probably lived in **hunter-gatherer bands**, often of about 30 people.

Farming brought new possibilities for settled development. The foundation of **small cities** followed. The earliest archaeological evidence is at Jericho (now Tell es-Sultan) north of the Dead Sea, Jordan, which was uncovered to its foundations of *c.*10,800BC by Dame Kathleen Kenyon (GB) (1906–78). Jericho expanded by 7800BC to support a population estimated to have been at least 3000. This population lived in large oval stone semi-subterranean structures and lived on crops and from hunting.

The era of living in bands was now over for some people, but as several millennia had yet to elapse before writing was born, we can only guess at the social structure of these early cities.

The first available documentary evidence on marital and social relationships comes from Sumerian cuneiform tablets and Egyptian hieroglyphs. The earliest fact we know is that the ruler Urukagina of Lagash, Mesopotamia *c.*2350BC, gave laws that were intended to protect **widows and orphans**.

In ancient Greece, marriage was monogamous. Being by purchase, the bride's consent was not necessary. Marriageable **women were sold** in auctions in the Babylonian civilization around 1430BC.

In Rome, two possible states were recognized – marriage or an alternative, less formal condition described as *semi-matrimonium* or **concubinage**. Men could choose between a wife or a concubine, but it was not legal to have both.

Divorce, which was legalized in 234BC, was also of two kinds—total divorce or divorce from bed and board.

Mother serves while sister pours. In the 19th and early-mid 20th century people often lived in extended families of more than one couple and generation. This family dinner took place in New Mexico, USA, in 1956. Families are getting smaller in the developed world. The change has often brought freedom from traditional roles for women.

Marriage and relationships

AD 1

Religious prohibitions

In Christian society, priests were forbidden to marry after ordination in AD235. Lent was then strictly observed and the marriage ceremony was not permitted to be performed during the period of Lent.

AD 1000

The king's decree

In 1073, priests were required to swear **vows of celibacy**. The reign of Henry VIII in England (r.1509–47) proved to be a decisive time for religion in English society. Henry wished to divorce his first wife, Catherine of Aragon, in order to marry Anne Boleyn. When the Pope refused to permit this, Henry declared himself head of the English Church and England became a Protestant State in 1533. He divorced Catherine and married Anne Boleyn and later also divorced his fourth wife, Anne of Cleves.

In 1533, an act was passed defining the forbidden degrees of affinity for lawful marriage, that is, that certain people who are closely related to each other may not marry.

During the Commonwealth in England (1649–60), **civil marriages** were legal, with a local magistrate administering the vows. In 1695, marriage in England was taxed at a rate varying from £50 for a duke all the way down to 2s 6d for a 'common person'.

Marriages performed by a **Registrar** without a religious ceremony were first authorized in England in 1836.

The laws regarding marriage have always followed what society or its leaders find useful. The church either accepted or,

in the rare cases of opposition, was forced to submit. In 1872, marriage to a deceased wife's sister was made legal in Australia, followed by New Zealand in 1880 and Canada in 1882. This, apparently popular, ruling probably reflected the relative **shortage of women** in the colonies at the time.

AD 2000

Differing attitudes

Divorce was legalized in the French Republic in 1793, an early result of liberty. In England divorce was only possible by Act of Parliament before 1857. Separation or divorce could only be sought by men until 1878, when English magistrates were empowered to grant legal separation to a wife who suffered violence from her husband.

Colour and race have also sometimes been factors in the legality of marriages. In some southern states of the US, marriage was illegal between black and white people before 1967. Similarly, 'Europeans' and 'non-Europeans' were not permitted to marry in South Africa before 1985.

Women's rights within a marriage were often very few. In England, married women could not own property before 1882. In Portugal, a married woman had to have her husband's written agreement before she could open a bank account or obtain a passport until 1965.

At the end of the 20th century in the developed world, women tend to have children later, and **families are smaller** than they once were. Single-parent families are increasingly common.

In more than 40 US states, **divorce** can be granted without fault on either side. The Roman Catholic church still does not permit divorce, although marriages can be annulled by the Pope. In strict Muslim society, a woman cannot divorce her husband, but he can divorce her.

Marriageable age varies widely in different societies. In the USA, marriage with parental consent is permitted at age 14 for males in Alabama, Massachusetts, New Hampshire, Texas, Utah and Vermont, and at 12 in Massachusetts for females. But in Puerto Rico, both parties to the marriage must be 21.

When it comes to marriage ceremonies, the pull of tradition is strong. Couples often choose to follow custom by wearing formal clothes and celebrating their wedding with large gatherings of relatives. This wedding picture was taken in Yokohama, Japan, in 1992.

Education and childcare

Maria Montessori, Italian doctor and educationalist, inspired a revolutionary movement in education. Beginning with retarded children and then from 1907 working with the offspring of Rome's working classes, she developed a system in which the children were given freedom to move about and choose activities – many of them academically demanding – using specially designed materials. Montessori schools have been set up across the world, especially in Europe and North America.

BEFORE AD 1

Learning to write

Education was known in the first recorded civilization – that of Sumeria (now southern Iraq). In *c*.3300BC scribe schools grew up to instruct pupils in pictographic **writing**.

The world's first institute of higher learning was founded by the Greek philosopher **Plato** (*c*.428–347BC) in *c*.385BC in a grove outside the western wall of Athens. It was named Plato's Academy and was a school for statesmen; its portals bore the sign 'Let no one ignorant of mathematics enter here'. It survived for more than nine centuries, until closed down in AD529 by the Emperor of the Eastern Roman Empire, Justinian (*c*.482–565).

In Greece **elementary** education had three branches: *poidatribes* — gymnastics, games, deportment and (for girls) dancing; *kitharistes* – music and lyric poetry; and *grammatistes* – reading, writing, arithmetic and learning poetry by heart.

Such education was neither compulsory nor competitive. **Discipline** was enforced with a forked stick in the classroom. Education for older children was confined to those intent on being trained for law, medicine, philosophy or rhetoric.

In 335BC, one of Plato's pupils, the Greek philosopher **Aristotle** (384–322BC), opened a school in the Lyceum – a garden near the temple of the Greek god Apollo in Athens – to teach astronomy, biology, ethics, literature, logic, mathematics, meteorology, metaphysics, physics and politics.

In ancient **China**, civil service exams were instituted in 165BC. People who wanted jobs in the civil service had to study the Chinese classics.

AD 1

Monastic teaching

After the disintegration of the Roman Empire, education became the province of the Church. Most schools were run by monasteries.

Charlemagne (742–814), the Holy Roman Emperor, never himself learned to read but he invited the Northumbrian monk Alcuin to help him found **monastic schools**. The curriculum included grammar, logic, rhetoric, arithmetic, geometry, music and astronomy.

AD 1000

The first universities

The **first university** in Europe was founded in Salerno, Italy, in the 9th century. University College, the oldest Oxford college, was founded in 1249 and the Sorbonne in Paris was founded in 1253 by Robert de Sorbon, who was Louis IX's chaplain.

Henry VIII (*r*.1509–47) ordered all clergymen with more than £100 a year to sponsor a pupil at grammar school or university.

Grammar schools were first established *c*.1550 for the teaching of Latin, knowledge of which was a prerequisite for entering any profession. In 1570, Roger Ascham, tutor to the young Elizabeth I, wrote *The Scholemaster*, one of the first English treatises on education.

Education for girls was considered to be a waste of money until well into the 19th century. In 1640, it is estimated that 80 per cent of women in London were illiterate.

In 1660, a boy at Eton College was beaten for not smoking. Tobacco smoke was supposed to have a fumigatory effect in preventing the plague. Until the advent of modern hygiene, many children had only a small chance of surviving their early years.

England's **Queen Anne** (1665–1714) had 17 children, only one of whom survived infancy – only to die at the age of 12. Parents had large families either to ensure an heir if they were rich or to provide labour on farms if they were poor. In 1778, Emily Lennox (1731–1814) gave birth to her 22nd child at the age of 46. Only half of her children survived into adulthood.

In 1762, French philosopher Jean-Jacques **Rousseau** (1712–78) published *Emile*, a treatise in the form of a novel on raising children. In the book, the character Emile is brought up apart from other children 'according to nature' This influenced Swiss educationalist Johann Heinrich **Pestalozzi** (1746–1827), whose school at Everdun attracted teachers from all over Europe.

The first **illustrated children's book** published in English was *Goody Two Shoes*, which appeared in 1765. It was possibly written by the Irish dramatist Oliver Goldsmith (1728–74).

Primary education was first made a legal requirement in Prussia in the mid-18th century. In France, the Guizot Law of 1833 established a primary school in every settlement.

In 1842, Edwin **Chadwick** (Eng) (1800–90) published *An Enquiry into the Sanitary Conditions of the Labouring Population of Great Britain*, which revealed that 57 per cent of the infants of the labouring class in Manchester died before the age of five.

In 1865 Elizabeth Garrett Anderson (1836–1917) became the **first English woman doctor**. The medical schools of the time would not admit her, but she took the examination for the Society of Apothecaries. She was awarded the degree of MD (Doctor of Medicine) by the University of Paris and became Britain's first Lady Mayor.

In the same year, **Lewis Carroll** (Charles Lutwidge Dodgson) (Eng) (1832–98) published *Alice's Adventures in Wonderland*, one of the first books written for children which did not have a moralizing didactic purpose.

In 1867, Thomas John **Barnardo** (1845–1905), an Irish philanthropist, opened his first home for destitute children in Stepney, London.

AD 2000

Education for all

Attendance at school by children under 10 was made **compulsory** in Britain in 1870. The National Society for the Prevention of Cruelty to Children (NSPCC) was founded in 1889.

Austrian philosopher and educationalist Rudolf **Steiner** (1861–1925) pioneered his educational method in a school in Stuttgart, Germany, in 1891. Steiner was interested in Eastern philosophy and mysticism and believed that education should aim to develop the whole child. The first Steiner school in Britain was founded in Streatham, in southwest London, in 1925.

In 1918, a British Education Act raised the school-leaving age to 14, in response to reports that children had lost education in the war because they had been working under-age in the booming wartime industries.

The pioneer of birth control, Marie **Stopes** (Scot) (1880–1958), opened her first clinic in 1921, in London. Her book *Married Love* (1916) argued that women should take pleasure in sex within marriage. It was banned in the USA.

In Britain, **comprehensive schools** replaced selective grammar schools and secondary moderns in the 1960s and 1970s. These schools aim to provide teaching for children of all abilities in mixed groups.

The Open University, aiming to enable any adult to study for a degree at home by coursework, correspondence, summer schools and lessons broadcast on television or radio, was founded in 1969.

Effective methods of **family planning** now give people control over the size of their families, but at the end of the 20th century this was still a privilege of developed countries. In Britain in 1999, the birth rate was 12 births per year per 1000 people. In Bangladesh, however, it was 25 and in Nigeria, 42.

Britain's oldest university – in Oxford, central England – grew from informal collections of students and masters in the 12th century. The University's picturesque spires and reputation for excellence have not protected it from harsh economic reality in the last decades of the millennium.

An ancient Egyptian scribe prepares to set down a message. In c.3000BC members of elite families could train as scribes – learning was by rote and by memorizing and discipline was severe. The great majority of the population remained illiterate.

Beliefs, rituals, religions

The earliest religion we can know anything about is **Shamanism**. The baffling geometric patterns (chevrons, dots, curves, grids, spirals and zigzags) in Upper Palaeolithic cave art, whether in Franco-Iberia or in the Kalahari in southern Africa, were unexplained until 1988. J. David Lewis-Williams (S. Af.) and Thomas A. Dowson (Zam) then published their theory that these were symbols deriving from Shamanic trances. The trance induces entoptic images – which are produced by the mechanism of the eye itself. Moving into a yet deeper condition of hallucination, shamans experienced both entoptic images and visions of bizarre and terrifying monsters – part beast, part human – known as therianthropes (from the Greek. *therion*, small wild beast; *anthropos*, man).

Cave art dates from at least 30,000BC. The most famous therianthropes are the 15,000-year-old, owl-faced, horned sorcerers in the Trois Frères cave in Ariège, France, found in 1914. It is also possible that the worldwide obsession with dragons has been perpetuated through entoptic phenomena.

The earliest known surviving religious **shrine** is in the El Juyo cave, northern Spain where there is a sculpted chimerical stone face, half male primate, half feline. It is dated from *c*.12,000BC and was discovered in 1978/79 by Dr Leslie G. Freeman (US) of Chicago University.

The earliest-dated still free-standing religious monuments are megalithic **menhirs** (Breton *men*, stone; *hir*, long) in north-western Portugal *c*.4800BC. The Grand Menhire Brisé at Locmariaquer in Brittany, France once stood 66ft 7in *20.3 metres* tall and weighs 256 tons *258,000 kilograms* – proof of the religious fervour of people willing to erect it. The stone circles of **Stonehenge** in Wiltshire, England were being built even before Zoser's Pyramid of 2900BC in Egypt. The axis of Stonehenge is oriented to midsummer sunrise *c*.1840BC.

The first civilizations were all deeply religious. In Sumeria (Iraq/Iran) from 3600BC the priests actually ruled the state. The principal gods or *dingir* were Enki (Water), Ki (Earth), An (Heaven) and Enlil (Air). Their divine laws or *me* were immutable and unchallengeable. Each Sumerian also had a personal god or 'good angel'.

EGYPT

Animal deities

From 5000BC, the ancient Egyptians used **animals** as totems or symbols of their clans. These animals then became identified with gods. **Ra** the creator god is represented with a falcon's head. **Hathor**, a nursing mother-goddess is often depicted with a cow's head.

A Nigerian shaman uses rattle and charms to access the spirit world. The word shaman is Slavonic but shamanism, the oldest known religion, is found all over the world. A shaman is a priestly witch-doctor, believed to have power through trances to influence the spirits – good and bad – who govern human life.

The earliest identified Egyptian god is **Min**, which has been dated from before 3400BC.

HINDUISM

One god takes many forms

Of the existing major religions of the world, that with the earliest roots is Hinduism, which arose in India from the Gangetic and Indic civilizations of *c.*2500BC. In Hinduism, the divine spirit is **Brahman** and all other gods are manifestations of him. These include **Vishnu** and **Shiva**, **Krishna** and the goddess **Shakti**. Vishnu represents the force of life and Shiva that of destruction.

The scriptures were all written in Sanskrit. The earliest is the *Rigveda*, composed *c.*1700BC, which is a collection of hymns. The *Upanishads*, written between 800 and 400BC, are a series of meditations on the nature of Brahman, the supreme being. The *Bhagavad Gita*, written in *c.*500BC, is in the form of a dialogue between Krishna and Prince Arjuna on the eve of a great war.

The central beliefs of Hinduism are **reincarnation** and **karma**. Karma is the sum of past actions, which result in reincarnation as lower or higher beings.

JUDAISM

Religion of the Old Testament

Judaism was formulated *c.*2000BC among the **Hebrews** who had migrated west from Mesopotamia (Iraq/Iran) to Palestine (Canaan). They were led by **Abraham**, who entered into a covenant with God who promised his protection to the Jews in return for their recognition of him as the one true god.

This covenant was renewed by **Moses**, who rescued the Jews from captivity in Egypt in the 13th century BC and led them to the Promised Land, where he received the Ten Commandments.

The **Torah** is the first five books of the Bible and consists of history and laws. These are written in Hebrew and are very ancient, traditionally ascribed to Moses. The **Talmud** (*c.*AD200) and the **Midrash** (AD400–1200) are collections of commentaries on the laws and scriptures.

The Hebrew word *Yehudi* may mean a descendant of Judah, founder of the greatest of the 12 tribes. David, the second king of Israel (*r. c.*1000–*c.*962BC), established Jerusalem as his capital with his palace on the city's highest hill, Mount Zion.

Palestine was invaded by the Babylonians in 586BC, by the Romans in AD70, and by followers of Islam in the 7th century AD. These invasions led to the **Diaspora**, a scattering of Jews into many countries, and to divisions in their religious practices. Jews in central Europe became known as Ashkenazi and those in the Mediterranean countries as Sephardic. In the 19th and 20th centuries, Jews could choose between the Orthodox wing and a more liberal **Reform Judaism**. Today, there are some 18 million Jews worldwide.

The first Zionist Congress to establish a state in the Holy Land for Jewish migrants was held in Basle, Switzerland in August 1897. The **State of Israel** was finally declared on 14 May 1948.

A Hindu woman prays as she performs ritual bathing in the sacred waters of the Ganges River in Varanasi in northeastern India. There are over 660 million Hindus worldwide, making it the fourth most popular religion, behind the combined branches of Christianity, Islam and Buddhism.

ISLAM

Teachings of the Prophet

Islam was founded by **Muhammad** (*c.*570–632) who was born in **Mecca** in the Arabian peninsula. He proclaimed himself a prophet and claimed that the scriptures of the **Koran** had been revealed to him by God. His flight from persecution to Medina in AD622 – known as the **Hegira** – marks the beginning of Islam.

Islam became a militant and missionary faith. Muhammad entered Mecca in triumph as the recognized prophet in 630 and Islam spread throughout North Africa, the Middle East and the Iberian Peninsula between 711 and 1492. During the 10th to the 13th centuries, Christian **crusades** were continuously mounted against Islam, specifically to rescue the Christian holy places. Jerusalem was retaken by the First Crusade in 1099 but lost again to Saladin in 1187.

In the 14th to 16th centuries, Islam also spread to northern India and remains the dominant religion there and in Pakistan. The fundamental ethos of Islam is embodied in

In the holy city of Jerusalem, a Jewish boy helps to carry the sacred Torah – the first five books of the Bible. It is part of the bar mitzvah ceremony that marks his entry into adulthood at the age of 13.

A Buddhist in Tibet holds a prayer wheel. The wheel contains a holy text and releases a prayer each time it spins. Tibet is home to a very distinctive style of Buddhism.

Muslims prostrate themselves during prayers. They face towards the Saudi Arabian city of Mecca, the birthplace of the Prophet Muhammad, founder of Islam. Each year 2 million of the world's 1.15 billion Muslims make a pilgrimage to Mecca.

the statement 'There is no god but **Allah** and Muhammad is his Prophet'.

The Five Pillars of Faith must be performed by all adult males and include **prayer** five times daily, dawn to sunset **fasting** during Ramadan, and making the **pilgrimage** to Mecca at least once in a lifetime.

BUDDHISM

Enlightenment offers an escape from suffering

Buddhism was founded near Benares, India c.524BC by the Indian prince Siddhartha (c.563–483BC), later named **Gautama Buddha** (the enlightened one), who had achieved enlightenment through **meditation**: after 49 days, he achieved the annihilation of desire, known as *nirvana*. He recognized suffering and taught that the way of deliverance from it is through the Eightfold Path of right conduct, right effort, right intentions, right livelihood, right meditation, right mindfulness, right speech and right view.

There are no gods in Buddhism, only **enlightened beings**, but the spread of

Buddhism to Tibet, China, Sri Lanka and Myanmar has meant that it has developed many different forms. In particular, Japan received Buddhism from China in the 12th century AD and developed the tradition known as **Zen**.

The scriptures are divided between those of the Sri Lankan Buddhists, which are written in Pali, and those written in Sanskrit, but they teach a similar doctrine.

The world's Buddhist population now stands at 330 million.

CHRISTIAN FAITH

Followers of Jesus

Christianity began with **Jesus** who was born c.5BC in Bethlehem, in Roman-controlled Palestine. He gathered a band of **disciples** who believed him to be the son of God, or Messiah. He taught followers to love God and one another and offered forgiveness of sins to those who repented. The Romans crucified him, but he is said to have risen from the dead.

Twelve appointed teachers, or apostles, began to spread Jesus's teaching. The first four books of the **New Testament** of the Bible are accounts by early Christians of the life of Jesus. The oldest copy of the New Testament, written in Syriac-Aramaic, dates from c.AD367.

Christianity spread to **Rome** and became the official religion of the Roman Empire in AD380. The church in Rome was founded by the disciple Peter who was subsequently identified as the first Bishop of Rome. His

successors became known as **Popes** and are the heads of the **Catholic** sect of Christianity.

However, in the 16th century, the German priest Martin Luther triggered off the **Reformation** when he protested in 1517 against the corruption of the church. He was followed by John Calvin in 1541 in Geneva, Switzerland and John Knox in Scotland in 1559. These men began the revolt against the Pope's authority which became **Protestantism**.

The total number of Christians exceeded 2000 million during late 1998.

PHILOSOPHY

The pursuit of wisdom

Philosophy as we know it began in Greece in the 5th century BC with the teaching of **Socrates** (469–399BC). Socrates taught his pupils through the 'Socratic method' of questioning everything. We know Socrates' teachings through his most famous pupil, **Plato** (c.428–347BC). In the *Symposium* and *Phaedo*, Plato expounds his theory that every transient object on earth is an imperfect reflection of an ideal form. His *Republic* explores the ideal political state, ruled over by a philosopher-king.

Aristotle (384–322BC) attended Plato's Academy in Athens in 367. Later, he became the tutor to the young Alexander the Great. Aristotle, known as the 'father of natural science', wrote on biology, zoology, ethics and politics.

Greek philosophy had a great influence on early Christian thinkers through the neo-Platonists. **Plotinus** (Egypt) (*c.*AD205–270) taught in Rome where his writings were organized by his pupil Porphyry into the *Enneads*.

In the Christian world, philosophy until the Renaissance was concerned with expounding the **nature of God** and man's relationship to him. The most influential writers were **St Augustine of Hippo** (*b.*Tunisia) (AD354–430) who wrote *The City of God* which is about the conflict between spiritual and worldly values, and **St Thomas Aquinas** (It) (1225–74), who in his great work, *Summa Theologiae*, tried to reconcile Aristotle's ethical thought with the ideals of Christianity.

At the same time, the **Arab world** produced a number of thinkers who had been influenced by Greek philosophy and who, in turn, influenced Western philosophers by way of Spain. **Avicenna** (Iran) (980–1037) interpreted Aristotle to the Arab world and was also a doctor of medicine. **Averroës** (Sp) (1126–98) was a doctor as well as a philosopher.

The **Renaissance** in Europe opened doors to science and the classical thought and literature of Greece and Rome, which had been suppressed by the Church. Desiderius **Erasmus** (Neths.) (*c.*1466–1536) wrote widely on various subjects, including criticism of the narrowness of the Catholic Church.

Many writers were concerned with politics and statecraft. The Italian statesman Niccolò **Machiavelli** (1469–1527) was led to write *The Prince*, a study in the achievement of political success through exercise of self-interest, by his experiences of Cesare Borgia and the Medici ruling

family in Florence. He was one of the first to separate the interests of the Church and the State, a process brought to a head in England by Henry VIII. This opened the way for more speculative philosophy. Thomas **Hobbes** (GB) (1588–1679) held the view that man is wholly selfish but that the sovereign state functions on enlightened self-interest.

René **Descartes** (Fr) (1596–1650) took thought back to its first principles and asked how we can know anything. The question of the nature of knowledge (epistemology) remained central to philosophy. Two important British philosophers who believed that all knowledge derives from experience (empiricism) were John **Locke** (1632–1704) and David **Hume** (1711–76).

From this time, philosophy followed different paths in different countries and was deeply concerned with politics. Jean-Jacques **Rousseau** (Swiss/Fr) (1712–78) believed that man's natural state was good and that he was corrupted by society. Rousseau's masterpiece *The Social Contract* proclaimed that 'man is born free but is everywhere in chains' and made him a forerunner of the French Revolution.

In Germany, philosophy followed a more abstract path. Immanuel **Kant** (1724–1804) was one of the first thinkers to realize that what we think or observe is influenced by who we are. Georg Wilhelm Friedrich **Hegel** (1770–1831) was concerned to build and define a system of logic while Arthur **Schopenhauer** (1788–1860) harked back to

Kant in describing the influence of the will on what we think or can know.

But the most influential political philosophy of our age came from the German Karl **Marx** (1818–83) who, in 1848, wrote (with Friedrich Engels) The **Communist Manifesto** as a programme for revolutionary action. It advocated class struggle by the oppressed proletariat against the bourgeoisie.

Friedrich Wilhelm **Nietzsche** (Ger) (1844–1900) opposed the Apollonian (rational) and the Dionysian (passion and will to power) and celebrated the übermensch (superman). Ludwig **Wittgenstein** (Aust/Eng) (1889–1951) concentrated on the use of language in formulating thought.

In the 20th century, French thinkers have moved beyond the previous boundaries of philosophy to write about literature, psychology and history. **Existentialism**, the logic propounded by Jean-Paul **Sartre** (1905–1980), was as much a moral and aesthetic view of mankind as a philosophy and emphasized the responsibility of the individual.

Michel **Foucault** (1926–1984) wrote on the history of ideas and Jacques **Derrida** (*b.*1930) coined the term 'deconstruction' to describe his approach to literature; he looks at the things texts say that their authors often did not intend.

St Thomas Aquinas was a theologian and a philosopher. One of his contentions was that God's existence can be proved by argument – creation must have a first cause. This likeness is from an altarpiece by Venetian artist Carlo Crevelli (1430/5–*c.*1495).

Crime and punishment

BEFORE AD 1

Rule of law

The first surviving set of laws established by precedent – that is, from actual cases – is the **Hammurabi Code**. Hammurabi was ruler of the Amorite dynasty in Babylon from c.1792–1750BC and he had 282 of his legal judgments carved on *stelae* (pillars of stone). The laws covered aspects of trade, family life and crime.

From c.600BC, the Romans established **magistrates** to judge disputes. The magistrates used freed men called **lictors** to summon and punish offenders.

AD 1000

For the common good

In early medieval times, major cities had Watch Committees to oversee law and order and health and safety for the citizens. The **London Watch** was instituted c.1253. In the USA, the Common Council of New York authorized a **uniformed police force** as early as 1693.

The London police force developed rapidly in the 18th and 19th centuries. In 1753, the novelist and magistrate Henry **Fielding** (Eng) (1707–54) founded a team of regular police and detectives known as the **Bow Street Runners**. The French *Sûreté* detective agency was founded in 1810, on the suggestion of ex-convict and safe-breaker François-Eugène **Vidocq** (Fr) (1775–1857).

The Bow Street Runners were remodelled by the Home Secretary Sir Robert Peel (Eng) (1788–1850) in 1829 into the London Police Force. In a reference to his name, they were known as 'bobbies' or 'peelers'.

The **first state police force in the USA** was the Texas Rangers, formed in 1835. The first specific police traffic squad was deployed in New York City in 1860.

Babylonian king Hammurabi claimed divine inspiration for his code of law; on this stele he is depicted receiving the code from sun god Shamash. The king used military might to win a great empire for Babylon.

AD 2000

Detective methods

Alphonse Bertillon (1853–1914) was chief of the Paris police from 1880 and developed an amalgam of body measurements and photographs, which he called **anthropometry**, to give an accurate description of people. This was largely superseded by fingerprinting for identification but remains useful for physical descriptions.

Fingerprinting was developed by Francis Galton (Eng) (1822–1911) in 1892 and the classification method was adopted by Edward Henry, chief commissioner of the London Metropolitan Police. The Galton-Henry method was introduced to Scotland Yard in 1901.

Another method was independently developed by Juan **Vucetich**, a Dalmatian immigrant to Argentina, in 1888 and is still used in Spanish-speaking countries.

London's Metropolitan Police Fingerprint Branch was set up on 1 July 1901. In the first six months of operations its three officers made 93 identifications by fingerprints. The first criminal convicted on fingerprint evidence was Harry Jackson in June 1902. Jackson left a thumbprint when he burgled a house in Denmark Hill, South London.

In 2000, 38 out of the 50 US states used the death penalty and of these 11 use the electric chair. Some 1,813 criminals were executed worldwide in 1999, including 98 in the USA.

In 1904, the Czech born psychologist Max Wertheimer (1880–1943) invented the **lie detector** or polygraph, based on a series of measurements of a subject's involuntary body functions such as temperature and sweating.

The International Criminal Police Organisation **(Interpol) was founded in 1923** to hold centralized records of criminals and fingerprints. Its headquarters were in Vienna, but moved to Paris after World War II.

The USSR state **secret police**, known as the KGB, existed for 68 years between 1923 and 1990. From 1921 to 1960 it sent an estimated 19 million people to prison and labour camps.

The repression of criminals and those accused of being 'counter-revolutionaries' in **Communist China** from 1949 to May 1969 was estimated by the KGB to have led to 26.3 million deaths.

Surveillance methods developed during World War II (1939–45), and the subsequent development of solid-state electronics, made possible rapid advances in detection. Miniaturisation brought microphones small enough to tap telephones and bug rooms in order to record private conversations.

Identikit portraits were first used in the UK in 1961. They were invented by Hugh McDonald (*b.* 1913) in the USA to produce a likeness from artists' drawings of faces. In 1969, Identikit was replaced by Photofit, based on photographs instead of drawings.

In 1984, the technique of **genetic fingerprinting** or 'DNA typing' was developed by Dr. Alec Jeffreys (UK). The method examines fragments of genetic code (DNA) from any body cells – including blood, hair and saliva – found at the scene of a crime. As each individual has a unique DNA pattern, this can be a powerful aid to identification.

In the USA, in 1999 there were 1,531,040 violent crimes committed, including 16,910 homicides, 93,100 rapes and 446,630 robberies. These figures represent a decline from a 1991 peak of 24,700 homicides, 106,590 rapes and 687,730 robberies.

There were 13,865 US State, County and City police agencies, employing some 641,000 officers. Sixty-one law enforcement officers were killed on duty in 1998.

CAPITAL PUNISHMENT

An eye for an eye

The **first recorded use of capital punishment** following a crime occurred in Nippur, Mesopotamia, *c.*1850BC. Two men were killed following the murder of temple official Lu-Inanna.

Capital punishment remained standard in many parts of the world for the next four millennia. In 2000 executions were still carried out in China (by shooting), South Africa (by hanging), Iran, Turkey and Saudi Arabia (by sword), Malaysia and the USA, where the death penalty was reintroduced in 1977.

Capital punishment was first **abolished** in the British Isles in the reign of William I (1066–87) but reimposed by his son Henry I (1100–35), reaching a peak with Edward VI (1547–53), when an average of 560 people were executed per year.

By 1801, the number of British **capital offences** – those for which the offender could be put to death – had grown to 223, but by 1834 these had been reduced to 15 and by 1861 to four (murder, treason, piracy and arson in a naval dockyard). The death penalty for murder in the UK ceased after 13 August 1964.

EXECUTION LANDMARKS

Landmark	Event	Date
Last burning at stake	Christian Murphy at Newgate, London	18 Mar 1789
Last boiling	Margaret Davy	28 Mar 1542
Crucifixion	Abolished by Emperor Constantine	AD330
Last guillotining	Hamida Djandoubi at Marseilles, France	10 Sept 1977
First electrocution	William Kemmler at Auburn Prison, NY	6 Aug 1890
First gas chamber	Gee Jon at Carson City, Nevada	8 Feb 1924
First lethal injection	Charlie Brooks at Huntsville, Texas	6 Dec 1982

Money

BEFORE AD 1

The first currency

Before coins were made as such, pieces of precious metal (gold or silver) were used to pay for goods or services and these were described by weight. In *c*.600BC Croesus, king of Lydia in Asia Minor (now Turkey), minted what may have been the **first coins** from electrum, a natural alloy of gold and silver.

Coinage in China began at much the same time. **Chinese coins** were made of bronze with a square hole in the middle from the 4th century BC until the early 20th century. In Chinese mythology, the earth is square and heaven dome-shaped, so the coins bore symbols of heaven and earth.

In the 5th century BC, Aegina, Athens and Corinth were the first **Greek** centres to mint their own coinage from silver. Within 100 years the first **bronze coins** appeared for lower denominations. Rulers and politicians habitually lowered the gold, silver or copper content of coins. Solon of Athens (Gk) (*c*.638–559BC) recorded the earliest known debasement of the currency.

In **Rome** the head of an emperor appeared on coins for the first time when Julius Caesar was declared 'perpetual dictator' in 45BC. After that, Roman coins all bore the portrait of the emperor or one of his close family.

AD 1

Inflation hits Rome

As it grew and its resources became stretched, the later Roman Empire had serious inflation problems, and increasingly **debased** its currency. Gold coins eventually ceased to have a fixed relationship to silver ones but were 'floated' so that their value was pegged to the price of gold.

With the collapse of the Roman Empire in the 5th century AD, different kingdoms began to issue their own coins. In England, Offa of Mercia (*d*.796) struck **silver pennies**, and this coin – also known as the *pfennig* – spread to countries on mainland Europe.

Japan began to issue coins similar to Chinese ones in 708. These were made of copper and were called *wado*, meaning soft copper. They replaced the previously used but rather inconvenient method of payment in rice.

AD 1000

Paper notes

Paper currency first appeared in Chengdu in Szechuan province, western China, during the Song dynasty (960–1279). Because the many regions of China all used different currencies, exchange notes were used in trade. During the Yuan dynasty (1206–1367) paper money was used exclusively; metal coins were not permitted.

The discovery of new silver mines in Germany and Bohemia in the Middle Ages made **silver coinage** more common. In Venice, the silver *grosso* (worth 24 *denarii* or pennies) was introduced in 1202. The Florentine *florin* (1251) and the Venetian *ducat* (1284) were the most important gold coins for international trade.

The first US silver dollars – known as 'Liberty' dollars from the image of Liberty stamped on them – were issued in 1794 in Philadelphia. These golden 'Liberty' coins ($20) and 'Indian Head' pieces ($10) date from the early 20th century.

The St Joachimsthal silver mine in Bohemia, discovered in 1512, issued its own 1 oz *30g* silver coins called *Joachimsthalers*, later known as thalers – from which the word '**dollar**' is derived.

The gold and silver mines of Central and South America produced a flood of precious metal in the 15th and 16th centuries. '**Pieces of eight**' were worth eight *reals*, the Spanish currency at the time.

Milled coins, with serrations around the circumference to make 'clipping' – the removal of chunks of precious metal – glaringly obvious, were first struck in France in 1639.

In the 1650s Sweden issued '**plate money**' – sheets of copper which could be up to 11 by 25.5 inches *28 by 65 cm* and weigh 30lb *14kg*. The plates were stamped with their equivalent value in silver but were too cumbersome to use.

This led to the first real **banknotes**, bearing a promise to redeem their value in coins at the bank, being issued by the Stockholm Banco in 1661. The first issue of paper money in the US was of Spanish dollars by the Massachusetts Bay Colony in 1690. The Bank of England – founded in 1694 – began to issue its own notes shortly afterwards.

The Scot John Law (1671–1729) tried to persuade the Scottish Parliament to issue paper currency, but they were not convinced. Undeterred, he moved to France, founded the **Banque Générale** in 1716 and issued paper currency guaranteed by the Crown.

Both the Stockholm Banco and the Banque Générale **collapsed** after issuing too many notes and their founders were imprisoned or exiled.

Perhaps the most unwieldy currency ever made was found by travellers to Yap Island (now in Micronesia, western Pacific) in the 19th century. The islanders used **discs of limestone** which could be up to 13ft *4m* in diameter.

The first '**Greenback**' dollar bills were issued after the cost of the American Civil War (1861–65) exhausted government reserves of gold and forced the US off the 'gold standard', according to which each unit of currency is exchangeable for an agreed amount of gold. American Express issued the first **traveller's cheques** in 1891.

AD 2000

Plastic money

In 1950, the world's first **credit card**, the Diners' Club Card, was introduced by Ralph Schneider (US) in New York City to enable members to dine on account in certain New York restaurants. The Bank of America issued the first bank credit card in 1958, and American Express produced its first credit card in 1963.

In the late 1990s, shopping via the **Internet** became common. Consumers could order goods using their personal computers and pay by credit card.

Banking and finance

BEFORE AD 1

Business in Babylon

The Sumerian and Babylonian cities *c.*2200BC began to use **bills of exchange**. Inscribed on clay tablets, these were payable either to the original creditor or, alternatively, to a third party if this had previously been arranged.

Secured loans were legally formalized in the code of the Amorite King of Babylonia, Hammurabi (1792–50BC). They were recorded

on clay tablets as laid down in his code. The **earliest known bank** is the Egibi Bank, established during the reign of Nebuchadnezzar II (604–562BC) in Babylon. It had numerous branches.

The **first known banker** was the Athenian Pasion (*c.*480–370BC) who started life as a slave but died worth 60 talents or 360,000 drachmae.

Athenian banks provided loans and safe deposits. Borrowers paid interest on loans but the bank did not give interest on any deposits.

The bank run by the Ptolemies of Alexandria *c.*290BC had a monopoly within Egypt. It was the first ever **central bank**.

AD 1

Inflationary crisis

In the last days of the Roman Empire silver became scarce and coins were **debased** until they contained only a few per cent of silver. Around 250BC, banks in Egypt were closing rather than accept these coins and the government had to issue a decree forcing them to stay open and keep dealing.

AD 1000

Italian finance

The Italian cities of **Florence** and **Genoa** were the great banking centres of the Middle Ages. They used bills of exchange to facilitate international trade.

Thousands lost their life savings on Thursday 24 October 1929, when the New York Stock Market crashed. In the aftermath of Black Thursday many banks failed: the crash began a global economic depression that was only reversed by rearmament prior to World War II.

However, it was a high-risk business financing kings who defaulted on loans. **Edward III** of England (r.1327–77) caused the ruin of the banking house of the Peruzzi in Florence in 1343 and the house of Bardi in 1346 by his constant wars with France and Scotland.

The world's first **stock exchange** for the buying and selling of stocks and shares opened in Antwerp in 1460. In London Sir Thomas Gresham (1519–79) founded the Royal Exchange – later known as the Stock Exchange – in 1568.

Share certificates were first issued by the Dutch East India Company in 1602 at the time of the opening of the Amsterdam Stock Exchange, Netherlands.

Pope Paul V (1552–1621) founded the *Banco di Santo Spirito di Roma* ('Bank of the Holy Spirit') in 1605 to support charities and to provide **low-interest loans** for the poor.

The **Bank of England** was founded in 1694. The **New York** Stock Exchange on Wall Street opened in 1790.

In Britain the principle of **limited liability** companies was established by law in 1856. The use of the terms Limited (Ltd) or Public Limited Company (plc) warns creditors of the limit upon the liability of the company's members.

The **Hongkong and Shanghai Banking Company** (later Corporation) opened in 1865. Shanghai had become the centre of foreign trade in China when the Treaty of Nanjing (1842) opened the country to foreign merchants.

The mythological 19th century Chinese **Bank of Hell** issued banknotes to be burned as an offering to the dead at the Chinese New Year.

AD 2000

Going global

The Bretton Woods Conference was a United Nations financial conference held in 1944 in Bretton Woods, New Hampshire, USA, to discuss post-war economic reconstruction. One outcome was the foundation of the International Monetary Fund (**IMF**), established to facilitate international monetary dealings and trade.

The International Bank for Reconstruction and Development (normally called the '**World Bank**') was founded in 1946.

Nasdaq (National Association of Securities Dealers Automated Quotation), set up in 1971, was **the first all-electronic stock exchange**. In the late 20th and early 21st century, Nasdaq became a hotbed for the high-technology companies that have driven strong, but volatile, stock market growth.

On 4 April 2000, for the first time, over 1.5 billion shares a day were traded on the New York Stock Exchange.

Business and trade

BEFORE AD 1

How to make money

The earliest approximation to a **business school** was established by Bai Guei in central China c.400BC. The training was in management, particularly how to make profits.

The first **consumer's guide**, *How to Buy in the Market* by Lynceus, was published in Samos, Greece, c.350BC.

Life insurance was initiated by the Collegium Tenulorum in Rome c.50BC. The heirs to the deceased collected triple the amount of the joining fee.

AD 1000

Quality control

In England, **customs and excise taxes** can be traced back to the Port of London under the Kings of Mercia (mid-7th to early 9th centuries).

The Mayor and Aldermen of London in 1238 instituted **hall-marking** of all gold or silver objects to preclude any 'of metal inferior to that of the coinage'.

The earliest recorded **patent** in England was granted by King Henry VI (r.1422–61, 1470–1) in 1449 for the design of the stained glass windows of Eton College.

One of the first recorded **pawn shops** opened in Brussels in 1618. The practice of pawning is much older. In 1338 King Edward III of England (*r*.1327–77) pawned royal jewels with Lombard Merchants, to raise money for a war against France. The pawn shop's sign of triple brass balls had even by then become traditional.

The oldest **chamber of commerce** was founded in 1650 in Marseilles, France.

The 18th century saw the expansion of London as a commercial centre. In 1707 William **Fortnum** – a former footman of King George III – and friend Hugh **Mason** opened their grocery shop in Piccadilly, West London. This was extended after 1920 into a more general department store. Sotheby's Auctioneers of London and New York were founded by John Sotheby, bookseller, as the Covent Garden Sale Rooms, London, in 1744.

Thomas Cook (1808–92) ran the world's first excursion (by train) in 1841. In 1856 he organized the first Grand Tours of the major European capitals.

The Irish born Alexander T. Stewart (US) (1803–76) opened New York's first **department store**, the Marble Dry Goods Palace, on Broadway, New York City, in 1848. By 1876 his annual turnover was $70 million.

In Britain, Boot's the Chemist chain was started by John **Boot** (Eng) (1816–60) who opened his store for 'vegetable remedies' at 6 Goosegate, Nottingham, in 1850. His son, Jesse Boot (1850–1931), had nearly 1000 branches when he died as Lord Trent aged 81.

Shopping began to change beyond all recognition in the late 19th century. In 1856, I. M. Singer & Co. of Boston, Massachusetts, first allowed old sewing machines to be **traded in** against new purchases and Edward Clark (US), a partner of Singer's, devised a system of **hire purchase** with down payments of $5 and monthly instalments of $3.

In 1879 the **cash register** was first patented by James J. Ritty (US) (*b*.1844), the owner of a saloon in Dayton, Ohio, to combat pilferage by bar staff. In the same year Franklin W. **Woolworth** (US) (1852–1919) opened his Nickel (five-cent) self-service store in Utica, New York. Woolworth lived

to see stores in nine countries and died worth $27 million.

The first recorded **car-hire** firm started in Chicago in 1918. The company was bought in 1923 by John D. Hertz and renamed **Hertz** Self-Drive.

Supermarket trolleys were inaugurated by the Humpty Dumpty store of Oklahoma City, USA, in 1937.

AD 2000

Shopping by numbers

On 26 June 1974 at 8.01am the first recorded purchase (a packet of Wrigley's Chewing Gum) was made via a scanner equipped to 'machine read' Uniform Product Codes, known as **bar codes**.

In 1985 the West Edmonton Mall, Alberta, Canada was completed as the world's largest **shopping centre**, housing more than 800 stores in a 121-acre *49-ha* site with parking for 20,000 cars and annually serving more than 20 million customers.

The rapid growth of **Internet shopping** at the close of the 20th century opened a new chapter in the ever-changing world of retail sales. Amazon, an on-line bookstore based in Seattle, Washington, was by 1999 already the world's largest bookseller.

An army of female clerks keep the well-oiled machine of US mail-order giant Sears, Roebuck running at the company's Chicago HQ. Sears, Roebuck was founded in 1893; it had 50 million customers 100 years later.

At the end of the second millennium computer software tycoon William 'Bill' Gates (US) (*b*.1955) was the world's richest individual, with a peak wealth of $94 billion. Gates founded the Microsoft Corporation aged 19 and became a billionaire at the age of 31 in 1986. In the mid-1990s Microsoft operating software was running 80 per cent of desktop computers.

THE LIVING EARTH

How the North American Monarch butterfly finds its way across thousands of miles to the very same wintering spot that its great-great-grandparents used the previous year is one of the mysteries of the natural world. Its ability to do so is the result of millions of years of evolution, but the Monarch – among the Earth's most delicate and short-lived species – is at the mercy of the human race, whose industrial activities destroy habitats and threaten the very future of the planet.

The story of our Earth

Plant fossils discovered in Mazon Creek, Illinois, USA, date from the later part of the Carboniferous Period in the Palaeozoic Era. The widespread swampy forests of the period are the basis of most modern coal deposits.

The Earth came into being about 4.6 billion years BP, emerging from the primitive cloud of gases and dust that became our Solar System. Before the advent of life, and therefore of fossil remains, it is difficult to form a picture of what the Earth looked like.

Many geologists believe that the planet's crust was relatively thin and unstable up to 3.8 billion years BP. It suffered **constant bombardment** by meteorites and was at the mercy of convection currents strong enough to move land masses as the Earth cooled.

The rock laid down in the oldest geological era, the **Precambrian**, forms the basis of present continents. Where Precambrian rock can still be seen at the Earth's surface – for instance in Canada and much of Scandinavia – it is called a shield. If it has been covered by a layer of sedimentary rock (rock laid down in layers, usually by the action of water) it forms a **platform**.

During the succeeding eras, **the continents grew** by deposition of rock and were shaped by metamorphosis – the effect of heat or pressure on rock – and by a succession of ice ages. An ice age 2.3 billion years BP, which scientists identified from the appearance of glacial detritus, was followed by another 590 million years BP.

The **first living creatures** did not have hard body parts and therefore did not leave fossils, but their presence can be deduced in the late Precambrian era by the presence of stromatolites – webs of carbonate rather like coral left by the blue-green algae of the time.

In the Cambrian Period, there was **an explosion of marine life** that left rich fossil deposits. The Earth's atmosphere had at last accumulated enough oxygen for creatures to form skeletons and there was extensive **flooding of continents**, resulting in vast areas of shallow warm water surrounding inland deserts. The seas retreated and advanced again and again in the ensuing periods, leaving deposits of marine fossils hundreds of miles inland from the modern coast.

One great expanse of water, called by geologists the Iapetus Ocean, lay between the land masses of what is now North America and Europe. Between 430 and 360 million years BP, this ocean shrank until the land masses collided and, pushing up ridges of rock, produced the northern Appalachian Mountains in North America and the Caledonian Mountains of Scotland.

Fish first appeared some 500 million years ago. In the Devonian period, marine plants began to colonize the land and developed into fern forests. The Carboniferous Period, from 360-286 million years BP, was a period of great change. Plant life was developing rapidly with tree-ferns, mosses and horsetails. **Insect life** appeared and, towards the end of the period, **amphibians and reptiles** developed.

At the same time, a huge collision of land masses began the formation of the mega-continent that geologists call **Pangea**. The great mass of Laurasia – consisting of modern South America, Africa, Australia, Antarctica and India – moved north towards the northern landmass (Gondwana), producing by its pressure the southern Appalachians and the Ouachita Mountains in what is now North America.

During the Permian Period, the **Asian land mass collided with Europe**, forming the Ural Mountains in the process, and Pangea was almost complete – only Chinese land mass was perhaps still detached.

Pangea was surrounded by an ocean that geologists call **Panthalassa**, but the continent was also indented by the Tethys Sea, where the first split in Pangea was to occur in the Jurassic Period.

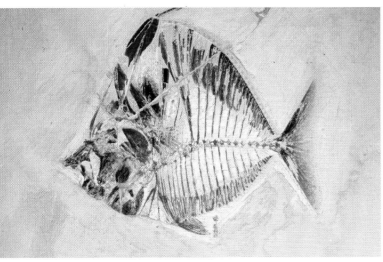

The fish that left this fossil remain was alive in the early part of the Eocene era, during the Tertiary Period, when a warm climate saw the first appearance of many modern flora and fauna.

Meanwhile, **the first mammals** appeared in the Triassic Period, some 230 million years BP. Reptiles were still the most common form of animal life with the spread of the **dinosaurs**.

Pangea began to dissemble again during the Jurassic Period, first splitting again into Gondwana and Laurasia, and then separating North America from Europe, and the southern continents from each other. In this period the **dinosaurs were dominant** and the Archaeopteryx had taken to the air.

In the Cretaceous Period, the **mega-continents further disintegrated** as the North Atlantic widened. The Tethys Sea – in the area of what is now the Mediterranean – narrowed as Africa moved northwards towards Europe, and India began its journey towards Asia, at an estimated speed of 6.5in *17cm* a year. The **dinosaur giants reached their peak** with the Tyrannosaurus, up to 40ft *12m* long; **flowering plants**

appeared and rapidly formed extensive deciduous forests.

At the end of the Cretaceous Period, some 65 million years ago, the **dinosaurs became extinct**, along with about 75 per cent of all other species. Geologists cannot explain this catastrophe, but have advanced theories that include a change in the amount of atmospheric oxygen or the collision of a huge asteroid with the Earth (see page 60). Whatever the reason, it cleared the way in the Tertiary Period for the development of more familiar animal species, including the early **man-apes** in Africa.

The continents were now approaching their present-day positions – with key differences that had a crucial impact on the distribution of animal life. In the Palaeocene Epoch, India floated free of the rest of Asia, while Australia and Antarctica were still joined and Europe and North America were still attached in the far north by a land bridge. This link was

broken in the succeeding Eocene Epoch, at around the same time that Australia drifted away from Antarctica.

India collided with Asia about 30 million years ago, forming the Himalayas. The Tethys Sea had shrunk into the Mediterranean by the Miocene Epoch and Africa was pushing up the Alps in Southern Europe. During the Pliocene Epoch, the isthmus of Panama rose out of the sea, cutting the Pacific Ocean off from the Atlantic and forming a land bridge between the Americas.

In the Quaternary Period came the most recent ice age, with the ice finally retreating to the poles about 10,000 years BP. The ice age saw creatures such as the woolly mammoth and reindeer. Between 5 and 10 million years BP, **hominids became distinct from apes**. *Homo erectus* appeared in the Pleistocene Epoch 1.5 million years BP and *Homo sapiens*, the first modern humans, about 200,000 years BP.

The lizard-like tuatara, native to islands off New Zealand, is very similar to reptile species known to have been alive 200 million years ago. Up to 26in *650mm* long, it is usually green or orange-brown and eats birds' eggs, small vertebrates and invertebrates.

GEOLOGICAL ERAS

Era	Period	Epochs	Span in years ago
Cenozoic (Gk. *kainos*, recent, *zóe*, life)	Quaternary	Holocene (Gk. *holos*, whole) Pleistocene (Gk. *pleistos*, most)	10,000–present 2 million-10,000
	Tertiary	Pliocene (Gk. *pleión*, more) Miocene (Gk. *meión*, less) Oligocene (Gk. *digos*, few) Eocene (Gk. *eós*, dawn) Palaeocene (Gk. *palaios*, ancient)	5–2 million 25–5 million 38–25 million 55–38 million 65–55 million
Mesozoic (Gk. *mesos*, middle; *zóe*, life)	Cretaceous Jurassic Triassic	Senonian, Gallic, Neocomian Malm, Dogger, Lias Tr3, Tr2, Scythian	144–65 million 213–144 million 248–213 million
Palaeozoic (Gk. *palaios*, ancient; *zóe*, life)	Permian Carboniferous Devonian Silurian Ordovician Cambrian	Zechstein, Rotliegendas Gzelian, Kasimovian, Moscovian *etc* D3, D2, D1 Pridoli, Ludlow, Wenlock, Llandovery Ashgill, Caradoc, Llandeilo, Llanvim *etc* Merioneth, St David's, Caerfai	286–248 million 360–286 million 408–360 million 438–408 million 505–438 million 590–505 million
Proterozoic (*Gk.proteros*, earlier; *zóe*, life)		Neo-, Meso- and Palaeoproterozoic	2.5 billion–590 million
Archean (Gk. *archaeos*, ancient)			4.6–2.5 billion

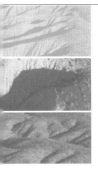

Geology

Geology (Gk. *geó*, earth; *-logy*, [subject of] study) is the science of the Earth's crust. The crust, or lithosphere (from Gk. *lithos*, stone), ranges from 3 to 40 miles *5 to 64km* in thickness.

To trace changes in the lithosphere, scientists need to be able to date rocks. Nicolaus Steno (Den) (1638–86) formulated **relative dating** in 1669, on the assumption that, with sedimentary rock, younger rock overlaid older rock.

James Hutton (Scot) (1726–97) propounded the **igneous** origin of rocks – that they have solidified from a molten state – in a *Theory of the Earth* (1785). He was the first to realize the immense age of the Earth.

The 19th century was the 'Golden Age' of geology. Canal engineer William Smith (Eng) (1769–1839) saw that sequences could be built up by **comparing fossil remains** in rock strata. He produced a geological map of England and Wales in 1815.

Adam Sedgwick (Eng) (1785–1873) worked out the way fossils in the rocks of North Wales were deposited in layers and named the oldest 'Cambrian' – from Cambria, the ancient Latin name for Wales.

After Antoine **Becquerel** (Fr) (1852–1908) discovered radioactivity, geologists could **date rock deposits** by making calculations of the decay of radioactive isotopes in samples of the rock.

The theory of **continental drift** was pioneered by

The 600-mile *950-km* San Andreas Fault in northern California, USA, is a fracture in the Earth's crust, running where the Pacific and North American tectonic plates meet. The two plates are sliding past one another at an average 0.4in *1cm* each year. If they move suddenly, an earthquake occurs.

James Lovelock worked for the National Institute of Medical Research in London and for NASA in the USA before setting up as an independent scientist. It was English novelist William Golding's idea to use the name of the Ancient Greek Earth goddess Gaia for the whole-Earth ecosystem in which Lovelock believes.

German meteorologist Alfred Wegener (1880–1920), who was struck by the apparent 'fit' of the east coast of South America with the west coast of Africa. In 1915, he published *The Origin of the Continents and Oceans*, in which he theorized that some 300 million years BP there was one super-continent, Pangea (Gk. *pan*, all; *gé*, earth), and one surrounding ocean, Panthalassa (Gk. *thalassa*, sea).

His idea was more or less ignored by scientists until, in the 1950s, **palaeomagnetism** was discovered. The Earth's magnetic field is produced by movements in the planet's outer core of liquid iron; the north and south magnetic poles move over time and are different from the geographic poles, which cannot move because they lie on the Earth's fixed axis of rotation .

Most rock contains particles of magnetic material, which are magnetized in the direction of the Earth's magnetic field at the time the rock was formed. By comparing the magnetic

alignment of the particles to the Earth's current magnetic field, geologists can establish that the rock has moved and work out its original position.

Using this discovery and the theory of **plate tectonics** – which proposes that the features of the Earth's surface are caused by the movements of rigid tectonic plates in the crust – geologists have tracked the steady movement of continents over millions of years (see pages 52–53).

Probably the most radical of all geological theories is that of James Lovelock (Eng) (*b.*1919), who argued that the Earth, plants and animals make a working whole, called **Gaia**. Lovelock saw Gaia as functioning like a giant organism whose parts regulate the whole to keep it adapted for life. He published his book *Gaia* in 1979.

Changing weather patterns

Geological evidence indicates that several **ice ages** have occured since the Proterozoic Period (*c.*2500–1800 million years BP). The most recent was 18,000 years BP when a sheet of ice some 10,000ft *3km* thick covered much of North America and Scandinavia, parts of the British Isles and most of Argentina and New Zealand.

By 7000 BC, most of the ice over North America and Scandinavia had melted, the sea level had risen and coastlines took on their familiar modern shapes.

During the birth of the ancient human civilizations, the earth was *c.*2°C *4°F* warmer than it is today and rainfall was also higher. The Sahara area of Africa, now inhospitable desert, provided **pasture for large herds of cattle**, as archaeologists have seen in cave paintings dated *c.*6000BC from Tassili N'Ajjer in Algeria. During the following centuries, the global **temperature probably fell** to around today's levels, but the Sahara was cultivated in the time of the Roman Empire (*c.*100BC–AD400).

In the 14th century there was a succession of **cold, wet summers**. During this period Norse settlement on Greenland, which had grown to a population of *c.*5000, was wiped out by disease and starvation because contact from Iceland ceased with the growth of pack ice between the two countries. Iceland itself suffered a famine.

The period from *c.*1450 to 1850 is known as the 'Little Ice Age'. There were **harsh winters**, recorded in many paintings of the period of frozen rivers and canals.

The **average global temperature** has risen 0.5˚C *1˚F* since 1900. The years 1920–40 were warm and sunny; from 1975–2000 the average has been warm.

This **global warming** may be due to human activity. The atmosphere is mostly made up of the gases oxygen and nitrogen, with some carbon dioxide and water vapour. When the Earth's surface absorbs sunlight, it reflects some of it as heat, which generally passes through the atmosphere into space. But 'greenhouse gases' – water vapour, ozone and carbon dioxide – absorb the radiation, preventing its escape into space.

The greenhouse effect makes the Earth warm enough to support life, but the rise in levels of carbon dioxide in the atmosphere – greatly increased by the burning of fossil fuels – has made it more extreme. Carbon dioxide **emissions could double** by the year 2060, and might lead to a temperature rise of 1.5–4.5˚C *3–8˚F*. Then the ice caps would melt, **raising sea levels** and causing coastal flooding.

El Niño ('the Christ Child') is a periodic warm ocean current that appears off the northern coast of Peru every two to three year. It is so called because it usually peaks around Christmas. This temperature rise may reach 4˚C *7˚F*. Not only does the warmer water **kill marine life** and affect fishermen and bird life, but the warm current **triggers heavy rainfall** and affects global wind patterns, which in turn affects sea temperatures further afield.

In 1982–83 and 1997–98 El Niño caused devastating **floods and droughts**, with crop losses from Australia to Argentina, Central America and the southern USA.

Bonfires were lit and frost fairs held on the frozen River Thames in London on occasions during the extremely cold European winters of the 17th–19th centuries. This engraving shows 'City Road', a street of shops set up on the ice near St Paul's Cathedral in 1813–14. Today's milder winters mean that the Thames no longer freezes over.

Meteorology

Meteorology – the study of atmospheric phenomena – began with the first farmers. Needing to predict the weather, they began to recognize and note patterns of clouds, winds and temperature. Rainfall was one of the easiest phenomena to be measured; **rain gauges** were in use in India by 300BC.

The word 'meteorology' was coined by the Ancient Greek philosopher and scientist Aristotle (384–322BC) as the title of his work describing the atmosphere and the Earth. One of his pupils, Theophrastus (372–287BC), noted indicators of storms, wind or fair weather in *On Weather Signs*.

In 1643, Evangelista Torricelli (It) (1608–47) **invented the barometer**. The Duke of Tuscany had asked him to discover why suction pumps could not raise water more than *c*.30ft *9m* from his well. Torricelli argued that the pressure exerted by the atmosphere to hold up the water must be matched by that of the weight of the column of water.

Italian physicist Evangelista Torricelli, inventor of the barometer, was assistant to the great scientist Galileo, and later became professor of mathematics in Florence. The unit of atmospheric pressure is called the 'torr' in his honour.

He went on to show that Mercury – about 14 times heavier than water – would support a column one-fourteenth the height; small variations in the height of the column would indicate changes in atmospheric pressure. The barometer he made had a 4ft *1.2m* glass tube containing mercury. French mathematician Blaise Pascal (1623–62) made the connection between air pressure and the weather.

Temperature was first accurately measured with the development of alcohol thermometers and a scale to calibrate them. This was the invention of Gabriel Daniel Fahrenheit (Ger) (1686–1736), who also showed that the point at which water boils varies with atmospheric pressure.

The American polymath Benjamin Franklin (1706–90) first established that thunderstorms are electrical in nature. The lightning is a relaease of charge built up because of the presence in cumulo-nimbus clouds of particles carrying opposite electrical charges.

Clouds were first classified in a scientific way by Luke Howard (Eng) (1772–1864). He divided them into cumulus ('a heap'), stratus ('a layer'), cirrus ('a lock of hair') and nimbus ('rain cloud').

The movement of **winds** was described by Gustave-Gaspard de Coriolis (Fr) (1792–1843). Hot air rises in the Tropics and spreads out towards the Poles, but it does not move in a straight line because of the rotation of the Earth, which deflects winds clockwise in the northern hemisphere and anti-clockwise in the southern hemisphere.

The first **weather maps** were made in the USA in the 19th century. Joseph Henry (US) (1797–1849) established a network of volunteer weather-watchers, linked by telegraph. Their information was collated in a map used in predicting weather patterns.

Scales of comparison help in weather analysis. The **Beaufort Scale** of winds, devised in 1805 by Admiral Sir Francis Beaufort (Ire) (1774–1857), ranges from Force 0 (calm) to Force 12 (hurricane, above 74mph *120km/h*) and describes winds by their effects – for example, 'twigs snap off trees'.

A more accurate measure could be obtained from pressure-tube wind gauges or **anemometers**, which were invented in the 18th century; the one developed in 1891 by William Henry Dines (UK) (1855–1927) is still in use.

The strength of **tornadoes** is measured on the Fujita Scale, developed by Dr T. Theodore Fujita (US) (*b*.1921). It classifies speeds from F0 (40–73mph *64–117km/h*) to F5 (over 261mph *418km/h*).

Hurricanes have, since the 1970s, been measured on the Saffir-Simpson Scale, devised in the USA by Herbert Saffir and Robert Simpson. The scale runs from 1 (74–95mph *118–152km/h*) to 5 (more than 155mph *248km/h*).

The advent of computers has contributed to the growth of international weather-research bodies. The **World Meteorological Office** was established in 1951.

World Weather Watch collects data from satellites, 12,000 land stations, 7000 ships, oil-rigs and aircraft. It transmits them into the Global Telecommunications System that feeds the World Meteorological Office.

By tracking movements of pressure belts and cyclones, satellites give early warning of natural disasters like hurricanes and floods.

Volcanoes

There are about 500 active volcanoes in the world, but many more dormant ones that could erupt at any time.

Magma, the molten rock that is ejected from a volcano, comes from immensely hot pockets in the Earth's crust, usually less than 70 miles *112km* from the surface. The magma pushes through weaknesses in the crust as lava or, if it has cooled and then partly solidified while still below the surface, erupts as rock fragments, which form volcanic ash.

Volcanic activity follows lines of weakness in the Earth's crust. One weak line runs around the circumference of the Pacific Ocean, through Japan, many Pacific island chains and the west coast of the Americas. Another runs north-south down the Atlantic Ocean.

In around 1626 BC, the explosion of Santoríni in the Cyclades islands between southern Greece and Turkey created shock waves that washed 160ft *50m* high on the neighbouring islands. On Crete, the **Minoan civilization** received its

deathblow as cities and agriculture were devastated.

When **Vesuvius** in southern Italy erupted in AD79, the town of Pompeii, *c.*5 miles *8km* downwind, was covered in 10ft *3m* of ash. Around 2000 people died where they stood from the effect of the poisonous sulphur fumes that accompanied the ash.

In 1783 the 15-mile *24km* Laki fissure in south-east Iceland erupted, spewing out a 100ft *30m* deep stream of molten basalt that flowed over 220 sq miles *570 sq km*. Thirteen farms were buried and three-quarters of the island's livestock died; around 10,000 people perished in the ensuing famine.

In the 20th century, scientists developed ways of limiting the damage caused by eruptions. In Hawaii in 1935 and 1942, **aircraft bombed the lava flow** from Mauna Loa, diverting it from the town of Hilo. **Water sprayed on lava** will cool it sufficiently to stop or slow the flow; this method was used in 1973 when the Kirkefell volcano erupted on Heimay, off Iceland.

The Soufrière volcano on the Caribbean island of Montserrat became active in 1995 after four centuries of dormancy. It erupted in 1997, and made the entire southern half of the island, including the capital Plymouth, uninhabitable.

Scientists are now able to monitor and predict volcanic activity. **Mount Usu** on the island of Hokkaido in northern Japan threatened to erupt in 2000, giving off gas and a small amount of lava that flowed harmlessly into the sea. As a precaution, more than 13,000 people were evacuated from their homes for several weeks. No lives were lost.

In May 1883 the volcano on the uninhabited island of Krakatoa in the Sunda Straits between Java and Sumatra erupted in four explosions. It set off *tsunami* (tidal waves) that took 36,000 lives on neighbouring islands.

The church tower is all that remains of San Juan Parangaricutiro in western Mexico after the town was buried in lava from the nearby Paricutin volcano on 20 February 1943. Paricutin continued erupting for nine years, but has been silent ever since.

Natural disasters

The Biblical story of Noah and the Mesopotamian Epic of Gilgamesh both tell of a **great flood** that killed the majority of humankind. Geologists have found evidence of severe flooding in the upper Persian Gulf that correspond to the time of Noah and Gilgamesh (*c.*2700BC), but historians cannot agree on whether there was, in fact, a single

A South African Defense Force helicopter rescues people forced to take refuge on a rooftop from the flooding that hit Mozambique, southeastern Africa, in February 2000. The floods rose fast, forcing people to flee to dwindling patches of high ground and even tree tops to escape drowning.

especially severe flood. The area was, however, frequently inundated.

Floods drown people and livestock, and also destroy crops (leading to famine) and pollute drinking water, (causing many diseases). The flooding of the Hwang Ho river in China in 1931 killed 3.7 million people; many more died of starvation as crops were destroyed.

One common effect of earthquakes and volcanoes in coastal regions is to set up *tsunami* (tidal waves) that may cause as much damage and loss of life as the quake

itself. The former capital of Jamaica, Port Royal, was built on the end of an 8 mile *12.8km* spit of sand and gravel curving out round a bay. On 7 June 1692, the region was hit by an earthquake. Most of the town slid into the bay, then the water in the harbour was driven out in a great wave. When it surged back in again it swept the remains of the town under the sea. More than 2000 people died.

Flash floods occur when sudden torrential rain is focused in a narrow channel. A flash flood near Johnstown, Pennsylvania, USA, on 31 May 1889 overloaded a 72ft *22m* dam, which finally gave way, sending a wall of water and debris 30ft *9m* high into Johnstown, where 2209 died.

The **greatest recorded vertical movement** resulting from an earthquake was at Yakatut Bay, Alaska, in 1899, when the coast rose by 47.5ft *14.5m* in some areas.

Japan is a seismic hot-spot on the Pacific belt with regular earthquake or volcanic activity. The **worst earthquake in modern times** took place in 1923 in Sagami Bay, and it reached 8.3 on the Richter scale. Tokyo and Yokohama were badly damaged and the death toll was 142,800. This, however, was overshadowed by the quake that shook Shensi, China, on 2 Feb 1556, in which 830,000 died.

In May 1970 Peru was hit by an earthquake whose epicentre was miles off shore beneath the Pacific Ocean. The nearest coastal town, Chimbote, was badly damaged, but did not suffer

great loss of life. However, 30 miles *48km* inland, the quake knocked a 0.5 mile *0.8km* crust of snow off the 21,860ft *6663m* Nevado Huascarán mountain, bringing down millions of tons of rock that destroyed the village of Ranrahica and half of the town of Yungay. The death toll was an estimated 40,000.

Four major natural disasters struck in the period from late summer 1999 to spring 2000. On 17 Aug 1999 around 17,000 people died when a 7.4 Richter-scale earthquake hit Izmit, an industrial town 65 miles *105km* east of **Istanbul** in Turkey.

On 29 Oct 1999 a 190mph *300km/h* **supercyclone** hit the state of Orissa in eastern India, driving a 30ft *9m* tidal wave that obliterated entire villages. Around 10,000 people were killed and 15 million left homeless.

Mudslides in Venezuela in December 1999 were Latin America's worst natural disaster of the 20th century. The slides, which came in the wake of torrential rains that began on Dec 15, killed up to 50,000 people.

Between Feb 4 and mid-April 2000, a tropical low-pressure system off the coast of Mozambique brought **violent rain** and the worst flooding for 40 years. Hundreds of thousands were made homeless and 700 killed by three cyclones – Eline, Gloria and Huda – in three months. Eline was measured gusting at 74.5mph *120km/h*. At the same time, the Horn of Africa was suffering the **worst drought for 15 years**.

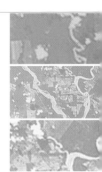

Human impact on the Earth

Three millennia BP, most of the globe – save the tundra or desert – was covered with **forest** of one sort or another. The chief effect of humans on the environment before the Industrial Revolution of the 18th–19th centuries AD was in the **destruction of the Earth's forest cover**.

When populations were small, forests could survive human use of trees. In the time of Roman Emperor Julius Caesar (100–44BC) more than half of France – c.140,000 sq miles *363,000 sq km* – was covered in forest. By the 1780s, on the eve of the French Revolution, this had been reduced to c.23,000 sq miles *60,000 sq km*.

The gradual **loss of the Earth's forests** leads to erosion as topsoil is exposed

NASA's Satellite Terra, launched in Dec 1999, uses banks of sensors to monitor environmental variables including greenhouse gas concentrations and pollution. This image is of Argentina.

to rain, and therefore to a gradual loss of fertility. One of the first to recognize this was George Perkins Marsh (US) (1801–82) who observed that in landscapes damaged by extensive tree-felling,

rivers dry up more quickly in summer and in winter collect torrents whose strong flow further changes the shape of the landscape.

Estimates in 2000 reveal that on arable land in the USA, **soil is being removed** eight times more quickly than it is being formed and that 4 billion tonnes are swept into rivers every year.

The changing balance between living organisms and agricultural and industrial processes has disrupted the carbon cycle – the sequence in which carbon released by respiration is reabsorbed by plants during photosynthesis.

Carbon dioxide (CO_2) produced by the burning of fossil fuels in industry and car engines has led the CO_2 content of the Earth's atmosphere to rise from 280 parts per million (ppm) in the pre-industrial era to more than 350 ppm now, helping to create the **greenhouse effect** (see page 55).

The emission of greenhouse gases is also linked to the depletion of the **ozone layer**, a band of ozone gas (O_3) in the upper atmosphere that prevents ultraviolet solar rays reaching the Earth. Ozone is destroyed by chlorofluorocarbons (CFCs) and other gases: a NASA satellite survey of 1991 revealed that the ozone layer had reduced by 4-8 per cent in the northern hemisphere and 6-10 per cent in the southern hemisphere between 1978 and 1990.

The resulting increase in ultraviolet radiation reaching the earth's surface may have contributed to higher rates of skin cancer in humans.

The nations emitting most greenhouse gases are the USA, followed by China, Russia, Japan, India, Germany, the UK, Indonesia, France (despite 70% of her electricity generation being nuclear), Italy and Canada.

Heads of state meeting at the Dec 1997 UN summit on global warming, held in Kyoto, Japan, agreed to limit emissions of industrial gases such as methane, nitrous oxide, sulfur hexafluoride, hydrochlorofluorocarbons and perfluorocarbons. Percentage reductions below the 1990 levels were agreed by the EU (8%), the USA (7%) and Japan (6%). This summit failed, however, to agree penalties for non-compliance with the treaty.

Pollution in the Arabian Sea shows as a red area in this NASA Terra satellite image. The red corresponds to areas where pollutants have prevented microscopic plankton from making the chlorophyll they need to flourish.

US Vice President Al Gore greets Japanese Prime Minister Ruyutaro Hashimoto at the start of the 1997 Kyoto convention on global warming. Rich nations with high rates of environmentally damaging emissions agreed to buy 'pollution rights' from less industrialised nations.

Evolution and extinction

In the 19th century, evidence from palaeontologists, zoologists and the naturalist Charles Darwin (Eng) (1809–82) demonstrated that life on Earth had evolved from simple forms to more complex ones.

The work on **genetics** of Augustinian monk Gregor Johann Mendel (Austria) (1822–84), rediscovered in 1900, explained how acquired characteristics passed from one generation to the next.

Measured in terms of species lost, evolution is an expensive process. Since the first multicellular organisms evolved 500–600 million years BP, an estimated 30 billion species have lived on Earth: only 30 million are still with us, which implies that **99.9 per cent of all species have become extinct**.

In ancient times, for reasons not yet clear, there were phases of **mass extinctions**. A third of plant and animal species alive at the start of the Palaeozoic Permian Period (286–248 million years BP) were extinct by its close. Most were marine invertebrates, and the phenomenon may have been related to the assembly of the mega-continent Pangea (see pages 52–53) and resulting changes in the extent, and probably depth and salinity, of the ocean.

At the end of the Cretaceous Period (65 million years BP), the **dinosaurs became extinct**, along with some three quarters of all known

By showing that mammoth bones were quite different from elephant bones, the anatomist Baron Georges Cuvier (Fr) (1769–1832) demonstrated for the first time that species become extinct rather than evolving into something else.

species. Various causes have been proposed, including a possible change in temperature accompanying the break-up of Pangea into separate continents.

Luis Alvarez (US) (1911–88) proposed in 1980 that the event coincided with the impact of an **asteroid** up to 6.2 miles *10km* in diameter, causing giant atmospheric dust-clouds that blocked sunlight and led to the death of plant and animal life. Evidence for the impact of the asteroid is provided by the layer of iridium-rich rock found at the Cretaceous level, typical of the level of iridium found in asteroids.

A mass of microscopic marine creatures became extinct at the end of the Palaeocene Epoch (55 million years BP), when world temperatures rose by 6°C *10.5°F*. Palaeoceanographer Gerald Dickens (Aus) argued that this global warming was caused by the eruption of a gigantic **bubble of methane gas** from the seabed.

In February 2000, a layer of mud associated with the fossil foraminifera from the Palaeocene Epoch was discovered in the seabed off Florida, USA. Dickens suggested that the mud derived from an underwater landslide triggered by the explosion of gas.

The single clearest present cause of extinction of species is the impact of human beings, who bring about extinction in three main

ways. The first is by **hunting**. Polynesians colonized New Zealand sometime before 1350 AD, and within a few centuries 50 per cent of the island's species were lost. They included flightless birds such as the giant moa, over 10ft *3m* tall and weighing up to 530lb *240kg*.

Humans had an equally damaging effect in North America. Before the arrival of Europeans in the 15th century, there were about 50 million plains bison. In 2000, there were about 500.

Destruction of habitats is a second agent of extinction. In Ecuador, the clearance of a single forested hillside in the 1980s for cultivation caused the overnight disappearance of 90 species of plants.

The third way that humans cause extinction is by **transporting species**. In many Pacific islands, native creatures were wiped out by the introduction of rats which also contributed to the loss of flightless birds in New Zealand. In Lake Victoria in East Africa, 200 species of fish disappeared in ten years after the introduction in 1985 of the Nile perch for commercial fishing.

The end of the 20th century saw a **rapid rise in the rate of species extinction**. The base rate calculated by scientists is one species per year across the entire history of life on Earth – but in Brazil, an estimated four species have been lost every day since 1965.

Animal longevity

Certain life forms can survive to immense ages. Scientists have made remarkable claims for Procaryota – bacteria and algae – particularly in the case of bacteria extracted from subterranean salt layers. Geologists claimed that bacteria found in Irkutsk, Russia, were 600 million years old, while the US Dry Valley Drilling Project in Antarctica claimed an age of up to a million years for some rod-shaped bacteria. Experts found live bacteria in an 11,600-year-old Mastodon carcass in Ohio, USA, in 1991.

Few creatures have longer lifespans than humans. However, a Marion's tortoise (*Geochelone sumeriei*) that died in Mauritius in 1918 was said to have lived to 152 years. In 1982 an Ocean quahog or clam (*Arctica islandica*), taken from mid-Atlantic waters, had a shell with 220 growth rings, which are formed annually and are

therefore measures of age. As the table below shows, animals can live to more than twice the average lifespan of their species.

Monarch butterflies make an epic round flight of up to 3000 miles *4800km* every year. They live about nine months – much longer than most species of butterfly.

ANIMAL LIFESPANS

	Average	Extreme		Average	Extreme
Human	40	122	Giraffe	10	36
Asian elephant	40	81	Cat (domestic)	13	34
African elephant	35	70	Sea-lion (California)	12	34
Horse	20	62	Bat	6	32
Hippopotamus	41	61	Deer	8	31.6
Chimpanzee	20	55.5	Lion	15	30
Gorilla	20	54	Dog (cattle dog)	12	29.4
Slow-worm	10	54	Moose	12	27
Grizzly bear	25	50	Pig (domestic)	10	27
White rhinoceros	20	50	Elk	15	26.7
Camel	12	50	Tiger	16	26.3
Beaver	5	50	Kangaroo (grey)	7	24
Termite	20	50	Squirrel (grey)	10	23.5
Zebra (Grant's)	15	50	Leopard	12	23
Goose (domestic)	25	49.6	Puma	12	20
Monkey (Capuchin)	15	49	Sheep (domestic)	12	20
Ass	12	47	Goat (domestic)	8	18
Baboon	20	45	Guinea pig	4	14.9
Black rhinoceros	15	45	Fox	7	14
Polar bear	20	42	Chipmunk	6	10
Bison	15	40	Mouse (house)	3	7.6
Cow	15	40	Mouse (field)	3	4
Black bear	18	36	Butterfly	18 days	9 months

The longest-lived mammal after humans is the Asian elephant. Smaller than its shorter-lived African counterpart, it has a single lip at the end of its trunk where the African elephant has two lips. There are at most some 50,000 of these elephants surviving in the wild.

THE ARTS

- **Music**

- **Theatre**

- **Dance**

- **Visual arts**

- **Decorative arts**

- **Art prices**

These Syrian bottles of lustreware glass date from the first millennium BC. Made from 'blue glass' – a mixture of sand and soda or potash – similar objects were being made as long ago as the 3rd millennium BC. The arts are an expression of Man's unique creativity and many examples remain to chart his progress from pre-history to modern times.

Music

BEFORE AD 1

The birth of music

The first **sound-making instruments**, two single-holed whistles, date to around 60,000 years ago and were found in the huge Haua Fteah cave in northern Libya. Bull-roarers, flat oval pieces of bone or wood with a hole for a string which are whirled rapidly in the air, have also been found in sites of the Palaeolithic era (*c*.30,000BC). These early instruments were probably used for signalling or in **religious or magic ceremonies**, rather than for making music as such.

The earliest evidence for music was the discovery in 1996 of an end-blown bone **flute** capable of producing the notes of the pentatonic scale – a scale of five notes to the octave still used in folk music. This was found in a cave at Nova Garica, Slovenia, which had been occupied by Neanderthal man *c*.43,000BC. This date was in fact some 5000 years earlier than the apparent first known arrival of man in that locality.

The earliest depictions of musicians in recent civilizations come from ancient Egypt. Musicians playing **harps, flutes, lyres and drums** are represented in tomb decorations *c*.3000BC.

Until only a few centuries ago, musicians played without written **scores** but the rudiments of musical notation were developed long before. A clay tablet of *c*.1800BC discovered in the city of Nippur, Sumer (now southern Iraq) was found to bear a heptatonic – or seven-note – scale.

Bagpipes were depicted on Hittite carvings in eastern Turkey *c*.1300BC. Known to the ancient Greeks as *askaulos*, they came to Britain, apparently with the Roman army, sometime between AD55 and AD400.

The Greek philosopher **Pythagoras** (*fl*.5th century BC) set out the basics of Western music with his discovery of the mathematical relationship between the musical intervals, the octave, the perfect fourth and fifth and so on.

AD 1000

Music thrives under the patronage of the Church

Early Christian music was called **plainsong** or Gregorian chant after Pope Gregory I (*c*.540–604) and comprised a single line of unaccompanied repetitive melody.

The present **notation system** was pioneered by the monk Guido d'Arezzo (It) (*c*.990–1050). He invented the **four-line stave** and the *sol-fa* method of sight-singing.

One of the first pieces of music written down to have **several voices** singing different lines simultaneously is the English *Summer is Icumen In*, a **four-part dance-song** from *c*.1250.

In secular song, the **lute** was used to accompany the voice for centuries before keyboards became common. The Muslims who overran Spain in 711–12 brought the lute with them from the Middle East. By the early 15th century it had spread to the rest of Europe.

The idea of **orchestral music** was conceived by Giovanni Gabrieli (It) (*c*.1555–1612), the organist at St Mark's Church in Venice. In 1597 his innovation was to

For centuries religious music was the only kind to be preserved. The monks of the Christian Church sang the Mass and other services in *cantus firmus* or plainsong, which followed a free melodic line without harmony, regular rhythm or accompaniment by instruments. Pope Gregory I 'The Great' (*c*.540–604) collected and encouraged the use of plainsong, so this type of music is often known as Gregorian Chant. This detail is from a 14th-century illuminated manuscript.

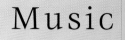

The standard arrangement of the modern orchestra comprises four groups – woodwind, brass, percussion and strings. Keyboard instruments such as harpsichords or pianos are occasionally added.

get musicians to play all together (*tutti*) when accompanying his choral *Symphoniae Sacrae*. Claudio Monteverdi (It) (1567–1643) introduced orchestration for 40 instruments in his opera *L'Orfeo in Mantua* (now Mantova) in 1607.

Ballet and masque were the precursors of **opera**. The earliest example of opera, a representation of a story on stage by vocal and instrumental music, was *La Dafne* (1597) by Jacopo Peri (It) (1561–1633) with a libretto by Ottavio Rinuccini (It) (1562–1621). This piece was lost, but Peri wrote a second opera, *Euridice* (1600), which survives.

In 1605, Adriano Banchieri (It) (1568–1634) wrote the first organ **sonata**. The earliest concerto – a piece for solo instrument and orchestra – was by Giulio Radino (It) in 1607.

The composer of the earliest **symphony** – an orchestral work in several sections, or movements, made especially for live performances, or concerts – has not been pinpointed. A candidate is Guiseppe Torelli (It)

INSTRUMENTS JOIN THE ORCHESTRA

Instrument	Earliest orchestral use and piece	Origin
Percussion		
Bass drum	**1705** Godfrey Finger (Cz) (*fl.*1685–1717), *Concerto alla Turchesa*	Ancient Orient
Bells	*c.***1730** G. M. Hoffman (Ger) (1690–*c.*1756)	Pre Pharaonic Egypt *c.*3400BC
Snare drum	**1749** George Frederic Handel (Ger/Eng) (1685–1759), *Music for the Royal Fireworks*	Prehistoric
Triangle	**1774** Glantz *Turkish Symphony*	Ottoman military
Timpani or kettle drum	*c.***1780** Various	Ancient Orient
Gong (tam tam)	**1791** Gossec, *Funeral March*	Indonesia ante 300BC
Tambourine	**1820** Carl von Weber (Ger) (1786–1826), *Preciosa*	Levant; first modern mention 1579
Anvil	**1825** Daniel Auber (Fr) (1782–1871), *Le Maçon*	Iron Age tool, first used for musical effect, 1528
Tenor Drum	**1842** Richard Wagner (Ger) (1813–83), *Rührtrommel*	Military
Xylophone	**1852** Jean Georges Kastner (Alsace) (1810–67), *Livre Portition*	Probably African
Castanets	**1877** Camille Saint-Saëns (Fr) (1835–1921), *Samson and Delilah*	Egypt, 8th century BC
Marimba	**before 1914** Percy Grainger (Aust/US) (1882–1961), *In a Nutshell*	African origin
Chinese temple blocks	**1923** Sir William Walton (Eng) (1902–83), *Façade*	Ancient Orient
Vibraphone	**1934** Alban Berg (Aus) (1885–1935), opera *Lulu*	Marimba type but with electric motor to keep resonators in motion
Strings		
Double Bass	**1607** Claudio Monteverdi (It) (1567–1643), *Orpheus*	Origin – bass viol
Harp	**1607** Monteverdi, *Orpheus*	Prehistoric Egypt, modern form 1792
Viola	**1607** Monteverdi, *Orpheus*	Known in Italy by 1530
Violin	**1607** Monteverdi, *Orpheus* **1609** King's band of 22 (Henri IV of France, 1589–1610)	Lombardic origin (three-stringed) 1508 Name derived from It. *vitulari*, to skip
Violoncello	**1607** Monteverdi, *Orpheus*	Known in Italy by 1530 Usually abbreviated to cello
Brass		
Trumpet	**1607** Monteverdi, *Orpheus* *c.***1800** (keyed), 1835 (valved); Jacques Halévy (Fr) (1799–1862), *La Juive*	Tomb of Tutankhamen, d. 1327BC
Trombone	**1607** Monteverdi, *Orpheus*	Roman Buccina; mediaeval, *sackbut*. Example recorded in Bruges, 1468.
Horn	**1639** Francesco Cavalli (It) (1602–76)	Prehistoric
Tuba	**1830** Hector Berlioz (Fr) (1803–69), *Symphonie Fantastique*	Pat. by W. F. Wieprecht (Prus) (1802–72), 1835
Woodwind		
Flute	**1607** Monteverdi, *Orpheus*	End-blown *c.*43,000BC; modern transverse form,1832 (Boehm)
Bassoon	*c.***1619** various	Italy *c.*1540, as a fagotto; possibly *c.*1520, north western Europe
Oboe	**1657** Jean Baptiste Lully (It/Fr) (1632–87), *L'Amour Malade*	France, 1511
Piccolo or octave flute	**1717** Handel, *Water Music*	Name dates from only 1856
Cor Anglais	**1722** Volckmar, *Cantata*	Uncertain; English or 'angled' horn
Clarinet	**1726** Faber, *Mass*	Invented. by J. C. Denner (Ger) (1665–1707)
Saxophone	**1844** Kastner, *Last King of Judah*	Invented by Adolphe Sax (Bel) (1814–94) *c.*1846
Keyboard		
Organ	**1607** Monteverdi, *Orpheus*, included his small organ and a regal (portable reed-organ)	Hydraulus or water organ invented *c.*270BC by Ctesibius (Gk) (*b.c.*300BC) with 19 keys and a keyboard
Virginal	**1611** First music - *Parthenia*	Known from pre 1530
Harpsichord	*c.***1720** Mainly concerto (until *c.*1800)	Earliest surviving, 1521, made in Rome
Pianoforte	**1732** Lodovico Giustini (It) (1685–1743), *Sonate*	Invented by Bartolomeo Cristofore (It) (1655–1731), Florence *c.*1709
Harmonium	*c.***1858** César Franck (Fr) (1822–90), various	Invented by G. J. Grenié (Fr) (1756–1837)
Celesta	**1880** Charles Marie Widor (Fr) (1845–1937), *Der Korrigane*	Invented. by V. Mustel, Paris, 1888

(1658–1709) of Bologna. Symphonies followed in the Netherlands (1698), England (1703) and Austria (1709).

Johann Sebastian **Bach** (Ger) (1685–1750) published 48 preludes and fugues in the *Well-Tempered Clavier* in 1722 and 1738 to demonstrate a system of tuning which allowed a keyboard player to play in tune in any of the **12 major and minor keys**. This was the beginning of Western harmony as we know it.

The 19th century was the era of the touring **virtuoso performer** and of great technical advances in instrument-making. The amazing career of the pianist and composer Franz **Liszt**

Trumpeter and singer Louis Armstrong (US) (1900–71) pioneered a new style in jazz centred on improvisational solos. He was born in New Orleans, the home of jazz, and as a young man played the cornet on Mississippi riverboats. In 1922 he joined the Chicago-based band of Joseph 'King' Oliver (US) (1885–1938) and was soon leading his own bands in Harlem, New York. Armstrong's nickname 'Satchmo' is short for 'satchel mouth'.

(Hun) (1811–86) was aided by Sébastian Erard's invention in the 1820s of the 'double escapement action' for the grand piano. It enabled performers to play a series of notes in rapid sequence for the first time.

AD 2000

An explosion of styles

Until the beginning of the 20th century, the only music that was not in the classical tradition was folk music. But then popular music developed in a variety of directions.

Charles Joseph 'Buddy' Bolden (US) (1877–1931), an innovative but unrecorded cornettist in New Orleans, has been described as 'the first man of **jazz**' *c.*1901. The **earliest jazz bands** featured clarinets, cornets, saxophones and drums. 'Jelly Roll' Morton (real name Ferdinand Joseph Lamothe) (US) (1890–1941) falsely claimed to be the inventor of jazz in 1902 but was arguably the originator of the '**blues**' in 1905. His jazz orchestrations, published *c.*1915, were the earliest in book form.

Classical harmony was taken to its farthest extreme by the Russian Igor **Stravinsky** (1882–1971). His *Rite of Spring* caused a riot at its first performance in 1913. Classical

music then began to explore new modes of expression. The first works of Arnold **Schoenberg** (Aus) (1874–1951) were almost totally free of harmony; he later invented the 12-note method to give his music some structure. He used the 12 notes of the chromatic scale in a particular sequence and manipulated the sequence in a variety of ways. His first piece using this technique was the *Piano Suite Op.25*, written between 1921 and 1923.

The next development came with the introduction of **electronics** into music. *Musique concrète* was developed in 1948 by a group of composers in Paris, who were later joined by Karlheinz **Stockhausen** (Ger) (*b.*1928). They used prerecorded sounds which were then manipulated electronically. They often did not use instruments at all.

'Aleatory' or chance music was invented by John **Cage** (US) (1912–1992) in the 1940s and used also by Pierre **Boulez** (Fr) (*b.*1925). Players are allowed certain freedoms of pitch and rhythm, often expressed via graphic notation in which music is sketched rather than specified exactly.

In the 1950s popular music took a new turn with **rock 'n' roll**. Elvis **Presley** (US) (1935–77) became known as the 'King of Rock'n'Roll' with hits such as *Love Me Tender* in 1956. The 1960s saw the arrival of the British **Beatles**, whose albums and singles topped the charts for most of the decade.

In the 1980s **Madonna**, **Michael Jackson** and **Prince** (all born in 1958) dominated the pop music scene with an accent on outrageous performances while the 1990s saw the rise of harder-edged rock and dance styles.

Theatre

BEFORE AD 1

Playing at being gods

The origins of theatre appear to arise from the very ancient rituals of **fertility** or **hunting rites**. Ancient Egyptian theatre featured dramatizations of the god Osiris's death at the hands of his evil brother Set which re-enacted the tearing of Osiris's corpse into 14 pieces. The earliest fully documented reference to Egyptian ritual drama with priests portraying the story of Osiris are only from the 12th dynasty (*c*.2155–*c*.1946BC) at Abydos.

On the island of Crete, the Minoan palaces of Knossos, Phaestus and Khania contain what appear to be **theatrical areas** dating from *c*.1900BC.

The earliest reference to **theatre in China** dates from the 8th century BC and refers to the variety of acrobatics, dancing, pantomime and singing during the Zhou (Chou) Dynasty (1027–221BC).

Theatre has enjoyed a continuous history from the time of **Greek comedy and tragedy**. The poet Archilocus of Paros (*fl*.711–676BC) appears to have been the innovator of metre and language in early comedy.

Thespis of Icaria, from whose name 'thespian' derives, invented the role of the **speaking** – as opposed to miming – **actor** *c*.535BC. The actor's mask was established shortly before his time. Later, around 509BC, comedy in Greece became the subject of competitions in Athens.

AD 1

Chorus explains all

Roman theatre *c*.AD50 adopted the pantomime (Gk. *pantos*, all; *mimos*, imitating), in which the masked actor's dumb show, was accompanied by a '**chorus**' describing his meaning.

In Japan, *kagura*, Shinto-based celebratory dance and skits, were introduced from China around AD540. In 720, the earliest known **drama school**, the Pear Garden, was established in Chang-an, China, by the T'ang Emperor Ming Huang (713–756).

AD 1000

French and Japanese pioneers

The earliest extant French play that was not actually part of a church service was the *Jeu d'Adam* (the Play of Adam), which played on the steps of French cathedrals in 1170.

Noh lyrical drama was developed in Kamakura, Japan, for the Shogunate of Yoshimitsu by Kiyotsugu Kwanami (1333–84) and performed on polished cedar podiums. Kabuki theatre had largely replaced the Noh tradition by 1590.

In 1494, England's King Henry VII (1457–1509) appointed the first Master of the Revels to the English court in London.

The Hôtel de Bourgogne, Paris, became in 1548 the first covered public playhouse of the post-Roman era . It was merged with Le Théâtre du Marais for the world's first **national theatre** — La Comédie Française in Paris in 1680.

James Burbage's (*c*.1530–1597) Theatre was opened in 1576 in Shoreditch, in east London. When demolished, some of its timbers were used

Plays were performed in Athens at the Festival of Dionysus, Greek god of wine, from the mid-6th century BC. The actors, who were all men, concealed their faces behind masks. Greek dramatists such as Sophocles (c.496–406BC) and Euripides (c.480–c.406BC) preserved many myths of Greek gods and goddesses.

The Italian *commedia dell'arte* ('comedy of skill') first emerged in the mid-16th century and had a great influence on the development of theatre – especially comedy – throughout Europe. Travelling players put on an improvised show based on a rudimentary plot outline and featuring stock characters. One character, the large-nosed, food-crazed Pulcinella (Italian, 'small chicken'), lives on as Punch in the Punch and Judy shows of modern times. It was called 'comedy of skill' because the improvisation required very talented actors.

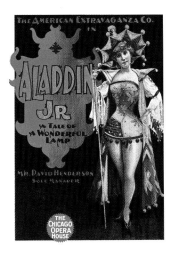

A 19th-century American variety show promises saucy thrills as well as laughs. In the 1860s American promoter Tony Pastor launched the first vaudeville shows – in which vulgar acts were banned – as an attempt to make variety respectable.

Russian actor-director Konstantin Stanislavsky, who argued that actors should avoid theatrics and aim to identify closely with the characters they were playing. His theories were the basis of the method acting taught at New York's Actors' Studio, where 20th-century icons Marlon Brando (b.1924) and James Dean (1931–55) studied.

for the nearby 1900 capacity **Globe Theatre** founded in 1599 by his son Cuthbert. Here many of the plays by **William Shakespeare** (Eng) (1564–1616) were first performed.

The **earliest use of the curtain** in the theatre was in 1585 in a performance of *Oedipus Rex* – by the ancient Greek dramatist Sophocles – in the world's oldest purpose-built theatre, the Teatro Olympico, Vicenza, Italy.

Women did not appear on the stage until the 17th century. Before that, men played the parts of women. George Jolly (*fl.*1640–73) included women in his English Comedian Players in 1654 in Germany.

Theatres were closed by Act of Parliament in England from the outbreak of the Civil War in 1642 until the Restoration of King Charles II in 1660. The Puritans, led by Oliver Cromwell, thought that theatre was immoral.

Private boxes appeared in London's new Restoration theatres, built to replace those closed down. At the Killigrew Theatre, Vere Street on 8 December 1660, Desdemona (from Shakespeare's tragedy *Othello*) was played by a woman – probably Mrs Hughes.

The Restoration also re-opened England to influences from the Continent. The **Punch and Judy** Show was first recorded in London by Samuel Pepys (Eng) (1633–1703). It derives from the Italian 16th-century *commedia dell'arte* style of theatre in which actors improvised comic situations round stock characters, such as Harlequin (the jester), Columbine (the young girl) and Pantaloon (the old man).

In 1716 the first **Christmas Pantomime** was introduced on 22 December by John Rich (*c.*1682–1760) with *Lilac Time* at Lincoln's Theatre, London. Pantomime was also at first based on the Italian harlequinades, but soon adopted burlesque versions of fairy stories such as Cinderella. In pantomime, women's roles are, as in classical theatre, once more played by men, but the women play the men's parts.

State funding for theatre (using taxpayers' money) was introduced by the Portuguese government in 1798 with a grant of £6500 (worth £483,000 in 1999) for the San Carlos Opera House, Lisbon. The earliest British grant was £17,500 (worth £663,000 in

1999) to the Covent Garden Theatre, London in 1930.

AD 2000

Bright lights, new styles

The 19th century saw the beginning of a spate of technical innovations. In 1816, **lime lights** were developed for stage lighting. They produced an intense white light by heating lime in an oxyhydrogen flame and were also called Drummond lights after their inventor Thomas Drummond, a Scottish engineer. The lighting cast strong lights on the principal characters and created very strong shadows, still commemorated in the phrase 'in the limelight'. Drury Lane Theatre was the first to be entirely gas-lit on 6 September 1816. In previous centuries, theatres were lit by candles or lanterns and fires were common.

Music hall started in London's taverns as a mixture of entertainment – hence, 'variety' – including songs, usually sentimental or comic, conjurors and recitations. The earliest purpose-built Music Hall was The Star, Churchgate, Bolton, Lancashire, England in 1840. Music hall continued until World War I but was finally ousted by films.

In 1846, **electric arc-lights** were first used on stage in the Paris Opéra.

Adah Isaacs Menken (US) (1835-68) was probably the first actress to appear (almost) **nude on stage**. She starred in 1864 in the play *Mazeppa*, (based on a Cossack legend) in which role she was tied to the back of a wild horse.

The art of **striptease** was pioneered by a dancer known only as Yvette at the Divan

Fayouan Music Hall, Paris, on 13 March 1894.

Operetta or comic opera was developed from the Italian *opera buffa* (comic opera) but took an idiosyncratic turn in England in 1875 with the works of Sir William (Schwenck) Gilbert (Eng) (1836–1911), librettist, and Sir Arthur (Seymour) Sullivan (Eng) (1842–1900), composer. They formed a partnership with the impresario Richard D'Oyly Carte, who built the Savoy Theatre in London in 1881. They produced a series of works sometimes known as the Savoy Operas and including *HMS Pinafore* (1878), *The Pirates of Penzance* (1880) and *The Mikado* (1888).

Acting style at this time tended to be relatively unrealistic, either highly melodramatic or comically stylised. Konstantin Sergeivitch Stanislavsky (1863–1938), a Russian actor, director and producer, introduced the technique of **method acting,** embraced by Hollywood, in which actors studied the psychology of characters in order to play them truthfully.

Repertory theatre – that is, a theatre with a permanent resident company – was launched in 1904 by Annie Elizabeth Fredericka Horniman (1860–1937) at the Abbey Theatre, Dublin. Miss Horniman staged first performances of the *The Land of Heart's Desire* by poet William Butler Yeats (Ire) (1865–1939) and *Arms and the Man* by George Bernard Shaw (Ire) (1856–1950).

Pulitzer Prizes were inaugurated in 1918, endowed by the Hungarian-born US publisher Joseph Pulitzer (1847–1911). Awarded each year by Columbia University, New York City, they include a category for Drama. Eugene O'Neill (US) (1888–1953) won in 1920/22/28/57 and Edward Albee (US) (*b*.1928) in 1967/75/94.

In the 20th century, many playwrights and producers have tried to get away from the formalism imposed by the proscenium arch. **Theatre in the round** brings the acting space back to the centre, where it was in mediaeval mystery plays. It was first reintroduced in 1932 by Glenn Hughes of the University of Washington's School of Drama in a production at the Edmond Meony Hotel, Seattle.

The French playwright and producer Antonin Artaud (1896–1948) was not interested in realistic representations or plots but believed that theatre should express the inner life of dreams and repressed emotions. His theories of the so-called **theatre of cruelty** were proposed in his book *The Theatre and its Double* of 1938.

In the 1950s, a group of playwrights, including Samuel Beckett (Ire) (1906–89) and Eugène Ionesco (Fr) (1912–1994) wrote plays that came to be called the **theatre of the absurd**, as they explored grim themes such as the ultimate impossibility of communication and the pointlessness of existence. Beckett's most famous play is probably *Waiting for Godot*, first produced in 1956.

The term **fringe theatre** was first used in the London *Times* newspaper to describe the 'extra' events in the Bath Festival of 1958 and in 1959 of the annual Edinburgh Festival.

The Polish director Jerzy Grotowski (*b*.1933) has also had a fundamental influence on theatre with his emphasis on **poor theatre**, a theatre shorn of effects and the 'theatrical' to concentrate on immediacy. He wrote his manifesto *Towards a Poor Theatre* in 1968.

Theatre in England came full circle in June 1997 with the opening of a reconstruction of Shakespeare's Globe Theatre. This was the brainchild of American actor Sam Wanamaker (1919–93).

Because of the towering reputation of William Shakespeare, English theatre is a popular attraction for visitors – and has become entwined with the heritage industry that caters for tourists. A faithful reproduction of the round Globe Theatre in which many of Shakespeare's plays were first staged has been erected on the south bank of the River Thames in London, just 200 yards from the site of the 16th-century original.

Dance

Dance involves rhythmical steps – glides, leaps, revolutions – solo or with partners and usually to musical accompaniment. Children often dance in an unco-ordinated way within days of being able to walk. The earliest known **depiction of dancing** was found on 21 July 1914 in the French Elène-Le Tuc d'Audoubert Pyreneean cave system: a wall painting known as *Le Sorcier Masqué* and dated to *c*.18,000BC.

BALLET

Courtly entertainment

Ballet dancers combine physical strength with grace in a *pas de deux*. The word ballet probably derives from Italian *ballare*, meaning to dance.

Ballet originated in the dances performed at the courts of the Italian princes in the Renaissance era and was taken from Florence to France by Catherine of Medici (1519–89) when she married the future Henri II of France. The **first recorded ballet** is *Ballet Comique de la Reine*, performed in 1581 by the French courtiers with the ladies as a *corps de ballet*.

One of the first **treatises on dance** was written by Thoinot Arbeau, Canon of Langres in France. Called the *Orchesography*, it describes the courtly dances of the time: *pavane, galliard* and *volta*.

Louis XIV (Fr) (1638–1715) – the self-aggrandizing *Roi Soleil* ('Sun King') – was very fond of ballet and liked to perform ballets with himself featuring as the Sun in the centre of his revolving courtiers. He founded a Royal Academy of Dancing in France in 1661. These courtly dances were stately. The dancers were formally dressed and so could not be very expressive; indeed, they confined themselves to movements of the feet and arms. Dancing was held to be part of the education of every gentleman and lady.

Dancers wore ordinary clothes or long costumes until Maria Anna de Camargo (Fr) (1710–70), a dancer at the Paris Opera, shortened her **skirts** to allow herself greater freedom of movement. **Tights** for dancers were introduced by another French dancer, Maillot, in the early 1800s.

The 19th century saw the birth of some classics of the ballet repertoire, *La Sylphide* in 1832 and *Giselle* in 1841. The **ballerina** now became more important than her male partner. About this time, ballerinas first used the points of their shoes and the male dancers supported them. The **tutu** was first designed by the

All over the world humans feel the ancient and instinctive urge to dance. In Brazil, home of the carnival samba, a spontaneous celebration breaks out on a beach in Bahia state when people hear the rhythm of drums and tambourine.

French painter Eugène Lami (1800–90) for the Paris Opera's production of *La Sylphide* but was then a mid-calf white dress.

Ballet then travelled to Russia, where the composer Piotr Ilyich **Tchaikovsky** (1840–93) wrote the music for three major ballets at the heart of the classical repertoire: *Swan Lake* (1877), *The Sleeping Beauty* (1890) and *The Nutcracker* (1892). An Italian dancer, Virginie

Zucchi, first wore the now obligatory short **tutu** in 1885 at the Imperial Theatre in St Petersburg.

The next major development in ballet was the work of the Russian impresario, Sergei **Diaghilev** (1872–1929). He too went to France to found his Ballet Russe, later based in Monte Carlo.

The Ballet Russe was home to many of the era's famous dancers, including Vaslav **Nijinsky** (1890–1950),

Anna **Pavlova** (1885–1931) and George **Balanchine** (1904–83). Diaghilev presented many famous ballets, such as Ravel's *Daphnis and Chloe* (1912) and Stravinsky's *The Rite of Spring* (1913).

In Britain, Marie **Rambert** (Pol) (1888–1982) founded the company which grew into the Ballet Rambert in 1926 with the dancer Alicia Markova and the choreographer Frederick **Ashton** (Eng) (1906–88). Ashton went on to join the Vic Wells Ballet which became the Royal Ballet in 1956 under the direction of Ninette de Valois (1898–1998). His most celebrated ballet was perhaps *La Fille mal Gardée* in 1960.

In America, dance was given a fresh flavour by Martha **Graham** (US)

(1893–1991). In 1958 her Dance Repertory Theater performed a landmark ballet to the music of *Appalachian Spring* by Aaron **Copland** (US) (1900–90). One of Graham's most famous dancers was Merce **Cunningham** (US) (*b.*1919). He led his own company from 1953 and created ballets to the music of John **Cage** (US) (1912–92).

FAMOUS DANCES BY YEARS OF ORIGIN

c.1650 Mazurka
From Poland. A lively round dance resembling the polka, for eight couples.

1663 Minuet
A precise, slow and stately French court dance with small steps (*pas menu*), for two dancers. Fashionable throughout the 18th century.

1696 Gavotte
Provençal dance for couples, popularized by the court of Louis XIV. Similar to the minuet but more lively.

1781 Waltz
A rotating, flowing Austrian dance performed to music in triple time with smooth and even steps. (Ger. *wälzen*, revolve)

1828 Quadrille
A 'figure' square dance for four couples, developed in France in 19th century. (It. *quadriglia*, square)

1835 Polka
A bouncing Bohemian peasant courtship dance in duple time. Introduced into Paris 1843. Origin from Czech *pulka*, half-step, owing to its characteristic short steps.

1862 Lancers
Quadrille for eight or 16 pairs: a formal dance.

19th century Paul Jones
Named after John Paul Jones (1747–92), a Scottish-born US naval officer noted for his victories for the Americans during the War of Independence. A ballroom dance during which partners are exchanged after circling in concentric rings of men and women.

1885 Samba
A Brazilian ballroom dance in double time, originally from Africa.

1892 Barn Dance
Originally danced in, and to celebrate the building of, a barn. Usually a Scottish-style dance where the partners advance side by side for a few steps and then dance a waltz.

1896 Tango
Probably of African origin.

From 1896, a flamenco dance and from 1913 a ballroom dance in 2/4 or 4/4 time, introduced into Europe and North America from Argentina, characterized by slow gliding movement and pointing positions.

The long, sweeping steps of the tango are brought to a halt in a sudden, dramatic pose.

1898 Cakewalk
Dance modelled on walking competitions in southern states from 1872 and named from the cakes given as prizes.

1912 Fox-trot
Alternating long and short steps in quadruple time. Named in 1914 in New York City after music writer Harry Fox (1882–1959).

1922 Rumba
Derived from Afro-Cuban dance, known since 1850, it involves dancing on the spot with a pronounced sway.

1925 Charleston
The basic step is side-kicking from the knee. Named from the song of 1923 by James P. Johnson (US) (1894–1955) about Charleston, South Carolina.

1926 Black Bottom
Jerking, athletic form of fox-trot, originated in the USA c.1900. Named for Black Bottom, Nashville.

1927 Paso Doble
Quick, Spanish-style two-step South American dance of 20th century. (Sp. for 'double step').

1934 Conga
Originally from Congo dance (1803). Latin-American dance consisting of three steps forward followed by a kick and performed by a single file column of many people at carnivals.

1937 Jitterbug
Fast, athletic jazz dance, grew popular in 1942. Jive was its more jerky variation.

1948 Mambo
Off-beat rumba from Cuba, exported by Perez Praole (1916–89) to USA in 1948. Name is probably Haitian.

1953 Rock 'n' Roll
Popular high-energy free dance (from the Jive) with music characterized by a heavy beat. Popularized by Bill (John Clifton) Haley (US) (1925–81).

1954 Cha-Cha-Cha
Mambo-like variation of ballroom dance to Latin-American danzón rhythm.

1958 Twist
A lively, non-touching dance with knee-flexing and body torsion by Hank Ballard.

1960 Reggae
Highly accentuated, off beat Jamaican dance, name probably originating from Jamaican/English *rege-rege*, a quarrel.

1962 Bossa Nova
Samba-like variation from Brazilian *baiao*. (Portuguese *bossa*, tendency; *nova*, new)

1962 Salsa
Latin American music incorporating elements of jazz and rock. *Salsa*, Spanish, Sauce.

1965 Disco Dancing
Freestyle modern dance with exaggerated hand and arm movements, popularized by the film *Saturday Night Fever* (1977).

1965 Go-Go
Exhibitionist, repetitive, fast dance of verve and excitement, often deliberately erotic.

late 1970s Break Dancing
Originated in the south Bronx, New York City. Acrobatic and energetic style of dance popularized by US blacks, individually or competitively, sometimes spinning around on their backs when grounded.

Visual arts

BEFORE AD 1

Cave artists

Painting on rock is the earliest form of art known to us. Aboriginal rock art from Arnhemland, Northern Territory of Australia, may date from before 50,000BC. The most famous painted caves are at Lascaux, France, and Altamira, Spain, and date from *c.*15,000BC. These ancient frescoes depict animals in vivid line drawings with added colour made from earth pigments of ochre and manganese.

The **Ancient Egyptians** painted scenes on the walls of palaces and tombs. Some paintings were in relief – that is, raised above the flat surface. One tomb painting, *c.*1400BC, shows the nobleman Amanemheb of Thebes hunting birds accompanied by his wife.

Chinese painting *c.*2500BC onward was influenced by calligraphy – decorative handwriting – and often included brushed ideograms, using ink and water-colours on silk and, later, paper.

Greek painting was at its best on decorated pots. The colours were simple: most were either black on red ('black figure'), dating from *c.*625BC, or red on black ('red figure'), dating from *c.*530BC. The figures were most often lively cartoons showing famous scenes from mythology or history.

Painters in Imperial **Rome** *c.*30BC produced murals and wealthy Romans decorated their houses with scenes from mythology. Some of these delicately-coloured paintings survive on the walls of villas in Pompeii, Italy.

AD 1

Sacred images

The art of the Byzantine Empire (395–1453) was highly decorative. Early **Byzantine** artists produced **mosaics** made up of small pieces of stone and glass pressed into a base of wet cement. Some of the most famous survive in the churches and tombs of Ravenna, Italy, an outpost of the Byzantine Empire in the 6th century.

The art of **illumination**, as practised by early Christian monks to decorate scriptures, has never been surpassed. The *Book of Kells* was produced *c.*820, most probably at Kells Monastery, Co. Meath, Ireland, although it may have been carried there by monks fleeing from the Scottish island of Iona.

The monks in early mediaeval monasteries left a precious legacy in the form of illuminated – that is, decorated – manuscripts of the Christian scriptures. The art of illumination was widely practised and highly developed by the 8th century. This detail is from the 12th-century French Bible of Saint Andre au Bois.

The hand written text uses ink made from crushed oak galls and iron sulphate. Pigments include the beautiful blue of lapis lazuli which, in this era, had to be imported from Afghanistan.

AD 1000

Eleventh-century cartoon

Tapestry and embroidery were also used to tell stories. The Bayeux Tapestry is a depiction of the Norman invasion of England in 1066 embroidered in wool on linen. It measures 19.5in *49.5cm* wide and 231ft *70m* long and reads rather like a an early strip cartoon with 72 separate scenes with explanatory captions.

Gothic architecture provided the opportunity for **stained glass** to attain its highest perfection *c.*1150–1450 in the many cathedrals built in that period – including Wells in Somerset, England, and Chartres in France. Stained glass with its tracery of lead

The art of the Byzantine Empire had a major influence on Gothic painting of the 13th century onward. The anonymous 6th-century artists who created this mosaic from the Basilica of Sant'Apollinare Nuovo in Ravenna, Italy, depicted the three Magi Balthasar, Melchior and Gaspar bearing gifts for the infant Jesus.

holding brightly coloured glass pieces in place is more like mosaic than painting in appearance and technique.

The Renaissance saw a renewal of interest in the Classical world and was at its height in 15th-century Italy. The art of perspective in painting – representing three-dimensional depth on a flat canvas by the use of a vanishing-point – was first developed by Italian architect Filippo Brunelleschi (1377–1446), and later codified by Leon Battista Alberti (It) (1404–72) in his treatise *De Pictura* ('On Painting') (1436).

Leonardo da Vinci (It) (1452–1519) was a central figure of the Italian Renaissance. His *The Last Supper*, a fresco measuring 14ft by 30ft *4.2m by 9.1m* on the refectory wall of the convent Santa Maria delle Grazie, Milan, depicts Jesus's last meal with his disciples and was painted between 1495 and 1497.

The **Baroque** era in painting (c.1585–1715) was characterized by the vigour and drama of its scenes and the exuberance of its painting style. The pioneer in Rome was Caravaggio (It) (1573–1610) whose paintings use bold light and shadow.

The **Rococo** style (c.1700–1760) was highly decorated and frivolous in tone. The word amalgamates French *barocco* (baroque) and *rocaille* (fancy rock-work for fountains) and was coined as a criticism of the art fashionable under King Louis XV of France (r.1715–74). Jean-Antoine Watteau (Fr) (1684–1721) is regarded as perhaps the most outstanding exponent of Rococo.

In the 18th and 19th centuries **Romanticism** was a reaction against the grime of the Industrial Revolution. In France, Théodore Géricault (1791–1824) and Eugène Delacroix (1798–1863) painted subjects full of drama and action. In England, J. M. W. Turner (1775–1851) painted bold landscapes rendered almost abstract by his use of light and his sweeping brushwork.

Realism countered the poetic licence of Romanticism with a choice of everyday subjects. Gustave Courbet (1819–77) led the movement in France.

Impressionism was the most influential movement of the late 19th century. It was the work of young artists turned down by the old-fashioned French Royal Academy of Painting and Sculpture for the annual exhibition, or *Salon*, so they held a *Salon des Refusés* – exhibition of works that had been refused – in 1863. Among the artists were Edouard Manet (Fr) (1832–83), Claude Monet (Fr) (1840–1926), Pierre-Auguste Renoir (Fr) (1841–1919) and Alfred Sisley (GB) (1839–99).

Post-Impressionism was a term coined by the English critic Roger Fry in 1910–11 to describe the work of painters such as Paul Gauguin (Fr) (1848–1903), Paul Cézanne (Fr) (1839–1906), and Vincent van Gogh (Neth) (1853–90) who moved away from the Impressionists' preoccupation with effects of nature.

The **Fauves**, too, were christened by a critic. Louis Vauxcelles likened their exhibition at the Salon d'Automne, Paris, in 1905 to the work of 'wild beasts' (Fr *fauves*). The painters at the exhibition included Henri

Matisse (Fr) (1869–1954) André Derain (Fr) (1880–1954) and Raoul Dufy (Fr) (1877–1953), whose 'wildness' lay in their exuberant use of non-naturalistic colours.

Cubism was originated by the Spanish painter Pablo Picasso (1881–1973) and by Frenchman Georges Braque (1882–1963). Picasso's famous work *Les Demoiselles d'Avignon* ('The Young Women of Avignon'), painted in 1906–7 was the epoch-making Cubist experiment in depicting a three-dimensional subject on a flat surface without perspective.

Dadaism was founded in Zürich, Switzerland, by a group of artists in revolt against what they saw as the smugness of society. The word Dada was said to have been found by inserting a penknife into the pages of a dictionary at random. Hans Arp (Fr) (1887–1966), Marcel Duchamp (Fr) (1887–1968) and the photographer Man Ray (US) (1890–1976) were among the central figures in the movement.

French Impressionist artist Claude Monet painted this work, *Gladioli*, in 1876, a time when he was working in Argenteuil, a suburb of Paris, and mostly painting in the open from a floating studio boat. It was from Monet's 1872 work *Impression: Sunrise* – a view of Paris – that the Impressionist movement got its name.

THE ARTS

French artist Edgar Degas (1834–1917) turned to sculpture in his later years, when his eyesight was failing: he said sculpture was a 'blind man's art'. He is celebrated for his impressionistic paintings of ballet dancers and racetracks and also for his intensely lifelike later work in bronze – such as this statue of a young ballerina.

Surrealism (1920–1940) used scenes from dreams and the subconscious to produce a 'super-reality'. The best known surrealists are the Spaniards Joan Miró (Sp) (1893–1983) and Salvador Dali (Sp) (1904–89) and the Italian Giorgio de Chirico (1888–1978), who all worked in Paris.

Abstract Art in the early 20th century was concerned with the manipulation of colour and patterns. Wassily Kandinsky (Rus) (1866–1944) led the way, followed by Piet Mondrian (Neth) (1872–1944) who painted only in lines and primary colours.

Abstract Expressionism began in the US after World War II with the work of Jackson Pollock (1912–56), Willem de Kooning (b.1904), and Mark Rothko (1903–70). They dripped and splashed the paint, so that the physical act of making the painting was part of the 'expression'.

AD 2000

The art is in the concept

Pop Art was a style or movement of the 1950s and 1960s which used images from popular culture and modern life such as advertisements and packaging. Roy Lichtenstein (US) (b.1923) produced a painting of a *Hot Dog* (1963) in bright primary colours. The American Andy Warhol (Andrew Warhola) (1927–87) produced paintings made up of small pictures of soup cans and of celebrities such as actress Marilyn Monroe.

In the 1970s, a movement in the USA took art out into the landscape. Walter de Maria (b.1935) was one of the exponents of this 'American Land Art'.

Installation Art developed in the 1980s and 1990s. It is a term covering usually large-scale objects taken out of their usual context and composing a type of stage set. The installation can include sound or video. Jenny Holzer (b.1950) used advertising slogans or clichés in illuminated information strips in her *Installation in the Guggenheim Museum* (1986). Bruce Neumann (b.1941) used large video projections of talking heads in *World Peace (Projected)* (1996).

SCULPTURE BEFORE AD 1

Ancestors cast a shadow

The **oldest ceramic object** yet found is the Venus of Dolní Vestonice from the Czech Republic, found in 1927 by Karl Absolon (Cz) (1877–1960). This small statuette of a woman is now dated to *c*.28,000BC.

Ancient **Greek** sculpture was usually cast in bronze. The *Discus Thrower* by Myron, dating from *c*.450BC, now survives only in a Roman marble copy. The complex balance of the statue, which depicts the discus thrower at the height of his swing back, was ground-breaking as earlier statues had shown people in stiff poses. It was possible because of the Greeks' advanced techniques of bronze-casting.

Greek sculptors aimed at the depiction of an ideal beauty but the **Romans**, who inherited Greek techniques, produced more life-like forms. The statue of Emperor Augustus *c*.10BC depicts him with heroic dignity, but is recognizable as an individual likeness. Both Greeks and Romans produced works in

marble as well as bronze to adorn buildings and gardens.

AD 1

Religious prohibition

In 726, the Byzantine Emperor Leo III banned the making of images of Christ, the Virgin Mary or the Saints. **Iconoclasm** – opposition to or destruction of sacred images – lasted on and off for several centuries and had a profound effect on art.

In the early Christian era, most sculpture was associated with buildings, especially **Cathedrals**. The tympanum – a semi-circular panel over the main door – was richly carved. A fine example is in the Cathedral of Vézelay, France, *c*.1125.

The huge stone carvings of figures (moai) found on **Easter Island** 2340 miles *3765km* west of Chile were made by Polynesian colonists *c*.AD1000–1500. The 600 or so statues show stylized humans and may represent ancestors. The largest is 62ft *19m* tall and weighs 82 tonnes.

AD 1000

Carving the gates of Heaven

The **Renaissance** saw the flowering of all forms of European art. Lorenzo Ghiberti (It) (1378–1455) was one of the first major figures of Renaissance Italy. He won a competition to design a set of doors for the Baptistry in Florence in 1401, but the work to complete the set took 27 years. The gilded panels, which depicted scenes from the Bible, were cast in bronze. Italian artist **Michelangelo** Buonarroti (1475–1564) praised Ghiberti's work, saying it was fit for the gates of Paradise.

Donatello (Donato di Niccolo) (*c.*1386–1466) was also a Florentine. He marks the Renaissance's rediscovery of classical sculpture with his life-size bronze sculpture of *David*, the king of Israel in the 11th/10th centuries BC who may have written some of the Psalms in the Bible.

In the late 20th century artists have taken art out from the gallery into the street in often temporary presentations. In 1985 Bulgarian-born US sculptor Christo (Christo Javacheff) (*b.*1935) used 40,000 yards *36,000 metres* of canvas to 'wrap' the Pont Neuf across the River Seine in Paris.

Michelangelo also produced a famous *David* (1501–4), this time in marble and over 16ft *5m* in height. The *David* of Giovanni Lorenzo **Bernini** (It) (1598–1680), carved in 1623, depicts David in the moment of casting the stone with which he slew the giant Philistine Goliath.

Frenchman Auguste **Rodin** (1840–1917) created the most important body of sculpture of the late 19th–early 20th centuries, but his work was not always liked. His statue of French writer Honoré de Balzac was commissioned in 1891 but was rejected and not finally cast until 1939, well after the sculptor's death.

Romanian sculptor Constantin **Brancusi** (1876–1957) carved directly in stone and wood, creating beautiful, and sometimes severe, abstract forms such as *Sleeping Muse* (1910).

American-born British sculptor Jacob Epstein (1880–1959) met with outrage from the Establishment for his **Modernist** figures and his nudes, such as *Genesis* (1931).

AD 2000

Moving pieces, new materials

One of the first artists to experiment with **kinetic** (moving) pieces was Naum Gabo (Rus) (1890–1977). He was also one of the first to use transparent plastics.

Henri Gaudier-Brzeska (Fr) (1891–1915) worked in London from 1911 and became a member of the **Vorticist** movement which sought to reflect the rhythms of the industrial age in art.

Henry **Moore** (GB) (1898–1986) created monumental human figures, often designed to be placed on a specific site.

The most characteristic work of Swiss sculptor Alberto Giacometti (1901–66) dates from the 1940s when his figures, such as *Pointing Man* (1947) took on a spindly, endangered appearance – reflecting his conception of the life of modern man.

Barbara **Hepworth** (1903–75), turned entirely to abstract forms. Her *Pierced Form* (1931) introduced the concept of the 'hole' in a figure and she continued to explore the relationship between the inside and outside of shapes.

In the 20th century sculptors have had access to many **new materials** as well as the traditional stone, bronze and wood. César Baldaccini (Fr) (*b.*1921) used plastics and recycled materials. His *Transfigured Mountain* (1995) was made of hundreds of crushed cars.

Minimalist sculptors of the 1950s and 1960s moved toward elementary geometrical forms without emotional overtones. The American Donald Judd (*b.*1928) concentrated on rows of geometric units.

Nam June **Paik** (Korea) (*b.*1932) focuses on the effects of the media. His *TV Buddha* (1974) has the Buddha facing a television set.

An army of ancient Egyptian sculptors must have worked on the giant Sphinx – a mythological creature resembling a lion with human chest and head – that lies close to the pyramids at Giza, near Cairo. The Sphinx is 70ft *20m* high and 140ft *40 metres* long; it was cut from solid rock before 2500BC.

Decorative arts

BEFORE AD 1

The first pots

The earliest example of **ceramics** so far discovered dates from 27,000BC and is a 'Venus' figure found at Dolní Vestonice, Czech Republic. Pottery (ceramic vessels) date from 10,700BC in the case of Jomon cord ware from Fukui, Nagasaki, Japan.

Amber fossil resin has been found, dating to *c*.12,000BC

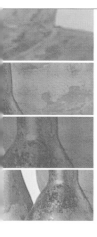

As long ago as the 3rd millennium BC Mesopotamian craftsmen in what is now Iraq were making objects from 'blue glass', a mixture of sand with soda or potash. A blue glass cylinder *c*.2600BC found at Tel Asmar, Iraq, is the oldest glass object in the world. These Syrian bottles of lustreware glass date from the first millennium BC.

before the Mesolithic period, around the Baltic and Jutland coasts. It was used for **amulets** (charms which are worn against evil). In about 9000BC, **trinkets** (pins or rings) were made from copper by cold hammering in Cayönü, Turkey.

The earliest dateable **mirrors** are polished bronze or copper discs used during the Old Kingdom of Egypt and dating from *c*.2940BC.

Tattooing, the permanent skin decoration made by puncturing and inserting pigments, has been found on Egyptian mummies dating from *c*.2000BC.

Lacquer, a varnish of shellac made from a resin exuded by insects on to the twigs of trees, was found at Shang ts'un

The ancient Egyptian fertility and love goddess Bastet is represented on this 2nd–1st century BC charm made of glazed pottery. As usual Bastet is shown with a cat's head. The charm, probably worn on a necklace, is about 5in *12cm* high.

ling, China, in the Eastern Chou dynasty *c*.650BC. The first dateable mirrors found in China are dated from *c*.500BC.

The oldest surviving fragment of **carpet** dates from *c*.400BC and was discovered in a frozen tomb at Pazyryk, Siberia.

AD 1

Fabrics and metalwork

Tapestry – thick, hand-woven fabric with designs formed by weft stitching across parts of the warp – was first recorded by Pliny (AD23–79) in Gaul. Samplers, small pieces of **embroidery**, are first found in Egyptian funerary goods *c*.AD350. **Knitting** originated in Arabia at about the same period.

In *c*.400, niello (mediaeval Lat. *nigello*, black) dark alloys was used to **inlay engraved designs** on polished metal, usually silver. This was first used in Early Christian period church plate.

Cloisonné, a form of decoartive **enamelling** in which colours are kept apart by thin metal strips, originated with Byzantine work, in Turkey *c*.550.

The earliest **stained glass** dates from St Paul's Church, Jarrow, County Durham, England from *c*.850. The origin of **porcelain** is dated to the time of the T'ang Dynasty (*c*.875) in Kiangsi Province, China.

AD 1000

The spread of luxury goods

English **samplers** date from one supplied to the Queen Elizabeth of York (1465–1503) in 1502. The first **glass mirrors** were made by craftsmen in the Italian city of Venice *c*.1670.

Mahogany first arrived in Europe from the West Indies in 1584 and dominated English furniture from 1733. Impregnations for wood preservation were developed in the Netherlands in 1779.

Chippendale furniture was designed by Thomas Chippendale (Eng) (1718–79), who published the first comprehensive trade guide in 1754. His neoclassical chairs were mainly of mahogany.

Josiah **Wedgwood** (1730–95) established a pottery called 'Etruria', near Hanley, Staffordshire, in 1759 where he initiated the use of neoclassical designs. In 1763 he dedicated his delicate new blue-and-white range to Queen Charlotte, wife of King George III (*r*.1760–1820); it was known as Queen's Ware.

The **rocking chair** first appeared in the USA *c*.1770.

Some historians have credited the great American scientist, writer and statesman Benjamin Franklin (US) (1706–90) with its invention.

Willow pattern, the blue and white transfer-printed china pattern, is attributed to Thomas Turner of Caughley in about 1780, although Thomas Minton (Eng) (1765–1836) is credited by other historians. The famous chinoiserie pattern became standardized by *c*.1830.

Fabergé, jewellers and goldsmiths, were established in St Petersburg, Russia, in 1842. Peter Carl Fabergé (1846–1920) took over his father's business in 1870 and began to diversify it. His fabled jewelled Imperial Easter Eggs were commissioned annually by Russian Czar Alexander III (*r*.1881–94) for his tsarina, Dagmar, from 1884 onward.

AD 2000

Old and new

In the late 19th and the 20th centuries, style in manufactured goods alternated between a harking-back to handmade craftsmanship in natural materials and an embrace of industrial processes and new materials.

William **Morris** (Eng) (1834–96) was a central figure in the first tendency and a leading light of the **Arts and Crafts** Movement. In 1861 he was one of the founders of a company to make stained glass, wallpapers and fabrics and in 1890 set up the Kelmscott Press, which produced books on handmade paper using typefaces that had been designed by Morris himself.

Morris's movement had a strong influence on the early

English potter Josiah Wedgwood was at the forefront of an 18th-century revival of interest in Greek and Roman decorative style. In his blue jasper and black basalt ware he imitated the shape of classical pots. A room in Dublin Castle commemorates Wedgwood's aesthetic achievement.

American husband-and-wife team Charles and Ray Eames had a great influence on 20th-century design, especially of furniture. Charles Eames first trained as an architect; he designed this house in California in 1949.

An artist exhibits great delicacy in carving a piece of ivory with a nautical scene. The art of 'scrimshawing' – carving on shells or whales' ivory – originated among English sailors in the 17th century. The oldest surviving scrimshaw is a decorated ivory tobacco box dated 1665. The origin of the unusual word scrimshaw is lost to history.

exponents of the **Art Nouveau** style, which developed in Europe between 1890 and 1910. Frenchman Emile **Gallé** (1846–1904) produced artistic, often sinuously formed glassware. Aubrey **Beardsley** (Eng) (1872–98) used flowing, elegant lines in his book illustrations such as for *Morte d'Arthur* (1893).

Charles Rennie **Mackintosh** (Scot) (1868–1928) combined Art Nouveau lines with traditional Scottish architectural style in his Hill House, Helensburgh, Scotland (1902–3). The Glasgow School of Art (1896–1909) is celebrated as his greatest achievement.

In the USA, Louis **Tiffany** (US) (1848–1933) – son of Charles Louis Tiffany, founder of the New York jewellers – applied the Art Nouveau style to stained glass windows and lamps. The movement left a enduringly popular legacy in the designs by Hector Guimard (Fr) (1867–1942) of station canopies and signs for the **Paris Métro**.

Another major influence on design was the German **Bauhaus** school from 1919–33 under its director, Walter Gropius (Ger) (1883–1969). The school was

a breeding ground of talent: German architect Ludwig Mies van der Rohe (1886–1969), Hungarian designer Laszlo Moholy-Nagy (1895–1946) and Swiss painter Paul Klee (1879–1940) all worked there.

The Bauhaus moved away from handcrafts to the use of **machinery**. Its exhibition of 1923 included murals, sculpture and stained glass.

In the UK in 1944, the **Design Council** was inaugurated by the government to encourage design in industry.

American Charles **Eames** (1907–78) with his wife Ray (1916–88) pioneered the use of new materials in furniture design, producing a simple, easily stacked chair made of steel tubing and plywood in 1940. Its comfort and clean lines made it very popular after it went into mass production. The Eames also designed a fibreglass armchair (1950–3) and a celebrated leather lounger (1956) as well as toys and tables.

Eero **Saarinen** (Fin) (1910–61), a collaborator of Eames' in the early 1940s, later produced several popular designs, among them the fibreglass Womb chair (1948) manufactured by the Knoll Furniture Company.

Studio pottery was revived by Bernard Leach (Eng) (1887–1979), who produced handmade pots as art forms.

Plastics and polyurethanes (petroleum products) were used in furniture-making in the late 20th century. In 1990 Biopol, a biodegradable plastic, was developed. PVC (poly-vinyl-chloride), invented in 1913, has been used in the manufacture of washable wallpapers.

The world's oldest surviving chair was painstakingly rebuilt from pieces found in the tomb of the Ancient Egyptian Queen Hetepheres, (mother of Kha fu) (c.2600BC) at Giza, near Cairo. The wide seat slopes towards the backrest. The carvings beneath the arms show three flowers tied together while the legs represent those of a lion.

Art prices

The creation of an art market at which paintings were auctioned began in the first half of the 18th century and so has existed for more than 250 years. In this unique table both the price paid and its 1999 equivalent are shown. The Mona Lisa (*La Giaconda*) by Leonardo da Vinci (It) (1452–1519) was bought (for his bathroom) by King François I of France in 1517 for 4000 gold florins or 37.35lb *16.94kg*. In 1962 it was valued for insurance purposes at $100 million, then £35,715,000, or in 1999 value £417 million.

Portrait of Dr Gachet by Dutch artist Vincent Van Gogh broke all records at auction in 1990. Dr Gachet was responsible for the mentally unstable Van Gogh in the last months of the artist's life in 1890.

PAINTINGS—PROGRESSIVE SALE PRICE RECORDS

Date	Artist, title, sold by and sold to	Price paid	Equivalent 1999 value	1999 $ value
1746	Antonio Correggio's (It) (c.1494–1534) *The Magdalen Reading* (in fact spurious), sold to the Elector Augustus II of Saxony (1696–1763)	£6500	£785,000	$1,282,700
1759	Raphael's (It) (1483–1520) *The Sistine Madonna*, sold to the Elector August II of Saxony (1696–1763)	£8500	£900,000	$1,470,600
1821	Jan Van Eyck's (Flem) (c.1389–1441) *Adoration of the Lamb* (six outer panels of the Ghent altarpiece) by Edward Solby to the Government of Russia	£16,000	£965,000	$1,576,800
1852	Bartolomé Murillo's (Sp) (1618–82) *The Immaculate Conception* by estate of Marshal Soult (1769–1851) to the Louvre, Paris	£24,000*	£1,877,000	$3,067,000
1885	Raphael's *Ansidei Madonna* by 8th Duke of Marlborough to the National Gallery, London	£70,000	£4,905,000	$8,015,000
1901	Raphael's *The Colonna Altarpiece* by Seidermeyer to J. Pierpoint Morgan (US) (1837–1913)	£100,000	£6,700,000	$10,948,000
1906	Van Eyck's *Elena Grimaldi-Cattaneo* (portrait) by Knoedler to Peter Widener (1834–1915)	£102,880	£6,815,000	$11,136,000
1911	Rembrandt's (Neths) (1606–69) *The Mill* by the 6th Marquess of Landsdowne to Peter Widener (1834–1915)	£102,880	£6,600,000	$10,784,000
1913	Raphael's smaller *Panshanger Madonna* by Lord Duveen (1869–1939) to Peter Widener	£116,500	£7,315,000	$11,953,000
1914	Leonardo Da Vinci's (It) (1452–1519) *Benois Madonna* to Czar Nicholas II (1868–1918) in Paris	£310,400	£19,490,000	$31,847,000
1961	Rembrandt's *Aristotle Contemplating the Bust of Homer* by estate of Mr & Mrs Alfred W. Erickson to New York Metropolitan Museum of Art	$2.3 million*	£10,400,000	$16,994,000
1967	Leonardo Da Vinci's *Ginevra de'Benci* (portrait) by Prince Franz Josef II of Liechtenstein to National Gallery of Art, Washington DC	£1,785,714	£18,465,000	$30,173,000
1970	Diego Velazquez's (Sp) (1599–1660) *Portrait of Juan de Pareja* by the Earl of Radnor to the Wilderstein Gallery, New York City	£2,310,000*	£20,415,000	$33,358,000
1980	J. M. W. Turner's (Eng) (1775–1851) *Juliet and her Nurse* by Trustees of Whitney Museum, New York City to an undisclosed bidder at Park Berret, New York City	$6.4 million*	£6,775,000	$11,072,000
1984	J. M. W. Turner's *Seascape: Folkestone* by estate of Lord Clark (1903–83) to Leggatt's, London	£7,470,500*	£13,265,000	$21,657,000
1985	Andrea Mantegna's (It) (c.1431–1506) *The Adoration of the Magi* by the Marquess of Northampton to J. Paul Getty Museum, Malibu, California	£8,100,000	£13,558,000	$22,692,000
1987	Vincent Van Gogh's (Neths) (1853–90) *Sunflowers* by Lady Beatty to Yasuda Fire and Marine Insurance Co. Tokyo	$24,750,000*	£34,970,000	$57,141,000
1987	Van Gogh's *Irises* by John Whitney Payson to Alan Bond (Eng/Aust) (b.1938) [not released by Sotheby's owing to failure to pay]. Resold to Getty Museum in 1990.	$53.9 million*	£51,225,000	$83,700,000
1990	Van Gogh's *Portrait of Dr Gachet* by Christie's, New York	$82.5 million*	£64,570,000	$105,507,000

*sold at auction; other pictures were sold by private treaty

SCIENCE

- **Mathematics**

- **Timekeeping**

- **Astronomy**

- **Physics**

- **Chemistry**

- **The chemical elements**

- **Automata and robots**

Jupiter in all its glory reveals the storms that
rack its atmosphere, creating the swirling
bands of acids that circle the planet. Since
time immemorial Man has struggled to make
sense of the beauty of the heavens.
Astronomers, delving ever deeper into the
cosmos, have confirmed and confounded the
predictions of mathematicians, and chemists
and physicists have begun to learn how our
world was formed and how life first began.

Mathematics

BEFORE AD 1

Counting in twos

The science of mathematics (Gk. *mathematikos* from *mathema*, science) – studying the relationships between numbers and forms – began with the Ancient Greeks. But far earlier civilizations had their own methods of measuring and counting.

As soon as people needed to start counting things, they had to break up large numbers into multiples of a 'base' number. Primitive peoples used the **base two**, so that counting went: 'one', 'two', 'two-one', two-two', and so on. This method is still used by African bushmen, some Amazon tribes and Australian Aborigines. But its use for large numbers is impossible, and other bases were developed.

One of the earliest artefacts indicating some sort of numeracy is a wolf bone found in Vestonice, Czechoslovakia, dating from *c.*30,000BC. The bone is about 7in *17cm* long and bears a

The abacus – beads strung on wires in a wooden frame – is the world's oldest calculator and was probably developed in China or Japan. The abacus was taken up by the Greeks and Romans and continued in widespread use in Europe until the 17th century. At the end of the 20th century the devices are still used in parts of Asia and in Asian communities worldwide. Here a Chinese herbalist calculates a bill in San Francisco's Chinatown.

row of carved notches in two groups. It was clearly a **tally stick** for some sort of numerical recording and it appears that the notches are grouped in sets of five.

In *c.*3300BC the Sumerians of ancient Mesopotamia (modern South Iraq) used cuneiform writing on clay tablets and there is evidence that they began with a 'base two' system. Later, they developed a system based on a combination of **decimal** (base ten) and **base sixty**, the number sixty being called *gesh*. This system was adopted by the Babylonians and the Assyrians. The base sixty, with its many factors, lingers in the division of the circle into 360 degrees and in the French numbers *soixante-dix* (70), *quatre-vingts* (80) and *quatre-vingt-dix* (90).

The Great Pyramid of Cheops in Egypt was built *c.*2950BC. The building of such monuments called for the next development in mathematics: **practical geometry**. The Ancient Egyptians were not acquainted with sophisticated geometry, but they used a system of stretched ropes knotted at intervals to achieve right angles and other proportions.

Much early mathematics is concerned with accounting. Around 2500BC the Chinese had a widespread civil service that was in charge of taxation and public spending. They had **two sets of numbers**. One system, of pictograms, was used by accountants and civil servants; the other, of 'scientific' numbers, was built up of horizontal and vertical strokes derived from bone or

bamboo counting rods. The latter was a decimal system, so that a horizontal stroke (–) represented 10, while two horizontal strokes (=) represented 20 and so on.

The *Chui-chang suan-shu* ('Nine Chapters on the Mathematical Art') was one of the earliest Chinese mathematical works, *c.*250BC. It consists of 246 problems on practical geometry and calculation for engineers, surveyors, and accountants.

The Greeks were not only builders but also passionate theoreticians and it is they who developed the study of mathematics as an abstract or 'pure' science.

The origin of the science has been attributed to Thales of Miletus (*c.*625–*c.*547BC) who founded **trigonometry** (Gk. *trigonon*, triangle; *metria*, measurement) when measuring the height of Egyptian pyramids.

Their earliest geometer (*geo*, earth; *metres*, measurer) was Thales' pupil Anaximander (610–546BC). He thought the Earth was cylindrical rather than spherical.

The first to assert that it was spherical was **Pythagoras** of Samos (*c.*560–480BC); it is to Pythagoras that we owe the famous theorem which states that the square of the hypotenuse is equal to the sum of the squares of the length of the other two sides of a triangle.

Euclid (Gk) (*fl.*300BC) wrote his textbook *Elements*, primarily on geometry, in Alexandria. When his patron Ptolemy I (*r.*323–285BC) required him to make his demonstrations easier to follow, Euclid is reputed to have retorted: 'There is no royal road to geometry'. **Euclidean geometry** was the basis of all further work until 1829, when Nicolai Lobachevski (Rus) (1793–1856) published *On the Foundations of Geometry,* the first account of non-Euclidian geometry of a kind later confirmed by Einstein.

The Greek astronomer Hipparchus (*c*.190–*c*.120BC) compiled the first known **trigonometrical tables** of ratios, in order to calculate parallaxes for measuring the distance of the Moon from the Earth. His estimated figure of 30 times the diameter of the Earth – 238,855 miles *384,400km* – was remarkably accurate.

AD 1

The birth of algebra

The Romans were more interested in practical achievements in engineering and building than in theory. In any case, Roman numerals – I, II, V, X and so on – did not lend themselves to advanced calculation: firstly, the Romans did not use a zero; secondly, their numbers are not arranged so that the place of a figure signifies a multiple of ten, as in our numbers (thus, in 21, the number is 2 x 10 + 1). In Roman numerals, the figures (XXI) are merely additive.

Algebra – the use of symbols to work out general equations – was pioneered by the Greek mathematician Diophantus of Alexandria (*c*.210–*c*.280) in *Arithmetica, c*.250. Before him, the Babylonians had used the principle of equations, but only to solve concrete problems.

Algebra was later developed in the Arab world and derived its name from the Arabic *al,* the; *jabr,* reunion (of broken parts). During the caliphate of al-Mamun (809–33) in Baghdad, many Greek and Hindu mathematical treatises were translated. Muhammad ibn Musa Al-Khwarizmi (*c*.780–*c*.850) wrote a book, *On the Hindu Art of Reckoning,* in which he expounded the Hindu numerals which are the basis of our numbers today. The word *al-jabr* formed part of the title of the book *Al-jabr wa'l muqabalah* ('The Science of Transposition and Cancellation'), also by Al-Khwarizmi.

The Mayan civilization (*c*.325–925) of Yucatan, Central America, used a counting system with a base of 20, so that larger numbers are **multiples of twenty**. This is thought to derive from the use of both the toes and the fingers for computation. The method became widespread throughout the Americas, even reaching the Inuit of the Arctic North.

The work of Greek mathematician Euclid remains central to basic geometry 2300 years after his death. His book *Elements,* which ran to 13 volumes, was studied by scientists throughout the Classical world.

AD 1000

Theories of numbers

One of the great Persian mathematicians is known in the West as a poet. **Omar Khayyam** (*c*.1050–1123) wrote a book called *Algebra* in which he described the geometrical solution to cubic equations – that is, equations employing cubic figures such as x^3 – by using intersecting conic sections.

Mathematicians have found that the 'Fibonacci sequence' of numbers discovered by the 13th-century Italian mathematician of that name appears frequently in organic structures such as shells and pine cones. In the sequence each number is the sum of the previous two: 0–1–1–2–3–5–8...

SCIENCE

The 18th-century Swiss mathematician Leonhard Euler standardized the use of much mathematical notation – such as *e* for the base of natural logarithms and *i* for the square root of -1.

Arabic mathematics was passed on to Western European scholars in the early Middle Ages, among them Leonardo of Pisa (It) (*c*.1170–1250), better known as **Fibonacci**. His book *Liber abaci* ('The Book of Calculations') (1202) is a treatise on algebra.

François Viete (Fr) (1540–1603) was the first mathematician to make use of vowels for unknowns and consonants for constants in his book *In Artem Analyticam Isagoge* ('Introduction to the Analytic Art').

Scottish landowner John Napier (1550–1617) was primarily interested in problems of computation. 'Napier's bones' were sticks on which were carved parts of the multiplication tables to aid multiplication and division. Napier moved on to invent the **logarithmic tables** which permit multiplication and division to be carried out by the addition or subtraction of the powers of numbers.

Analytical geometry – the application of algebra to geometry – was the brainchild of two great Frenchmen, René Descartes (1596–1650) and Pierre de Fermat (1601–65). Descartes believed that the whole universe could be described in mathematical terms. He invented '**Cartesian co-ordinates**' to enable geometrical shapes to be described by algebraic expressions. Points can be described by where they lie in relation to x and y axes (in two dimensions) plus the z axis for three dimensions.

Fermat's *Introduction to Loci* described the 'locus' of points created by two unknown quantities which can be drawn as a straight or curved line. Fermat also created the modern **theory of numbers** – the investigation of the properties of numbers – and with Blaise Pascal (Fr) (1623–62) the **theory of probability**. Pascal was an extraordinary combination of mathematician, physicist and theologian. He invented a calculating machine on which

The 19th-century English mathematician George Boole is hailed as the father of computer science. He developed a binary decision-making method with a five-term logic – Yes, No, And, Or, Not – that became central to computer programming.

he did his father's tax work. A friend asked him about the mathematical likelihood of throwing certain numbers on dice and his correspondence with Fermat on the problem formed the basis of what later became known as **probability theory**.

The next two mathematical giants were Isaac Newton (GB) (1642–1727) and Gottfried Wilhelm Leibnitz (Ger) (1646–1716), who independently discovered the method of **differential calculus**, used to calculate the rates of change of varying quantities (called 'fluxions' by Newton) in 1675–7.

Leonhard **Euler** (Swiss) (1707–83) was one of the most prolific mathematicians in history, with more than 800 papers over a vast range of both pure and applied mathematics and physics and astronomy. He became professor of mathematics and physics at the Academy of Sciences in St Petersburg under Russian Empress Catherine II (*r*.1762–96).

Euler was so impressed by the work of Comte Joseph Louis de Lagrange (Fr) (1736–1813) that he held back some of his own publications to give the younger man a chance. In 1793 Lagrange was appointed to the Commission that drew up the metre-kilogramme-second or **metric system**, which has become the universal system of scientific measurement.

Johann Karl Friedrich Gauss (Ger) (1777–1855) was a notable mathematician from boyhood and for years kept a diary of his discoveries in Latin. His most important mathematical work was done in the theory of numbers and the **geometry of curved bodies** (non-Euclidean geometry), but he also made contributions to electrical and magnetic theory.

A radical addition to thought was the application of mathematics to **logic**. George Boole (GB) (1815–64) was largely self-taught but became professor of mathematics at Cork, Ireland, in 1849. His *An Investigation of the Laws of Thought* (1854) uses algebraic symbols to describe logical relationships.

The Mathematical Theory of Communication by Claude E. Shannon (US) (*b*.1916) was published in 1948. It followed Booleian logic and confirmed the proposition that all information could be represented as '**bits**' and so analyzed using the strict binary mathematics as understood in the emerging field of computing.

AD 2000

Back to basics

Much modern mathematics is concerned with **questioning** things previously regarded as self-evident. Georg Cantor (Rus) (1845–1918) worked on transfinite arithmetic – the concept of infinity in the theory of numbers – and his ideas were a precursor of the modern theory of **topology**, which studies what happens to a figure when it is transformed – twisted or turned inside out.

David Hilbert (Ger) (1862–1943) redefined the traditional basis of Euclidean geometry. Euclid had based his geometry on axioms which he treated as self-evident truths. Hilbert replaced Euclid's 10 axioms with 21 assumptions (since called **Hilbert's axioms**) and redefined the axiom as something not true in itself but merely an assumption for the purpose of argument.

This questioning of axioms was also applied to the bases of **arithmetic**. Bertrand Russell (GB) (1872–1970) and Alfred North Whitehead (GB/US) (1861–1947) published in 1910–13 the monumental *Principia Mathematica* in which they attempted to derive the whole of arithmetic from basic axioms. But in 1931 Kurt Gödel (Aus/Czech) (1906–1978) showed that this logical system contains statements which can be neither proved nor disproved.

Set theory began in the 19th century with the work of Cantor and

The ideas of 17th-century French mathematician Pierre de Fermat are still bearing fruit at the end of the millennium – his manipulations of prime numbers were the basis of the encryption systems developed to prevent computer hackers breaking into electronic mail messages.

SOME MATHEMATICAL SIGNS

Zero	0	The concept of zero or nought, which made positional notation practical, was the innovation of an unknown Hindu mathematician, probably in Ujjain in west-central India *c*.700. It was later adopted by the Persian mathematician Al-Khwarizmi (*c*.780–*c*.850).
Plus and minus	+ −	Both the plus (+) and the minus (-) signs were first published by John Wideman (Ger) *c*.1489 in Leipzig, Germany.
Equals sign	=	Devised by Robert Record (*c*.1510–58), Fellow of All Souls College, Oxford, in his algebra text *The Whetstone of Witte*, published in London in 1556. He chose this sign because 'no 2 thynges can be moare equalle' than two short parallel straight lines.
Decimal point	•	Introduced by John Napier (Baron Merchiston) (Scot) (1550–1617) in his *Mirifice Logarithmorum Canonis Descriptio* ('Description of the Marvels of Logarithms'), 1614.
Multiplication sign	×	First used by William Oughtred (Eng) (1575–1660) in his book *Clavis Mathematica* ('The Key to Mathematics'), 1631.
Infinity	∞	The sign for infinity, thought to derive from the Greek letter *phi*, first appeared in 1656 or 1665 in *De Sectionibus Conicis* ('On Conic Sections') by John Wallis (Eng) (1616–1703).
Division sign	÷	Invented by John Pell (GB) (1611–85) while he was working as a professor of mathematics in Amsterdam in 1668.
Ångström unit	Å	Introduced to indicate the ten thousandth part of the millionth of a metre, viz. 10^{-10}m. Named in 1905 after Anders Ångström (Sw) (1814–74).

POWERS OF NUMBERS

10^{63}	This number of 64 digits is a vigintillion.
10^{87}	Is an estimate of the number of atoms in the Universe.
100^{100}	The name googol was, in 1959, given to the 101 digit number by Dr Edward Kasner's nine-year-old nephew. Ten to the power of a googol was termed a googol plex.
10^{140}	An *asankhyeya* was the name given to this number by the Jains of India *c*.100BC.
10^{303}	This number of 304 digits is a centillion.
$10^{3000003}$	This number of 3,000,004 digits is a milli-millillion.

The prefixes used for positive and negative powers of ten in counting are:-

deca- (or deka-), x 10^1 (da)	deci-, x 10^{-1}, (d)
hecto-, x 10^2 (h)	centi-, x 10^{-2}, (c)
kilo-, x 10^3 (K)	milli-, x 10^{-3}, (m)
mega-, x 10^6 (M)	micro-, x 10^{-6}
giga-, x 10^9, (G)	nano-, x 10^{-9}, (n)
tera-, x 10^{12}, (T)	pico-, x 10^{-12}, (p)
peta-, x 10^{15}, (P)	femto-, x 10^{-15}, (f)
exa-, x 10^{18}, (E)	atto, x 10^{-18}, (a)

has been one of the most useful logical tools of the 20th century. Elements can be assigned to different sets or groups which are mutually exclusive, overlap or contain each other. This theory allowed Cantor to propose **infinite sets**, and so manipulate the concept of infinity. Nonetheless, Cantor could not show that all sets of numbers could be treated in the same way. In 1963 his Continuum Hypothesis was shown to be insoluble by student Paul Cohen.

Mathematical logic has also taken a new turn with the use of **computers**. At first mathematicians assumed that the computer would merely enable them to calculate much faster, but the solution of the 'four-colour problem' seemed to indicate that the computer was itself 'thinking' of approaches more subtle than its programmers were able to devise.

The **four-colour problem** had first been proposed in 1852 by a student attempting to colour a map of the counties of England. He asked whether it could be shown that four colours would suffice to distinguish all the divisions on any map.

This problem proved surprisingly hard to solve and various flawed proofs were proposed over the years. In 1970, two American mathematicians, Wolfgang Haken and Kenneth Appel, approached it by listing the types of map for which four colours might not work. The list was so long that the only way to work through it was by devising a computer program. In 1976, their program appeared to show that it had tested every one of the possible cases and that, therefore, the hypothesis was proven: four colours *would* always be enough.

The complex problem known as **Fermat's Last Theorem** states that $x^n + y^n = z^n$ cannot be true if n is an integer greater than 2. Pierre de Fermat noted it down before his death, but the theorem defied attempts to prove it until 1993, when English mathematician Andrew Wiles (*b*.1953) offered the first real progress in 356 years in solving the enigma. His first solution proved to be false but in less than a year Wiles came up with a solution that is now widely accepted.

A contemporary bust of Roman Emperor Julius Caesar, conqueror of Gaul, Britain, Egypt – and time. His calendar prevailed for over 1500 years, but it failed to synchronize the calendar year with the time taken for the Earth to orbit the Sun.

Timekeeping

BEFORE AD 1

Taking a cue from nature and the heavens

Natural events such as blossom-time, bird migrations, the rising and setting of the sun and the phases of the moon made it inevitable that early humans would have a basic awareness of the passage of time. Human knowledge of the fundamental principles behind time-keeping, namely astronomical observation and a counting system, appear to date from *c*.850,000BC and *c*.35,000BC respectively.

Marks found on bone artefacts and fragments, analyzed by Alexander Marshack (US) of Harvard University, suggest that the **period from new moon to new moon** was carefully tracked by the Aurignacian civilizations of *c.*35,000BC and by cave-dwellers in southwestern France in *c.*10,000BC.

The human menstrual cycle and the lunar cycle both take about 29 days, which may also have encouraged the Sumerian, Mycenean, Greek and Roman civilizations to adopt a **lunar calendar**.

The **Egyptians** reckoned their calendar from the heliacal rising (the rising closest to the Sun, as viewed from Earth) of Sirius A, the brightest (Mag -1.4) of all stars. The appearance of this star, which they called Sothis, and identified with the goddess Sopdet, presaged the annual inundation of the River Nile.

The Egyptians probably also first established that the Sun took **365 days** to make its apparent passage through a complete circuit of the stars. They divided the year into **twelve months**, each of which consisted of three 10-day **weeks**; five extra days were added at the end of the year to make a total of 365.

The Egyptians also appear to have been the first to divide the day into **24 hours** (*c.*2100BC), allocating one hour to dawn, 10 hours to day, one hour to dusk and 12 hours to night.

Because these civilizations measured the day as the period from sunrise to sunset, the **length of a day** varied and with it, the size of any divisions such as hours. The 2nd-millennium BC definition of the day as the period from midnight to midnight probably stemmed from a convention adopted by Babylonian astronomers after 1800BC.

AD 1

The Julian calendar and the idea of a seven-day week

By 46BC the Roman calendar had drifted so far away from the seasons that Julius Caesar (*c.*101–44BC) abolished it. He decreed a new length for the year of 365 days, 6 hours – and added 67 days to the current year to bring the months back into synchronization with nature. This new Julian calendar was conceived by the Greek scholar Sosigenes.

The **Old Testament** laid down a pattern of work and rest, based on a seven-day cycle. However, the general adoption of

This magnificent gold-cased 'bras en l'air' pocket watch from *c.*1810 shows that watchmakers of the 19th century regarded their craft as both science and art. The gilt figure on the bridge indicates the time by delicately raising and lowering her arms.

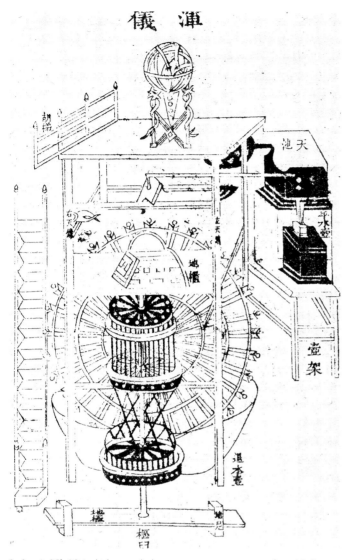

渾儀

Su Song's 35ft *10.6m* high water-clock in Kaifeng, China, was powered by a central waterwheel. A five-tiered pagoda concealed the complex escapement that regulates the time, which was displayed by puppet figures at irregular intervals.

AD 1000

The Lord's time

In Europe years began to be measured from the believed date of Christ's birth starting in the reign of Pope St John I (*r*.523–526). Pope John commissioned a Roman abbot, Dionysius Exiguus (died 556) to compile a new table of dates for Easter.

Dionysius was unwilling to use the existing system of counting the passage of years from AD284, the accession of the Roman Emperor Diocletian, because Diocletian had been a determined persecutor of the early Christians. He began his reckoning *ab incarnatione* (from the Incarnation of Christ). The use of the term **anno domini** ('in the year of Our Lord') was established by the early 9th century.

The Laws of Ina, king of Kent in AD690–3, used the term **fortnight** (Old English *feowertyne niht*, 'fourteen nights'), meaning two weeks, for the first time.

seven-, as opposed to 10-day weeks, was another Roman innovation.

In *c.*AD80, the **seven-day week** was adopted by both the Greeks and the Barbarian tribes; Christian, Muslim and other calendars followed suit. The custom of referring to days of the week, as opposed to dates in the calendar, originated in the Middle East in *c.*AD250, and spread into Western Europe.

Jews gave each year a number denoting the number of years since the giving of the Ten Commandments on Mount Sinai; Romans since the founding of Rome or the accession of the Emperor.

The most sophisticated clocks were **clepsydra,** or water-powered clocks. In 976–9, Zhang Sixun (China) devised a **water-wheel escapement** in which a stream of water filled a sequence of buckets fixed to a wheel.

In 1088 Su Song (China) (1020–1101) built a water-driven mechanical clepsydra in a clock tower in Kaifeng.

Water-driven clocks were of limited accuracy because it was difficult to set up a water supply that flowed absolutely regularly. In 991, Gerbert d'Aurillac (Fr) (*c.*983–1003), later Pope Sylvester II, completed **Europe's first weight-driven clock**. He

learned about the technique of using weights to drive machinery while in Spain.

The **earliest mechanical clock** of which detailed record has survived was built by Richard of Wallingford (Eng) (1291–1336), at St Albans, Hertfordshire.

The **minute**, originally a geometrical term meaning a sixtieth part of a circle, was first applied to the 60 divisions of an hour in *c.*1377, coinciding with the appearance of public clocks.

AD 2000

Accurate timekeeping

The **Gregorian calendar** was introduced by Pope Gregory XIII (*r*.1572–85) when it became clear that the Julian calendar no longer synchronized with the seasons. On 24 February 1582 he issued a papal bull, ordaining that Thursday 4 October would be followed by Friday 15 October, and that every year must begin on January 1 instead of the old date of March 25.

To prevent further slippage, Joseph Scaliger (Fr) (1540–1609), the theoretician behind the new calendar, devised the system of **leap days**. An extra day is added at the end of February in all years divisible by four, except century years (1800, 1900 and so on) unless the century is divisible by 400.

The terms **decade** and **century** came into use in the early 17th century. The term **millennium** for 1000 years first appeared in 1711, and in 1968 the ancient Greek word **aeon** was adopted by the world's astronomers to represent a period of 1000 million years.

Small weight-driven **household clocks** appeared in Europe in *c.*1400, and in 1410 the Florentine architect Filippo Brunelleschi (1377–1446) built the first spring-driven portable clock. Peter Henlein (Ger) (*c.*1485–1542) built the first watch in around 1504.

Christiaan Huygens (Neth) (1629–95) harnessed the pendulum, which always swings in the same amount of time, to a spiral spring and balance wheel to regulate a clock precisely. He built the first **pendulum clock** in 1657. Previous clocks lost up one hour in every 24, but Huygens's clock was accurate to within five minutes a day.

The technology improved in the 17th–19th centuries. **Balance springs** (1658), **minute hands** (1670), **jewelled movements** (1704), **self-winding watches** (1775) and **alarm clocks** (1847) helped to make clocks more useful and ever more accurate.

Astronomers and physicists believe that **time began** some 15,000 million years ago at an instant in which the universe exploded from an infinitely condensed state.

This theory was first postulated by Aleksandr Friedman (Russ) (1888–1925); in 1929 Edwin Hubble (US) (1889–1953) showed that other galaxies are moving away from our own, so establishing that the universe is expanding. In 1950 the astronomer Fred Hoyle (Eng) (*b.*1915) coined the term by which the explosive event is generally known: the **Big Bang**.

20TH CENTURY BREAKTHROUGHS

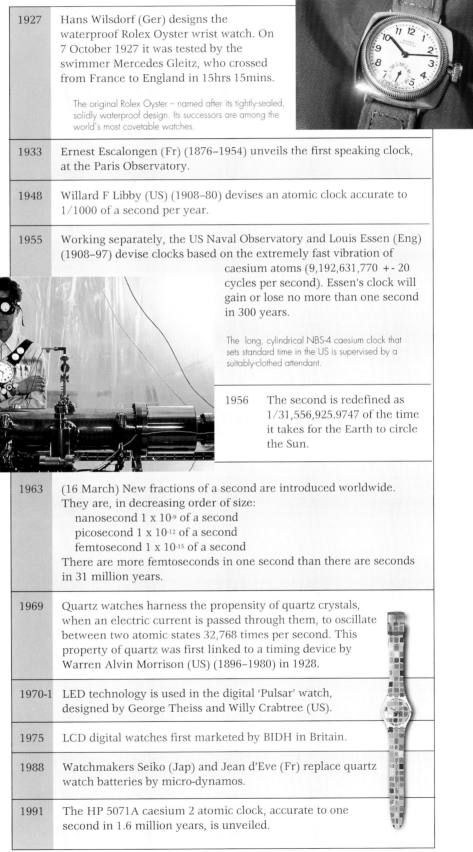

1927	Hans Wilsdorf (Ger) designs the waterproof Rolex Oyster wrist watch. On 7 October 1927 it was tested by the swimmer Mercedes Gleitz, who crossed from France to England in 15hrs 15mins. *The original Rolex Oyster – named after its tightly-sealed, solidly waterproof design. Its successors are among the world's most covetable watches.*
1933	Ernest Escalongen (Fr) (1876–1954) unveils the first speaking clock, at the Paris Observatory.
1948	Willard F Libby (US) (1908–80) devises an atomic clock accurate to 1/1000 of a second per year.
1955	Working separately, the US Naval Observatory and Louis Essen (Eng) (1908–97) devise clocks based on the extremely fast vibration of caesium atoms (9,192,631,770 +- 20 cycles per second). Essen's clock will gain or lose no more than one second in 300 years. *The long, cylindrical NBS-4 caesium clock that sets standard time in the US is supervised by a suitably-clothed attendant.*
1956	The second is redefined as 1/31,556,925.9747 of the time it takes for the Earth to circle the Sun.

1963	(16 March) New fractions of a second are introduced worldwide. They are, in decreasing order of size:
	    nanosecond 1×10^{-9} of a second
	    picosecond 1×10^{-12} of a second
	    femtosecond 1×10^{-15} of a second
	There are more femtoseconds in one second than there are seconds in 31 million years.

1969	Quartz watches harness the propensity of quartz crystals, when an electric current is passed through them, to oscillate between two atomic states 32,768 times per second. This property of quartz was first linked to a timing device by Warren Alvin Morrison (US) (1896–1980) in 1928.
1970-1	LED technology is used in the digital 'Pulsar' watch, designed by George Theiss and Willy Crabtree (US).
1975	LCD digital watches first marketed by BIDH in Britain.
1988	Watchmakers Seiko (Jap) and Jean d'Eve (Fr) replace quartz watch batteries by micro-dynamos.
1991	The HP 5071A caesium 2 atomic clock, accurate to one second in 1.6 million years, is unveiled.

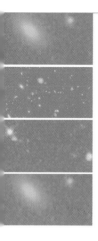

Astronomy

BEFORE AD 1

When the stars helped people to navigate and to keep time

Observations of the **patterns of stars** in constellations were used for navigation long before scientific study. Seafarers probably steered by the stars tens of thousands of years ago in the waters off southeast Asia.

Human interest in the **Moon's phases** can be seen in some notched bones found in France. These tallies apparently denote successive lunar months of 27.32 days and are thought to date back to c.30,000BC.

Entire galaxies form small circles of light in this composite photograph taken by the Hubble Space Telescope. Because it is in orbit high above the Earth's atmosphere, the Hubble can take clearer pictures than land-based telescopes. It was put into Earth orbit by the US Space Shuttle *Discovery* in April 1990.

Astronomical records (Gk. *astron*, star; *nomos*, a law) were kept in many early civilizations. In the reign of Chinese Emperor Chuan Hu, the five nearer planets could be seen in conjunction, or close together. Such a conjunction took place in either 2449BC or 2446BC.

The Egyptians moved from recording data to constructing **calendars**. Owing to their total dependence on the annual flooding of the Nile for their crops, it was vital for the Egyptians to have accurate calendars. They based these on the rising of the star Sirius A.

Scientific astronomy was developed by the ancient Greeks. Thales of Miletus (Gk) (624–546BC), who had probably learnt astronomy in Egypt, made the first accurate **prediction of a solar eclipse** in 585BC. Soon afterwards Pythagoras of Samos (Gk) (c.560–c.480BC) was the first to contend that the **Earth was a sphere**.

The 4th century BC Greek explorer and geographer Pytheas of Massila – now Marseilles – **attributed tides to the Moon**. He also witnessed the 'midnight sun' that in summer never sets in the northern polar regions.

Aristarchus of Samos (Gk) (c.275BC) was the author of both the **heliocentric hypothesis** – that the Earth revolved round the Sun – and that of the **Earth's rotation** on its axis.

Hipparchus (Gk) (c.190–c.120BC) was the first to estimate the **distances of the Sun and the Moon from the Earth**. In 134BC he made the first star chart according to a grid of celestial latitudes and longitudes and devised the grading of the brightness of stars according to magnitudes – a star of magnitude 1.0 is six times brighter than a star of magnitude 6.0. He also discovered the **precession of the equinoxes** (the slow circular movement of the north celestial pole) now known to require about 26,700 years per cycle.

AD 1

Earth at the centre

The Egyptian astronomer Ptolemy (c.AD100–170) proposed that the **Earth was the centre of the universe** with the Sun, Moon and stars revolving around it. This scheme was widely accepted, and violently defended, for the next 1600 years, despite the work of Copernicus.

The Arab world inherited the work of the Greeks and Egyptians. In 813, Al-Mamun founded a **school of astronomy** in Baghdad and many more stars were charted, notably by Al-Sufi (c. 903). Arab astronomy reached Europe via the Moorish invasion of the Iberian peninsula.

AD 1000

Sun back in its rightful place

The Spanish king Alfonso X (1221–84) was called 'the Astronomer' because he drew up a book of planetary tables.

Heliocentricity was again expounded by Nicolaus **Copernicus** (Pol) (b. Mikotaj Kopernik) (1473–1543), who published in 1543 in Nuremberg his great work *De Revolutionibus Orbium Coelestium* ('On the Revolutions of the Celestial Spheres').

The **invention of the telescope** is usually attributed to Hans Lippershey (Ger/Neths) (1570–c.1619) or his apprentice who found in 1608 that two lenses correctly spaced in a tube could magnify distant objects. The

These images of Jupiter and three of its 16 moons were taken by the *Voyager I* space probe in March 1979. Launched in 1977, *Voyager I* has investigated the outer planets of our solar system. Currently at the edge of the system, it will send back data well into the 21st century.

telescope collects light in the large objective lens and magnifies the image in the smaller eyepiece lens.

The **laws of planetary motion** were formulated by German scientist Johannes **Kepler** (1571–1630) in his *Astronomia Nova* published in Heidelberg in 1609. The first law was that the planets move round the Sun, not in circles, but in ellipses, with the Sun as one of the foci.

In 1609 **Galileo Galilei** (It) (1564–1642) heard that a telescope had been invented in the Netherlands and constructed his own telescope with eight-fold magnification which he demonstrated in Venice in August that year. In Jan 1610, he discovered with his newer 20x telescope that Jupiter had

four moons. He also observed that Venus like the Moon, had phases, which he realized implied that Venus was orbiting the Sun, confirming Copernicus's heliocentric theory of the universe.

The Christian Church taught that God had created the Earth and not the Sun at the centre of the universe; in 1616, Pope Paul V declared that the ideas of Copernicus were heretical.

On 22 June 1633 Galileo, who had published his theories in pamphlets of 1610 and 1632, was **tried in Rome for heresy** and was forced to recant. Some witnesses maintained that as he rose from his knees Galileo, now almost blind and in his 70th year, muttered 'Eppur si muove!' ('And yet it moves').

The first discovery of the principle of the **reflecting telescope** (which uses a concave mirror to collect light) was by James **Gregory** (GB) (1638–75) in 1663. In 1671 Isaac **Newton** (GB) (1643–1727) presented his first reflecting telescope to his fellow scientists of the Royal Society, London.

The **velocity of light** was first measured in 1675 by the

Danish astronomer Ole Römer (1644–1710) by using the eclipse times of the satellites of Jupiter.

In 1687 Sir Isaac **Newton** published his *Philosophiae Naturalis Principia Mathematica* in Latin. Newton held that every particle in the universe attracts every other particle with a force that is directly proportional to the product of their masses and inversely proportional to their distance apart. The acceleration due to gravity at the Earth's surface is often expressed as 32ft per sec per sec. It is more accurately 32ft 2.08ins/sec^2 *9.80665m/sec^2.*

Edmond **Halley** (GB) (1656–1742) was British Astronomer Royal from 1720–42. He is best known for his work on **comets**, especially the comet which bears his name. He predicted its return in 1758. Sure enough, it was sighted on Christmas Day 1758 by the astronomer Palitzsch, 16 years after Halley's death. **Halley's comet** was first definitely recorded in 240BC. The

Englishman Isaac Newton (1643–1727) identified the force that holds the universe together: gravity. He was supposedly inspired when an apple fell on his head from a tree in c.1665. Newton used his theory to calculate the movements of the Moon. He also investigated the qualities of light and used the first reflecting telescope. He was Master of the English Mint from 1699–1727.

THE PLANETS

Name	Average distance from Sun (millions of km)	(miles)	Relative gravity	Discovered by
Mercury	58	36	38.0%	known from antiquity; earliest known observation is 265BC passed on to us by Ptolemy (AD90–168)
Venus	108	67	90.3%	known from ancient times, earliest known observation is the Babylonian 'Venus tablet' dating from *c.*650BC
Earth	150	93	100%	–
Mars	228	142	38%	known to the ancient Egyptians, Chinese and Assyrians
Jupiter	778	483	264%	known from antiquity
Saturn	1427	887	116%	known from antiquity, first recorded observations date from Mesopotamia *c.*650BC
Uranus	2870	1783	117%	William Herschel (GB), 1781
Neptune	4497	2794	120%	Johann Galle (Ger), 1846
Pluto	5900	3666	6%	Clyde Tombaugh (US), 1930

The world's largest optical telescope became operational on Mauna Kea, an extinct volcano in Hawaii, in 1992. The telescope, named the Keck I, was built by the California Institute of Technology. It has 36 interlocking segments forming a 33ft *10m* mirror and enables observers to detect stellar objects 200 million times smaller than is possible with the naked eye.

comet's first return to Earth in the third millennium will take place in 2061.
In 1784, John Goodricke (GB/Neths) (1764–86), from his observations of the star Delta Cephei, discovered that **variable stars** fluctuate in brightness with a regular periodicity. Delta Cephei varies from magnitude 3.4 to 5.1 over a period of just over five days.

Sir William Herschel (Ger/GB) (1738–1822) discovered the planet Uranus in 1781. In 1789, he built a 4ft *124.5cm* telescope in Slough, Berkshire, the largest in the world at the time. With it, he established that our galaxy – the Milky Way – was lenticular (lens-shaped).

The first **asteroid** (minor planet) was discovered in 1801. Giuseppe Piazzi (It) (1746–1826) discovered Ceres (Mag. 7.4) from Palermo, Sicily, on 1 January 1801. Ceres, which has a diameter of 940km *584 miles*, is now known to be the largest of a total that may exceed 40,000.

Friedrich Bessel (Prus) (1784–1846) of Königsberg Observatory was the first to measure the **distance to a star**. In 1838, he used trigometrical parallax to calculate the distance from the Earth to 61 Cygni. This method uses the apparent change in position of a

Asteroid 243 Ida was the first asteroid found to have its own moon. This image, taken by the *Galileo* space probe in 1993, shows the moon at the far right. Ida – named after a mountain on the island of Crete – is in orbit between Mars and Jupiter at an average 162 million miles *270 million km* from the Sun. Its moon – called Dactyli after the mythological *Dactyli*, a group of smiths who lived on Mt. Ida – measures just 1 × 0.87 × 0.7 miles *1.6km × 1.4km × 1.2km*.

distant object when viewed from two different spots. 61 Cygni has now been found to be the 16th nearest star to our Sun at 11.2 light years or 65.8 million million miles *105.95 million million km.*

In 1863 the Director of the Bonn Observatory in Germany, Friedrich Argelander (1799–1875), published his **star atlas** of the northern stars with the positions of 324,198 stars.

In 1912, Henrietta Leavitt (US) (1868–1921) formulated the Period-Luminosity Law of variable stars. It enables observers to ascertain the distance of a variable star by timing its periodicity; astronomers can then use the variables as 'standard candles' to measure the distances of other nearby bodies.

AD 2000

Everything is flying apart

Between 1912 and 1925 Vesto M. Slipher (US) (1875–1969) found that almost all galaxies showed a **'red shift'** in their spectra. This is the result of the **Doppler Effect**, discovered in 1842 by Austrian physicist Christian Johann Doppler (1803–53), which describes the change in wavelength of light received from a moving body. If the body is approaching the observer, the wavelength is

apparently shortened, producing a shift to the blue end of the spectrum. If the body is receding, it produces a red shift. The red shift demonstrates that **the universe is expanding**.

Edwin P. Hubble (US) (1889–1953) confirmed the the **expanding universe** in 1923 when he discovered that spiral nebulae were in fact galaxies. Hubble formulated the law which states that the further away the galaxies are, the faster they are moving.

In 1927 Abbé Georges Lemaître (Bel) (1894–1966) published the '**Big Bang** theory' of the origin of the universe. This envisages the beginnings of matter squeezed into a super-dense state which exploded outward. The rate of the red shift suggests that the Big Bang may have occurred 15 billion years ago.

In 1932, Karl Guthe Jansky (US) (1905–50) detected **extraterrestrial radio waves** – 'a steady hiss type static of unknown origin'. He later demonstrated that these waves came from the Milky Way and opened the way to **radio astronomy**. Many heavenly bodies emit radio waves, including the Sun and Jupiter. Radio 'telescopes' are in fact aerial dishes; the first was made with a 31ft *9.5m* dish in 1937 by Grote Reber (US) (*b.*1911).

REFLECTING TELESCOPES

Date	Aperture	Name	Observatory
1668	1in *2.54cm*	Newton	Cambridge, England
1789	49in *124.5cm*	Herschel	Slough, England
1845	72in *189.9cm*	Rosse	Birr Castle, Parsonstown, Ireland
1917	100in *254cm*	Hooker	Mount Wilson, California
1948	200in *508cm*	Hale	Palomar, California
1976	236in *600cm*	Mt. Semirodriki	Zelenchutskaya, Caucasus, USSR
1992	396in *1000cm*	Keck I	Mauna Kea, Hawaii

The first **quasar** (quasi-stellar object) was identified in 1963 by Maartin Schmidt (Neths/US) (*b*.1929) at Palomar, California. Quasars are remote, dim bodies that emit very powerful energy and are thought to be the centres of galaxies. The powerful radio emitter 3C–273 in Virgo was the first to be identified.

In 1968, Dr Jocelyn Bell Burnell (GB) (*b*.1943), of Cambridge University, detected a star, CP1919, that mysteriously emitted bursts of radio waves and other radiation at precise intervals of 1.3373 seconds. Since then, several similar '**pulsars**' – thought to be rapidly spinning super-dense stars composed of neutrons – have been identified.

The satellite *Hipparcos*, launched in 1989, accumulated data on the position of 100,000 stars with a precision 100 times better than results from Earth.

The limiting effect of the Earth's atmosphere on optical telescopes was circumvented with the positioning of the first optical telescope in space. The **Hubble Space Telescope** was launched into Earth orbit on 24 February 1990 aboard the US space shuttle *Discovery*.

This 94 inch *2.4m* orbiting instrument proved defective, and was repaired by a special mission of the space shuttle *Endeavour* on 2–13 December 1993. Astronaut Ackers set a new US duration record for EVA (Extra-Vehicular Activity) of 29 hours 40 mins.

Results from the Hubble Telescope indicate that a number of galaxies now appear to be **10 per cent more distant** than previously thought.

A **brown dwarf** is a star without enough mass to ignite nuclear reactions in its core; such failed stars give off a fading light as they shrink. For many years astronomers were certain that they existed, but none were discovered until scientists at the Astrophysics Institute on the Canary Islands and at Mauna Kea on Hawaii began to look for the metallic element **lithium** in stars. Most stars destroy lithium in their cores but brown dwarfs are too cool to do so. In 1995, the lithium test confirmed the existence of brown dwarf PP1 15 in the Pleiades cluster.

The **Sloan Digital Sky Survey** (SDSS) is a project run jointly by several academic and research organizations to map 10,000 square degrees (one-quarter) of the sky in detail using electronic light detectors and a 8ft *2.5m* telescope at the Apache Point Observatory in Sunspot, New Mexico, USA.

In 2000 the SDSS discovered a quasar with a red shift (see page 92) of 5.8 as measured by the Keck Telescope at Mauna Kea, Hawaii. It is the **most distant known heavenly body**.

Calculating the quasar's distance is a complex procedure, as the universe is constantly expanding. The light emitted by the star took 13 billion years to reach Mauna Kea. At that time, the universe was *c*.0.95 billion years old, and the distance between the Milky Way (our galaxy) and the quasar was *c*.4 billion light years.

But the further away a part of the universe is from the original location of the Big Bang, the faster it is moving. The distance between the Milky Way and the quasar is

increasing all the time – at the rate of 336,000 miles/sec *540,000km/sec*. Scientists have calculated that if they could halt the expansion and measure the distance today between the Milky Way and the quasar it would be 27 billion light years.

1999–2000 were the years of new space observatories. NASA launched the **Chandra X-ray Observatory** in July 1999. It will observe X-ray emissions to try to discover more about the history of the cosmos. The European Space

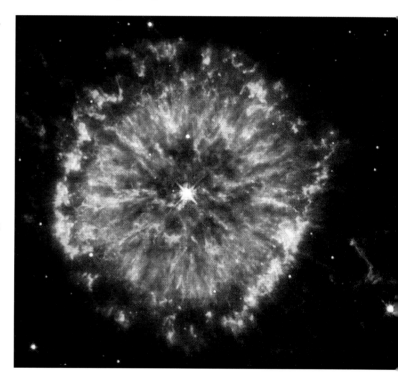

Agency's **XMM satellite observatory**, also launched in 1999, will investigate what happens in the vicinity of black holes (see page 97).

The **Gemini North observatory** at Mauna Kea opened in 2000. Its primary mirror is 26.5ft *8.1m* wide and 7.8in *20cm* thick. It will collect information from the infrared end of the spectrum from star-forming areas that are occluded by dust that absorbs visible light.

This composite of three images taken by the Hubble Space Telescope in 1998 shows a cloud of gas emitted by a star (centre) in the Aquila galaxy *c*.6500 light years from Earth. Stars with a mass similar to that of our own Sun give off gas in this way, exposing the hot stellar core, as they near the end of their lives. Our Sun will 'explode' like this in *c*.6 billion years.

Physics

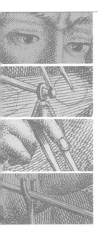

By ancient tradition, Archimedes suddenly understood the physical law of the displacement of fluid when the public bath overflowed as he lowered himself into it. He supposedly ran naked into the street shouting 'Eureka! Eureka!' (Gk: 'I have found it! I have found it!'). He also invented a device – a screw within a cylinder – for raising water.

ARCHIMEDE de Syracuse
Mathematicien né 550 ans avant
Jesus-Christ.

BEFORE AD 1

How the world works

Physics (Gk. *phusika*, natural things) covers the scientific laws of matter and energy and of their relationship to each other. Traditionally this was divided into the six fields of electricity, heat, light, magnetism, mechanics and sound. Many applications of physical laws have been exploited before the laws themselves were discovered.

The ancient **Egyptians** had to harness the waters of the River Nile to irrigate their crops every year. They understood enough about

practical hydraulics to build a dam on the Nile in *c*.3000BC and to extract the water with simple pumps.

The Greek Thales of Miletus (*c*.625–*c*.547BC) described the effect of **static electricity** using a piece of amber found on the seashore. While Archytas of Tarentum (*c*.420–*c*.350BC) has been credited with the invention of the **pulley** block and tackle which enabled the effort put into moving a weight to be reduced proportionally to the number of parts of the tackle.

Perhaps the finest Greek thinker, **Archimedes** (287–212BC) formulated his

principle that a body floating in water will weigh less by the amount of water it displaces in *c*.235BC. He was asked by Hieron II, the ruler of Syracuse in Sicily, to check that a crown was solid gold. Archimedes did this by comparing the displacements of gold and of the crown. He proved that the king's goldsmith had adulterated the gold when making the crown.

Archimedes was also the first to determine the **centres of gravity** of solids such as the cylinder and the cone.

AD 1

Progress in the East

Arab scholars from the golden age of the Islamic Empire (711–1492) studied various branches of practical physics. The scientific methods **Avicenna** (ibn Sina) (979–1037) later had great and long-lasting influence on western scientists.

The Arab mathematician **Alhazen** (ibn al-Haytham) (*c*.965–1038) wrote a book on optics in which he described the structure of the eye and reflection and refraction from curved surfaces. **Al-Jazari** was an engineer and theoretician who lived in Mesopotamia *c*.1200. Among other inventions detailed in his *Book of Knowledge of Ingenious Devices*, was a reciprocating water pump.

AD 1000

The nature of light and matter

Dutch mathematician Willebrord van Roijen Snell (1581–1626) published his law of **refraction** of light in 1621, describing the way a beam of light will bend in passing from one medium to another. The principle of refraction is used in lenses.

In the 17th century many discoveries were made about the nature of solids, liquids and gases. In 1643, Evangelista Torricelli, an Italian physicist, was the first to measure **air pressure**, using a column of mercury.

In 1661 Robert **Boyle** (GB) (1627–91) discovered that the volume of a given mass of gas at constant temperature is inversely proportional to its pressure – this is known as Boyle's Law.

British scientist Isaac **Newton** (1642–1727) first published his law of universal gravitation in *Philosophiae Naturalis Principia Mathematica* ('Mathematical Principles of Natural Philosophy') (1687).

Newton also experimented with the refraction of light through a prism and discovered that differently coloured rays – that is, different wavelengths of light – refracted at different angles. This led him to replace the lens with a mirror in a **telescope** because a beam of light (made up of several colours) would never produce a clear image when refracted through a lens. Discoveries in electricity were made many years before electricity itself could be harnessed for practical use. Stephen Gray (GB) (*c.*1696–1736) was the first to realize that materials conduct **electrical current**. In his experiment, the electricity was produced by rubbing a tube of glass and the current travelled down a silk thread.

The terms 'conductor' and 'insulator' were first used by John **Desaguliers** (Fr/GB) (1683–1744). Charles de Coulomb (Fr) (1736–1806) gave his name to the **coulomb**, a unit of electrical current, in 1785.

J. A. C. **Charles** (Fr) (1746–1823) made a major discovery about the properties of gases when he realized that the volume of a fixed mass of gas is directly proportional to its absolute temperature, if the pressure remains constant. This was later confirmed by Joseph Gay-Lussac (Fr) (1778–1850). Both men were pioneering balloonists.

It was John Dalton (GB) (1766–1844) who first proposed a picture of the **atom**, which he thought of as the smallest possible particle of matter. He noticed that two gases always combine in the same proportions and deduced that this was because the synthesis happened at the atomic level.

In 1827, Georg **Ohm** (Ger) (1789–1854) published his discovery that the electrical current that flows through a conductor is directly proportional to voltage applied and inversely proportional to resistance.

The electrical researches of Michael **Faraday** (GB) (1791–1867) enabled him to invent the dynamo, the transformer and the electric motor in a single year, 1831.

James Clerk Maxwell (GB) (1831–79) was a pupil of Faraday. In his *Treatise on Electricity and Magnetism* (1873), he developed the theoretical basis of their work by postulating the existence of **electromagnetic waves**.

In 1897 J. J. Thomson (GB) (1856–1940) showed that cathode rays consist of electrically charged particles and discovered a constant ratio between the particles' charge and mass. He called the particles 'corpuscles', but they have since become known as **electrons**.

In 1911 physicist Ernest Rutherford (NZ) (1871–1937) discovered a central core to the atom: the **nucleus**. He went on to describe the atom as being like a tiny solar system with electrons orbiting the central nucleus.

AD 2000

New basis for physics

German physicist Max **Planck** (1858–1947) demonstrated in 1900 that the emission or absorption of energy by matter does not happen in a smoothly continuous way but in 'quantum' changes – perceptible and indivisible leaps. It was the beginning of the 20th-century science of quantum theory.

In his special theory of relativity (1905) Albert **Einstein** (Ger) (1879–1955) was concerned with the blurring between an object's mass and energy under certain conditions. When bodies approach the speed of light, their size and mass are

Werner Karl Heisenberg (Ger) (1901–76) helped to establish the modern science of quantum mechanics. He conceived of a central order in nature, expressible in a mathematical equation. As a public figure he was active in promoting the peaceful use of nuclear energy after World War II and, in 1957, led other German scientists in opposing a move to equip the German army with nuclear weapons.

Scientists use a bubble chamber to examine the behaviour of subatomic particles in a laboratory. As the number of known particles has grown in the 20th century, theory has often led practice: theoretical scientists use calculations to 'prove' the existence of a new particle and their colleagues then try to identify it by experiment.

subject to change. In his general theory of **relativity** (1915) Einstein suggested that the properties of space-time would be modified by the effect of the mass of heavenly bodies.

The first proof that Einstein's contentions were valid came on 29 May 1919 during a total solar eclipse seen from Príncipe Island, in the Gulf of Guinea. As light from stars passed the sun it was bent by the sun's gravity to the precise extent that Einstein had calculated, and thus the stars could be observed even when behind the sun.

German physicist Werner Karl Heisenberg (1901–76) formulated his principle of **indeterminacy** in 1925. He realized that it is impossible to measure the position or behaviour of a particle accurately without affecting the very parameters which are being measured – and therefore it is not possible to be certain of either the exact position or the direction of individual particles.

Every subatomic particle has an antimatter equivalent, an **anti-particle**, in which the electric charge is reversed.

The first to be discovered was the anti-particle of the negatively charged electron.

This discovery was made in 1932 by Carl D. Anderson (US) (1905–91) in a cloud chamber (a vessel filled with air or hydrogen which is supersaturated with water). The anti-particle was christened a **positron** with the symbol e^+.

Niels **Bohr** (Den) (1885–1962) further developed the picture of the atom by applying the quantum theory to Rutherford's ideas. Bohr argued that electrons circling the atomic nucleus could follow a number of orbits and that when they shifted from one orbit to another, radiation was emitted at a fixed frequency. This frequency corresponded, he said, to the spectrum of the element.

Subatomic particles are divided into **leptons** and **quarks**. Leptons include the electron, the muon and the tau and are not affected by the force of the nucleus. The existence of **quarks** was deduced in 1964 by Murray Gell-Mann (US) (*b.*1929). Independently, Russian-born physicist George Zweig (US) (*b.*1937) also proposed the existence of these particles, which he called 'aces'.

Quarks are the basic constituent of hadrons which respond to the nuclear force. Quarks are believed to have a charge equal to either one-third or two-thirds that of an electron. There appear to be six types of quark, and they have been given the names Up, Down, Strange, Charm, Bottom and Top. Mann took the name quark from the novel *Finnegans Wake* by 20th-century Irish novelist James Joyce.

German-born scientists Max Planck (left) and Albert Einstein confer in June 1930. Planck's quantum theory and Einstein's two theories of relativity were profoundly revolutionary and broke with the principles of physics that had been accepted since the time of Isaac Newton. Both men won the Nobel Prize for Physics: Planck in 1918 and Einstein in 1921.

Physicists found experimental evidence for the existence of a number of **new subatomic particles** in the last decades of the 20th century. Working independently in the USA in 1974, Samuel Ting (US) (*b.*1936) and Burton Richter (US) (*b.*1937) discovered the J-psi particle, a type of **meson**. A meson consists of a quark and an antiquark (the quark's anti-particle) held together by exchange of other particles named **gluons**.

In 1977 at Fermilab (the Fermi National Accelerator Laboratory) in the US, Leon Lederman (US) (*b.*1922) discovered the **upsilon** particle, a massive meson consisting of a bottom-antibottom quark pair.

In 1983 Carlo Rubbia (It) (*b.*1934) and Simon ven der Meer (Neth) (*b.*1925), studying collisions between particles at CERN (the Centre for Nuclear Research) in Geneva, Switzerland, identified the **W and Z particles**, also known as 'weakons' or W and Z bosons.

In 1984 research carried out at CERN found the first evidence for the existence of the 'top quark'.

Efforts to find a **unified theory** consistent both with quantum mechanics and the general theory of relativity have led physicists to propose pictures of the universe that are suggestive of science fiction. The existence of **black holes** – very dense concentrations of matter with gravitational fields so strong that they curve space and time around on itself, and allow nothing (not even light) to escape – was proposed as long ago as 1783 by John **Michell** (Eng) (1724–93), who called them 'dark stars'. Both

black holes and **wormholes** – tiny black holes running like tunnels through space and time, connecting one black hole to another – became favourites of science fiction.

In the 1980s, physicists at the California Institute of Technology (Caltech) in the USA were surprised to find that wormholes broke none of the rules of Einstein's general theory of relativity; the scientists could not prove that wormholes did not exist.

In 1985 Kip Thorne (US) at Caltech argued that a wormhole could be kept open for a long period of time. Because a wormhole connects black holes in different parts of space and time, Thorne's contention suggested that another sci-fi theme, **time travel**, was theoretically achievable.

Also in the 1980s, different versions of the **superstring theory** – the contention that the basic matter of the universe does not consist of particles but string-like objects existing in 10 or more dimensions — held sway. In 1995, Edward Witten (US) (*b.*1951) of the Institute of Advanced Study at Princeton, USA, developed the **M-theory**, in which he suggested that, instead of strings, these elements were membranes. The membranes can exist either as rolled-up cylinders (when they act as strings) or as bubbles.

In 1989 US physicists Martin Fleischmann (*b.*1927) and Stanley Pons (*b.*1943) reported that they had produced energy by **cold fusion** – nuclear fusion achieved at or near room temperature, rather than at the extremely high temperatures of millions of degrees Centigrade found in

stars or created in nuclear bombs. However, Austrian-born physicist Harold Furth (US) (*b.*1930) subsequently refuted their claim.

Scientists at CERN reported in April 2000 that they might have created **conditions similar to the 'Big Bang'** (see page 92) — on a minute scale. In the Large Electron Positron collider they fired lead nuclei (which are composed of 208 protons and neutrons) at a thin lead foil at almost the speed of light.

At sufficiently high energy, the collision produced a fireball of thousands of separate quarks and CERN scientist Ulrich Heinz

A computer display at CERN exhibits particle behaviour immediately following a collision between an electron and a positron – creating a Z boson or weakon. This weakon exists so briefly that it does not make a track of its own, so scientists deduce its existence from the behaviour of other particles, shown here as yellow, red and green lines.

The Large Electron Positron collider at CERN is the world's largest particle accelerator. It is housed in a circular tunnel 17 miles *27km* long 330ft *100m* underground. In October 2000 it will be replaced by the Large Hadron Collider; its first task will be to search for the Higgs boson – an elusive particle whose existence has so far only been inferred from the behaviour of quarks and leptons.

referred to this as a 'soup' or quark-gluon plasma (QGP); Heinz proposed that this may be the form taken by matter 10 microseconds after the 'big bang' that began the universe *c.*15 billion years ago.

and electrolyzed water. He gave it the name ozone but it was Dr Thomas Andrews (Ire) (1813–85) who identified it as a form of oxygen.

In 1845 Schönbein was working in the kitchen when by chance he discovered the explosive ester (acid-derived organic compound) called **nitrocellulose**. He spilled some nitric acid and because his wife had banned him from using the kitchen for experiments quickly mopped up the spillage using a cotton apron, hanging it above the stove to dry. There was a flash and the apron vanished. The ester is used in modern plastics and explosives.

The **Industrial Revolution** stimulated much chemical research. The textile industry called for the synthesis of **dyes** which had previously been derived from plant material. In 1856 alizarin – an orange-red

colour – was synthesized by Karl Graebe (Ger) (1841–1927), who also coined the chemical terms meta-, ortho- and para- to describe different configurations of molecules.

Also in 1856 William Perkin (Eng) (1838–1907) discovered and patented the aniline mauve dye aged just 18. He promptly resigned from his position at London's Royal College of Chemistry and set up a factory to produce the dye. In 1868 he synthesized coumarin, the **first synthetic perfume**.

In 1863, Johann von Bayer (Ger) (1835–1917) discovered barbituric acid, which is used in the production of modern plastics and barbiturates (sedative drugs). He is said to have named the acid after his woman friend, Barbara. Some 13 years later, in 1879, he synthesized **indigo**.

The Russian chemist Dmitri Ivanovich Mendeleyev (1834–1907) first made some order out of the chaos of the properties of the 63 elements then known. In 1869, he formulated the **periodic table** in which the elements are arranged in order of atomic weights horizontally and in vertical rows according to their properties.

With this table he predicted the properties of undiscovered elements for which he had left gaps. The silvery metallic Gallium (discovered in 1875), and in 1879 the new metals Scandium and Thulium matched his predictions.

Antoine Henri Becquerel (Fr) (1852–1908) discovered in 1896 that potassium uranyl sulphate emitted penetrative **radiation** in all directions

The football-like fullerene – a new molecule of carbon with faces arranged symmetrically as 20 hexagons and 12 pentagons – was discovered in 1985. It was named after R Buckminster Fuller, the American polymath who invented the geodesic dome. Chemists later found that other molecules in this class have properties of shock resistance and superconductivity.

without a stimulus of any kind. Marie Curie (Pol/Fr) (1867–1934) named this phenomenon **radioactivity** in 1898. It was the earliest indication that atoms included subatomic particles which had electrical charges. Marie Curie and her husband Pierre isolated the elements radium and polonium.

Swedish chemist Svante August **Arrhenius** (1859–1927) was awarded the 1903 Nobel Chemistry Prize for his work on electrolysis – the division of a compound into its constituent parts when electricity is passed through it. In 1905 he was the first to warn that carbon dioxide emitted from the burning of fossil fuels could raise the temperature of the Earth's atmosphere in a potentially dangerous way.

Leo Hendrik Baekeland (Belg) (1863–1944) created **Bakelite**, the first completely synthetic plastic, in 1905 by mixing formaldehyde and phenol. It was used for many years in the production of radio sets and telephones. In the same year Germany's leading industrial chemist, Heinrich **Caro** (1834–1910),

Polish-born scientist Marie Curie won two Nobel Prizes – the first for physics in 1903, shared with her husband Pierre and Frenchman Henri Becquerel for work on radioactivity; the second for chemistry in 1911, for her work on the properties of the element radium. She paid the highest price for her triumphs, dying of leukaemia caused by prolonged exposure to radiation.

developed the process for making calcium cyanamide – used in fertilizers – from calcium dicarbide.

In 1909 Søren Peter Lauritz Sørensen (Den) (1868–1939) first measured the 'potential of hydrogen' (**pH**) – the level of hydrogen ions in a substance – to determine its acidity or alkalinity.

In 1913, Henry Gwynn-Jeffreys Moseley (Eng) (1887–1915) used a technique called x-ray spectroscopy to examine the x-ray spectra of the elements. On the basis of this he devised a list of the elements' **atomic numbers** – that is, the number of protons in the nucleus – and revised Mendeleyev's Periodic Table, arranging the elements by their atomic number rather than by atomic weight.

Moseley stated that there were 92 elements between hydrogen and uranium, of which 85 were then known. He predicted the existence of the unknown element 72 (**hafnium**), which was discovered in 1923.

The protein hormone **insulin**, produced by the human pancreas, was first isolated by the Canadians Frederick Grant Banting (1891–1941) and Charles H. Best (1899–1978) in 1921. Insulin was obtained in pure form in 1926. Its isolation and subsequent manufacture have transformed the lives of millions of diabetics.

In 1932 Harold Clayton Urey (US) (1893–1981), who went on to direct the atomic bomb project in World War II, isolated **heavy water**, a liquid in which the heavy hydrogen isotope deuterium (symbol D) substitutes for normal hydrogen. Heavy water (D_2O) proved an

important moderator of neutrons when setting up **atomic chain reactions** – it slows down high-energy neutrons so that fission is more controlled and continuous.

Robert Burns Woodward (US) (1917–79) had a productive career **synthesizing organic substances**. In 1944 he synthesized quinine, in 1951 cholesterol and in 1954 lysergic acid – from which the hallucinogenic drug LSD is derived. He went on to synthesize chlorophyll in 1960 and vitamin B^{12} in 1971. His work won him the Nobel Prize for Chemistry for 1965.

AD 2000

Secrets of life

Biochemists Francis Crick (Eng) (*b.*1916) and James Watson (US) (*b.*1928) – building on the work of Rosalind Franklin (Eng) (1920–58) – published their findings on the molecular structure of deoxyribonucleic acid (better known as **DNA**) in 1953. The molecule forms two interwoven spirals – a double helix.

Roger Guillemin (Fr/US) (*b.*1924) and Andrew Schally (Pol/US) (*b.*1926) discovered the **hormones of the pituitary gland** in the brain in 1968. Hormones are the body's chemical messengers and the pituitary gland controls many of the body's functions. In 1976 Guillemin discovered **endorphins**, substances also produced by the pituitary which appear to reduce the perception of pain by interfering with the transmission of signals between nerve cells.

Molecules and crystals once thought to be stable have revealed new formations. In

1984, chemists in Israel, the US and France discovered a structure of crystal symmetrical on five axes – previously thought impossible. These so-called **semi-crystals** enable the synthesis of extremely light new alloys which have been used, among other things, on the hot-plates of cookers.

In 1988 the **Human Genome Project** – an international collaboration to map all of the 100,000 known genes in human DNA – was launched in the USA. By identifying the position and function of the genes, scientists hope to uncover the mechanisms of disease and heredity.

Much research in biochemistry in the 1990s has centred on manipulating the complex molecules that determine genetic inheritance. Here a research scientist studies banding patterns made by DNA samples. Canadian biochemist Michael Smith perfected the splicing of segments of foreign genetic material into DNA in 1993, making it genetic modification of life forms possible.

CHEMICALS IN THE EARTH'S ATMOSPHERE

The Earth's atmosphere comprises 13 constituent gases and some water vapour. Measured in parts per million of dry air, these gases are:

Constituent	Symbol	Parts per million
Nitrogen	N	780,836
Oxygen	O	209,475
Argon	Ar	9340
Water vapour	H_2O	5300
Carbon dioxide	CO_2	322
Neon	Ne	18.18
Helium	He	5.24
Methane	CH_4	1.5
Krypton	Kr	1.14
Hydrogen	H	0.5
Nitrous oxide	N_2O	0.27
Carbon monoxide	CO	0.19
Xenon	Xe	0.087
Ozone	O_3	0.04

SCIENCE

THE 112 CHEMICAL ELEMENTS IN THE ORDER OF THEIR DISCOVERY

Date	Element name	Symbol	Name derived from	Physical description	Discoverers
	Carbon	C	Latin *carbo*, charcoal	Colourless solid (diamond) black solid (graphite) or fullerenes	Prehistoric
	Gold (Aurum)	Au	Anglo-Saxon gold	Lustrous yellow metal	Prehistoric
	Lead (Plumbum)	Pb	Ango-Saxon lead	Steel-blue metal	Prehistoric
	Sulphur*	S	Sanskrit *solvere*; Latin *sufrum*	Pale yellow solid	Prehistoric
c.8000BC	Copper (Cuprum)	Cu	Cyprus (Cuprum)	Reddish-bronze metal	Prehistoric (earliest known use)
c.4000BC	Iron (Ferrum)	Fe	Anglo-Saxon *iren*	Silvery-white metal	Earliest smelting
c.4000BC	Silver (Argentum)	Ag	Anglo-Saxon *seolfor*	Lustrous white metal	Prehistoric (earliest silversmithery)
c.3500BC	Tin (Stannum)	Sn	Anglo-Saxon *tin*	Silvery-white metal	Prehistoric (intentionally alloyed with copper to make bronze)
c.1600BC	Mercury (Hydrargyrum)	Hg	Hermes (Lat. Mercurius) the divine patron of the occult sciences	Silvery metallic liquid	Near historic
c.1000BC	Antimony (Stibium)	Sb	Mediaeval Latin *antimonium*	Silvery metal	Near historic
c.1220	Arsenic	As	Latin *arsenicum*	Steel-grey solid	St Albertus Magnus (Ger) (1193–1280)
1669	Phosphorus	P	Greek *phosphorus* 'light bringing'	Yellowish or red solid	H. Brand (Ger) (c.1630–c.75)
1737	Cobalt	Co	German *kobold*, 'goblin'	Reddish steel metal	G. Brandt (Swe) (1694–1748)
1746	Zinc	Zn	German *zink*	Blue-white metal	A. S. Marggraf (Ger) (1709–82)
1748	Platinum	Pt	Spanish *platina*, diminutive of silver	Bluish-white metal	A. de Ulloa (Sp) (1716–95)
1751	Nickel	Ni	German abbreviation of *Kupfernickel* ('devil's copper') or niccolite	Silvery-white metal	A. F. Cronstedt (Swe) (1722–65)
1753	Bismuth	Bi	German *weissmuth*, 'white matter'	Reddish-silvery	C-F. Geoffroy (Fr) (c.1729–53)
1766	Hydrogen	H	Greek *hydro genes*, 'water producer'	Colourless gas	H. Cavendish (Eng) (1731–1810)
1772	Nitrogen	N	Greek *nitron genes*, 'saltpetre producer'	Colourless gas	D. Rutherford (Scot) (1749–1819)
1772–4	Oxygen	O	Greek *oxys genes*, 'acid producer'	Colourless gas	C. W. Scheele (Swe) (1742–86) and J. Priestley (Eng) (1733–1804)
1774	Chlorine	Cl	Greek *chloros*, 'green'	Yellow-green gas	C. W. Scheele (Swe)
1774	Manganese	Mn	Latin *magnes*, 'a magnet'	Reddish-white metal	C. W. Scheele (Swe)
1781	Molybdenum	Mo	Greek *molybdos*, 'lead'	Silvery metal	P. J. Hjelm (Swe) (1746–1813)
1783	Tellurium	Te	Latin *tellus*, 'earth'	Silver-grey solid	F. J. Muller (Baron von Reichenstein) (Austria) (1755–1833)
1783	Tungsten (Wolfram)	W	Swedish *tung sten*, 'heavy stone'	Grey metal	J. J. d'Elhuyar (c.1755–c.1783) and F. d'Elhuyar (Sp) (1740–1828)
1787	Strontium	Sr	Strontian, a village in Highland region, Scotland	Silvery-white metal	W. Cruikshank (Scot) (c.1743–1810/11)
1789	Uranium	U	The planet Uranus (discovered 1781)	Bluish-white metal	M. H. Klaproth (Ger) (1743–1817)
1789	Zirconium	Zr	Persian *zargun*, 'gold-coloured'	Steel-white metal	M. H. Klaproth (Ger)
1794	Yttrium	Y	Ytterby, in Sweden	Steel-grey metal	J. Gadolin (Fin) (1760–1852)
1795	Titanium	Ti	Latin *Titanes*, 'sons of the earth'	Silvery metal	M. H. Klaproth (Ger)
1798	Beryllium	Be	Greek *beryllion*, 'beryl'	Grey metal	L. N. Vauquelin (Fr) (1763–1829)
1798	Chromium	Cr	Greek *chromos*, 'colour'	Silvery metal	L. N. Vauquelin (Fr)
1801	Niobium[1]	Nb	Latin Niobe, 'daughter of Tantalus'	Grey metal	C. Hatchett (Eng) (1765–1847)
1802	Tantalum	Ta	Tantalus, a mythical Greek king	Silvery metal	A. G. Ekeberg (Swe) (1767–1813)
1803	Cerium	Ce	The asteroid Ceres (discovered 1801)	Steel-grey metal	J. J. Berzelius (Swe) (1779–1848), W. Hisinger (Swe) (1766–1852) and M. H. Klaproth (Ger)
1803	Palladium	Pd	The asteroid Pallas (discovered 1802)	Silvery-white metal	W. H. Wollaston (Eng) (1766–1828)
1804	Iridium	Ir	Latin *iris*, 'rainbow'	Silvery-white metal	S. Tennant (Eng) (1761–1815)
1804	Osmium	Os	Greek *osme*, 'odour'	Grey-blue metal	S. Tennant (Eng)
1804	Rhodium	Rh	Greek *rhodon*, 'rose'	Steel-blue metal	W. H. Wollaston (Eng)
1807	Potassium (Kalium)	K	English potash	Silvery-white metal	Sir Humphrey Davy (Eng) (1778–1829)
1807	Sodium (Natrium)	Na	English soda	Silvery-white metal	Sir Humphrey Davy (Eng)
1808	Barium	Ba	Greek *barys*, 'heavy'	Silvery-white metal	Sir Humphrey Davy (Eng)
1808	Boron	B	Persian *burah*, 'borax'	Dark brown powder	L. J. Gay-Lussac (1778–1850) and L. J. Thénard (Fr) (1777–1857) and Sir Humphrey Davy (Eng)
1808	Calcium	Ca	Latin *calx*, 'lime'	Silvery-white metal	Sir Humphrey Davy (Eng)
1808	Magnesium	Mg	Magnesia, a district of Thessaly	Silvery-white metal	Sir Humphrey Davy (Eng)
1811	Iodine	I	Greek *iodes*, 'violet'	Grey-black solid	B. Courtois (Fr) (1777–1838)
1817	Cadmium	Cd	Greek *kadmeia*, 'calamine'	Blue-white metal	F. Strohmeyer (Ger) (1766–1835)
1817	Lithium	Li	Greek *lithos*, 'stone'	Silvery-white metal	J. A. Arfwedson (Swe) (1792–1841)
1818	Selenium	Se	Greek *selene*, 'moon'	Greyish solid	J. J. Berzelius (Swe)
1824	Silicon	Si	Latin *silex*, 'flint'	Dark grey solid	J. J. Berzelius (Swe)
1825-7	Aluminium	Al	Latin *alumen*, 'alum'	Silvery-white metal	H. C. Oerstedt (Den) (1777–1851) and F. Wöhler (Ger) (1880–82)
1826	Bromine	Br	Greek *bromos*, 'stench'	Red-brown liquid	A. J. Balard (Fr) (1802–76)
1829	Thorium	Th	Thor, the Norse god of thunder	Grey metal	J. J. Berzelius (Swe)
1830	Vanadium	V	Vanadis (or Freyja), the Norse goddess of beauty and youth	Silvery-grey metal	N. G. Sefström (Swe) (1789–1845)
1839	Lanthanum	La	Greek *lanthano*, 'to conceal'	Metallic	C. G. Mosander (Swe) (1797–1858)

[1] Formerly Columbium

Yellow sulphur burns fiercely, and is associated with Hell.

Nickel balls alongside the US 5-cent coin that takes its name from the element. However, the nickel coin is in fact made of copper and nickel alloy.

Date	Element name	Symbol	Name derived from	Physical description	Discoverers
1843	Erbium	Er	Ytterby, in Sweden	Greyish-silver metal	C. G. Mosander (Swe)
1843	Terbium	Tb	Ytterby, in Sweden	Silvery metal	C. G. Mosander (Swe)
1844	Ruthenium	Ru	Ruthenia (in Ukraine)	Bluish-white metal	K. K. Klaus (Estonia) (1796–1864)
1860	Caesium	Cs	Latin *caesius*, 'bluish-grey'	Silvery-white metal	R. W. von Bunsen (1811–99) and G. R Kirchhoff (1824–87) (Ger)
1861	Rubidium	Rb	Latin *rubidus*, 'red'	Silvery-white metal	R. W. von Bunsen and G. R. Kirchhoff (Ger)
1861	Thallium	Tl	Greek *thallos*, 'a budding twig'	Blue-grey metal	Sir William Crookes (Eng) (1832–1919)
1863	Indium	In	from the indigo lines in its spectrum	Bluish-silvery metal	F. Reich (1799–1882) and H. T. Richter (Ger) (1824–98)
1868	Helium	He	Greek *helios*, 'sun'	Colourless gas	Sir Joseph Lockyer (Eng) (1836–1920) and P. J. C. Jannsen (Fr) (1824–1907)
1875	Gallium	Ga	Latin Gallia, France	Grey metal	F. de Boisbaudran (Fr) (1838–1912)
1878	Ytterbium	Yb	Ytterby, in Sweden	Silvery metal	J. C. G. de Marignac (Swiss) (1817–94)
1878–1879	Holmium	Ho	Holmia, a Latinized form of Stockholm	Silvery metal	J-L Soret (Swiss) (1827–90) and P. T. Cleve (Swe) (1840–1905)
1879	Samarium	Sm	Named after Col. M. Samarski	Light grey metal	F. de Boisbaudran (Fr)
1879	Scandium	Sc	Scandinavia	Metallic	L. F. Nilson (Swe) (1840–99)
1879	Thulium	Tm	Latin and Greek Thule, Northland	Metallic	P. T. Cleve (Swe)
1880	Gadolinium	Gd	Johan Gadolin (1760–1852)	Silver-white metal	J. C. G. de Marignac (Swiss)
1885	Neodymium	Nd	Greek *neo didymos*, 'new twin'	Yellowish-white metal	C. Auer von Welsbach (Austria)
1885	Praseodymium	Pr	Greek *prasios didymos*, 'green twin'	Silvery-white metal	C. Auer von Welsbach (Austria)
1886	Dysprosium	Dy	Greek *dysprositos*, 'hard to get at'	Metallic	F. de Boisbaudran (Fr)
1886	Fluorine	F	Latin *fluo*, 'flow'	Pale greenish-yellow gas	F. F. H. Moissan (Fr) (1852–1907)
1886	Germanium	Ge	Latin Germanica, Germany	Grey-white metal	C. A. Winkler (Ger) (1838–1904)
1894	Argon	Ar	Greek *argos*, 'inactive'	Colourless gas	Sir William Ramsay (Scot) (1852–1916) and Lord Rayleigh (Eng) (1842–1919)
1898	Krypton	Kr	Greek *kryptos*, 'hidden'	Colourless gas	Sir William Ramsay (Scot) and M. W. Travers (Eng) (1872–1961)
1898	Neon	Ne	Greek *neos*, 'new'	Colourless gas	Sir William Ramsay (Scot) and M. W. Travers (Eng)
1898	Polonium	Po	Poland	Metallic	Mme. M. Curie (Pol/Fr) (1867–1934)
1898	Radium	Ra	Latin *radius*, 'ray'	Silvery metal	P. Curie (Fr) (1859–1906), Mme. M. S. Curie (Pol/Fr) and G. Bemont (Fr)
1898	Xenon	Xe	Greek *xenos*, 'stranger'	Colourless gas	Sir William Ramsay (Scot) and M. W. Travers (Eng)
1899	Actinium	Ac	Greek *aktis*, 'a ray'	Metallic	A-L Debeirne (Fr) (1874–1949)
1900	Radon	Rn	Latin *radius*, 'ray'	Colourless gas	F. E. Dorn (Ger) (1848–1916)
1901	Europium	Eu	Europe	Steel-grey metal	E. A. Demarçay (Fr) (1852–1904)
1907	Lutetium	Lu	Lutetia, Roman name for Paris	Metallic	G. Urbain (Fr) (1872–1938)
1917	Protactinium	Pa	Greek *protos*, 'first', plus actinium	Silvery metal	O. Hahn (Ger) (1879–1968), Lise Meitner (Austria) (1878–1968), F. Soddy (Eng) (1877–1956) and J. A.Cranston (Scot)
1923	Hafnium	Hf	Hafnia, Copenhagen	Steel-grey metal	D. Coster (Neths) (1889–1950) and G. C. de Hevesy (Hun/Swe) (1885–1966)
1925	Rhenium	Re	Latin Rhenus, the river Rhine	Whitish-grey metal	W. K. F. Noddack (1893–1960), Ida Tacke (1896–1976) and O. Berg (Ger) (1874–)
1937	Technetium	Tc	Greek *technetos*, 'artificial'	Black metal	C. Perrier (Fr) and E. Segré (It/US) (1905–1989)
1939	Francium	Fr	France	Metallic	Marguerite Perey (Fr) (1909–75)
1940	Astatine	At	Greek *astos*, 'unstable'	Metallic	D. R. Corson (*b*.1914) and K. R. Mackenzie (US) (*b*.1912) and E. Segré (It/US)(1905–89)
1940	Neptunium	Np	The planet Neptune	Silvery metal	E. M. McMillan (1907–91) and P. H. Abelson (US) (*b*.1913)
1940–41	Plutonium	Pu	The planet Pluto	Metallic	G. T. Seaborg (*b*.1912), E. M. McMillan, J. W. Kennedy (*b*.1917) and A. C. Wahl (US) (*b*.1917)
1944	Curium	Cm	Pierre Curie (1859–1906)	Metallic	G. T. Seaborg, R. A. James (US) and A. Ghiorso (Fr) and Marie Curie (1867–1934) (Pol)
1944–45	Americium	Am	America	Metallic	G. T. Seaborg, R. A. James, L. O. Morgan (US) and A. Ghiorso (Fr)
1945	Promethium	Pm	Greek demi-god Prometheus – the fire stealer	Metallic	J. Marinsky (*b*.1918), L. E. Glendenin and C. D. Coryell (*d*.1971) (US)
1949	Berkelium	Bk	Berkeley, California	Metallic	S. G. Thompson, A Ghiorso and G. T. Seaborg (US)
1950	Californium	Cf	California	Metallic	S. G. Thompson, A. Ghiorso, K. Street Jr. and G. T. Seaborg (US)
1952	Einsteinium	Es	Albert Einstein	Metallic	A. Ghiorso *et. al.*
1953	Fermium	Fm	Dr Enrico Fermi (1901–54) (It)	Metallic	A. Ghiorso *et. al.*
1955	Mendelevium	Md	Dmitri I. Mendeleyev (1834–1907) (Rus)	Metallic	A. Ghiorso, B. G. Harvey, G. R. Choppin, S. G. Thompson and G. T. Seaborg (US)
1958	Nobelium	No	Alfred B. Nobel (1833–96)	Metallic	E. D. Donets, A. Shchegolev, V. E. Ermakov (USSR)
1961	Lawrencium	Lr	Dr Ernest O. Lawrence (1901–58) (US)	Metallic	E. D. Donets, A. Shchegolev, V. E. Ermakov (USSR)
1969	Dubnium[2]	Db	Research centre in Moscow	Only a few atoms of these transuranic elements have been created with minuscule half-lives. Their physical descriptions have yet to be determined.	A. Ghiorso, M. Nurmia, K. Eskola, J. Harris and P. Eskola (US/Fin)
1970	Joliotium	Jl	Frédéric and Irène Joliot-Curie		A. Ghiorso, M. Nurmia, K. Eskola, J. Harris and P.Eskola
1974	Rutherfordium	Rf	Ernest Rutherford (1871–1937) (NZ)		A. Ghiorso et al (US)
1981	Bohrium	Bh	Niels Bohr (1885–1962) (Den)		G. Münzenberg (Ger)
1982	Meitnerium	Mt	Lise Meitner (1878–1968) (Swe, *b*. Austria)		G. Münzenberg (Ger)
1984	Hahnium	Hn	Otto Hahn (1879–1968) (Ger)		G. Münzenberg (Ger)
1994	Unnnilium	Unn	Un-un-nil (1-1-0) – the 110th element		Sigurd Hofman (Ger)
1995	Unununlium	Uuu	Un-un-un (1-1-1) – the 111th element		Sigurd Hofman (Ger)
1996	Element 112				Sigurd Hofman (Ger)
1999	Element 114				Lawrence Berkeley National Laboratory (US)
1999	Element 116				Lawrence Berkeley National Laboratory (US)
1999	Element 118				Lawrence Berkeley National Laboratory (US)

[2] International Union of Pure and Applied Chemistry name, but called Hahnium in the USA

In 1941 the first isolated sample of plutonium was kept in this cigar box. Four years later, an isotope of the same element powered two bombs that devastated Japan.

Automata and robots

The idea of a machine that looks and behaves like a human being has fired the imagination of writers for thousands of years. The idea was current in the era of Ancient Greek poet **Homer** (*fl.* 8th century BC), who in the *Iliad* described maidens constructed of gold but resembling living, breathing women.

The modern robot – a self-controlling and at least partly mobile machine that can be programmed or operated from a remote command centre – is far from this poetic vision, and is unlikely to look like a human.

Its oldest precursors, however, lie in the history of **automata**, mechanical devices and toys that were made to resemble people or animals. One of the earliest automata is the **wooden pigeon** said to have been made by the scientist and mathematician Archytas of Tarentum (Gk) (*fl.*400-350BC), and powered by steam or compressed air.

Automata were popular in China as early as the Han dynasty in the third century BC, when the Emperor was reportedly delighted by the performance of a mechanical orchestra.

In the 13th century AD Arab inventor al-Jazari made **water-powered automata**, among them moving peacocks, for the Urtugid princes of Mesopotamia. In Europe Roger Bacon (Eng) (1220-92), the Franciscan philosopher and alchemist, is reported to have built a **mechanical talking head**, although this may be one of many tall stories told of a man who was seen by his contemporaries as a worker of wonders.

In Renaissance Europe there was a great fashion for water-powered automata built around garden fountains, and subsequently a thriving craft industry in the production of spring-powered automata of people and birds for the amusement of gentlefolk.

In the 18th century, remarkable **tableaux méchaniques**, larger scale clockwork-powered entertainments, were popular; a mechanical theatre built at Hellbrunn near Salzburg, Austria, in 1748–52 contained 113 hydraulically driven figures.

The production of automata for entertainment largely died out in the 20th century although goldsmith Peter Carl **Fabergé** (Rus) (1846–1920) made a few remarkable, ornate examples.

The word **robot** (from Czech *robota*, heavy labour) entered

The strikingly human-looking Honda P-3 android robot from Japan weighs 285lb 130kg and is 5ft 2in 1.6m tall. It can open doors and manoeuvre around furniture.

the English language in 1923, when the play *R.U.R* ('Rossum's Universal Robots'), written three years earlier by Czech writer Karel Capek (1890–1938), was performed in London. The play, set in a future world of '1950–60', describes a revolt by mechanical drudges who somehow learn human emotions and rebel against their human masters.

The first **remote-controlled vehicles** had been developed in the 1890s by Croatian-born engineer Nikola Tesla (US) (1856–1943), the inventor of the alternating current motor. He patented a radio-controlled motor boat in 1898. The first working **model robot** was designed by Englishmen Captain Rickards and AH Refell in 1928 and exhibited at the London Model Engineering Exhibition of that year.

In 1950 neurophysiologist W. Grey Walter (US) (1910-77) in Bristol, England, built two **mobile autonomous robots** capable of making simple decisions; he likened them to tortoises and named them 'Elmer' and 'Elsie'. Each had three individually motorized wheels (two for propulsion and one for steering), all powered by a telephone battery at the rear of the tortoise 'body'. They responded to 'sense data' received through a light sensor and a contact sensor. The decisions they made involved avoiding obstacles and approaching or retreating from light sources. Walter's reports of the experiments in the journal *Scientific American* and a book, *The Living Brain* (1953), had a profound influence on subsequent robot-makers.

The **first robot arm** was created by US inventor

George C. Devol in 1954. In association with businessman Joseph F. Engelberger he then developed the **first industrial robot**, Unimate, in 1959. It was a mechanical device programmed to move parts in a die-casting factory. Devol and Engelberger together set up the **first robot manufacturing business**, Unimation, in Dambury, Massachusetts.

Devices based on Devol's robot arm have become well established in industry. The great majority are mechanical arms programmed to perform a repetitive action such as car assembly or spray-painting; others are remotely controlled devices used to perform tasks hazardous to humans, such as bomb disposal, minefield surveys and nuclear power plant inspections. Robots were used to clear up debris in the wake of the Three Mile Island nuclear accident in the USA in 1979 (see page 157).

In 2000 an estimated 650,000 industrial robots were in use worldwide.

Robots are also playing a major role in **exploration**, especially in environments where the conditions are too difficult for humans to stay very long. One such is the ocean floor. In 1985 Robert Ballard (US) discovered the wreck of the SS *Titanic* in the north Atlantic, using a remote-controlled robotic device named *Argo*; four years later the same robot found the wreck of the German battleship *Bismarck*, sunk in May 1941.

In 1993 a team at the Massachusetts Institute of Technology tested a 6ft *2m* submersible, *Odyssey*, which can descend to 16,000ft *5000m*. It was used in 1997 off

New Zealand in a search for the legendary giant squid. When NASA's *Pathfinder* mission landed on Mars on 4 July 1997, the *Sojourner rover*, a six-wheeled robot vehicle controlled from Earth, went out to explore the surface of the red planet near the landing craft. *Sojourner* took 550 pictures which it sent back to Earth via the main *Pathfinder* craft.

With the rapid advance of computer power in the late 20th century, **robotic vehicles** became possible. In October 1995, the *Navlab V*, built by the Robotics Institute of Carnegie Mellon University, drove itself from Washington, D.C., to San Diego. The vehicle was governed by a laptop computer.

Robots have also been developed to perform **domestic duties** such as vacuuming and cleaning. In June 2000 five companies offered models of domestic robot for sale in the US.

The **most advanced self-contained robot** in 2000 was the P3 Robot built by Honda Motors of Japan. It walked, but only could only keep going for about 25 minutes before its batteries needed recharging.

The remote-controlled robotic explorer *Argo* is lowered into Atlantic waters in 1985 on its successful quest to become the first vessel to find the wreck of the great ocean liner SS *Titanic*, which sank in April 1912.

MEDICINE AND HEALTH

- **Human extremes**

- **Medicine and surgery**

- **Vision**

- **Dentistry**

- **Public health**

An 18th century cartoon depicts patients of English surgeon Edward Jenner sprouting cows, after being treated with a bovine disease to protect against the deadly killer disease, smallpox. Having discovered that infection with cowpox stopped smallpox in humans, Jenner set to work infecting patients in a process called vaccination and saw the death rate plunge. Despite huge advances in medical science, Jenner's method remains a cornerstone of preventive medicine for public health.

Human extremes

A reporter uses a stepladder to chat with Robert Pershing Wadlow, history's tallest known man. Wadlow's armspan was 9ft 5.75in *2.88m*. In 2000 the tallest man in the USA is Sudan-born former pro basketball player Manute Bol (US) (b.1962), at 7ft 6.75in *2.31m*; tallest in the UK is Christopher Greener at 7ft 6.25in *2.29m*.

Scientific estimates for the **average height** of different human species are shown in the table below. Surprisingly, the male *Homo erectus* was on average taller than the male *Homo sapiens sapiens*. An estimated 63,000 million *Homo sapiens sapiens* have lived up to the end of the second millennium AD.

The earliest known **study of human stature** was that

carried out by Frenchman Count Philibert de Montbeillard starting in 1777. Evidence from graveyards indicates that poor nutrition stunted growth – and shortened life – very widely until the 20th century.

The global **average male height** in 1950 was less than 5ft 6in *1.68m*. By 2000 it had risen – in the course of just two well nourished generations in the developed world – to 5ft 9in *1.75m*. The rate of increase is, however, beginning to taper off.

Only ten human males are known to have **surpassed a height of 8ft** *2.43m*. The tallest was Robert Pershing Wadlow (US) (1918–40), who at the time of his death measured 8ft 11.1in *2.72m*.

The only female reliably recorded to have exceeded 8ft was Zeng Jinlian (China) (1964–82) who, allowing for her spinal curvature, would have stood 8ft 1.5in *2.48m*.

The **shortest known mature human** was Gul Mohammed (India) (1961–97) who, aged 29, measured only 1ft 10.5in *57cm*. He suffered from ateliotic dwarfism, caused by lack of secretions from the pituitary gland, which controls growth and maturation.

Frenchwoman Jeanne Calment celebrates her 122nd birthday in Arles, southern France. As a girl she met Dutch painter Vincent Van Gogh (1853-90) when he visited her father's art supply shop in 1888. Mme Calment said that olive oil was the secret of her longevity, and smoked cigarettes until she was 120.

The **heaviest recorded human** was John Brouwer Minnoch (US) (1941–83), the 6ft 1in *1.85m* tall Seattle taxi-driver who is known to have exceeded 100 stone (1400lb *635kg*). In 1981 Minnoch gained 200lb *91kg* in just seven days.

The **greatest proven age** attained by any human is 122 years 164 days, by Jeanne Louise Calment (1875–1997) of Arles, France. In 2000 the world average life expectancy was about 64.5 years.

AVERAGE HEIGHTS OF HUMAN SPECIES

Species	Date Span	Male		Female	
		ft/in	cm	ft/in	cm
Homo habilis	2.5m – 1.2m	4ft 4in	132	3ft 10in	117
Homo erectus	1.9m – 50,000BP	5ft 10in	178	5ft 3in	160
Homo sapiens (archaic)	700.000 – 100,000BP	5ft 8in	172.5	5ft 2in	157.5
Homo neanderthalis	200,000 – 25,000BP	5ft 5in	165	5ft 2in	157.5
Homo sapiens sapiens	200,000 – the present	5ft 9in	175.1	5ft 3in	160

Medicine and surgery

BEFORE AD 1
Driving out sick spirits

Trepanning, cutting a hole in the skull with a flint tool, was practised as early as 10,000BC, probably to release evil spirits thought to cause migraine or epilepsy. A surprisingly large number of skeletons found with trepanned skulls clearly survived the operation.

Ancient papyri reveal that the Egyptians *c*.2000BC knew and used about one-third of the **plant medicines** known today. The ancient medical technique of **acupuncture** was devised in China *c*.1500BC. Practitioners insert fine needles at points along lines of energy on the body called 'meridians'.

Hippocrates of Cos (Gk) (460–375BC) is still known as the 'father of medicine'. The writings ascribed to him or his followers include descriptions of splints for broken bones and the cauterization of wounds.

AD 1
Diseases identified

Aretaeus the Cappadocian (*c*.81–138) was the first to recognize and describe many conditions including arthritis, jaundice, sciatica, tetanus and leprosy. Claudius Galenus (**Galen**) (Gk) (*c*.130–201) was physician to several Roman emperors. He learned about the organs from dissection of animals, and was the first physician to describe diagnosis from the pulse.

Early Christians treated diseases with holy water, relics or prayer. Most monasteries had sick wards and herb gardens to make potions. St Benedict (It) (*c*.480–*c*.547), founder of the Benedictine Order in 527, placed care of the sick above every other duty.

Arab physicians were expert at distillation and developed many drugs, including **laudanum** and the purgative **senna**. Rhazes (*c*.850), an alchemist from Baghdad, founded a hospital in that city and wrote a Graeco-Arabic medical encyclopaedia. He distinguished between measles and smallpox.

AD 1000
How the body fits together

The study of **anatomy** was re-established by the Flemish physician Andreas Vesalius (1514–64). He published his great study *De Humani Corporis Fabrica* ('The Fabric of the Human Body') in 1543.

Battlefield surgery in the Middle Ages was rough and painful: wounds were cauterized with a red-hot iron to stop bleeding and many patients died of shock. French surgeon **Ambroise Paré** (1510–90) realized that this drastic treatment was not necessary. He invented salves for wounds and ligatures to stop bleeding. Later, he founded the first school for midwives, in Paris.

William Harvey (Eng) (1578–1657), physician to Kings James I and Charles I of England, demonstrated that blood in the arteries always flows away from the heart and in the veins it flows towards the heart. He saw that the heart acts like a pump, constantly circulating the same blood. Harvey's discoveries were expanded by the Dutch scientist Anthony van Leeuwenhoek (1632–1723), who also developed the **microscope** to study the corpuscles in a blood sample.

Powerful **painkillers and anaesthetics** were discovered in the 19th century. German chemist Friedrich Sertürner (1783–1841) first isolated **morphine** from opium. Humphry Davy (GB) (1778–1829) discovered the painkilling effects of inhaling

A practitioner of the ancient Chinese healing art of acupuncture – puncturing the body with long needles in order to counter particular ailments – will use a diagram like this as a reference aid. By Chinese tradition acupuncture works because the needles change the balance of yin (the female principle) and yang (male) in the body. Western scientists think that the needles may stimulate the brain to release pain-killing substances called endorphins.

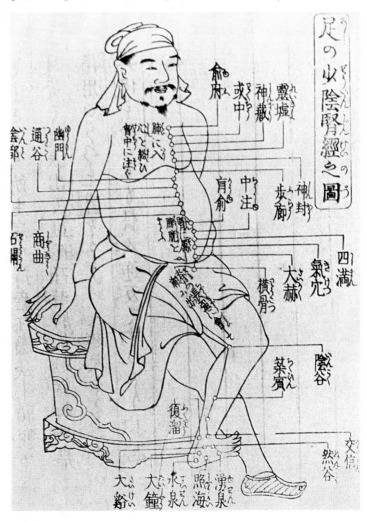

nitrous oxide but its use as an anaesthetic was the idea of the American dentist Horace Wells (see page 114). **Ether** and **chloroform** were first used in childbirth and were championed by Scottish obstetrician James Young Simpson (1811–70).

A major breakthrough in the understanding of infectious disease came with the 'germ theory' of **Louis Pasteur** (Fr) (1822–95). Pasteur was a chemist who became interested in industrial problems, first in winemaking and then in the silk industry. He believed that the diseases of silkworms were caused by micro-organisms and identified **bacteria**, such as streptococci and staphylococci, by use of a microscope. Building on the work of Edward Jenner (see page 116) Pasteur developed inoculation against anthrax and rabies.

Pasteur's work was studied by **Joseph Lister** (1827–1912) in England. Lister was familiar with the use of microscopes from an early age, and became professor of surgery at Glasgow Royal

Infirmary. He realized that bacteria in the air caused infection in wounds and used **carbolic** acid as a sterilizing agent. The carbolic was sprayed on the wound during surgery and then included in the dressing. His first experiment with sterilizing was in 1865.

At the same time, Robert Koch (1843–1910) in Germany laid the foundations for a scientific approach to **bacteriology**. He developed a solid nutrient-jelly on which to culture bacteria and identified tuberculosis and cholera bacteria in 1882–3.

Until the late 19th century, surgeons could only learn what was wrong with a patient internally from the patient's description of the symptoms. In 1895, German physicist Wilhelm Conrad Röntgen

Centuries separated the medical figures shown here in debate. All three left significant legacies: Galen (2nd century AD) and Avicenna (10th century AD) wrote voluminous medical books; Hippocrates (5th century BC) composed the 'Hippocratic Oath', a statement of ethics for physicians.

(1845–1923) discovered the electromagnetic waves later called **X-rays** and found that he could take a picture of bones within the body.

Despite advances in operating conditions, surgeons remained reluctant to open up the chest or abdomen. But slowly the list of successful operations grew. **Appendectomy** – removal of the appendix – became fairly common in the 1880s and in 1901 was carried out on King Edward VII before his coronation.

It was the work of French biologist **Alexis Carrel** (1873–1944) on blood vessels that made possible major surgery on internal organs. Carrel developed methods of sewing (suturing) blood vessels and of replacing sections with material from another artery or vein. This paved the way for **organ transplants**.

Meanwhile, Austrian-American pathologist Karl Landsteiner (1868–1943) had

Surgeons in Salt Lake City, USA, transplant an artificial heart into a calf during trials in 1974. The Dutch-born pioneer of artificial organs, Willem Kolff, took his expertise to the USA in the 1950s and one of his pupils, Robert Jarvik, designed a pneumatically operated artificial heart in 1976. Doctor William de Vries successfully transplanted this device, the Jarvik 7, into a human volunteer in 1982. The patient survived 112 hours.

studied the composition of blood and realized that people had blood of different types, dictated by their genes. He identified the **blood groups** A, O, B and AB in 1901, the M and N groups in 1927 and the Rhesus factor in 1940. The first blood transfusions were directly from person to person, but in the 1930s scientists developed storage techniques and blood banks were established.

AD 2000

New body parts

The first organ replacements were 'artificial' ones. Willem Johan Kolff (Neths) (*b.*1911) developed a renal **dialysis machine**, made of aluminium, wood and cellophane, during World War II. It performed the blood-filtering work of the kidney and enabled damaged kidneys to recover.

The first successful **kidney transplant**, performed in 1954 in Boston, was from one identical twin to another. This meant the operation did not have the problem of rejection – when the body's own immune system attacks 'foreign' material. But widespread organ transplants had to wait for a solution to the rejection of body parts from another person.

By 1960, drugs to suppress the body's autoimmune defences had been developed and in 1967 South African surgeon Christiaan Barnard (*b.*1922) performed the first **heart transplant**, sewing the heart of a 24-year-old woman into a 54-year-old man named Louis Washkansky. This patient died of pneumonia after only 18 days but, by the 1990s, one patient had lived for 20 years after a heart

THE WORLD'S WORST EPIDEMICS

Date	Disease	Location	Death toll
AD165–90	'Antonine Plague'	Europe	1 in 4 of population
*c.*1347–51	Bubonic Plague	Europe and Asia	*c.*75 million
1493 onwards	Syphilis	Spain, Italy, France	Unknown
1518 onwards	Smallpox	Mexico and S.America	Unknown
1551	Sweating sickness	Shrewsbury, England	900
1590s	Typhus	Mexico	2 million
1665	Bubonic Plague	London	100,000
1812	Typhus	Russia	300,000
1918-19	Influenza	Worldwide	21.6 million
1976	Ebola virus	Zaire	274
1979 onwards	AIDS	Worldwide	24 million
1988	Malaria	Brazil	500,000 cases
1991	Cholera	Peru	258

transplant and the operation was almost routine.

Cryomedicine developed from cryogenics, the science of very low temperatures from –150°C *–238°F* to –273°C *–460°F* at which molecular motion has almost stopped. In **cryosurgery** a scalpel or probe is dipped in liquid nitrogen (at –209.86°C *–345.78°F*) and used to freeze target tissue, such as tonsils, haemorrhoids, cataracts or tumours. The method was first used successfully to remove cells in an operation for prostate cancer in 1968.

X-ray scanning took a leap forward when it was linked to a computer to produce computer-assisted axial tomographs (**CAT scans**). A sectional X-ray of the body is taken and the computer converts data on the amount of radiation absorbed by each tissue into a three-dimensional picture that is of immense diagnostic value.

The technique was developed by Sir Geoffrey Hounsfield (Eng) (*b.*1919) in the 1960s and was first installed at the Atkinson Morley's Hospital, in Wimbledon, south London. It was used to diagnose a brain tumour in 1971.

Cancer is one of the key unsolved diseases of the 20th

century. Chemotherapeutic drugs have been developed to inhibit the proliferation of malignant cells, but the cancer cells eventually become resistant to this type of treatment.

César Milstein (Arg/GB) (*b.*1927) in 1975 developed monoclonal antibodies (MABs), cultures that can produce antibodies specifically directed at the cancerous antigens. These MABs can be packaged in 'magic bullets' that are directly targeted on a cancer.

A further method of internal examination was developed with the **endoscope**, a flexible tube with an eyepiece and lens which can be introduced into the patient's

English doctors Robert Edwards (*b.*1925) and Patrick Steptoe (1913–88) face the press on 14 February 1969 after they achieved the first fertilization of a human ovum outside the body. The world's first 'test-tube baby' – fertilized in a laboratory and then restored to the mother's womb – was born less than a decade later, on 25 July 1978.

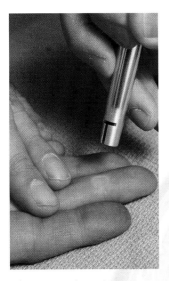

In laser surgery, diseased tissue is destroyed by an intense beam of light, which burns off targeted cells. For internal surgery, the laser is directed along an optical fibre carried within an endoscope. This method was first used in 1986 by Ludwig Demling (Ger) to destroy gallstones.

body. The smallest endoscope yet developed is the ocular endoscope made by the French surgeons Claude and Joseph Léon in 1990 to examine the socket of the eye behind the iris.

In 1988, the **Human Genome Project** was launched, with scientists in 20 centres around the world collaborating to map the 80,000 different genes in the human genome (see page 101). Each gene contains millions of nucleotides or bases, the building blocks of DNA (deoxyribonucleic acid).

As the genes are mapped, the specific ones responsible for various medical conditions are isolated, opening the possibility of modifying the genes in the near future. In 1989 Francis S. Collins (US) found the gene that, if mutated, can give rise to **cystic fibrosis**, a hereditary disease of mucous and sweat glands. The discovery made it possible to develop tests for prenatal diagnosis.

In December 1999, US researchers announced that they had **sequenced the first entire human chromosome** – chromosome 22. It is made up of 33.5 million bases, and is associated with the mechanism of the immune system, congenital heart disease, mental retardation and other conditions.

In 1999–2000 rapid progress was made with mapping the human genome and the projected completion date, originally set for 2005, was brought forward to 2003.

Laser scissors and tweezers are finely focused beams of laser light that surgeons can use to manipulate micro-tissues such as chromosomes

inside cells or the structure of cell walls. In the 1990s, this technique was used to increase fertility in women by changing the surface of their ova and reimplanting them.

The PowderJect company was founded in 1993. It markets a machine that introduces drugs into the body by means of a a **needle-free** burst of high-velocity helium gas. The patient feels little more than a light finger tap on the skin.

Organ regeneration took a new direction in the 1990s with the possibilities of **tissue engineering**. The human embryo in the mother's womb has unspecialized or 'stem' cells, which have the potential to become different types of tissue if given the appropriate chemical stimulus. At the Harvard Medical School, researchers have grown neural stem cells in culture and shown that they can produce all the different types of cells found in the brain. Eventually, it may be possible to use tissue engineering to repair damage caused in the brain by such degenerative diseases as Parkinson's.

Specialists may also be able to make 'bioartificial' organs on demand. Scientists working at many centres including the Massachusetts

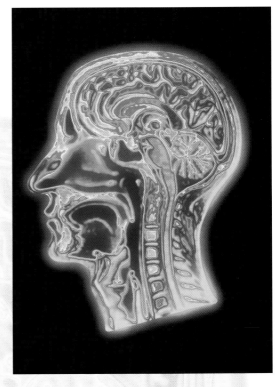

Magnetic Resonance Imaging (MRI) is a method of scanning that uses low-frequency radiation, passed through the body while it is in the field of a large magnet. Magnetic realignment in the nuclei of the elements within the body is plotted by computer on a visual display unit. MRI can produce images of the organs and soft tissue such as the brain and spinal cord shown here.

Institute of Technology and the Harvard Medical School are confident that whole organs will be grown in the 21st century.

At Brigham and Women's Hospital in Boston, USA, **Magnetic Resonance Imaging** (MRI), first developed in the USA in the 1970s by P.C. Lauterbur and Raymond Damadian, was in 1996 used in the removal of tumours with great accuracy.

MRI scans can build up a three-dimensional computer-generated image of the relevant part of the patient's body. Also, surgeons can generate fresh scans while they operate; these give them an updated picture of the tissues involved.

Vision

This 17th-century Dutch engraving attempts to explain some of the basic principles of vision and optics, as outlined by the Arab scientist Alhazen.

BEFORE AD 1

Short sight means a short life

Nearly half of the sensory input from the external world into human mind comes from the mind. In pre-historic times, short-sightedness would have been a handicap to any hunter-gatherer, and no doubt **traditional medicine** – or magic – would have been invoked in an attempt to cure or alleviate the problem. On the other hand, the relatively short human lifespan of that era would have given this usually progressive condition less time to develop.

The **use of a sighted person's eyes** to act as a guide – as in the ancient Greek story of Oedipus – would have been a common strategy to deal with severe loss of vision.

AD 1

No help in sight

Roman Emperor Nero (*r*.AD54–68) is reported to have squinted through a green crystal, most likely a large emerald. This could have had sight-correcting properties, but may have been a pioneer sunglass.

The Greek astronomer Ptolemy (*c*.100–170) wrote a substantial treatise on optics. It was later lost, but it dealt with **refraction** – the phenomenon harnessed by spectacles – at some length. He also advanced the view that vision was achieved by means of rays emitted by the eye and reflected from the seen object.

AD 1000

The right theory

The Arab scientist Alhazen (full name Abu-'Ali al-Hasan ibn al-Haytham) (963–1039) dismissed Ptolemy's theories and advanced the correct view – that light issues from a luminous source such as the Sun or a flame, and is reflected from various parts of an object before being focused in the eye.

AD 2000

From simple glasses to intricate laser surgery

Aids to correct vision first appeared in Italy *c*.1286. The inventor of the first *roidi da ogli* ('little discs for the eyes') is unknown, but the most likely candidates are two Italian glassworkers: Salvino degli Armati of Florence and Alessandro de Spina of Pisa.

The first portrait of anyone wearing **spectacles** was of Hugues de Provence (Fr), painted by Tommaso Barisino (It) in 1352.

The earliest spectacles were all made with **convex lenses** to correct long sight. The first reference to spectacles for the commoner condition of myopia, or short sight, was made by Nicholas of Cusa (It) (1401–64) in *c*.1450.

In 1780, at the age of 74, Benjamin Franklin (US) (1706–90) invented **bifocal lenses**, so that one part of the spectacles corrected for near vision and the other part for distant vision.

Contact lenses were devised in 1887 by A. E. Fick (Ger) but did not appear commercially until the

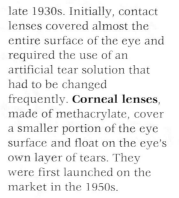

late 1930s. Initially, contact lenses covered almost the entire surface of the eye and required the use of an artificial tear solution that had to be changed frequently. **Corneal lenses**, made of methacrylate, cover a smaller portion of the eye surface and float on the eye's own layer of tears. They were first launched on the market in the 1950s.

The use of **laser surgery** to cut away sections of the cornea and so correct eyesight began in the 1980s.

The thin, soft modern plastic contact lenses of the 1990s are water absorbent for greater flexibility. Many modern contact lenses are also gas permeable, allowing sufficient oxygen to reach the cornea – which, because it has no blood vessels, must get all its oxygen from contact with the air. This allows wearers to keep the lenses in for a long period of time.

Dentistry

BEFORE AD 1

The first toothbrushes

A sacred Indian text *c.*1000BC recommends using twigs of different sizes from the Bead Tree *Melia azedarach* or Mango *Mangifera indica* for cleaning all the surfaces of the teeth.

The ancient Greeks, on the other hand, recommended cleaning teeth with a small ball of wool moistened with honey and rinsing with a mixture of dill, aniseed, myrrh and white wine.

Erasistratus of Alexandria (Gk) (300–260BC), at one time court physician to the Macedonian-born Persian emperor Seleucus I, is believed to have invented the first **dental pliers**.

A gold **dental plate** was found in a grave in Tanagra, Greece, which appears to date from *c.*250BC. The plate contained two incisors.

AD 1

Toothpicks and fillings

Pliny the Younger (*c.*61–113) advised against using the quill of a vulture for a **toothpick** as he said this led to halitosis. He recommended using a porcupine quill instead.

The Muslim Abu Zakariya Yuhanna Ibn Masawaih (776–855) is said to have invented the practice of **filling cavities** in teeth with gold.

AD 1000

At the barber's mercy

In mediaeval times, dentistry was limited to extraction of a tooth if it was giving trouble. This service was provided by **barbers** who combined haircutting with crude surgery. Dentures made from bones dated *c.*1490 have been found in Switzerland.

The Italian dentist Giovanni Arcolani (*c.*1390–1458) used gold leaf instead of a piece of gold to fill cavities, making it possible to fill the cavity more tightly.

King Henry VIII of England (*r.*1509–47) granted a charter in 1544 to the newly formed Guild of Surgeons and Barbers, laying down the provision that surgeons and barbers should pursue their professions separately. But barbers in England continued to perform dentistry.

The Frenchman **Pierre Fauchard** (1678–1761) and the Scottish surgeon **John Hunter** (1728–93) were the founders of modern dentistry. Fauchard was an ex-naval surgeon who had given much thought to dental problems as sailors on long voyages used to suffer from scurvy which causes deterioration of the gums. In *Le Chirurgien Dentiste* ('The Surgeon Dentist') he cautioned against use of tooth-powder containing brickdust.

John **Hunter** wrote the *Natural History of Human Teeth* in 1771. The first scientific description of the **physiology of teeth**, it was translated into several European languages and also published in America. Hunter was the first to use the terms molar and incisor.

Dentures were commonly made by sticking teeth from dead people into ivory 'gums'. Teeth from the corpses of the Napoleonic Wars (1800–15) were known as 'Waterloo' teeth from the battle (1815) of that name. Impressions of teeth and jaw were usually made using beeswax at this time.

Horace Wells (US) (1818–97) of Hartford, Connecticut, was the first to use **nitrous oxide** – or 'laughing gas' – as a dental **anaesthetic**. In 1844 he attended a demonstration on the exhilarating effect of the gas; returning home, he persuaded his assistant to help. The assistant extracted one of Wells' teeth when Wells had inhaled enough of the gas to make him unconscious.

In 1845 the American Claudius Ash invented the porcelain tooth which could be set in a plate. Nevertheless barrel-loads of dead men's teeth were

In the days before painkilling injections and local anaesthetics, a dentist takes a good grip on his patient's head prior to yanking out a rotten tooth. According to some accounts, in the 16th century an Italian, Giovanni Plateario, pioneered the use of a low chair such as this for his clients. Previously it was common for dentists to use their knees to clamp the patient's head in position while they investigated his mouth.

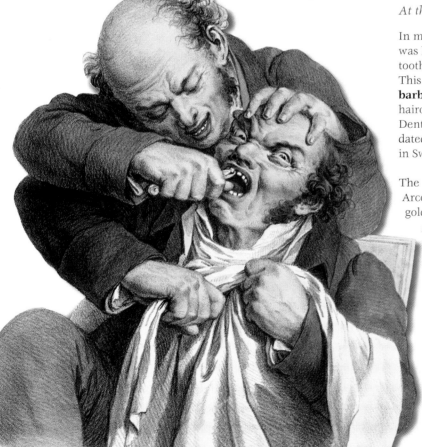

shipped to England after the American Civil War (1861–65).

The first power **drill** was devised by George Fellows Harrington (Eng) (1812–95) in 1863. He also experimented with the use of aluminium dental plates.

Nylon toothbrushes were first marketed in the US by Du Pont in September 1938. In 1945 US authorities began to add **fluoride** to drinking water supplies after research showed that one part per million in water reduces tooth decay.

AD 2000

Teeth on screen

The dental **scanner** was invented by the Americans Rob Golden and William Maness in 1987. The scanner is roughly the same shape and size as the human jaw and, as the patient bites into it, it transmits an image of the teeth on to an attached screen.

In the 1990s, scientists were using a modified strain of *Streptococcus mutans* to develop a **vaccine** against bacterial tooth decay. The proposed vaccine would be taken orally and would prevent harmful bacteria reproducing on the teeth.

American consumers were offered a new way to brush their teeth when the Squibb 'Broxident' electric toothbrush hit the market in 1961. The Broxident had a mains cord, visible in this promotional shot, but a cordless electric toothbrush running on a rechargeable battery was developed by General Electric the same year. The forerunner of the American models was invented in Switzerland just after World War II.

THE DEVELOPMENT OF TOOTHPASTE

Date	Inventor	Ingredients
c.AD50	Scribonius Largus	vinegar, honey, salt and ground glass
1562	Ambroise Paré	scuttle bones, purple shells, pumice, burnt alum, hartshorn and cinnamon
1600	Lazarus Riverius	snakeweed root, alum and white coral
1794	Bartholomew Ruspini	powdered oris root, Armenian bole, powdered crabs' eyes, pimento powder and rose pink
1850	Paterson Clark	Powdered charcoal and water

Public health

BEFORE AD 1

Ancient waterworks

Many ancient civilizations had systems of public sanitation. The city of Mohenjo Daro (*c*.2500–1600BC) on the Indus river in Pakistan had piped water, baths and sewers.

Airs, Waters, Places – a 5th century BC treatise by the Greek physician Hippocrates or one of his followers – was the first attempt at analyzing disease and attempting to identify the most important environmental factors. The treatise divides diseases into **endemic** (those always present in a country) and **epidemic** (occasional) and suggests that climate, altitude and a clean water supply are crucial factors that affect the spread of disease.

AD 1

A clean populace

The first work on **urban water supplies**, *De aquis urbis Romae* ('On the water of the city of Rome') was written by Sextus Julius Frontinus (It) (AD40–104) in AD97 in Rome. He laid down laws as *curator aquarum* ('Director of the water supply') on the proper

Public health campaigns often provoke suspicion and fear. In the 18th century English vaccination pioneer Edward Jenner's plan to inoculate against smallpox using cowpox inspired this satirical cartoon by James Gillray.

use and maintenance of the city's water supplies. The Romans built large and elaborate **public baths** throughout their empire.

AD 1000

The ignorance of hygiene and spread of disease

In most towns and cities throughout the Middle Ages, people emptied their chamber pots out of the window in the mornings. The refuse ran away down a

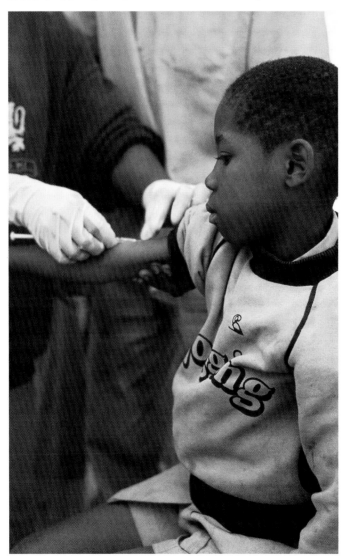

Vaccination campaigns have saved millions of lives around the world. In central Africa in 1994 a worker for the International Red Cross gives a measles vaccination to a Rwandan boy at a camp in Zaire. The child was a refugee from the horrific civil war in Rwanda.

gutter in the middle of the road and was eventually washed by rain into the nearest river.

The terrors of **leprosy** and **bubonic plague** – the bacterial disease that brought thousands to an early death in Europe in the 14th century – spurred city authorities to develop **quarantine** regulations.

The first systematic quarantine was implemented by Venice in 1348 when the city closed its gates to all transport, travellers and ships. As the plague swept Europe, the city authorities of Milan (1374), Marseilles (1383) and Majorca (1471) ordered that plague victims and all who had come into contact with them should be housed outside the city walls for a period of 40 days.

Mercury was discovered to be effective in treating the sexually transmitted disease of **syphilis** in 1493. In 1496 Joseph Grünpeck (Ger) (1473–1532) wrote the first medical treatise on the disease, *Tractactus de pestilenta scorra*.

The Tudor monarchs of England (1485–1603) were forced to move from one palace to another with all their courtiers and attendants while the palaces were cleaned of accumulated waste and filth. Sanitation improved in the reign of Queen Elizabeth I (*r.*1558–1603) when poet John Harington (1561–1612) invented the water closet. The first was installed in the Queen's House, Richmond, in 1596.

The 1604 Plague Act in England permitted local authorities to impose **house arrest** on entire families of plague victims. After a victim had died, all his or her clothing and bedding and those of the household would be burned in the street.

Francisca Henriquez de Ribera, Countess of Chinchón in Spain (1576–1639), recovered from a fever after being treated with a powder derived from the bark of a South American tree. She introduced the powder into Europe and it became known as *cinchona* after her, and later as quinine. It was widely used in the treatment of **malaria** from *c.*1630.

In the 18th century great strides were made against **smallpox**, endemic in Asia and Europe from earliest times. In 1718 Lady Mary Wortley Montagu (1689–1762), wife of the British ambassador to Constantinople (modern Istanbul), introduced **inoculation** to England.

Inoculation had been used in the East for centuries but was still fairly dangerous as it involved introducing the smallpox organism itself into the bloodstream. It was first practised on condemned prisoners and orphaned children. In 1796 Edward Jenner (Eng) (1749–1823) was the first to vaccinate against smallpox with a much safer preparation of the innocuous cowpox virus.

Baron Dominique Jean Larrey (Fr) (1766–1842) designed the first prototype **ambulance** – a sprung cart that conveyed the wounded from battlefields in the Napoleonic Wars (1800–15).

Louis René Villermé (Fr) (1782–1863) devoted himself to the study of the social causes of disease. He prepared a report (1826) after careful analysis of mortality rates in Paris, relating them to environment, crowding and so on. He found the overwhelming factor relative to the death rate was poverty.

A Red Cross poster warns against the dangers of the killer smallpox. The disease was endemic in 31 countries in 1967, but by 1978 had been eradicated. The triumph followed a major campaign led by the World Health Organisation and involving teams of public health workers in every country.

AD 2000

Governments step in

The first Public Health Act in Britain was passed in 1848, and was the work of Edwin Chadwick (Eng) (1801–90). It established a central Board of Health – led by Chadwick – to oversee local boards who would be responsible for drainage, cleansing, paving and drinking water.

The **Red Cross** International Agency was founded in 1864 by Swiss doctor Henri Dunant (1828–1910). Established to be a neutral agency to care for war wounded, it now also provides emergency services to areas of natural disaster and leads international vaccination and disease prevention campaigns.

The bacillus responsible for epidemic **typhoid** was first isolated by Georg Theodor August Goffky (Ger) (1850–1918) in 1884. Almroth Wright (Eng) (1861–1947) performed the first typhoid inoculation in 1896.

The first **motorized ambulance** came into use in Paris in December 1895.

The discovery of antibiotics – naturally produced chemicals capable of destroying microorganisms such as bacteria – was a great step forward in the fight against infectious disease. The first antibiotic, **penicillin**, was discovered by Scottish-born bacteriologist Alexander **Fleming** (1881–1955) in 1928.

In 1940 the Australian Howard **Florey** (1898–1968) and the German-born Ernst **Chain** (1906–79) proved the powerful effectiveness of penicillin against bacteria. The drug began to be produced in large quantities in the following year and saved the lives of many servicemen in World War II.

In the UK, Welshman Aneurin ('Nye') Bevan (1897–1960), minister of health in the Labour government elected in 1945, instituted the **National Health Service**, which was established in 1948. The service aimed to provide free medical, dental and optical care as a basic human right.

In 1946, the **World Health Organisation** was instituted to study disease and work towards its eventual worldwide eradication.

Two previously unknown diseases struck in 1976. **Ebola**, a haemorrhagic virus, killed 274 out of 300 inhabitants of a village in Zaire. In July that year a pneumonia-like respiratory disease swept the delegates at the American Legion convention in Philadelphia, USA. The sickness, which became known as **Legionnaire's disease,** kills one in eight of its victims.

The **AIDS** epidemic, first recognized in the 1980s and widespread through the world in the 1990s, raised the possibility that infectious disease will never be wholly eradicable. Public health structures proved inadequate to deal with the social and political aspects of the disease and the apparently mutable nature of the virus.

Alexander Fleming discovered the first antibiotic, penicillin, by accident while experimenting on lysozyme, an enzyme found in body fluids such as tears and saliva. He found a mystery mould growing on a culture dish that proved to be a very powerful antibacterial agent. Fleming's discovery won him a share in the 1945 Nobel Prize for Physiology.

POLITICS AND GOVERNMENT

- **Living in cities**

- **Political systems**

- **Empires**

- **Migration**

- **The 25 main civilizations of human history**

The flags of nations belonging to the United Nations outside the UN headquarters in New York symbolize the will of the member countries to maintain peace and security across the globe. The UN was formed in 1945 after the world had suffered two major wars in the space of thirty years. In the aftermath of the atomic bombs dropped on Japan, every nation was well aware that the stakes had been raised in the realm of international conflict.

Living in cities

BEFORE AD 1

First farming settlements

Urban living began in the 10th millennium BC, when Mesolithic men and women abandoned nomadic hunting and gathering and settled as agriculturists in the 'Fertile Crescent' – in Syria, Lebanon, Israel and Jordan, eastern Turkey and northern Iraq.

The world's earliest known **trading centre** was Jericho – now, Tell el-Sultan in the Jordan Valley – 10 miles *16km* northwest of the northern tip of the Dead Sea. Occupied from *c.*9000BC, it covered more than six acres *2.5ha*.

The Sumerian civilization of **Mesopotamia** (modern Iraq) built the world's oldest known cities, the most ancient of which is Eridu (modern Tell site at Abu Shahrain). Archaeologists have excavated a building, known as Temple I, that dates from 4900BC.

The city of **Uruk** (modern Warka) established itself on the left bank of the River Euphrates in southern Iraq in 3750–3400BC. Its population in this period has been estimated at 50,000 living on 1100 acres *445ha*. By *c.*2500BC it had been overtaken by the nearby city of **Ur**, which contained 250,000 on 1300 acres *525ha*.

Rome was founded by the Latins, a tribe of peasant farmers, in the eighth century BC. Ruled by Etruscan kings from *c.*610BC, it became the centre of the Roman Empire, growing fast until by *c.*310BC water supply had become such a problem that the first aqueduct, the Aqua Appia, had to be built to bring water into the city.

AD 1

Two million Romans and the destruction of Pompeii

Rome's burgeoning population had, it is believed, reached 1.1 million by 133BC and by AD90, at the zenith of the empire, the city may have had a population of two million.

The Roman city of Pompeii suffered two great disasters. In AD63 an earthquake struck, followed in 79 by an eruption of volcanic ash from nearby Mount Vesuvius that engulfed it, killing more than 2000 people, but preserving the city frozen at a moment in time.

AD 1000

Independence and the rise of city planning

In the Middle Ages and Renaissance, many **Italian cities** were independent states. Florence and Milan were ruled

by powerful families such as the Medici and the Visconti, and Venice had a Senate headed by the chief magistrate or doge.

In the US, Philadelphia – founded in 1681 by the Quaker William Penn (1644–1718) – was one of the **first planned cities**. Each house had its own plot of land, providing a pleasant garden area.

Lisbon was one of the first European cities to be 'modernized' in the 18th century. On 1 November 1755 a great earthquake flattened the city and it was followed by a fire and a massive tidal wave. The rebuilding of the city was masterminded by the Marquis of Pombal (1699–1782).

In England the Industrial Revolution led to the building of instant **slums** to house the workers who flocked to centres like Manchester and Birmingham to find work. The reformer Edwin Chadwick (Eng) (1801–90) reported that in 1845 in Preston, 2400 people slept in 853 beds. In Manchester at the same time, 700 people had only 33 lavatories. In Paris in 1854 sewage was still being removed at night by private 'nightmen' who charged households for the service.

The transformation of Paris by Baron Georges **Eugène Haussman** (1809–91) between 1853 and 1869 had a mixed political agenda. The French emperor, Napoleon III (1808–73), wanted to create a modern city in place of the narrow streets and crooked buildings of Paris as it then was. The new design helped to combat slum diseases such as cholera but also made it more

In the 6th century BC, Babylon was the world's most magnificent city. The ruins of King Nebuchadnezzar's palace overlook a processional road (right) that once led to the 38ft *12m* tall Gate of Ishtar, named for the Babylonian goddess of war and love. The Hanging Gardens of Babylon – hailed by the Ancient Greeks as one of the Seven Wonders of the World – rose alongside the Gate.

difficult for the Paris crowd to erect barricades across streets as they had in the 1789, 1830 and 1848 revolutions.

Rome's peak population of two million at the height of its Empire was not overtaken anywhere until the 19th century. In the period 1801–1939 **London** was the world's biggest city, growing from 1,117,270 in 1801 to a peak of 8,615,050 at the outbreak of World War II.

In 1900 there were just 20 cities worldwide with populations exceeding one million. Britain had five (London, Birmingham, Manchester, Glasgow and Liverpool) and the USA four (New York, Chicago, Philadelphia and Boston).

Garden cities were the concept of Sir Ebenezer Howard (Eng) (1850–1928). He formed the Garden City Association in 1899; England's first garden city, Letchworth, was founded in 1903.

Urban **green belts** – areas surrounding cities that are kept free of development – were initiated in Britain in 1935 in the Great London Plan of pioneer town planner Patrick Abercrombie (1879–1957).

As the great cities grew in the 20th century, the urban centres were referred to as **inner cities** while the larger conurbation was indicated by the term 'Greater'. The word '**megalopolis**' described the conurbation formed where one city merged with another.

By 1950 Greater New York had a population of 12.3 million, compared with Greater London's 10.4 million and Greater Tokyo's 6.7 million. In 1975 the top two were Greater New York (19.8 million) and Greater Tokyo (17.7 million). By 1996 **Tokyo** had overtaken the north American city: with 29.4 million resident in Tokyo, and 24.4 million in the New York Megalopolis.

Increasing motor traffic and industrialization brought the problems of urban **smog** – with lead and sulphur in the air causing widespread disease. The worst recorded smog in London was in 1952, when transport ground to a halt and pedestrians could hardly see to walk. About 4000 people died of heart and lung diseases over the following weeks. The Clean Air Act was subsequently introduced in an effort to cut pollution.

AD 2000

Urban explosion

The percentage of the world's population living in cities has grown from 29.4 in 1950 to an estimated 48.2 in 2000. The United Nations believes it may reach 61 per cent by 2025.

Brazil has experienced one of the most rapid of urbanization processes. In 1940, 31 per cent of Brazil's population lived in cities; by 1989, this figure had reached 74 per cent. In 1983, Cubatão in the state of São Paulo, Brazil, was called the most polluted place on earth. In this heavily industrial city, there were no birds or trees left alive and four per cent of babies were born dead, with a further four per cent dying within a week of birth.

Another aspect of rapid city growth in some countries has been the appearance of **shanty towns** of the poorest residents living in makeshift housing. In 1988, thousands of people were made homeless and many died in Rio de Janeiro, Brazil, when torrential rain caused mud slides to wash poor shanty housing down steep hillsides.

These problems have led to research into solutions. The city council of Curitiba, the capital of the state of Paraná in southern Brazil, revolutionized city transport in the 1990s with high-speed buses and cleaned up the city's slums.

In 1997, 320 cities worldwide had populations of over one million; of these, 180 were in developing countries.

This alabaster bust of a Sumerian priest dates to c.3300BC. By this time the Sumerians – possibly originally a central Asian people – had established several city states in the fertile plain of Mesopotamia between the Euphrates and Tigris rivers (modern Iraq). Each city belonged to a patron deity and contained a temple in his or her honour.

New York's thrusting skyscrapers symbolize for many the energy and style of urban life at its best. In the late 20th century the city – celebrated in music, cinema and literature for its vitality – has enjoyed the reputation of being the foremost modern metropolis. The Lower Manhattan skyline shown here in 1949 is today dominated by the imposing 110-storey twin towers of the World Trade Center.

Political systems

BEFORE AD 1

Hunters gather in tribes

The earliest **communal organization** was the tribe, at first just an extended family, with a chief. Organization in Palaeolithic society *c*.30,000BC was simple, but necessary for hunting expeditions against large animals such as mammoths or bison. In Périgord in southern France, Upper Palaeolithic sites in cave shelters show that reindeer bones form up to 99 per cent of the animal remains. This implies that the people hunted reindeer, and in the French Dordogne and Vézère river valleys the settlements were probably on reindeer migration routes. These settlements may have housed 30 to 100 people.

In the Copper Age of *c*.4000BC onward there was a spread of larger **settled communities** practising agriculture. One notable example, at Dobrovody in the Ukraine, dates from *c*.3700BC and may have housed about 2000 people. It consists of 200 houses, grouped together for defence.

The priestly class was very powerful in Ancient Egypt. In the 14th century BC, Pharaoh Amenophis IV – also known as Akhenaton – challenged the priests, abandoning the conventional pantheon of gods and initiating the cult of the sun deity, Aton. Following Amenophis's early death the priests used the puppet king Tutankhamen to restore the old faith.

Bronze Age Crete (*c*.3000–100BC) is best known for its royal palaces. There is no proof that the King Minos of legend existed, but the elaborate buildings and throne room imply an aristocratic leadership and sophisticated lifestyle whose complex administrative details are revealed on tablets discovered there that bear the scripts known to modern scholars as Linear A and B.

Fragments of an epic poem from **Mesopotamia** (modern Iraq) in the third millennium BC give a glimpse of an early form of governmental assembly. The poem describes the conflict *c*.2780BC between two city states: Kish – ruled by Agga, son of Enmebaragesi – and Erech, ruled by Gilgamesh. In the poem Gilgamesh takes counsel from both a senate and Erech's lower house. It is the earliest known example of the **bicameral** – or two chamber – system of government that is common today.

In Ancient Egypt the **pharaohs** were revered as living gods who ruled by divine right. In the Second Dynasty (*c*.3200–2950BC) they ruled with the aid of chief ministers or viziers. The office of Chancellor of Lower Egypt was even earlier and was filled by Hemaka at Saqqara in the reign of Den (in the period 3300–3250BC). By the Fourth Dynasty (*c*.2850–*c*.2725BC) the powers of the viziers – who were then always the sons of pharaohs – became very wide, and in the New Kingdom (from *c*.1567BC) that office, too, became a hereditary one.

Democracy (Gk. *demos*, the people; *kratos*, power) had its

birth in Athens *c*.505BC. Its foundation stems from Cleisthenes, the Archon (holder of public office with judicial and executive power) of Athens in 525–24BC. He made an alliance with the people of Athens to overthrow his rival, Isagoras. All major decisions were taken by an **assembly of all the citizens**, which met at least 40 times a year – a system called direct democracy by historians because decisions were taken by citizens themselves rather than by their elected representatives, as in most modern democracies. The day-to-day running of the city-state was carried out by a Council of 500 citizens.

The Athenian system had its critics, chief among them the Greek Plato (*c*.428–348BC) whose tract, the *Republic*, argues that the ordinary citizen does not know enough to shoulder the responsibility of government and that the best form of rule is that of the 'philosopher-king' – basically a benevolent tyrant. Plato got the chance to try this system on Dionysius II of Syracuse but failed to exert sufficient influence on the tyrant, who had Plato imprisoned.

Rome became a **Republic** in 510BC with a **Senate** consisting of a council of ex-magistrates and members of the patrician class of noble families. But with the expansion of the Empire, military leaders became more powerful than the Senate.

The triumvirate of Pompey, Crassus and Julius Caesar was formed in 60BC and Caesar assumed total power in 46BC. From the time of Augustus (reigned 27BC–AD14) on, power was in the hands of **emperors**.

In Athens, birthplace of democracy in the 6th century BC, an orator argues a point with his fellow citizens. Democracy – Greek for 'rule by the people' – did not extend to the entire population. Women and slaves, of whom there were around 20,000 in Athens, were not considered to be citizens and so did not have the right to vote in the citizens' Council where policy was agreed.

AD 1

Legal system restores order

After the disintegration of the western half of the Roman empire in the fifth century, Europe was at the mercy of barbarian tribes for many years until the Frankish king **Charlemagne** (742–814) imposed order on much of western Europe by campaigns against the Saxons and Danes.

Charlemagne founded a **legal system** with jury courts. Alfred the Great (*c*.848–900), King of Wessex in England, also established a legal code.

The earliest **parliament** (Old Fr. *parlement*, speaking) in the world is the Icelandic *Althing*, founded *c*.930 by Norse settlers. From 930 to 1263, Iceland was a republic but then came under the rule of the king of Norway.

AD 1000

King's freedom charter

The **Magna Carta**, sealed at Runnymede (now Surrey, England) in 1215, was an agreement forced on King John by his barons to limit the demands he could make on them. It guaranteed a degree of justice to all freemen.

The Swiss Federation of **cantons** began in 1291, when Schwyz, Uri and Lower Unterwalden formed the Everlasting League. In 1513, there were 13 cantons. The constitution formed in 1874 provides for two houses—a National Council of elected members and a Council of States, consisting of representatives of the cantons.

Sir **Thomas More** (Eng) (1478–1535) wrote his *Utopia* – a vision of an ideal society – in Latin in 1516. The book has given its name to the utopian literary genre, which envisages a perfect political and social system.

In 1649, the English beheaded King Charles I (1600–49), following his trial by Parliament. This was the first time a king had been tried judicially and undermined the long-held principle of the Divine Right of Kings, which argued that monarchs held their power from God.

Royal absolutism still held sway in France, however, until the **Revolution of 1789**. The revolution began as a movement for constitutional reform but the extremist Jacobins became more powerful and King Louis XVI was executed in 1793. The cause of *Liberté, Egalité, Fraternité* (Liberty, Equality and Brotherhood) became subsumed in terror and violence. The political use of the terms 'left' and 'right' originated from the seating in the French National Assembly of 1789 in Paris, where the 'reactionaries' sat on the right, the 'moderates' in the centre and the 'democrats' and reformists on the left.

Thomas Jefferson (US) (1743–1826) was the main author of the **American Declaration of Independence** (1776), in which America threw off its

The French Revolution saw the emergence of a new political force: the mob. From the day – 14 July 1789 – on which the citizens of Paris stormed the hated Bastille prison, mass unrest played a crucial role in the Revolution. Leading radicals such as Maximilien Robespierre (1758–94) and Georges Danton (1759–94) whipped up the fervour of the people of Paris.

colonial ties to Britain. The Declaration contains a statement of the radical new political principles on which the Republic would be founded: 'that all men are created equal and independent' with a 'right to life, liberty and the pursuit of happiness'. The American Constitution of 1787 is the earliest written political constitution, formulated by the Constitutional Convention presided over by George Washington (US) (1732–99), who went on to become first president of the United States.

The Englishman William Godwin (1756–1836) was one of the first exponents of **anarchism** in his book *Enquiry Concerning Political Justice* of 1793, in which he questioned all types of authority, including that of marriage. He married Mary Wollstonecraft (1759–97), an early campaigner for the rights of women. Their daughter married the poet

On 2 April 1917 US President Woodrow Wilson asks Congress to pass a resolution placing the US at war with Germany; four days later, with the backing of both chambers of Congress – the House of Representatives and the Senate – he declared war. The US Constitution divides power between President, Congress and Supreme Court. The President has often found himself in conflict with a Congress controlled by his political opponents. In the mid-1990s Senate Republicans prevented President Clinton, a Democrat, from achieving his legislative goals.

In 1840, the French political theorist Pierre Joseph Proudhon (1809–65) published *Qu'est-ce que la propriété?* ('What is Property?'), which advocated the idea of **mutualism**, the mutual support of small groups of workers by exchange of goods, thus avoiding the dangers of **capitalism**.

The Russian Mikhail Bakunin (1814–76) was the most active **anarchist** of the 19th century. He joined the **First International** (the first socialist organisation) but was expelled in 1872 as his views differed from those of Karl Marx (Ger) (1818–83).

Marx prepared the **Communist Manifesto** with Friedrich Engels (Ger) (1820–95) in 1848 and wrote *Das Kapital* ('Capital'), which was published in three volumes 1867–94, the second two posthumously. Marx believed that historical development can be analyzed in terms of social class and economic factors. The capitalists control the wealth which is actually created by the working class. Marxist Communism seeks to return the control of wealth and power to those who create it.

In Britain, the **Labour Party** was founded in 1900 and first rose to power in 1924. **Nationalist parties** have been a feature of British politics since Plaid Cymru was formed in 1925 for Welsh independence. The Scottish Nationalist Party, formed in 1934, was granted support for its aims by Britain's Labour government in 1997.

The **Communist Party of the Soviet Union** had a monopoly of power for 73 years (1917–1990). The Party arose from the *Iskra* ('Spark'), group, which was established by Vladimir Il'ich **Lenin** (*b.* Ul'yanov) (1870–1924) within the Russian Social Democratic Labour Party. It came to power in the **1917 Revolution** when Lenin led the overthrow of the provisional government. After the death of Lenin, Iosif Vissarionovich **Stalin** (*b.*Dzhugashvili) (1879–1953), Secretary General of the Party's Central Committee, was effectively a dictator by 1929.

Stalin introduced economic development programmes dubbed **Five Year Plans** from 1928 to 1955. **Purges**, to cleanse the Party of 'unreliable elements' began in 1928, culminating in the Great Purge in which an estimated eight to ten million were slaughtered in 1936–38.

The 1920s and 1930s saw the rise of **fascism** in Europe. Adolf Hitler (1889–1945) in Germany and Benito Mussolini (1883–1945) in Italy initiated violent nationalist movements with purges against minority races notably Jews and Gypsies. Fascism was nourished by the economic difficulties of the Depression of the 1930s – and similar movements had some support in Britain and the US.

In Spain, after the Civil War (1936–39) fought between Republicans, anarchists, communists and Nationalists, General Francisco Bahamonde (**Franco**) (1892–1975) took power with the aid of fascists in Germany and Italy and remained in control until his death. In Portugal, Antonio

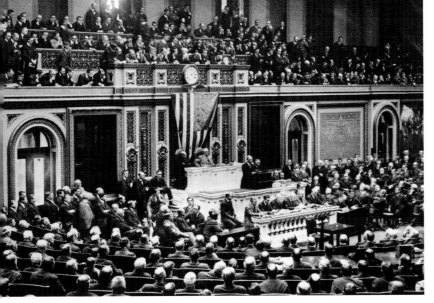

Percy Bysshe Shelley (Eng) (1792–1822) who did not hesitate to adopt the ideas of his father-in-law.

Salazar (1889–1970) also established a fascist dictatorship, which lasted until 1974.

AD 2000

Nationalism and racial tensions breed conflict

The post-World War II period saw the rise of **nationalism** as a political force in eastern Europe after the collapse of the Communist bloc, and in African states newly liberated from being colonies of European powers. Diverse mechanisms arose to govern mixed-race countries. One of the most hated was **apartheid** – the segregation of races – in South Africa. It was routed in 1994 with the country's first multiracial elections.

In Eastern Europe, blocs formerly held together by a common socialist principle – as in Yugoslavia where Marshall Tito (1892–1980) pursued his own liberal communism – fell apart into racial fighting on his death. In December 1991, the Union of Soviet Socialist Republics (USSR) rapidly fell apart in the face of nationalist and economic unrest.

The late 20th-century emphasis on competitive trade led to a softening of hardline Socialist countries such as **China**, visited by US President Clinton in 1998, and to the close co-operation of the eleven countries of the **European Union**, who joined in a common currency in 1999.

KEY POLITICAL WRITINGS

*c.*400BC Plato	*The Republic* Described a just society governed by a philosopher-king.
AD529–533 Justinian I	*Corpus Juris Civilis* (The Body of Civil Law) Codification of all existing Roman law and commentaries.
1513 Niccolò Machiavelli	*The Prince* A guide for rulers claiming that the end justifies the means.
1516 Sir Thomas More	*Utopia* A portrait of an ideal commonwealth with perfect justice and freedom.
1651 Thomas Hobbes	*Leviathan* Describes the social contract in terms of the necessary subsuming of the individual's naturally self-centred interests to those of the state.
1762 Rousseau	*The Social Contract* Explains the idea of a 'General Will' that will promote the greatest good for all.
1776 Adam Smith	*The Wealth of Nations* The first statement of economic liberalism, advocating free trade and the abolition of monopolies.
1791 Tom Paine	*The Rights of Man* Statement of liberal republicanism and egalitarianism inspired by the American War of Independence and the French Revolution.
1840 Proudhon	*What is Property?* An indictment of property ownership as 'theft'.
1859 John Stuart Mill	*On Liberty* Definition of individual liberty within the state.
1867–95 Karl Marx	*Das Kapital* (Capital) Expounds the idea that the quest for profit can only be pursued at the expense of the worker.
1902 V. I. Lenin	*What is to be Done?* Advocates the formation of a vanguard revolutionary movement to guide workers.
1912 P. Kropotkin	*Fields, Factories and Workshops* Advocates anarcho-communism, with small decentralised self-determining units.
1964 Herbert Marcuse	*One Dimensional Man* Condemns the narrowness of industrial society.
1973 E. F. Schumacher	*Small is Beautiful* Emphasises that economics should put people first.

Fascist dictator Adolf Hitler salutes his Nazi cohorts in 1934, the year he took the title of *Der Fuehrer* ('The Leader') and became head of the German state. Hitler, who ruthlessly promoted the cult of the strong leader, dismissed democracies as 'decadent'. Under his rule trade unions and opposition parties were declared illegal and in the 1935 Nuremberg Laws Germany's Jews were deprived at a stroke of their citizenship – a grim step towards the horror of genocide that was to come in the following decade.

Empires

Citizens of the ancient city of Mohenjo-Daro used this public bath in the mid-third millennium BC. Mohenjo-Daro and Harappa were the two great capitals of an empire that spread out from the valley of the River Indus. Remains of the cities – which had brick houses and impressive sanitation systems – were discovered beneath layers of river mud in 1922.

BEFORE AD 1

Power of the pharaoh

The **earliest empire** dates from *c*.3200BC, when Meni (Gk. Menes), the first pharaoh, unified the Upper and Lower Egyptian Kingdoms. He made Memphis, at the apex of the River Nile delta, his capital.

In the Egyptian 5th Dynasty (*c*.2725BC), imperialistic ambition led to **military expeditions** to the west into Libya, into Sudanese Nubia to the south and to the north into the territories of Canaan and Syria.

In the pre-Christian era, the world saw eight more empires. The first was the **Akkadian** Empire in which Sargon (*r*.2334–2279BC) dominated all the city-states of Mesopotamia, embracing the whole of Akkadia (north) and Sumeria (south), extending into what is now northern Syria and western Iran. The Akkadian Empire survived until 2004BC, when Elamites took the Akkadian city of Ur and captured its

last ruler, Ibbi-Sin.

The **Indus Valley** Civilization, centred on the cities of Mohenjo-Daro and Harappa, may be described as an empire. It is dated from *c*.2500BC and its area, stretching from the Himalayas to the Arabian Sea, exceeded 390,000 square miles *1 million sq km*. This mysterious civilization appears to have been destroyed by invading warrior-nomads, the Aryans, *c*.1500BC.

The **Assyrian** Empire began in the valley of the Tigris river *c*.2500BC. Ashur-uballit (*c*.1363–1328BC) began military campaigns against the neighbouring Babylonians, and succeeding rulers expanded the empire to include Egypt and the territories between present-day Israel and the Persian Gulf. A coalition of Babylonians and Medes finally destroyed the capital, Nineveh, in 612BC.

The **Babylonian** Empire had two brief lives. The first, under Hammurabi (*c*.1795–1750BC), was defeated

by the Hittites. A second empire was built by Nebuchadnezzar II (*r*.604–562BC). But this fell to a new empire-builder – the Persian Cyrus – who entered Babylon in 539BC.

Cyrus II the Great (559–530BC), *Shahanshah* ('King of Kings') of **Persia**, established an empire from the River Indus in the east to the Aegean Sea in the west. His son, Cambyses II (*r*.529–522BC), added Egypt to Persian conquests, while Darius I (522–486BC) invaded Greece but was defeated in the Battle of Marathon in August 490.

The **Seleucid** Empire (312–64BC) was established by Alexander the Great's general, Seleucus Nicator (*c*.358–280BC), by capturing Mesopotamia, Syria and most of Persia. It fell to the Romans in 64BC.

The **Carthaginian** Empire, so named from the Latin name Carthago for the Phoenician colony of Qrthdst on the north-eastern coast of Tunisia, was founded *c*.770BC. Its influence by *c*.400BC extended from Libya to Morocco, into Sardinia, southern Spain and western Sicily.

The **Roman Republic** launched the first of the three Punic Wars against the Carthaginians in 264BC when the Romans wrested back control of Sicily. In the Second Punic War of 218–210BC, the Carthaginian general Hannibal (247–*c*.182BC) crossed the Alps from Spain to inflict severe defeats on the Romans before being forced out in 203. In the third and final war of 149–146BC the Romans razed Carthage and incorporated the entire region into their empire.

The **Chinese Empire** predates the first Ch'in or Qin Emperor, Shih Huang-Ti (r.221–210BC). Its zenith was reached in the Western Han Dynasty c.100BC under Emperor Hsiao-wu-ti, with conquests in Vietnam, Manchuria, Korea and Japan.

AD 1

The glory that was Rome

Of all the nine pre-Christian empires, none remotely approached the might of the **Roman Empire**. Beginning with Sardinia, from the First Punic War (264–241BC), Rome's accretion of territory was remorseless. By the second century AD the Empire extended from Scotland's Antonine Wall into Arabia as far as the River Euphrates, and from Armenia to Morocco.

The first Roman ruler to be proclaimed emperor was Octavianus, the great-nephew of Julius Caesar (100–44BC). Octavianus assumed the name **Augustus** and reigned from 27BC for 41 years. The last emperor was Theodosius I (r.379–395), after whose time the Eastern Empire was given to his son Arcadius, while

another son, Honorius (r.395–423), took the Western Empire of Italia, Africa, Hispania, Illyria, Gaul and Britain. In 410 Rome was sacked by Germanic Vandals and Visigoths, and the Western Empire came to end.

Arcadius was the first ruler of the **Byzantine Empire**, which developed from the eastern half of the Roman Empire. The capital Constantinople (modern Istanbul), was founded by the Roman Emperor Constantine in 330 as a Christian city. Justinian (r.527–565) was its greatest emperor; he retook northern Africa from the Vandals and captured much of present-day Italy, including Rome.

Justinian laid the legal foundation of much modern civil law in the *Pandectae* of 533. The basilica of **Hagia Sophia** (Gk. 'Holy Wisdom') in Constantinople was completed in 533.

In May 1453, the 198th and last Byzantine Emperor, Constantine XI, fell fighting an invading Turkish army at the gates of Constantinople.

A large part of western Europe was loosely held together in the **Holy Roman Empire** for 1008 years between 800 and 1808. Charlemagne (747–814), king of the Franks, received the title of Holy Roman Emperor at the hands of Pope Leo III in 800.

The title of emperor and the centre of power moved to the German princely states from 1138, first with the Hohenstaufens, then the House of Luxemburg and finally the Habsburgs from 1278 until the final fall of the empire.

The 57th emperor, Francis II (1768–1835), who was also Emperor of Austria and King of Hungary, was defeated and **deposed** by Napoleon I, French Emperor 1804–15, and only reinstated after the

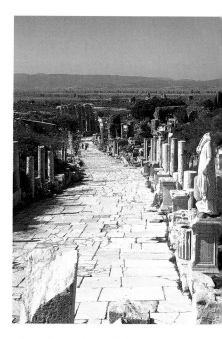

Curetus Street in Ephesus, Turkey, was part of the road network that held the vast Roman Empire together. Good, straight roads helped trade and enabled the Roman army to move swiftly when order was threatened. There were more than 48,000 miles 77,000km of major roads spanning the empire.

Charlemagne, King of the Franks from 768, overpowered the warlike Saxons and created a western European empire running from the Mediterranean to the Baltic Sea. He helped Pope Leo III in a campaign against the Lombards in what is now northern Italy and as a reward the pope crowned him Holy Roman Emperor on Christmas Day 800. The title and the empire survived for more than a millennium. This magnificent 14th-century reliquary holds part of Charlemagne's skull.

The 19th century British Empire had its origins in the time of Queen Elizabeth I of England (r.1558–1603). The first acquisition of land for the Crown was the occupation of the island of Newfoundland in 1583 by Sir Humphrey Gilbert, a half-brother of the great Elizabethan adventurer and poet Walter Raleigh (1552–1618).

In the early 13th century Mongol leader Genghis Khan created a vast Asian empire. His mounted warriors, armed with sabres, lances and bows, were famed for their speed and fierceness. This image is from a 17th-century Mongolian painting.

Congress of Vienna in 1814–15. By that time the Holy Roman Empire had no political reality.

AD 1000

Mongol terror

One of the most dramatic phenomena of the Middle Ages was the rise of the Mongolian **Genghis Khan** (meaning 'Universal Ruler') (c.1162–1227). Born Temüjin, he succeeded his father at 13 and then spent 30 years crushing all Mongol resistance, emerging in 1206 as Great Khan of all the Mongols.

His army overran northern China in 1211, slaughtering any who stood in its path. Genghis Khan's ruthlessness paralyzed all opposition as his territories expanded eastward to the Pacific coast and westward to the Black Sea – the **largest empire** the world had ever known.

He died in 1227, succeeded by his third son Ogödei, who reigned until 1242. From 1260 Genghis's grandson **Kublai Khan** (1214–94), based in Kaanbaligh (Beijing), ruled the vast empire for its last 34 years. It now extended also from the Arctic to Malaya and from Korea to Hungary.

Kublai Khan became the first emperor of the Yuan dynasty of **China** and made Buddhism the state religion, but after his death the Mongolian nations broke away from the empire, leaving only a relatively unified China.

In the New World, the first emperor of the **Incas** was Manco Capac c.1200. The Inca empire, with its capital at Cuzco, eventually stretched most of the way along the chain of the Andes mountains, all the way from present-day Chile in the south to Ecuador in the north. The emperors were regarded as semi-divine descendants of the Inca sun-god, Inti. The empire was eventually destroyed by the Spanish in 1532 and the last of the Inca emperors, Atahualpa, was killed in 1533.

In Mexico, the **Aztec** state was founded in the 12th century and began to expand into an empire under Montezuma I (c.1390–1464). The Spanish conquistador (conqueror) Hernando Cortés (1485–1547) invaded Mexico in 1519 and killed the last Aztec emperor, Montezuma II (1466–1520).

The discovery of the New World by **Christopher Columbus** (It) (1451–1506) in 1492 gave rise to another phase of imperialism. The great wealth in gold and silver of these vast territories financed the much smaller European powers of Spain and Portugal for over two centuries. Fabulous argosies of treasure crossed the Atlantic, carrying silver from northern Mexico and Upper Peru (now Bolivia), and gold from the Minas Gerais region of Brazil.

The Spanish and Portuguese powers had to appeal to the Pope to arbitrate their division of the **new lands**. Pope Alexander VI (r.1492–1503), himself a Spanish Borgia, drew up a line in 1493 at a longitude 100 leagues west of the Azores (a league was roughly 3 miles 5km).

But the Portuguese

demanded that the line be moved further west and the Treaty of Tordesillas, signed in 1494, was to give them the as yet unknown land of **Brazil**, which was only discovered in 1500 by the Portuguese explorer Pedro Alvares Cabral (c.1467–1520).

The expansion of **Russia** into a formidable empire began with Tsar **Peter the Great** (1672–1725), who devoted his enormous energies to westernizing the fairly primitive conditions in Russia and to expanding into Turkish and Swedish territories.

Catherine the Great (1729–96) increased the Russian empire further with the partition of Poland, and wars against Turkey and Sweden.

This expansion was checked by the rise of **Napoleon Bonaparte** (1769–1821) in France, who took the lead after the French Revolution of 1789 and swept across Europe in a series of whirlwind campaigns, subduing large parts of Italy, Austria, Spain and Portugal, as well as Egypt and Syria.

But his empire was of short duration. Napoleon was finally defeated by a combination of British, Prussian, Dutch and German Allies in 1815 at Waterloo and the boundaries of France reverted to close to what they had been before.

France's Second Republic was also brief. **Napoleon III**, the nephew of Napoleon I, was proclaimed emperor in 1852. He attempted to strengthen his position by annexing Savoy and Nice in 1860 and tried to set up a puppet government in Mexico. His short-lived empire collapsed

after his defeat in the Franco-Prussian war of 1870–71.

The **British** Empire was the most extensive and powerful of modern empires. In 1945 it covered 14,435,060 sq miles *37,386,632 sq km*. From beginnings in the reign of Queen Elizabeth I (r.1558–1603), it grew in the 17th century with the acquisition of islands in the West Indies and Canada. In the 18th century, it expanded to the east with India, Singapore and New South Wales, Australia. The 19th century saw the division of Africa between the European powers and the addition of Burma and Ceylon (Sri Lanka).

In the 20th century, most of the former British Empire has been granted **independence** – including the dominions of Australia, Newfoundland, Canada, New Zealand and South Africa in 1931 and India in 1947.

The former dominions of the empire formed the British **Commonwealth** in 1931, which by the 1990s was a growing organization for mutual aid and support with 53 member states.

AD 2000

Political freedom, economic dependence

The '**scramble for Africa**' in the 19th century was the last great surge of European imperialism. Ports had been established around the African coast and slaves exported for centuries, but it was not until the late 19th century that explorers, missionaries and traders began to penetrate into the interior.

By 1900, the continent was

divided between Britain, France, Portugal, Spain, Italy and Germany. By the start of World War I, the only independent nations in Africa were **Liberia** and **Ethiopia**. After World War II, the German and Italian colonies were confiscated and most African nations were granted independence in the 1960s. The last European nation to hold imperial territories was Portugal, which retained **Mozambique** and **Angola** until 1975.

But in the late 20th century a new type of imperialism can be said to be in force in many of the developing countries of the world. The dictates of economic liberalism have made these countries once again satellite states, this time to the demands of **multinational companies**, who provide capital and jobs in return for cheap labour and tax incentives. Today, car manufacturers, oil companies and multinational banks are seen as the new emperors.

The world's last surviving emperor is Emperor **Akihito** of Japan (r.1989–). Akihito is said to be the 125th in direct line from Jimmu (660–581 BC), traditionally the first Emperor of Japan. But he is a purely ceremonial head of state.

Until Emperor Hirohito (r.1926–89), Japanese emperors were believed to be divine, but Hirohito renounced his divinity after Japan's defeat in World War II. The Japanese 'empire' consisted only of the islands of Japan until expansion into Manchuria, Korea and Russia in the early years of the 20th century.

Migration

BEFORE AD 1

Out of Africa

The **first great migration** in human history was that of tool-using *Homo habilis*, ancestors of modern humans who began to move outward from their homeland in East Africa to colonize Europe about 1.9 million years BP. By 500,000BC, their descendants – either *Homo erectus* or later modern humans (*Homo sapiens*) – were established in China. After fossil remains of these people were found from 1927 onward at a site near Beijing (Peking) in China, they were known as Peking Man.

Australia was settled from Southeast Asia *c.*60,000BC. The ancestors of the modern Aboriginals must have used rafts to cross what was then a 44 mile *70km* strait between Java and Australia.

Waves of adventurers from East Asia **populated the Americas** by crossing a land bridge in the region of what is now the Bering Sea between Siberia and Alaska. There were three separate periods of low sea levels in *c.*45,000, 30,000 and 20,000BC.

Towards the end of the 2nd millennium BC in Mesopotamia neighbouring peoples became strongly competitive over pockets of fertile land for cultivation. Abraham led the Hebrews away from Mesopotamia to found a new homeland in Canaan, between the Mediterranean and the Dead Sea, around 1300BC. Once there, the Hebrews became subject to a forcible migration as many were captured and taken into slavery in Egypt.

They were led out of Egypt by Moses *c.*1300BC, but suffered another episode of slavery from 586–458BC, after Nebuchadnezzar (605–562BC), King of the Babylonian Empire based in lower Mesopotamia, captured their capital Jerusalem and deported them into exile.

Migrations in the South Pacific were over thousands of miles of ocean in open canoes or catamarans. The islands of Polynesia were populated over millennia.

The Pacific peoples derived from Indonesia and spread into the western islands of the South Pacific first. New Guinea was populated by 35,000BC, but other places were uninhabited for much longer. Eastern Polynesia was colonised in *c.*300BC; Easter Island and Hawaii in *c.*AD400 and New Zealand in *c.*AD800.

These first settlers of New Zealand were succeeded by a group from East Polynesia, the ancestors of the Maoris, by *c.*1350.

AD 1

Warrior bands

In the Northern hemisphere, **established civilizations faced a crisis** around 370AD with the onslaught of the Huns, fierce nomadic tribes of central Asia. The swift Hun cavalries swept into northern China, and drove many of the northern Chinese southward.

Other bands of Huns rode west and, under Attila (*c.*406–53), attacked Rome and Byzantium and invaded Gaul; still others invaded Persia and northern India.

Homo habilis, who appeared in East Africa about 2.5 million years BP and migrated northwards about 1.9 million years later, stood *c.*4–5ft *1.2–1.5m* tall compared to the 5ft 6in–5ft 8in *1.69–1.77m* of early modern humans. *Homo habilis* was skilled at making tools and lived as a hunter-scavenger-gatherer.

Historians calculate that at the peak of the New World slave trade in the 1780s, 78,000 Africans were forced to migrate each year to the Americas. They came from many tribes, including Bantu, Fon, Yoruba, Akan and Ibo. The majority came from west Africa, but many were from the east and south of the continent.

In the succeeding centuries, religious oppression and expansion gave rise to the greatest movements of populations. The Jews, marginalized by their Roman rulers in Judaea (now southern Palestine), spread to other countries, settling in enclaves throughout the Mediterranean region and Eastern Europe. They were often persecuted, but preserved their separate identity by adhering to their religious faith, Judaism.

Islam spread from 632 to *c.*1400 by means of an irresistible military campaign that took the Arab people eastward from Mecca, the birthplace of the faith, as far as northern India and Spain.

AD 1000

Slave trade

Between 1502 and 1870, European countries shipped **cargoes of slaves** from West Africa to the Americas and the Caribbean to work in sugar, coffee and cotton plantations. According to one estimate, 10.5 million slaves arrived in the New World and at least a million people died in transit.

The slave trade had a devastating effect both on its African victims and on the indigenous peoples of the West Indies and South and Central America. Like Europeans before them, Africans brought with them diseases to which the natives had no resistance, such as influenza and chicken pox. In the Caribbean, Africans entirely displaced Indians; in Brazil, the Indians retreated deep into the Amazon forests.

When slavery was abolished in the 19th century, the European empires had to find other sources of cheap labour. Thousands of Chinese and Indians were taken by the British to South Africa as **indentured labour** until the early years of the 20th century. This was effectively a form of slavery since indentured labourers had to perform many years of work for subsistence wages before earning their freedom.

AD 2000

Workers on the move

The availability of land in **the USA** and its emergence as an industrial nation attracted the poor of Europe. In Ireland **the potato famine** of 1847 drove 2 million people to the USA; a further million followed in the next decade. The Scandinavian countries saw a similar exodus. In 1825–1930, more than 2.5 million people left for the USA from Norway, Finland, Sweden and Iceland.

Around 350,000 Jews entered Palestine in 1932–48, many fleeing Nazi persecution in Europe. The state of **Israel** was declared on 14 May 1948.

The second half of the 20th century saw **waves of economic migration**, in many cases from newly independent colonies to their former 'mother country'. Hundreds of thousands of Algerians came to France from northern Africa and similar numbers of West Indians and Asians to the UK.

By contrast, Portugal saw a major outflow of labour. In 1995 Portugal had a home population of *c.*9.9 million, but there were *c.*4.5 million Portuguese abroad – with most living in Brazil, France and North America.

In the 1990s, wars in the former Socialist Federal Republic of Yugoslavia and religious oppression in Afghanistan forced thousands to flee their homelands. In 1991 some 3.7 million people from Serbia, Croatia and Bosnia in former Yugoslavia sought asylum in the countries of Western Europe.

Refugees from the bloody disintegration of the Socialist Federal Republic of Yugoslavia in the early 1990s found new homes in other parts of Europe, but have not always been welcomed: in many countries, people were suspicious that the refugees had migrated merely for economic reasons.

At the end of the 20th century, displaced Afghanis formed the world's **largest refugee population**, with more than 6 million having left their home since their country was invaded by the Soviet army in 1979. The Soviets quit the country in 1989, but the hard-line rule of the Islamic Taliban from 1996 drove more Afghanis abroad.

The USA has been by far the **recipient of the most immigrants**. Between 1820 and 1996, the USA received 63.1 million official immigrants including 7.1 million from Germany and 5.4 million from Italy.

In 1999, the USA's population of 272 million included an estimated 25.2 million people who were born overseas, of whom more than a quarter were from Mexico. There were 1 million each of Cubans, Vietnamese, Filipinos and Chinese.

THE 25 MAIN CIVILIZATIONS OF HUMAN HISTORY

	Name	Dawn	Final collapse	Duration in millennia	Cradle	Dominant states	Religion or philosophy
1	Sumerian	3600BC	1738BC	1.8	Euphrates-Tigris Delta (now Iraq)	Sumer and Akkad Empires 2334–2193BC and 2112–2004BC	Pantheon of gods including Enlil and Tammuz
2	Egyptian	c.3400BC	AD525	3.9	Lower Nile, Egypt	Middle Empire c.2210–1790BC	Pantheon of gods including Isis, Osiris and Horus
3	Indian	c.2500BC	1950BC	0.6	Mohenjo-Daro, Harappa, Indus and Ganges valleys	–	Unknown
4	Minoan	c.2000BC	c.1380BC	0.6	Knossos, Crete and the Cyclades	Thalassocracy of Minos c.1750–1400BC	Goddess worship
5	Hittite	1900BC	c.1200BC	0.7	Kushara, Anatolia, Turkey	Hittite Empire c.1450–1200BC	Pantheon of gods including Inar and Telpinu
6	Chinese	c.1600BC	AD220	1.8	Yellow River Basin	Qin and Western Han Empires 221BC–AD172	Buddhism, Taoism, Confucianism
7	Austronesian	1500BC	c.AD1775	3.2	Solomon Islands		Ancestor spirits, Mana (supernatural power)
8	Babylonic	1930BC	539BC	1.3	Lower Mesopotamia	Babylonian Empire 586–539BC	Judaism, Zoroastrianism, Astrology
9	Inuit	c.1400BC	c.AD1850	c.3.2	Beringia	Thule AD c.1150–1850	Pantheon including Sedna (seal goddess) and iceberg spirit
10	Greek and Roman	c.1300BC	AD558	1.8	Greek mainland and Aegean Islands	Roman Empire 31BC–AD378	Philosophies of Platonism, Stoicism, Epicureanism; Pantheon of gods including Mithras (Roman) and the Olympians (Greek); later Christianity (from AD64)
11	Central American	c.1200BC	AD1550	2.7	Gulf Coast of Mexico (Olmec)	Mayan Empire AD250–900	Human sacrifice and penitential self-mortification
12	Syrian	c.1200BC	AD970	2.2	Eastern Cilicia	Achaemenian Empire 547–331BC	Zoroastrianism
13	Spartan	c.650BC	AD395	1.0	Laconia, Peloponnese	Sparta c.620–371BC	*Eunomia* (good order) developed from the laws of Lycurgus (7th century BC)
14	Far Eastern (main)	AD589	Scarcely survives	1.4 to date	Si Ngan (Sian-fu), Wei Valley, China	Mongol Empire AD1279–1368; Manchu Empire AD1644–1912	Mahayana Buddhism
15	Khmer	AD600	AD1432	0.8	Cambodian coast	Angkor Kingdom AD802–1432, Yashodharapura	Hinduism, later Buddhism
16	Islam	AD632	Flourishes	1.3 to date	Madinat al-Nabi (Medina), Saudi Arabia	Kingdom of Hejaz and Nejd (Saudi Arabia since 1932)	Islam
17	Far Eastern (Japan and Korea)	AD645	Survives	1.3 to date	Japan via Korea Naniwa (Osaka)	Tokugawa Shogunate AD1600–1868	Mikado-worship, Shintoism, Buddhism and Zen Philosophy
18	Western	c.AD612	Flourishes	1.3 to date	Ireland; Iona, Scotland; Lindisfarne, England	Habsburg Monarchy AD1493–1918; French (Napoleonic) Empire AD1792–1815; British Empire AD1757–1931	Christianity
19	Orthodox Christian	c.AD680	Survives	1.3 to date	Anatolia, Turkey	Byzantine Empire AD395–1453	Orthodox Christian Church
20	Hindu	c.AD775	Survives	1.1 to date	Kanauj, Jumna-Ganges; Duab	Mughal Raj AD c.1572–1707; British Raj 1818–1947	Hinduism, Sikhism
21	Orthodox Christian (Russia)	c.AD950	Survives	1.0 to date	Upper Dnieper Basin	Muscovite Empire AD1478–1917	Orthodox Church
22	Zimbabwe	AD1150	AD1500	0.35	near Masvingo, Zimbabwe	Trading entrepôt AD1250–1450	Shona deities
23	Ottoman	AD1324	AD1922	0.6	Bursa, Turkey	Ottoman Empire AD 1372–1922	Islam
24	Andean (Inca)	AD1410	AD1533	0.1	Cuzco, Peru	Inca Empire AD 1438–1533	Pantheon of gods including Viracocha (god of rain), Inti the (Sun god) and Quilla (moon goddess)
25	Communist	AD1848	AD1991	0.15	Western Europe	USSR (1917) and China (1949)	Marxist-Leninism, Maoism

The 25 main civilizations of human history

Of the 25 great civilizations in world history, the most durable was that of **Ancient Egypt**. It existed in the Valley of the River Nile from *c*.3400BC to AD525 – just short of four millennia. Two others lasted more than three millennia – the Austronesian and the Inuit, both of which were remote from the rest of humankind.

Western civilization has its roots in Ancient Greece and Rome, but was virtually extinguished by the barbarian tribes of Central Europe in the 5th and 6th centuries AD – except for insular Christian enclaves in Ireland, on Iona, Scotland, and at Lindisfarne, England. From these embers, fanned by travelling monks, it began to flourish once more from *c*.AD675.

Islam arose with the Prophet Muhammad (*c*.570–*c*.AD632) in Medina, Saudi Arabia, in 632 and despite the schism between Shiites and Sunni, today holds ideological sway from northwest Africa eastwards into the Indian subcontinent. **Orthodox Christian** civilization rose from the 1000-year-old

Byzantine Empire (AD395–1453) in Anatolia *c*.680 and then spread to the Dnieper Basin of Russia from *c*.950. The **Hindu** Empire on the Indian subcontinent, though never militarily imperialist, marked its first millennium in *c*.AD1775 and with the ending of the British Raj of 1818–1947, revitalized itself well into its second.

No fewer than 10 major civilizations were lost to the western world and discovered or rediscovered by western explorers and archaeologists. In *c*.998 Leif Eriksson (Nor) (*c*.970–*c*.1020) first came across **Inuit** in Greenland.

In the 16th century Spanish conquistadors ('conquerors') found the **Inca** civilization of the Andes in 1532 and Portuguese colonisers of Africa reported the discovery of the Great **Zimbabwe** – 62 acres *25ha* of ruins, once the capital of a great African civilization – in 1552. The **Austronesian** or Melanesian civilization, embracing also the farflung Micronesians and Polynesians, became known to Europeans with the discovery of the Solomon Islands by Alvaro de Mendaña de Neira (Sp) (*c*.1542–95) in 1568.

In 1502 Christopher Columbus (Genoa) (1451–1506) first sighted a large sea-going cargo canoe crewed by

Mayans, leading to the eventual discovery by Europeans of this **Central American** civilization.

French diplomat Ernest de Sarzac (1832–1901) uncovered the first evidence of the **Sumerian** civilization in 1877. Europe's earliest civilization of *c*.2000–1380BC was found in Crete by Sir Arthur Evans (Eng) (1851–1941) in 1896–1900. He named it **Minoan** after the legendary local king, Minos.

Hugo Winckler (Ger) found the first archaeological signs of the 20th–13th century BC **Hittite** capital, Hattusas (at Boghazkoy in Turkey) in 1906. The most recently discovered civilization is that of the **Indus Valley**, Pakistan. Excavation at Mohenjo-Daro and Harappa, its urban centres, began in 1922, but the discovery of the Indus civilization was not announced until 1924.

As Rome extended its empire eastwards the cult of the Persian god Mithras became popular, especially among the military. Very little is known of the religion because its secrets were only revealed to initiates. Most of its relics show Mithras, as in this carving, killing a sacred bull.

Inti Raymi, the Inca Festival of the Sun, is re-created each June in Cuzco, Peru. In its original form it celebrated the winter solstice; a priest killed a black llama to propitiate the sun god. The Inca civilization thrived in the central Andes in the 15th century but was destroyed by 16th-century Spanish invaders.

BUILDING AND ENGINEERING

- **Architecture**

- **Building techniques**

- **Tallest structures**

- **Civil engineering**

- **Wonders of the World**

- **Electricity**

- **Energy production**

- **Atomic power**

Architects, builders and engineers have changed the face of the earth. Their work must provide practical solutions to difficult problems and should also be pleasing to the eye. Medieval stonemasons achieved both these aims triumphantly when they created magnificent cathedrals in major towns and cities across Europe. Today's builders aspire to the same perfect balance of engineering skill and aesthetic appeal.

Architecture

BEFORE AD 1

Remains of early houses

The earliest major **stone structures** to survive today are the foundations of the walls of Jericho (modern Ariha, Jordan), completed by *c*.7800BC. Evidence of **houses of sun-dried brick** date from some time after its foundation in 8350BC.

In 1959 a megalithic **chamber tomb** on Île de Carn, Finisterre, France was carbon-dated to 4100BC. Round chambers at the Beira Alta and Tras-os-Montes sites in northwest Portugal have been dated to 4900BC.

The earliest known **pyramid** is Zoser's 204ft *62m* tall stepped pyramid at Saqqara, Egypt. His reign is dated to 2940–2900BC and the architect was Imhotep, son of the world's first known engineer and architect,

The step pyramid erected to mark the tomb of the Ancient Egyptian pharaoh Zoser dates from the early 3rd millennium BC and is the world's oldest surviving stone pyramid. It stands in the desert close to the site of Zoser's capital, Memphis.

Greek builders gave the Parthenon in Athens its appearance of perfect strength and proportion by making the 50 columns lean in slightly and bulge at the top. If the columns had been built entirely straight, they would have seemed to an observer to be bending inwards. Built to honour Pallas Athena, patroness of Athens, the Parthenon was later used as a Church, a mosque and a store for ammunition.

Ka-nofer. Around 300 years later three pyramids were built at Giza, near Cairo. The Great Pyramid of Pharaoh Cheops built *c*.2650BC stands 480ft *144m* high and contains 6 million tons of stone.

The earliest known **castle**, or perhaps fortified military entrepôt, is the huge example excavated at Tell Brak, Syria in 1938 and dated to 2800BC.

The first square building to be capped with a circular **dome** was the church of Hagia Sophia in Constantinople (modern Istanbul), built by the Byzantine Emperor Justinian in AD532.

Classical Greek architecture was based on strict mathematical proportions. The diameter of a column was usually a third

of its height, but the columns of the **Parthenon** temple to the goddess Athena in Athens, built between 447 and 432BC, are six times as high as their diameter.

The **Great Wall of China** was completed in the Qin dynasty (221–206BC) as protection against the Mongols. It is 1450 miles *2250km* long and an average 25ft *8m* high. It has square watchtowers at intervals.

AD 1

Sacred buildings

The **pagoda** design was adapted by Chinese Buddhists in northern China *c*.AD150 from Indian Buddhist stupas.

Chichen Itza, the Mayan sacred site, which dates from *c*. AD900, includes the stepped pyramid of Kulkulkan (the Plumed Serpent). The Mayan civilization centred on the Yucatan peninsula did not have metal tools.

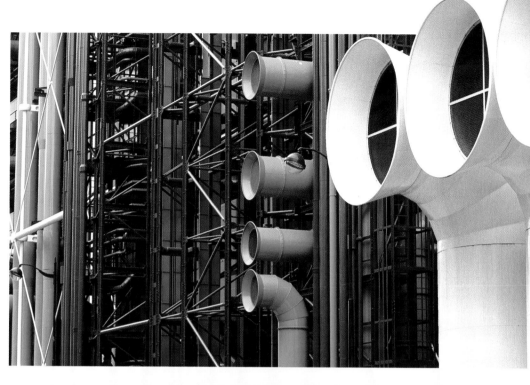

AD 1000

Sturdy fortifications and soaring spires

The Normans introduced two types of **castle** construction into England: the **motte and bailey**. The motte was an artificial mound protected by a stockade and perhaps a moat while the bailey was a stronghold built on one side of the mound. The White Tower of the **Tower of London**, built in 1086, is of the donjon type with a square keep about 100ft *30m* high, with towers at the corners.

Chartres Cathedral in France, built between 1194 and 1260, is the earliest example of the High **Gothic style** characterized by vertical lines of spires and pointed arches and a wealth of stained glass.

The great Florentine architect Filippo Brunelleschi (1377–1446) won a tough contest to build the spectacular dome of the Cathedral in Florence. It was built between 1420 and 1436, with an innovative structure of eight stone ribs filled in with brickwork.

Inigo Jones (Eng) (1573–1652) brought the ideas of the Italian Andrea Palladio to England. The first English **Palladian-style villa** was the Queen's House at Greenwich, London, dating from 1618. It shows Palladio's qualities of symmetry and restraint to perfection.

The industrial era produced new materials for architects to exploit. Its **first major structure in cast-iron** was the 100ft *30m* Iron Bridge at Coalbrookdale, Telford, England, dating from 1775. Welding and riveting had still not been invented, so the main ribs were jointed after the manner of woodworking joints and wedged.

Frenchman Alexandre Gustave Eiffel (1832–1923) designed the inner structure of the **Statue of Liberty** in 1855 and then began his **Eiffel Tower** in Paris, finished in time for the Paris Exhibition of 1889.

The British architect Sir George Gilbert Scott (1811–78) was a champion of the **Gothic Revival** in England and designed the **St Pancras Station Hotel** in London in 1865.

AD 2000

Secular style

In Barcelona, Spain, a **unique building style** was initiated by Antoni **Gaudi** (1852–1926). The walls of his blocks of luxury flats, Casa Mila and Casa Battló, which were begun in 1905, undulate like waves, the balconies seem to hang over the street and none of the rooms have straight lines or right angles.

In the USA, Cass Gilbert (1859–1934) applied the Gothic style to one of the **early skyscrapers**, the Woolworth Tower in New York (1913).

The US architect Frank Lloyd Wright (1867–1959) built one of the most revolutionary buildings of the post-war period. The **Guggenheim Museum** in New York, completed in 1959, is designed as an ascending spiral ramp which increases in diameter as it climbs.

In the 1970s **post-modern architecture** resulted in a deliberate playfulness in building, with architects quoting from styles and then undermining them. The American Robert **Venturi** (*b.*1925) designed a house at New Castle, Delaware, USA, in 1978 with a façade of cutout Greek columns. English architect Richard Rogers' (*b.*1933) **Lloyd's Building** (1986) in the City of London, is effectively inside out. The lifts and staircases are set in towers on the outside of the central atrium.

The external pipes of the Centre Georges Pompidou in Paris are carefully colour-coded: green for water, blue for air conditioning, red for elevator shafts. The building was designed by Italian Renzo Piano and Englishman Richard Rogers and completed in 1977. The Pompidou Centre's use of functional features such as pipes for decoration was extremely influential, and spawned the High Tech school of architecture.

Building techniques

BEFORE AD 1

Tents of animal hide

The **earliest man-made structure** of which we have record pre-dates the emergence of our own species. Stone footings of a circular shelter found by Dr Mary Leakey on the lowest cultural level of the Olduvai

Three levels of flying buttresses support the rib-vaulted 105ft *32m* high nave of the majestic Nôtre Dame Cathedral in Paris. These masonry arches, rising to the outer wall of the church from separate piers, push back against the outward thrust of the roof vaulting. The Cathedral's great weight has made it sink several feet into the ground of the Île de la Cité on the River Seine.

Gorge in Tanzania, eastern Africa date from the period of *Homo habilis* c.1.75 million years ago. The find comprised a loosely piled ring of lava blocks which may have been weights for the anchoring of a tepee-like structure.

The next evidence dates from 1.3 million years later. In 1965 Dr Henry de Lumley-Woodyear found numerous postholes round a settlement of 21 oval tent-like structures or hutments – together with the oldest known pebble-lined hearth pits – at the Terra Amata site in Nice, southern France. The site dated from the Acheulian period c.380,000 years ago

and appears to have been occupied in the summer by groups of hunter-gatherers for up to 15 seasons.

AD 1

Stone takes flight

The Romans were the first to exploit the building potential of the **arch**, seen in the three-tiered aqueduct at **Pont du Gard**, near Nimes, France, built in 19BC. This aqueduct is 30 miles *48 km* long.

The earliest **glazed windows** were of Syro-Palestinian origin, but the technique was adopted by the Romans c.AD50. The hot glass was rolled out on a hard flat surface but was not very transparent. The Romans also used brick and developed an early form of **concrete** called pozzolana (named from its source near Naples).

Islamic builders made use of many building techniques, but they perfected the **dome**. The most famous early example is the **Dome of the Rock** in Jerusalem of 688: a high structure clad on the interior with glass mosaic.

AD 1000

Glory of church architecture

Durham Cathedral, England, (*b.*1093) has one of the earliest examples of **rib vaulting** in its choir. Ribs allowed ceiling vaults to be lighter in construction as the spaces between could be filled with lighter material. The outward thrust of the ribs was later counteracted on the outside of the building by the addition of **flying buttresses**.

Later, rib vaulting flowered into the fantastic tracery of fan vaulting. Perhaps the most extravagant example is King's College Chapel, Cambridge built by master John Wastell in 1446.

In 1578, an early **prefabricated building**, Nonesuch House, was shipped from the Netherlands and erected on London Bridge, England.

Sash windows also came from the Netherlands. In the 1680s, French windows – casements carried to floor level – were installed at the Palace of Versailles, France. In 1743, the first pulley-powered passenger **elevator** was built at the Petit Cour du Roy, Versailles.

Semi-detached houses were first erected in 1790 on the southeast side of Regent's Street in central London.

Cast iron was beginning to be available for building use in the late 18th century but was at first only used in industrial sites. One of the first iron-framed buildings was the Benyon Marshall & Bage flax mill, in Shrewsbury, in western England.

Glass-making techniques were also developing. Plate glass was installed in 1801 in a men's outfitters at Francis Place, central London. Joseph Paxton (Eng) (1801–65) designed a 300ft *90m* long **conservatory** in cast iron and plate glass at Chatsworth, Derbyshire in 1836.

Portland Cement was patented by the English bricklayer Joseph Aspdin (1799–1855) in 1824. He used clay and limestone to make a hydraulic (waterproof) cement. Artificial stone was first used in 1832 in Brighton, Sussex, and in the building of the College of Surgeons, London.

Also in 1832, **corrugated iron**, was first used by John Walker at Rotherhithe, London. **Galvanized iron** was patented by Henry Crauford in 1837.

Reinforced concrete was first used in 1845 in Paris. J. L. Lambot (Fr) used rods and metal meshes to improve the strength. Joseph Monier (Fr) (1823–1906) received a patent in Paris in 1867. Pre-stressed concrete was introduced by P. H. Jackson (US) in San Francisco, California in 1880.

In 1884–85, the first major use of the new material **steel** was also the first 'skyscraper'. The ten storey Home Insurance Co. building, La Salle, Chicago was designed by William Baron Jenney (US) (1832–1907). The top four storeys were steel-framed.

In 1888, Georges Espitallier (Fr) patented the first **prefabricated panels**.

These were made of varnished compressed cardboard sandwiching slagwool, derived from blast-furnace slag.

In 1901, the first **multi-storey car park** (seven storeys, 19,000 sq ft *1765 sq m*) was built at 6 Denman Street, London. The first underground park was built at the Christian Science Church, Central Park, Manhattan, in 1901.

AD 2000

Futuristic materials for tomorrow's houses

Laminated glass was first developed for car windscreens. It has a layer of clear plastic material sandwiched between two layers of glass. The French chemist Edouard Benedictus patented this invention in 1909 but it was not used commercially until 1920.

The German firm Wulff developed **polystyrene**, one of the many thermoplastics, in 1933. Since then, it has been used in many applications, including insulation, suspended ceilings and in the 1990s in road building, a technique developed in Scandinavia.

In 1959, the principle of **float glass** was developed in England by Sir Alistair Pilkington. A ribbon of glass up to 11ft *3.3m* wide is floated on a bath of molten tin. The still plastic glass can be rolled to a uniform thickness.

Reflecting glass has been used in many city buildings such as the John Hancock Tower in Boston Massachusetts (1969–73) to give a sense of lightness.

Belgian company Saint-Roch patented Priva-lite – glass made with a **layer of liquid crystal** inside – in 1990. The crystals can be made transparent or opaque by passing an electric current through them.

House of the future? The geodesic dome was developed by American engineer and mathematician R. Buckminster Fuller (1895–1983) in 1947. The dome shape is the most efficient way of enclosing space because it shelters the maximum possible area with a given amount of building material. This dome is built of interconnecting triangles, which can be made from many materials; Fuller devised a low-cost option made of waterproofed paper. Today, self-build geodesic domes are available in kit form.

BUILDING AND ENGINEERING

FROM PYRAMIDS TO RADIO MASTS – THE WORLD'S TALLEST STRUCTURES OVER FIVE MILLENNIA

Height ft	Height m	Structure	Location	Material	Building or completion dates
204	62	Djoser step pyramid	Saqqara, Egypt	Tura limestone casing	c.2600BC
294	89	Pyramid of Maydum	Maydum, Egypt	Tura limestone casing	c.2575BC
336	102	Snefru Bent pyramid	Dahshûr, Egypt	Tura limestone casing	c.2400BC
342	104	Snefru North Stone pyramid	Dahshûr, Egypt	Tura limestone casing	c.2400BC
480.9[1]	146.5	Great Pyramid of Cheops (Khufu)	Giza, Egypt	Tura limestone casing	c.2940BC
525[2]	160	Lincoln Cathedral, central tower	Lincoln, England	lead sheathed wood	c.1307–1548
489[3]	149	St Paul's Cathedral spire	City of London, England	lead sheathed wood	1315–1661
465	141	Minster of Notre Dame	Strasbourg, France	sandstone from Vosges	1420–39
502[4]	153	St Pierre de Beauvais spire	Beauvais, France	lead sheathed wood	1568
475	144	St Nicholas Church	Hamburg, Germany	stone and iron	1846–7
485	147	Rouen Cathedral spire	Rouen, France	cast iron	1823–76
513	156	Köln Cathedral spires	Cologne, West Germany	stone	1880
548	167	Mole Antonelliana	Turin, Italy	stone and brick	1863
555[5]	169	Washington Monument	Washington, D.C., USA	stone	1848–84
985.9[6]	300.5	Eiffel Tower	Paris, France	iron	1887–9
1046	318	Chrysler Building	New York City, USA	steel and concrete	1929–30
1250[7]	381	Empire State Building	New York City, USA	steel and concrete	1929–30
1572	479	KWTV Television Mast	Oklahoma City, USA	steel	Nov 1954
1610[8]	490	KSWS Television Mast	Roswell, New Mexico, USA	steel	Dec 1956
1619	493	WGAN Television Mast	Portland, Maine, USA	steel	Sept 1959
1676	510	KFVS Television Mast	Cape Girardeau, Missouri, USA	steel	June 1960
1749	533	WTVM & WRBL Television Mast	Columbus, Georgia, USA	steel	May 1962
1749	533	WBIR-TV Mast	Knoxville, Tennessee, USA	steel	Sept 1963
2063	629	KTHI-TV Mast	Fargo, North Dakota, USA	steel	Nov 1963
2120.6[9]	646.38	Warszawa Radio Mast	Plock, Poland	galvanised steel	July 1974

[1]Original height. With loss of pyramidion (topmost stone) its height is now 449ft 6in 137m [2]Fell in a storm [3]Struck by lightning and destroyed 4 June 1561 [4]Fell April 1573, shortly after its completion [5]Has sunk 5in 12.7cm since 1884 [6]Original height. With addition of TV antenna in 1957, now 1052ft 320.75m [7]Original height. With addition of TV tower on 1 May 1951, now 1427ft 449m [8]Fell in gale in 1960 [9]Fell during renovations in 1991

THE WORLD'S TALLEST STRUCTURES IN AD 2000

This table combines a listing by country with one by height. The bold entries read alone comprise a list of the world's tallest structures in descending order of height.

Country	Height ft	Height m	Structure	Storeys	Dates	Location
Poland	**2120**	**646**	**Warszawa Radio Mast (guyed)**	–	**1974–1991**	**Plock, Poland**
	757	231	Palace of Culture and Science	42	1955	Warsaw
USA	**2063**	**629**	**KTHI-TV mast (guyed)**	–	**1983**	**Fargo, North Dakota**
	1454	443.17[1]	Sears Tower	110	1970–74	Chicago
	1368	417[2]	World Trade Center (One)	110	1973	New York City
	1362	415[2]	World Trade Center (Two)	110	1973	New York City
	1250	381[3]	Empire State Building	102	1929–31	New York City
	1046	318	Chrysler Building	–	1929–30	New York City
	555	169	Washington Monument	–	1848–84	Washington, D.C.
Canada	**1815**	**553.34**	**C.N. Tower**	**–**	**1973–75**	**Toronto**
Russia	**1794**	**547**	**Moscow TV Mast**	–	**1967**	**Moscow**
	1761	536.75	Ostankino Tower	–	1971	Moscow
	787	240	Moscow State University	26	1953	Moscow
	334	102	St Isaac	–	1818–58	St Petersburg
China	**1535**	**468[4]**	**Nina Tower**	**100**	**1998**	**Hong Kong**
	1535	468	Oriental Pearl TV Tower	–	1995	Shanghai
	1499	457[5]	Chongqing Tower	114	1997	Chongqing
	1253	382[6]	Jin Mao	93	1998	Shanghai
	1227	374	Central Plaza	78	1992	Hong Kong
Malaysia	**1482**	**451.9**	**Petronas Towers I and II**	**88**	**1996**	**Kuala Lumpur**
United Kingdom	**1272**	**387.1**	**ITV Belmont Mast**	**–**	**1969**	**Lincolnshire**
	800	244	Canary Wharf (Canada Square)	50	1991	City of London
	620	189	Telecom Tower	–	1966	London
	600	183	National Westminster Tower	52	1979	City of London
	525	160	Lincoln Cathedral	–	1307–1548	Lincolnshire
	518.7	158.1	Blackpool Tower	–	1894	Lancashire

Tallest structures

THE WORLD'S TALLEST STRUCTURES IN AD 2000

Country	Height		Structure	Storeys	Dates	Location
	ft	m				
Australia	1269	387	**North West Cape TV Tower**	–	**1967**	**North West Cape**
	899	274	Centre Point Tower	–	1979	Sydney
Netherlands	1256	383	**Gerbrandytoren (TV)**	–	**1959–60**	**Lopik**
	367	112	Cathedral	–	14th cent.	Utrecht
Germany	1197	365	**TV Tower**	–	**1969**	**Berlin**
	850	259	Commerzbank Tower	60	1997	Frankfurt
	528	160.9	Cathedral Spire	–	1890	Ulm
	513	156	Köln Cathedral	–	1880	Cologne
Taiwan	1138	347	**T & C Tower**	85	**1997**	**Kaoshiung**
Greenland	1210	369	**TV Tower**	–	–	**Thule**
Japan	1092	333	**TV Tower**	–	**1958**	**Tokyo**
	971	296	Landmark Tower	70	1993	Yokohama
Finland	1059	323	**Standardized TV Masts (33)**	–	**1955–77**	**nationwide**
	439	134	Belvédère de Näsinneula	–	1971	Tampere
Un. Arab Emirates	1053	321	**Chicago Beach Tower Hotel**	60	**1999**	**Dubai**
Thailand	1049	320	**Baiyoke Tower II**	90	**1997**	**Bangkok**
France	985.9	300.5[?]	**Eiffel Tower**	–	**1887–89**	**Paris**
	495	151	Cathedral of St Pierre	–	1568	Beauvais
	482	147	Cathedral	–	1823–76	Rouen
	465	141	Cathedral of Notre Dame	–	1420–39	Strasbourg
Indonesia	1040	330	**BDNI Centre Bldg (Twr A)**	62	**1999**	**Jakarta**
North Korea	984	300	**Hotel Ryugyon**	105	**1995**	**Pyongyang**
Singapore	918	280	**Overseas Union Bank**	66	**1986**	**Singapore City**
	918	280	**United Overseas Bank Plaza**	66	**1992**	**Singapore City**
	918	280	**Republic Plaza**	66	**1995**	**Singapore City**
	741	226	Stamford Westin Hotel	73	1986	Singapore City
South Africa	882	269	**Strijdom TV Tower**	–	**1971**	**Johannesburg**
Spain	879	268	**Collserola Tower (TV)**	–	**1992**	**Barcelona**
	492	150	Ville de los Caidos Cross	–	1940	Guadarrama
Venezuela	853	260	**Park Central Tower**	62	**1978**	**Caracas**
Austria	826	252	**Donauturm**	–	**1963–64**	**Vienna**
South Korea	817	249	**Korea Life Assurance**	60	**1985**	**Seoul**
Denmark	758	231	**Frejlev TV Tower**	–	**1956**	**Frejlev**
Mexico	718	219	**Torre Latino Americana**	–	**1972**	**Mexico City**
	206	63	Pyramid of the Sun	–	c.350	Teotihuacon
	151	46	Pyramid of the Moon	–	c.350	Teotihuacon
Switzerland	705	215	TV Tower	–	**1931**	**Beromünster**
	492	150	Centrale Nucléaire	–	1979	Däniken
Morocco	656	200	**Mosque of Hassan II minarets**	–	**1991**	**Casablanca**
Belgium	607	185	**Vlessart-Leglise TV Mast**	–	**1933**	
	492	150	Tour du Plan Incliné	–	1965	Ronquières
Italy	548	167	**Mole Antonelliana**	–	**1863**	**Turin**
	433	132	St Peter's Church	–	1626	Rome
	324	99	Campanile of St. Mark	–	13th/14th cent.	Venice
	186	56.7	Leaning Tower	–	1174-1280	Pisa
Brazil	528	161	**State Bank Building**	–	**1947**	**São Paulo**
Sweden	508	155	**TV Tower (Kaknäs)**	–	**1967**	**Stockholm**
	387	118	Cathedral	–	1435	Uppsala
Israel		140	**Shalom Tower**	–	**1966**	**Tel-Aviv**
Algeria		120	**Mosque (minaret)**	–		**Constantine**
Norway	387	118	**Tryvann Tower**	–	**1962**	**Tryvann, Oslo**
	360	110	Hotel Plaza	37	1990	Oslo
Hungary	344	105	**Parliament Building**	–		**Budapest**
Myanmar	324	99	**Shwe Dagon Pagoda**	–	12th/16th cent.	**Yangôn**
Senegal	285	87	**Minaret**	–	**1964**	**Touba**
India	242	74	**Taj Mahal**	–	**1629–53**	**Agra**
Turkey	190	58	**Obelisk (from Egypt)**	–	**AD390**	**Istanbul**

Note: The heights listed above for skyscrapers have, in many cases, been enhanced by the addition of TV masts or other superstructures, giving total heights as follows:

ft	m		ft	m	
[?]1558.7	475.10	Sears Tower	[?]1650	503	Chongqing Tower
[?]1558.7	475.10	World Trade Center	[?]1378	420	Jin Mao
[?]1473	449	Empire State Building	[?]1052	320.75	Eiffel Tower
[?]1706	520	Nina Tower			

The 984ft *300m* Eiffel Tower in Paris – named for its designer Gustave Eiffel (Fr) (1832–1923) – was built as the centrepiece for the 1889 Paris Exhibition. Its iron latticework sections were lifted into place by two cranes. It weighs around 7100 tons.

BUILDING AND ENGINEERING

Civil engineering

The term **civil engineering** refers to the building of dams, bridges, harbours and highways and dates only from 1818, when military engineering lost its pre-eminence after the Napoleonic Wars (1800–15).

But feats of civil engineering were in evidence as early as the 6th millennium BC, when **irrigation works** at Choga Mami in Iraq were begun – long in advance of the first major canal dug at nearby Mandali. It is clear that bridge-building, tunnelling and multi-storey building was well established in early times.

Success was very dependent on the harnessing of new tools and new materials. There is evidence of pulleys in use as early as 1500BC from Alalakh, Syria. But no date has been established for the vital introduction of cranes and hoists.

Early Christians carved an underground cemetery network called the 'catacombs' in the soft rock beneath Rome. Scholars believe the idea came from the cave burials of ancient Jewish tradition.

In the 6th century BC the Greek **Cherisphron** succeeded in raising stone blocks to a height equivalent to that of a modern six-storey building in the 64ft *19.5m* tall Temple of Diana at Ephesus (now Bodrum, Turkey). It is not known how he did this.

His temple, to the Roman goddess of the moon and hunting (Greek Artemis), was the third of the **Seven Wonders** of the Ancient World (see pages 124–5).

The use of **mine tunnelling** to conduct a water supply first appeared on the Aegean island of Samos c.530BC when, according to the Greek historian Herodotus (c.484–c.424BC), the engineer Eupalinos drove an almost square shaft c.8ft *2.5m* in height through Mount Castro to a length of 3600ft *1.1km*. The tunnel was drilled from either end by groups of slaves using hammers and chisels and it had to make a U-bend in the middle of the mountain, where the two work parties failed to meet exactly.

One of the first **closed-pipe water systems** was installed in the Greek city of

Pergamon (modern Bergama, Turkey) c.170BC. Water ran 600ft *183m* into a valley and then came 190ft *58m* over a lower hill, before rising 450ft *137m* into Pergamon itself. The pipe was probably lead.

Roman water engineers preferred open-channel **aqueducts** because they could be cleared, maintained and, if necessary, by-passed in ways not possible with enclosed pipework.

BRIDGES

The earliest bridges were probably fallen tree trunks across streams. Piles driven into mud and topped with timber gangways were used by lake dwellers in Stone or Bronze Age settlements at Obermeilen by Lake Zurich, Switzerland. The earliest Alpine examples, however, date to the Middle Neolithic before 3000BC.

With the growth of **trackways** between early settlements from around 6000BC, the need for bridges became greater. It grew greater still with the beginnings of wheeled transport in c.3500BC.

Pontoon or boat bridges appeared in the 1st millennium BC. Xerxes, king of Persia from 486–465BC, crossed the Hellespont (c.3 miles *5km*) with his army in 480BC on a total of 676 boats strung in two parallel rows.

The Euphrates at Babylon, where it was some 3000ft *915m* wide, was bridged by the Babylonian king Nebuchadnezzar II (d.562BC) with 150 stone piers only 20ft *6.1m* apart.

MILESTONES IN ENGINEERING

Date	Construction	Location
3200BC	Earliest arched sewer constructions	Sumeria (now Southern Iraq)
2800BC	Earliest qanaats for water supply	Western Iran
2700BC	Earliest stone-built bridging	Wadi el Garawi, Egypt
2300BC	Earliest reservoir	Moeris, al-Fayyum, Egypt
550BC	Earliest rock-cut water supply tunnel (by Eupalinos)	Island of Samos, Greece
270BC	Earliest lighthouse (Pharos) (by Sostratus of Cnidus)	Pharos, Alexandria, Egypt
AD65	Earliest iron bridging (traditionally accepted date)	Lantshang river, Yunnan, China
C.AD150	Earliest pagoda (Kanisaka's Buddhist pagoda)	Peshawar, Pakistan
C.AD250	Catacombs	St. Sebastiano, Appian Way, Rome
C.AD715	Minaret (converted by Muslims from church tower)	Damascus, Syria
AD990	Donjon or castle keep	Longeais, France

The landmark 4199ft *1280m* long Golden Gate Bridge in San Francisco, California, was the world's longest suspension bridge when it opened on 27 May 1937. Its construction took four years and cost $35 million.

The earliest reference to a **major bridge** is that across the River Nile at Sadd-el-Kafara, 19 miles *30km* south of Cairo in Egypt. It was built *c.*2650BC in association with a dam that was subsequently washed away by floods.

The dating of the primitive clapper bridges made of simple stone slabs and found on Dartmoor and Exmoor, southwest England, remains so uncertain that estimates range from Neolithic to mediaeval. The **oldest surviving bridge** in the world is at Izmir, Turkey, across the River Meles, dated to *c.*850BC. **Iron** was used in bridge-building by the Chinese as early as *c.*AD65.

The modern principle of the **suspension bridge** – where the roadway hangs from cables anchored at either side – was patented by James Finlay (US) (*c.*1762–1828). However, the world's largest spans for some time remained cantilever bridges in which the beams are fixed at one end only and supported midway.

TUNNELS

Progress in tunnel construction is summarized in the table overleaf from the laborious work of Greek and Spanish builders in the first millennium BC to the world's longest sub-aqueous tunnel, 23.60 miles *37.98km* under the **English Channel**, opened on 6 May 1994.

The greatest difficulty in tunnelling is not boring through rock but driving tunnels through soft ground that might easily cave in or flood. Mark Brunel (Fr/UK) (1769–1849) invented the **tunnel shield** in 1818, in the Wapping-Rotherhithe tunnel beneath the River Thames in London (first phase 1825–28). An enormous iron casing was pushed through the soft ground by screw-jacks, and the miners themselves worked through hatches in the casing.

The Mont Cenis rock tunnel through the Alps recorded progress of 9in *30cm* a day before the Italian engineer Germain Sommeiller introduced his **compressed air drill** in 1861. The tunnel was holed through on Christmas Day 1870 after a loss of 76 lives.

The **immersed-tube technique** – in which sections of tunnel were constructed on dry land and then sunk into a trench that was later filled in – was first unsuccessfully tried in the Wapping-Rotherhithe tunnel. In 1906 it was used by the US engineer W. J. Wilgur in the construction of the twin-tube railway tunnel crossing the 812m *2665ft* Detroit River between Detroit, Michigan and Windsor, Ontario.

In the world's longest tunnel, the Delaware Aqueduct, begun in 1939, **rock bolts** were used for the first time to pin the rock together. This method was faster and cheaper than installing steel ribs, enabling a speed of 120ft *36.6m* a week to be achieved through hard rock.

Workers pause in the 12.31 mile *19.82km* Simplon 2 rail tunnel in November 1922. Simplon 1 (1906) and 2 run through the Alps between Brig, Switzerland, and Domodossola, Italy. Before they were built the only way to make the journey was via a road constructed by command of French Emperor Napoleon over a 6581ft *2006m* mountain pass.

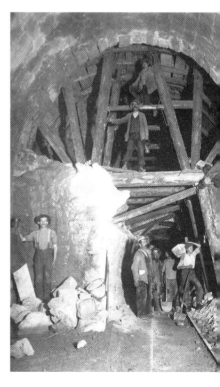

The 221m *726ft* tall Hoover Dam on the River Colorado on the Nevada/Arizona border, USA, was finished in 1936. Originally called the Boulder Dam, it was renamed in 1947 in honour of US President Herbert Hoover (1874–1964).

The 3769km *2342 mile* St Lawrence Seaway linking the Atlantic Ocean to the Great Lakes on the Canada/US border cost $750 million and was opened on 26 June 1959.

CANALS

The earliest vestiges of a canal were discovered near Mandali, Iraq, in 1968 and have been dated to the 5th millennium BC.

The world's first great canal was China's **Grand Canal** – 1060 miles *1700km* in length – parts of which were built in the 6th century AD. It was eventually finished in 1283.

It is calculated that at times a workforce of 4.8 million was deployed. The total length of its Y-shaped route, including parts of the Yellow River, is 1560 miles *2500km*. Today it is used extensively, with some ships of 2000 tonnes.

The first ship canal able to accommodate all ocean-going vessels of its era was the 49 mile *79km* long **Amsterdam canal** to Den Helder, which was completed in 1819–25.

During the cutting of the **Suez Canal** (Qana el Suweis) in Egypt, opened in 1869 but progressively widened and deepened since, an estimated 720 million cubic yards *550 million cu m* was excavated to create 91 miles *146km* of canal in an overall route of 108 miles *174km* from Suez on the Red Sea to Port Said on the Mediterranean. The canal was closed by the Suez War of 1956 and again in the Six Day War of 1967, but was reopened in June 1975.

The **Panama Canal** between the Atlantic and the Pacific Oceans required the digging of 41.5 miles *67km* within the overall route of 50.4 miles *81km*, if the Gatun and Miraflores Lakes and the Calebra Cut are included.

The promoter of the Suez Canal, Ferdinand **de Lesseps** (Fr) (1805–94), originally formed the Panama canal company and began work in 1881. But he ran into many difficulties, the company collapsed and the canal was taken on by the USA in 1904. It was opened on 15 August 1914 and continued under the control of the USA. It will be handed over to the Republic of Panama in 2000.

The **St Lawrence Seaway** from Gulf of St Lawrence, Canada, to Duluth, USA was completed in 1958. It measures 2342 miles *3769km* and includes the Welland and the Beauharois Canals.

DAMS

Neolithic man built small stone dams to make catching fish easier. The first massive dam was at **Sadd-el-Kafara**, Egypt, dated to *c.*2750BC near Helwan, south of Cairo. It was 37ft *11m* high and probably used to store water for a nearby alabaster quarry.

The earliest known **arch** or crescent-shaped dam was

PROGRESSIVE RECORDS – BRIDGE SPANS

Feet	Metres	Name and location	Date opened
142	43	Narni, River Nera, Italy	AD14
c.250	76	Lan Chin, Lantshang River, Yunnan Province, China	c.65
251	77	Trezzo, Adda River, Italy	c.1380
450	137	Chak-sem-ch-ri Lamasery, Brahmaputra, Tibet	1420
580	177	Menai, Menai Strait, Anglesey to mainland Wales	1826
870	265	Fribourg, Sarine Valley, Switzerland	1834
1010	308	Wheeling, Ohio River, West Virginia, USA	1849
1043	318	Lewiston-Queenston, Niagara River, Canada/USA	1851
1057	322	Cincinnati-Covington, Ohio River, Ohio-Kentucky, USA	1867
1268	387	Niagara-Clifton, Niagara River, Canada-USA	1869
1596	486	Brooklyn Bridge, East River, New York City, USA	1883
1710	521	Firth of Forth Road Bridge, Scotland	1889
1800	549	Quebec Cantilever Rail Bridge, St Lawrence River, Canada	1917
1850	564	Ambassador, Detroit River, Windsor, Canada/USA	1929
3500	1067	George Washington, Hudson River, New York	1931
4200	1280	Golden Gate, San Francisco, California, USA	1937
4260	1298	Verrazano Narrows, New York City, USA	1964
4626	1410	Humber Estuary road bridge, Humberside, England	1978
5840	1780	Akashi-Kaikyo (Honshu-Shikoku link) Japan	1998

PROGRESSIVE RECORDS – TUNNEL LENGTHS

Miles	Km	Name and Location	Dates completed
0.6	1.0	Isle of Samos water tunnel, Greece	c.550BC
1.4	2.2	Baebolo silver mining tunnel, Cazlana, Spain	c.250BC
0.9	1.4	Pausilippo road tunnel, Naples-Pozzuoli	36BC
3.5	5.6	Lake Fucinus drainage tunnel, near Rome, Italy	c.AD40–50
4	6.4	Nochistongo drainage tunnel, Valley of Mexico	1608–09
7.45	12	Noireu, Saint Quentin canal tunnel, N. France	1822
7.95	12.79	Mont Cenis rail tunnel, France-Italy	1871
9.26	14.9	St. Gotthard rail tunnel, Switzerland	1882
12.3	19.8	Simplon 1 rail tunnel, Switzerland-Italy	1906
12.31	19.82	Simplon 2 rail tunnel, Switzerland-Italy	1922
18.1	29.1	Shandaken (part of Catskill Aqueduct), New York	1923
105	168.9	Delaware water supply aqueduct, New York City	1944

The World's longest subaqueous rail tunnels are:-

Miles	Km	Name and Location	Date
14.48	23.3	Sekan rail tunnel (total length 33.46 miles 58.85km) under the Tsugaru Channel, linking Honshu and Hokkaido, Japan	1988
23.60	37.98	English Channel Tunnel (total length 31 miles 55yds 49.94km), linking Folkestone, England, and Calais, France	1994

PROGRESSIVE RECORDS – DAMS

Height		Name and Location	Date
ft	m		
37	11	Sadd el Kafara, Wadi el Garawi, Egypt	c.2750–2500BC
98	30	Gukow River, Shansi Province, China	c.250BC
130	39	Subiaco, River Aniene, Italy	c.AD50
151	46	Tibi, Rio Monegre, Alicante, Spain	1594
164	50	Puentes I, Rio Guadalentin, Spain	1791
233	71	Puentes II (see above)	1884
299	91	New Croton, Croton River, New York, USA	1905
325	99	Buffalo Bill or Shostone Dam, Wyoming, USA	1910
351	107	Arrowreck, Boise River, Idaho, USA	1916
364	111	Schräh Dam, Schwyz, Switzerland	1924
390	119	Diablo, Skagit River, Washington, USA	1929
417	127	Owyhee, Adrian, Oregon, USA	1932
446	136	Chambon, River Romanche, France	1934
726	221	Hoover Dam, Colorado River, USA	1936
778	237	Mauvoisin, Dranse de Bagnes River, Switzerland	1957
858	262	Vajont, Vajont River, Veneto, Italy	1961
932	284	Grand Dixence, Rhône tributary, Valais, Switzerland	1962
1017	310	Nurek Dam, Vakhsh river, Tadjikistan	1980

built c.AD560 by Chryses of Alexandria on the Turko-Syrian border. The arch dam is built with the convex side facing the water so that the water pressure forces the masonry joints tighter.

A gravity dam resists water pressure by its own weight. The **Grande Dixence** in Switzerland is 2296ft 700m long and contains 7,790,000cu yds 5,959,350cu m of concrete. It was the highest dam in the world until the completion of the 1017ft 310m Nurek Dam in 1980.

Embankment dams uses semi-permeable material to reduce water pressure, and controlled seepage is permitted. The 754ft 230m high and 6799ft 2073m long **Oroville Dam** (1968) in California, USA, was the highest embankment dam in the world before the Nurek.

The biggest dam-building project of the late 20th century is the **Three Gorges** dam in the Chang Jiang (Yangtze River), China. The project, begun in 1993, is scheduled for completion in 2009. It will create a deep water reservoir of 400miles 600km in length, which will entail the displacement of about 1.2 million people.

BUILDING AND ENGINEERING

Wonders of the World

The Seven Wonders of the Ancient World were listed by the Phoenician epigrammist **Antipater** (*fl.c.*120BC) from Sidon on the eastern coast of the Mediterranean. The constructions he chose ranged in age over more than two and a half millennia.

PYRAMIDS

The pharaohs' enduring monument

The **pyramids at Giza**, Egypt, were built *c.*2940BC onward. They are enormous stone funerary monuments raised to the pharaohs Khufu (written as Cheops by the Greeks), his son Khafra (Chepren) and Khafra's son Menkaura (Mykerinos).

The largest and earliest of the trio, built by the engineers Hemyuna and Ankhuf, succeeded four earlier Egyptian pyramids as the **world's tallest structure** (see pages 140–1)

The 29th-century BC pyramids at Giza near Cairo are the only one of the Seven Wonders of the World to survive in the 20th century AD. The largest or Great Pyramid contains 2.3 million blocks of granite and limestone, each averaging about 2.5 tonnes. It has been estimated that it would have taken 4000 men 30 years to cut, move and position these pieces.

standing 480.9ft *146.5m* tall. At an unknown date it lost its pinnacle or pyramidion, which may have been covered with gold leaf and was probably therefore looted. The theft reduced its height to 449ft 6in *137m*. With a base line of 765ft *230m* it covers 13.12 acres *5.3ha.*

The pyramids were built with extraordinary **precision** – as is reflected by the fact that the maximum discrepancy in the base line of the Great Pyramid is 7.9in *20cm* – less than one-tenth of 1%.

GARDENS

A proud king's gift to his homesick wife

The **Hanging Gardens of Babylon**, an ancient city-state near modern Baghdad, are not mentioned in any contemporary source, and there are conflicting accounts of their creation in later works of the classical era. It is possible that they only existed in the imagination of later writers.

The Jewish historian Flavius Josephus (*b.c.*AD37) said that the gardens were built

by **Nebuchadnezzar II** of Babylon (*r.*605–562BC). They imitated in their layout the mountains and trees of Media, a kingdom in what is now northern Iran. The gardens were supposedly intended as a gift to the Babylonian king's Median wife, Amytis.

Diodorus Siculus, the 1st-century BC classical author of a 40-volume history of the world, maintained that the gardens were built by **Darius I** (*c.*558–486BC) of the Persian Achaemenid dynasty in 522BC. It may be that a change in the course of the River Euphrates, which watered the gardens, required them to be wholly rebuilt.

A third possibility is that the gardens were built for Queen **Sammuramat**, wife of the Assyrian king, Shamsi-Adad V (*r.*823–811BC) – a woman known in Greek legend as Semiramis, daughter of a Syrian goddess.

TEMPLE

Towering shrine to the moon goddess

The **Temple of Diana** in Ephesus (then in Greek Asia Minor, now in Turkey) was reputedly built *c.*550BC. An illustrious marble edifice with columns the height of a modern six-storey building, it survived only two centuries before being damaged by fire in 356BC. It was eventually destroyed by the invading Goths in AD262 in one of their incursions from the lands they occupied to the north of the Black Sea.

The design of the temple has been attributed to the Greek

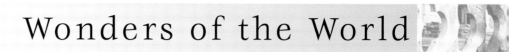

In Diodorus Siculus's account, the Hanging Gardens of Babylon climbed in terraces from the riverbank in the northern part of the city. Some archaeologists believe that the gardens were planted on the side of a vast stepped pyramid, with pumps sending water up from the river to cascade down through the luxuriant growth.

Cherisphron. His plan measured 452 x 234ft *138 x 71.5m* and the columns rose 64ft *19.5m*. Diana was the Roman goddess of the moon and hunting and was associated with fertility and childbirth; in Greek mythology she was known by the name of Artemis.

STATUE

Colossal figure of the great king of the gods

The great carved image of **Zeus**, king of the gods, that resided at Olympia in Greece was the most celebrated of all statues in antiquity. Completed some five years after 438BC, it was made by the renowned Greek sculptor Pheidias (or Phidias) of Athens (born *c.*490BC).

Although the figure of Zeus was seated, the statue is believed to have been 39–59ft *12–18m* tall. The best surviving visual evidence of its grandeur is on the coinage of Elis dating from the time of the Roman Emperor Hadrian (AD76–138).

MAUSOLEUM

Memorial of a short life

The white marble **tomb of Mausolus** was completed at Halicarnassus (now Bodrum), Turkey, shortly after 353BC. It measured 438ft *133.5m* in circumference and was 137ft *42m* tall.

The great monument was planned by Mausolus (377/6–353BC) just prior to his death aged 24 years. He was the satrap – a provincial governor within the Persian empire – of Caria, a mountainous area in the southwest of Asia Minor.

The architect of his tomb was **Pythius** of Priene, overseen by Artemisia, who was both the widow and sister of Mausolus. In the late 15th century AD crusading knights used the stones of the mausoleum – the word derives from Mausolos' name – to build a castle.

COLOSSUS

Bronze protector of a Mediterranean harbour

The **Colossus of Rhodes**, a huge bronze statue of the sun god Helios, is reputed to have been 105ft *32m* tall. It served also as a lighthouse.

The more fanciful accounts claim that the statue actually stood astride the harbour entrance at Rhodes, capital of the Mediterranean island of the same name. The architect was **Chares of Lindus**, a pupil of the great Lysippus of Sicyon (*fl.*328BC), who was a master of huge naturalistic bronzes. Completed in 282BC, however, the awe-inspiring statue stood for no more than 65 years before being destroyed by an earthquake in the year 226 or 224BC.

LIGHTHOUSE

North African beacon

The **pharos (lighthouse) of Alexandria** was probably begun in around 290–280BC. Its architect was named Sostratus. After the Macedonian Alexander the Great conquered Egypt and founded Alexandria in 332BC, one of his generals ruled the country as Ptolemy I (c.367–283BC). The lighthouse, begun under his

The towering statue of Zeus at Olympia shimmered with a covering of ivory platelets and gold leaf. Its creator Pheidias also carved the frieze for the Parthenon in Athens and the statue of Athene, Greek goddess of war and wisdom, that stood there.

rule, was dedicated to him and his spouse, Berenice.

It rose on the islet of Pharos, 1 mile *1.6km* off the coast but connected to the mainland by a dyke. According to some authorities it was 300ft *91m* tall, but others insist that it towered 439ft *134m* over the waves. The range of its light may have been increased by siting a polished bronze convex mirror behind it. It is said to have been visible 35 miles *50km* out to sea.

The pharos was demolished in an **earthquake** in AD1302. In 1477 the Mamluk sultan Qait-Bey (*r.*1468–95) used its ruins to build a fort.

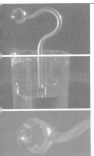

Electricity

BEFORE AD 1

Amber's special quality

The word electricity (Gk. *elektron* amber) is derived from the earliest method for generating **static electricity** by rubbing amber, particularly with fur. It was described by Thales of Miletus (Gk) (*c.*625–*c.*547BC).

AD 1

Glass attracts

Roman naturalist Pliny the Elder (AD23–79) also knew of the behaviour of static electricity in attracting objects to a piece of glass excited by friction. No one in the ancient world, however, studied the phenomenon any further.

AD 1000

Force of friction

The idea of electricity was first developed by the English physician William Gilbert (1540–1603). He first used the terms 'electricity' and '**electric force**' – the force between two bodies charged by friction.

Electrical **conductors** were discovered in 1729 by Stephen Gray (Eng) (1666–1736), who transmitted an electric current 492ft *150m* down a hemp thread.

Four years later, Charles François de Cisternay Dufay (Fr) (1698–1739), working at the Academy of Sciences, Paris, established that there were two types of electricity: he found

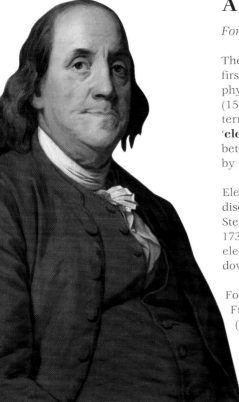

American polymath Benjamin Franklin was a scientist, a statesman and an author. As well as establishing that lightning is a form of electricity and developing the lightning conductor, he bought and ran the *Pennsylvania Gazette* newspaper (early 1730s) helped to draft the US Declaration of Independence (1776), invented bifocal spectacles (1784) and was a vigorous anti-slavery campaigner.

that an electrified glass rod could be made either to attract or repel pieces of cork. He called them 'vitreous' and 'resinous' electricity but they were renamed positive (+) and negative (–) by Benjamin **Franklin** (US) (1706–90).

In January 1746 Pieter van Musschenbroek (Neths) (1692–1761), working at the University of Leiden, discovered how to **store electricity** by charging water in a container. A brass wire protruding out of the sealed container was rubbed to generate static electricity which was transmitted to the water. His assistant was nearly killed by the first major recorded shock from what became known as a '**Leyden jar**'.

Benjamin Franklin also established that **lightning** was an electric charge – rather than one of the god Zeus's thunderbolts, as the Ancient Greeks had imagined – in a recklessly dangerous experiment flying a silk kite in a thunderstorm in Philadelphia in 1752.

Franklin collected the thundercloud's charge – which passed down the kite's line – in a Leyden jar on the ground. As a result, hundreds of sharp-pointed **lightning conductors** soon sprouted from the roof-tops of that and many other cities to protect buildings by conducting this celestial electricity safely to the ground.

The Italian physician Luigi Galvani (1737–98) came to believe that there was an electric force in living tissue which he called '**animal**

Many 19th-century scientists used the Leyden jar – a device for storing electricity by charging water in a container – in their physical experiments. It is now used mainly for teaching.

electricity'. In a series of experiments on the muscles of frogs' legs, he discovered that the muscle could be induced to twitch if two different metals – which came to be called electrodes – were brought into contact with it.

Galvani was mistaken in his concept of animal electricity, but his experiments laid the foundations for the principle of **storage batteries**.

Galvani's work was developed by Alessandro Guiseppe **Volta** (It) (1745–1827), who discovered that coins of two different metals placed above and below his tongue produced a weak electric activity. But the animal electricity theory was scotched when he realized that the same effect could be achieved by putting the two coins in a saline medium.

Volta had, in fact, discovered the principle of **electrolysis** and from there it was a short step to his development in 1800 of the first **electric batteries** with the Voltaic 'pile' of alternate discs of copper and zinc, between sheets of moistened cardboard. What came to be known as Volta's pile produced the first continuous and controllable, though weak, electric currents.

In 1803 Johann Wilhelm Ritter (Ger) (1776–1810) invented the **accumulator** or rechargeable battery. This new source of electric power enabled Humphry **Davy** (1778–1829) to discover the elements sodium and potassium (1807). When he immersed electrodes in different salt mediums, Davy found that these elements were released.

In 1820, Hans Christian **Oersted** (Den) (1777–1851) demonstrated that a compass needle twitched to point at right angles to the direction of flow of a current in any nearby wire.

Following this, André Marie **Ampère** (Fr) (1775–1836) began to work out the mathematical laws of electro-magnetic theory and developed an instrument for measuring electric current which was the forerunner of the **galvanometer**. The SI (Système Internationale) unit of electric current was named after Ampère.

The German physicist Georg Simon **Ohm** (1789–1854), working in Cologne in 1827, first discovered the relationship between potential difference (volts), resistance and current (amps); resistance came to be measured in ohms.

Electricity remained a subject studied by laboratory physicists and chemists until 29 August 1831. That was the day on which Michael **Faraday** (Eng) (1791–1867)

and his assistant Charles Anderson (1790–1866) discovered **electro-magnetic induction** – electric current produced by the rapid change of the poles of a magnet.

In 1830 Joseph Henry (US) (1797–1878) discovered **self-induction** – the generation of an electric arc jumping from a battery terminal to a wire. He later helped Samuel Morse (US) (1791–1872) to set up the first patented **electric telegraph** between Washington, D.C. and Baltimore on 24 May 1844.

The great 19th-century theoreticians of electricity were both Scots. William **Thomson** (later Lord Kelvin) (1824–1907) and James Clerk **Maxwell** (1831–79) were interested in developing a unified theory which could be applied to all the behaviour of matter and energy.

Kelvin was also a tireless practical scientist who actively participated in laying the first transatlantic cable – 3000 miles *4800km* between England and the USA – and calculated equations for the speed of transmission through it. Maxwell's enormous contribution was a set of equations bringing all wave forms – of electricity, light or radio – into one theory.

At the same time, inventors were harnessing electricity in a variety of practical applications.

In 1860, Gaston Planté (Fr) (1834–89) invented the rechargeable **electro-chemical cell**, made of sheets of lead in sulphuric acid. This cell is essentially the same as the battery used in modern cars.

In 1868 Georges Leclanché (Fr) (1839–82) devised a low-cost **dry cell** with zinc alloy and manganese dioxide electrodes in an ammonium chloride electrolyte. This is the type of battery used in torches, radios and so on.

Johann Philipp Reis (Ger) (1834–74) described his diaphragm-type microphone to the Frankfurt Physical Society on 26 October 1861. It employed the principle of **magnetostriction** – that is, minute changes in the length of a magnetized metal rod.

The great English scientist Michael Faraday followed his discovery of electromagnetic induction by inventing the first electric motor (1821) and the first electrical transformer (1831). In his lifetime he was celebrated for the popular lectures he gave at the Royal Institution, London, from 1825–62.

AD 2000

Progress on a small scale

The applications of electricity in the 20th century have been increasingly **miniaturized** as the behaviour of matter in different states is investigated at the molecular level.

Piezo electricity (from Gk. *piezo*, to press) was discovered by Pierre **Curie** (1859–1906) in 1880. He found that if a crystal of quartz is compressed between electrodes it will generate electricity and that when an electric current is passed through a crystal, the crystal will change dimensions. This last effect is employed in **quartz crystal watches** and clocks.

The Dutch physicist Heike Kamerlingh Onnes (Neths) (1853–1926) discovered in 1911 that a metal's resistivity suddenly vanishes when the metal is cooled to near absolute zero (0°K, –273°C). In the case of mercury this was at 4.15°K. This 'superconductivity' means that electric current will continue to flow freely as long as the temperature remains near zero.

In 1929, the Swiss physicist Felix

Clive Sinclair (*b.*1940) tried to interest the British public in his electrically powered three-wheel vehicle, the C5, in 1981 – without success. The C5 was designed for short trips of under 20 miles *32km* and was powered by a washing-machine motor.

Bloch (1905–83) described what became known as Bloch bands, the different levels of energy of matter when it is subjected to heat or light. Bloch based his theory on the behaviour of **semi-conductors**, materials with a conductivity between that of insulators and metals. Silicon, for example, acts as an excellent insulator at low temperatures but as a conductor if subjected to heat, light or an electric current.

This quality of semiconductors is the basis of the **transistor**, discovered in 1948 by US physicist John Bardeen (1908–91), which is most often made of silicon.

Transistors and other miniaturized electric devices can be assembled on printed **circuit boards**, first devised by Paul Eisler (Aus/Eng) (1907–92) in 1943. The printed circuit board consists of maps or tracks of conductor, commonly copper, laid out on a piece of insulation material.

Electronic circuits grew even smaller when Jack St Clair Kilby (US) developed in 1959 the **integrated circuit**, which consists of thousands of tiny components assembled on a crystal of semi-conducting material, usually of silicon – hence the common name '**silicon chip**'.

In 1957, John Bardeen, Leon N. Cooper and John Robert Schrieffer in the US together formulated the BCS theory (using the initials of their names).

Photographed through an electron microscope, copper oxide wires are used to test the electrical conductivity of this block of yttrium barium by scientists developing semiconductors. Transistors – used in radios, TVs and computers – are made by joining together semiconductors with differing electrical properties.

They proposed that the electrons in superconductors which would normally repel each other are in fact attracted and form what were known as **Cooper pairs**.

In 1962, Welsh physicist Brian David **Josephson** (*b.*1940) deduced that these Cooper pairs would flow between superconductors separated by a thin layer of insulating material and demonstrated that an electrical current across the gap could be measured.

Meanwhile, physicists continued to raise the **transition temperature** of superconductivity. The Swiss physicists Karl Alex Müller (*b.*1927) and Johannes Georg Bednorz (*b.*1950) discovered in 1986 that ceramic, a material normally thought of as an insulator, would act as a superconductor at 30°K.

In 1993 Hans R. Ott made a mercury amalgam with ceramic which lost all resistance at 133°K, –140°C. Ultimately, **zero resistance** may be achieved at room temperature of 300°K.

Energy production

The San bushmen of the Kalahari Desert are Africa's oldest surviving people. Their myths tell how the Sun once lived on Earth, but was thrown up into the sky by children. He left men knowledge of fire – the earliest form of man-made energy – as a legacy of his time on Earth.

Ancestors of *Homo sapiens* learnt the uses of fire *c*.1.5 million years ago, and their descendants have not rested in the search for energy sources. Since animals were first harnessed to traction in *c*.6800BC, humans have found ways to control and use natural forces and to release the energy locked up in matter.

Date	Energy source	Method	Uses/Pioneer	First used in
c.1.5 million BC	**Fire**	Controlled fire	Used for heating, cooking and lighting	Dering-Yurakh, Siberia, Russia and Swartzkrans, South Africa
c.4800BC	**Wind and air power**	Sailing boats	Transport	Eridu, Sumeria
644BC		Windmill	After 1421, widely adapted for corn grinding and drainage in northern Europe	Neh, Persia
AD1772			Andrew Meikle (Scot) (1719–1811) invented spring windmill sails in which hinged shutters replaced sail cloths	Dunbar, Scotland
1807		Calorific (hot-air) engine External combustion	Robert Stirling (Scot) (1790–1878)	Kilmarnock, Scotland
1833		Wind-powered generator	John Ericsson (Swe/US) (1803–89)built a 5hp example. By 1988 units had attained 3.2 megawatts	London, England
c.350BC	**Natural gas**	Fire wells (methane, CH_4)	Heating, lighting, cookery (distributed by bamboo piping)	Szichuan, China
1857			Revived for modern use for lighting and heating a leper colony	near Bombay, India
c.1780	**Solar power**	Solar furnace	Antoine Lavoisier (Fr) (1743–95)	Paris, France
1878		Solar generator	First exhibited by Augustin Mouchot (Fr); used by Mouchot and Abel Pifre (Fr) to power a printing press	Paris, France
1948		Solar heated house	Engineered by Maria Telkes (Hun/US) (1900–95)	Dover, Maryland, USA
1954		Solar power plant	Parabolic mirror system designed by Felix Trombe (Fr). Output 50 kilowatts	Odeillo, Pyrénées-Orientales, France
1991		Solar battery – silicon	Used as mobile low-power source by Gerald Pearman (US)	Bell Laboratories, New Jersey
1991		Solar panel (transparent)	Devised by Michael Gratzel – usable as windows	Lausanne, Switzerland
c.100BC	**Fossil fuels**	Coal	For iron-making, and later electricity generation. Even by 1900 still comprised 95% of the world's fossil fuel usage	North-eastern China
1603		Coke	Pioneered by Sir Hugh Plat (Eng) (1552–1608)	England
from 1875		Lignite (brown coal)	Mainly used in Russia and Eastern Europe with some in North America	Russia

> Windmills, originating in Persia, were not found in western Europe until the 11th century AD.

Date	Energy source	Method	Uses/Pioneer	First used in
c.50BC	**Water power**	Water mill (horizontal)	For grinding corn on River Lycus at Kabeira near Niksar	Kelkit, Turkey
1582		Water turbine for water supply	Designed by Peter Morice (Neths)	City of London, England
1884		Turbine for high head, low flow water sources	Designed by Lester A. Pelton (US) (1829–1908). Impulse turbine uses nozzles to direct water	California, USA
AD808	**Explosives**	Black powder		China
1847		Nitro-glycerine	Ascarlo Sobrero (It) (1812–88)	Turin, Italy
1863		TNT (Trinitrotoluene)	J. Wilbrand (Ger)	Germany
1867		Dynamite (addition of absorbent Kieselguhr)	Alfred Bernhard Nobel (Swe) (1833–96) (also invented gelignite in 1875)	Sweden
1889		Cordite (cellulose nitrate and nitroglycerine with plasticizers)	Frederick Abel (GB) (1827–1902) and James Dewar (Scot) (1842–1923)	Royal Institution, London
c.AD62	**Steam power**	Aeolipile (steam engine)	Hero of Alexandria invented a spherical 'engine',which rotated with the force of jets of steam expelled through nozzles.	Alexandria, Egypt
1671		Model steam car	Ferdinand Verbiest (Flan) (1623–88)	Beijing, China
1690		Steam piston engine	Denis Papin (Fr) (1647–1712)	Marburg, Germany
1698		Steam pump	Thomas Savery (Eng) (c.1650–1715)	British coalfields
1712		Improved piston action	Thomas Newcomen (Eng) (1663–1729)	Dudley Castle, Staffordshire, England
1769		Separate condenser	James Watt (Scot) (1736–1819), 5 January 1769 Conceived by Jacob Leupold (Ger) in 1725	Soho Works, near Birmingham, England
1769		Mobile steam engine	On 10 Oct., Nicholas Joseph Cugnot (Fr) (1725–1804). Steam powered *fardier* (wagon), the first powered vehicle tested	Paris, France
1769		High pressure engine	Richard Trevithick (Eng) (1771–1833), 24 March 1802	Cornwall, England
1800		Valve steam engine	George Henry Corliss (US) (1817–88). Also introduced spring valves	Providence, Rhode Island, USA
1884		Steam turbine (high speed)	Charles Parsons (Ire) (1854–1931), who also built the first vessel so powered – the 35 knot *Turbinia*	Newcastle-upon-Tyne, England
1746	**Electrical power**	Leyden Jar (electrostatic storage)	Pieter van Musschenbroek (Neths) (1692–1761)	Leiden University, Netherlands
1775		Electrophorus (static generator)	Alessandro Volta (It) (1745–1827)	University of Pavia, Italy
1796–99		Battery	Alessandro Volta. His voltaic pile comprised copper, zinc and brine saturated cardboard discs, piled in sequence to produce a current	
		Electric motor	Thomas Davenport (US) (1802–51). First patent granted 25 February 1837	Brandon, Vermont, USA
1834		Rechargeable battery	Gaston Planté (Fr) (1834–89)	Paris, France
1859		D.C. generator (Dynamo)	Zénobe Gramme (Bel) (1826–1901)	Paris, France
1869		A.C. generator (Alternator)	Zénobe Gramme	Paris, France

Scottish engineer James Watt improved the efficiency of the early steam engine by introducing a separate condenser in which the steam was condensed.

Date	Energy source	Method	Uses/Pioneer	First used in
1877	**Electrical power** (continued)	Hydro-electric generation	Brush generator (water wheel)	Paris, France
1881		Three phase induction motor	Nikola Tesla (Croat/US) (1856–1943)	Pullman's Mill, Godalming, England
1888		Transmission of electricity	Thomas A. Edison (US) (1847–1931). Building opened 4 September 1882	257 Pearl Street, New York City
			Westinghouse – 3000volts over 3 miles *4.8km*	Telluride, Colorado, USA
1928		Generation from dammed water	Connecticut Light and Power Co. fed 33,000hp turbine from reservoir	Rocky River, Waterbury, Connecticut, USA
1905	**Geothermal** (heat from inside the Earth)	Harnessed natural steam	Fumaroles (volcanic vent) yielding steam at up to 260°C at 27kg/cm² led to turbines yielding 3.75mW (1914), 135mW (1939) and 254mW by 1950. Also power generation at Taupo Hot Springs, New Zealand	Larderello, Tuscany, Italy
1930			Domestic and industrial use of hot springs Highly insulated piping supplies the capital city Reykjavik	Pvottalauger, Iceland
1926	**Liquid fuelled rockets**	Liquid oxygen and ethanol	Robert H. Goddard (US) (1882–1945), first trial (42ft *12.5m* altitude) (not revealed until 15 December 1929)	Auburn, Massachusetts, USA
1944		V2 rocket assault	Wernher von Braun (Ger/US) (1912–77), first V2 (*Vergeltungswaffe zwei*) (revenge weapon No. 2), 12.93 tonnes	Euskirken, Germany, delivered to Port d'Italie, Paris, France
1961		Vostok I orbit	Russian Yuri Gagarin (1934–68) became the first man in space and orbited the Earth	Russia
1969		US Apollo 11 lunar mission	Neil Alden Armstrong (US) (*b.*1930) set foot on the Moon at 02.56 GMT on 21 July from *Eagle*, which was lifted off by the 363.6ft *110.85m* tall Saturn V, 3-stage rocket which generated 175.6 million h.p. and weighed all-up 6876 tonnes	Cape Canaveral (then Kennedy Space Center), Florida
1937	**Jet aero-engine**		Sir Frank Whittle (Eng) (1907–96) tested his WU1 engine. Used in Gloster aircraft in 1941	Rugby, England
1939		Maiden flight of jet-powered Heinkel He178, 27 Aug.	Erich Karl Warsitz (Ger) (1906–83), Dr Hans von Ohain's engine	Marienehe, Germany
December 2 1942	**Atomic power**		First nuclear reactor built by Enrico Fermi (It/US) (1901–54)	Stagg Field, University of Chicago, USA
1955		Breeder reactor	US Atomic Energy Commission Laboratory ERB-1 (Westingthouse)	Arco, Idaho, USA
1970		Mox (mixed oxide)	Recycled nuclear waste	Germany
1966	**Tidal power**	First tidal generators	24 turbines, each of 10MW on 2400ft *750m* dam	Rance, Brittany, France
1998	**Biogas**	From cow dung	First dung-fuelled power station	Holsworthy, Devon, England

Well insulated against the cold, engineers check a geothermal installation in Iceland.

WORLD'S CRUDE OIL AND NATURAL GAS RESERVES (1997)

Country	Crude Oil in billions of barrels	Natural Gas in millions of units		Country	Crude Oil in billions of barrels	Natural Gas in millions of units	
1. Saudi Arabia	261.6			9. Libya	29.5	40.05 cu ft	1.31 m³
2. CIS (and from USSR)	120.4	1,958.1 cu ft	55.45 m³	10. China	29.0	40.5 cu ft	1.14 m³
3. Iraq (incl. Neutral Zone)	112.0	118.2 cu ft	3.34 m³	11. USA	22.0	166.5 cu ft	4.71 m³
4. Kuwait	95.6	52.8 cu ft	1.49 m³	12. Norway	19.0	88.5 cu ft	2.50 m³
5. Iran	91.7	776.9 cu ft	22.00 m³	20. UK	4.7	25.7 cu ft	0.73 m³
6. United Arab Emirates	80.6	204.2 cu ft	5.78 m³	– Rest of EU	2.2	88.0 cu ft	2.49 m³
7. Venezuela	68.7	142.3 cu ft	4.03 m³				
8. Mexico	48.6	65.8 cu ft	1.86 m³	**World Total**	**1,120.8**	**5,061.6 cu ft**	**143.32 m³**

Nuclear power

The story of the development of nuclear power begins with the discovery in Paris in 1896 of 'Becquerel rays'. The French physicist Antoine Henri **Becquerel** (1852–1908) described the fluorescent rays given off by certain uranium salts in pitchblende.

This process was called 'radioactivity' by Marie **Curie** (Pol) (1867–1934) and her husband Pierre (Fr) (1859–1906), who worked closely with Becquerel to isolate these active elements in pitchblende. They identified radium and polonium as radioactive elements. Marie named polonium after the country of her birth.

NUCLEAR ENERGY

As at 1998 eight nations were reliant on nuclear energy for **more than 40%** of their energy:

Lithuania	81.8%	Sweden	48.2%
France	78.2%	Bulgaria	45.4%
Belgium	50.1%	Slovakia	44.0%
Ukraine	46.8%	Switzerland	40.6%

Measured in millions of kilowatt hours (kwh), the **greatest generation of electricity** by nuclear reactions with the number of reactors operative is:

Country	Kw/hours	Number of reactors
USA	55,600	107
France	34,700	59
Japan	27,300	54
Germany	14,000	29
Russia	11,100	20
UK	10,100	35
Sweden	7,300	12
Canada	7,200	16
Ukraine	7,200	16
South Korea	6,700	12

In 1902, the New Zealand physicist Ernest **Rutherford** (1871–1937) with Frederick Soddy (UK) (1877–1956) – working at McGill University, Canada – formulated a theory of what was happening to cause radioactivity. They proposed that the atoms of one element were in fact spontaneously disintegrating and ending up as atoms of another element.

A major stage on the road to nuclear power was the Swiss-German scientist Albert **Einstein** (1879–1955)'s Special Theory of Relativity, formulated in 1907. It bore the key proposition that mass could be transformed into energy.

In 1910 Rutherford's experiments with alpha particles – a form of radiation given off by some radioactive elements – convinced him that atoms contain a tiny **nucleus** with a strong positive electric charge orbited by negatively charged electrons.

In 1913 Niels Bohr (Den) (1885–1962) gave his fellow-scientists a new understanding of atomic structure. He applied the quantum theory of German physicist Max Planck

Niels Bohr was a professor in his native Copenhagen when the German army invaded in April 1940. After fleeing in a fishing boat to Sweden in 1943, he went on to the USA where he took part in atomic research. In the years following World War II he campaigned against the threatened use of the nuclear weapons that he had helped to create.

(1858–1947) (see page 95) to Rutherford's model of the atom and argued that electrons orbiting the nucleus emitted radiation when shifting from one orbit to another. The frequency of the radiation corresponded to the spectrum of light emitted by the atom (see page 96).

Then in 1917 in Manchester Rutherford went on to **split the atom**. He fired alpha particles at nitrogen and found that some of them, hitting the nitrogen nucleus, made it break up, releasing positively charged particles named protons. In the process, the nitrogen atoms were transmuted into oxygen atoms.

In the following quarter century, research into the nature of the nucleus became a tool of national politics as scientists first realized the potential enormous **energy** released in atomic degradation.

In 1932 James Chadwick (Eng) (1891–1974) discovered the **neutron**, a new particle with no electrical charge within the atomic nucleus. It proved very useful for bombarding the nucleus because as an uncharged particle it could enter the nucleus without being attracted or repelled – and thus deflected – by the charges on the electrons or the nucleus itself.

Leo **Szilard** (1898–1964), a Hungarian physicist, fled from the Nazi threat in 1933, and in 1934 took out a patent on nuclear fission – splitting the nuclei of certain atoms, with the release of energy – in England. He emigrated to the USA in 1938.

On 17 December 1938, the Germans Otto Hahn (1879–1968) and Fritz Strassmann (1902–80) with the Austrian Lise Meitner (1878–1968) – working at the Kaiser Wilhelm Institute for Chemistry, Dahlem, near Berlin – induced nuclear fission by bombarding **uranium** with neutrons. They discovered that the fission could begin a **chain reaction**.

When the uranium nucleus split under bombardment it released two or three new neutrons. Each of these could then split another nucleus, which would release more neutrons

capable of splitting more nuclei – and so on. They did not immediately realize the significance of what they had achieved. But in the USA Szilard persuaded Albert Einstein to alert President Franklin D. Roosevelt to the major implications of this discovery.

On 9 October 1941, without consulting the US Congress or the judiciary, President Roosevelt as Commander-in-Chief of the US armed forces approved the top-secret **Operation Manhattan** to manufacture a nuclear bomb (see pages 204–5).

Scientists found that nuclear fission took place only in **uranium-235** (U-235) – a rare type of uranium. The more widespread form of uranium was **uranium-238** (U-238). Another fissile element, plutonium (Pu-239) could be made from U-238 (see page 204).

The first sustained and controlled **release of atomic energy** was on 2 December 1942 in a squash rackets court under the stands of the University of Chicago's Stagg Field Stadium, Illinois. The nuclear device was built by a team led by Italian physicist Enrico **Fermi** (1901–54).

The building of the $1 million graphite uranium pile, called CP-1 (Chicago Pile 1), had begun on 16 November. It comprised 57 layers of graphite (344.2 tons), uranium oxide (35.97 tons) and uranium metal (5.53 tons) and measured 20 x 25ft *6.10 x 7.62m*. The graphite acted as a moderator in reducing the speed of the bombarding neutrons so that, instead of being immediately absorbed by the non-fissile U-238 nuclei, they

remained free to cause fission within the small proportion of U-235.

The pile was controlled by sheets of **cadmium** which are able to absorb neutrons. The pile was increased until it reached 'critical size' when the chain reaction could begin. The control rods of

Chicago Pile 1 – the world's first nuclear reactor – was built inside a giant square balloon to contain the dust released when holes were drilled in its graphite bricks. There were 22,000 holes in which the uranium oxide and uranium metal were placed. When the pile was complete, the balloon was carefully deflated.

Enrico Fermi was a physics professor in Rome from 1926–38, but fled fascism to the USA. This is his official ID photograph for the Los Alamos project in New Mexico, where the first nuclear weapons were made.

The materials used in nuclear reactors must be treated with extreme care. Plutonium (Pu239), for instance, is probably the most dangerous substance known to man. It remains toxic for 24,000 years.

cadmium were removed and the atomic chain reaction was released. CP-1 remained in use as a research tool until 1953.

The USA turned its attention to the manufacture of the atomic bomb. The first reactors, called **production reactors**, were built to produce plutonium – which could only be obtained in any quantity synthetically from uranium – for use in the bomb. The first medium-sized reactor was at Oak Ridge, Tennessee, and the first large-scale reactor was at the Hanford Engineering Works on the Columbia River, Washington State, USA.

By the summer of 1945 the US atomic bomb was ready. The hitherto unprecedented force of the **two bombs** dropped in August on Hiroshima and Nagasaki (see page 181) effectively ended World War II.

After CP-1 in Chicago, the **first nuclear reactor actually to produce power** was the EBR-1 (Experimental Breeder Reactor) at the National Engineering Laboratory run by the US Department of Energy near Arco, Idaho, USA, in 1951. It was capable of producing 300 kilowatts (kW) of electricity.

In 1952 the **European Centre for Nuclear Research** (CERN) was established at Geneva, Switzerland. Niels Bohr was involved in its creation.

The Soviet Union inaugurated the world's first **working nuclear power station** at Obninsk on 27 June 1954.

In Britain, Calder Hall power station opened in Cumbria on 17 October 1956. Calder Hall was both a military production reactor and the first reactor to supply substantial quantities of electricity to the British National Grid. Its output was 200 megawatts.

The first **atomic power plant in the USA** opened at Shippingport, Pennsylvania, on 18 December 1957.

Scientists developed new types of reactor. The early power stations used up their initial supply of U-235, but in the **breeder reactor** the reaction itself produced more fissile matter. The first of the breeder reactors

Workers in a nuclear power plant inspect the reactor core while it is refuelled. In the 1979 near-disaster at Three Mile Island, Pennsylvania, a cooling pump and the core itself malfunctioned. In the 1986 catastrophe at Chernobyl, Soviet Union, one of the plant's four reactors exploded.

opened at Dounreay in Scotland in 1959.

Conventional nuclear reactors used a 'moderator' of graphite or heavy water – a denser form of water – to slow down neutrons and increase the effectiveness of the chain reactions. The **fast reactor** functioned without a moderator.

The core of the reactor was surrounded by a blanket of uranium carbide, and the uranium was converted into plutonium during the reaction. The plutonium could be extracted and used

power stations escalated after a series of accidents. The first major leak was in March 1979 from the reactor at **Three Mile Island**, Pennsylvania, USA. There was outcry over the fact that local residents were not warned of the potential danger for five hours after the first indications of problems within the plant.

On 26 April 1986, a leak caused by overheating at **Chernobyl** in the Ukraine, Soviet Union, sent clouds of radioactive material as far as Sweden. The effects of the leakage will continue for

Public reaction against nuclear power, coupled with a reduction in the rate of increase of demand for power, meant that fewer power stations were built in the 1990s. In Japan the first local referendum on construction of a reactor led to its decisive rejection by the citizens of Maki.

In the USA, the Department of Energy (DoE) was taken to court in 1996 by utilities companies demanding that the government should provide sites for the safe disposal of **nuclear waste**. The DoE's proposed site at

The North Anna nuclear power station near Fredericksburg, Virginia, contains twin pressurized water reactors. They came into operation in 1978–80 and produce c.14 billion kWh – roughly 20 per cent of Virginia's electricity.

TRANSPORT

The early 20th century was a golden era for the fortunate few lucky to own a motor car. Within 50 years, however, car ownership was no longer a luxury and the revolution in private transport had changed modern life fundamentally. By sending a man to the Moon, the pioneers of the technological age opened a new chapter and what was for over two millennia a dream, became for modern man a reality – at last we could explore the heavens.

TRANSPORT

Moving by sea

BEFORE AD 1

Egyptian reed boats and Greek galleys

The earliest surviving portrayal of a sail is on a painted pottery vase of the Gerzean or Naqada II period *c*.3500–3100BC in Egypt. The Ancient Egyptians used bundles of **papyrus reed** lashed together to make their shallow-draught boats.

This type of construction is still used on Lake Titicaca in Peru/Bolivia. In 1970 the Norwegian anthropologist Thor Heyerdal (*b*.1914) crossed the Atlantic from Morocco to the West Indies in a reed boat, *Ra II*, proving his theory that early Mediterranean peoples could have made a similar voyage.

Galleys were developed by the Egyptians and Greeks both as cargo boats and warships; they became the characteristic ship of the Mediterranean. The **bireme**, with two staggered banks of oars, dates from *c*.700BC, while the **trireme**, in which a third bank of oars was above and outside the others, dates from *c*.500BC. These boats were some 115ft *35m* long and it is estimated that they could be propelled at 9 knots over a brief stretch. (1 knot is a sea speed of 1 nautical mile per hour, equivalent to 1.15 statute miles per hour *1.85km/h*). During a battle, the galleys would be rowed at speed in line abreast with rams and grappling irons deployed from the bows.

The Pentekonter, which had a crew of 25 oarsmen per side, was mentioned by the Greek historian **Herodotus** (485–425BC). The galleys were sailed with a single square **sail** when the wind was astern.

AD 1

Oak warships

The **Viking longboats** are known from 300BC but reached their peak in AD800. They were built of oak, and could be rowed or sailed with a huge central square sail.

Because of their narrow, shallow-draught shape and double-ended construction – pointed at both front and back – they were **fast** and very manoeuvrable. The steering-oar was mounted on the starboard, or steering-board, quarter on the right-hand side of the ship.

The Vikings were great sea explorers. One, Leif **Ericsson**, sailed from Scandinavia to Greenland, Baffin Island and Newfoundland *c*.AD1000.

AD 1000

Explorers' favourite

Spanish and Portuguese explorers developed the versatile, hardy **caravel** in the 15th century. This was a relatively light and small ship, about 23m *75ft* in length, smaller than the more clumsy galleons, and rigged with lateens – long, narrow triangular sails that had been used on Arab boats in the Red Sea and Indian Ocean since at least the 2nd century AD.

The caravel was the earliest known **fore-and-aft rig** – the sail's leading edge was parallel to the mast so that it could be deployed almost in the same line as the boat's hull, allowing the boats to tack into the wind. Christopher Columbus took two caravels, the *Niña* and the *Pinta*, on his 1492 expedition to the New World.

An entirely different approach to sail-handling was developed by the Chinese. The **junk** sail is made up of separate horizontal panels of linen or bamboo matting rigged on bamboo spars. The whole sail is controlled by ropes so that it can be reefed – or rolled up – like a Venetian blind. In sudden storms, the rig can be reefed instantly to leave a tiny amount of sail to manoeuvre.

From *c*.1550 junks were the first ships to employ watertight **bulkheads** – partitions that divide the ship up. They ran not only athwartships (across the ship) but also fore-and-aft (from front to back) and greatly increased the strength and seaworthiness of the ship.

The first **yachts** – small, swift sporting craft called *jaghts* – were unveiled at a water festival in 1580 at Amsterdam, Netherlands. King Charles II of England (1630–85) enjoyed yachting while he was in exile in the Netherlands and, after he was crowned King of England in 1660, was given a 20m *66ft* yacht by the city of Amsterdam. He and his brother James, Duke of York, raced on the Thames from Greenwich to Gravesend and back in 1661.

Cornelis Jacobszoon van Drebbel (Neths) (1572–1633) tested the first successful

Simple but efficient felucca sailboats such as this have navigated the River Nile in Egypt for thousands of years. In the modern era, they share space on the river with vast tourist liners.

(man-powered) **submarine** on the River Thames in 1620. It is contended that he enriched the air inside with oxygen, using chemicals devised by Michael Senivogius (Sedziwój) (Pol) (1566–1636) but this would have been more than 150 years before the first accepted identification of oxygen.

Engineer and entrepreneur Robert Fulton (US) (1765–1815) was the first to run a successful **steamboat** service. His boat, the 150ft *45m Clermont*, had a single-cylinder engine and two paddlewheels of 15ft *5m* diameter and made the 150 mile *240km* trip from New York to Albany, near Boston, in 32 hours, when the journey took four days by sail.

English engineer Isambard Kingdom **Brunel** (1806–59) set up the Great Western Steamship Company in 1836 and his *Great Western* entered service on the transatlantic route to New York in 1838. Brunel's next ship, the *Great Britain* (1845) was the first iron-hulled transatlantic steamer.

In the *Great Eastern* of 1854 Brunel introduced bilge keels – beams along the lower part of the inner hull – to dampen the roll. The *Great Eastern* remained the largest ship ever built until 1899.

Sailing ships continued to be the main form of marine traffic until the end of the 19th century, but increasing costs and the competiton from steam powered ships stimulated some changes in design.

The **clippers** were most famous for their (commercially important) races to get the first tea crop to England and to the US from China. The first true clipper, the *Rainbow*, was built in New York City in 1845.

The *Sovereign of the Seas*, built by Donald Mackay (Can/US) (1810–80) in 1852, set a record from New York to Liverpool of 13 days 14 hours. The last and greatest, the *Cutty Sark*, was built in Dumbarton, Scotland, in 1869, many years after the introduction of steam.

In 1859, the French frigate *Gloire* (5600 tons), designed by Stanislas Dupuy de Lôme (Fr) (1818–85) and propelled by both sails and steam power (13.5 knots), became the world's first **iron-clad battleship**. It just beat the iron-built *HMS Warrior* (9210 tons), which was launched at Blackwall on the Thames in 1860, into the water.

S.S. *Atlantic* was the first **purpose-built tanker**. It was launched in 1863 on the River Tyne, northeast England. **Turbines** were developed in 1884 by Charles Parsons (Ire/Eng) (1854–1931). In 1897 the Parsons Marine Steam Turbine Co. built the turbine-powered 44.5 ton *Turbinia* whose nine propellors on three shafts gave her 34.5 knots. The first transatlantic crossing by an internal combustion engined boat was in 1902. The 38ft *11.58m Abiel Abbot Low* crossed from New York to Cornwall, England – 3100 miles *4989km* in 36 days.

A **schooner** is a ship with two or more masts, all fore-and-aft rigged. The largest ever schooner, the *Thomas W. Lawson* (5218 gross tons) uniquely had seven masts each 193ft *58.82m* high. This leviathan was built in 1902 but was lost off the Isles of Scilly in December 1907.

Trials in 1906 by Enrico Forlanini (It) (1848–1930) of the first **hydrofoil** – a boat lifted out of the water by foils or blades on its hull – were held on Lake Maggiore, Italy.

The water becomes a playground for a diver in search of fish or brightly coloured coral. The first aqualung or scuba equipment ('self-contained underwater breathing apparatus') was created in 1942 by Frenchmen Jacques Cousteau and Emil Gagnan.

In March 1940 RMS *Queen Elizabeth* – then the world's largest liner, at 82,998 gross reg. tons – arrived in New York after a hazardous wartime Atlantic crossing. She served as a wartime troopship, but reverted to a luxury passenger liner from 1946 until 1969. She was sabotaged in Hong Kong harbour in 1972 when being used as a floating university.

TRANSPORT

The vessel reached 38 knots. Commercial use of hydrofoils as ferries began later with the Swiss *Supromar PT10* in 1953 on the same lake.

Since the development of nuclear-powered submarines in the 1950s, these masters of the deep can stay underwater for far longer. The U-boats of World War II spent 80 per cent of their time on the sea's surface; in 1982–3 British submarine *Warspite* set a record by remaining submerged for 111 days in the South Atlantic, covering 30,804 nautical miles *57,085km.*

The 17,900-ton **battleship** HMS *Dreadnought* was launched at Portsmouth, England, in 1906. Completed in eight months with ten 12-in *304.8-mm* guns and a maximum speed of 21 knots with turbine engines, she rendered all the other battleships of the world obsolete at a stroke. By 1918 the Royal Navy had 48 and the Imperial German Navy 26 'Dreadnoughts'.

The steel-hulled, five-masted barque *France II*, built by Chantiers de la Gironde, Bordeaux, in 1911 was, at 5866 gross tons, the largest **solely sail-powered** vessel ever constructed. She was 418ft *127.4m* overall and was wrecked in 1922.

Between 1941 and 1945, **Liberty Ships**, all-welded pre-fabricated 10,500-ton merchant ships were mass-produced in US shipyards from a simple design of 1879 from the Sunderland Co. of Newcastle-upon-Tyne, England. Henry John Kaiser (US) (1882–1967) organized the mass production of these 11 knot (20km/h) vessels, some of which were built in under five days.

Roll-on Roll-off (Ro-Ro) ferries were introduced by Preston to Larne Transport Ferry Service for freight vehicles across the North Channel, Irish Sea in 1948.

The first **nuclear-powered submarine**, USS *Nautilus* – with a length of 324ft *98.75m* overall and a displacement of 4.040 tons submerged – was commissioned in 1954. On 3 August 1958 (under the command of Cdr. William R. Anderson USN (*b.*1921)) she reached the North Pole under the ice cap.

The world's first **nuclear-powered surface ship** was the *Lenin*, built in Leningrad (now St Petersburg) in 1957. She was built to be an ice-breaker of 16,000 tons with a length of 440ft *134m* and was powered by three nuclear reactors.

Hovercraft (Air Cushion Vehicles) were patented on 12 December 1955 by Christopher Cockerell (Eng) (1910-99). The maiden flight was by the 4-ton Saunders-Roe *SR-N1* at Cowes, Isle of Wight, in 1959.

The first public hovercraft service was across the Dee Estuary in north Wales by the 60 knot, 24-passenger Vickers-Armstrong *VA-3.* Regular flights of the craft started on 20 July 1962.

In 1980, the **tanker** *Seawise Giant* was lengthened in the Nippon Kokan shipyard in Japan to 1504ft *458.45m.* Her draught is 80ft 9in *24.61m* and beam 225ft 11in *68.86m.*

AD 2000

Underwater giant

In 1980, NATO revealed the launch of the first of the Soviet Union's monster 557.5ft *170m* long submarines of the

Typhoon class. They were believed to have a dived displacement of 20,000 tonnes, and to be armed with 20 55NX missiles with a 4800 nautical mile range.

A return to the romance of sail was made with the first ever sailing liners, *Wind Star* and *Wind Song*, built in France in 1986. The 440ft *134m* boats have four masts carrying 21,528 sq ft *2000sq m* of sail which is controlled by computer.

A hovercraft took the transatlantic speed record in June 1990. Hoverspeed *Great Britain* made the crossing in 3 days, 7 hours and 55 min.

A census of world shipping in April 1998 showed 28,073 ships of 1000 or more gross tons under 51 national flags, with an aggregate gross tonnage of 483,757,000. Of these, 6917 were tankers and 2238 were container ships.

By 2001, shipping could be revolutionized by the **FastShip**, designed by David Giles. These 750ft *228m* ships will be powered by water-jet engines, can reach 39 knots. They will ply a route across the Atlantic between Cherbourg, France, and Philadelphia, USA, where the harbours are being extended to take them.

At the end of the 2nd millennium, the gondola – a wooden, barge-shaped boat propelled by one or more standing oarsmen or gondoliers – is still in demand on the busy canals of the Italian city Venice.

Seamanship and navigation

BEFORE AD 1

Watching currents and stars

Early seafarers combined their extensive knowledge of local wind and sea current directions with observation of seabirds, sea fauna, water temperatures and many other factors to find their way. **Polynesian** peoples navigated thousands of miles following these indications and the positions of the stars.

The Ancient **Chinese** were the first to use the principle that a magnetized iron needle will swing toward magnetic north (close to but not identical with true north). They used pieces of magnetite – iron oxide or, as it was known, lodestone – as early as 2500BC.

Lighthouses to indicate dangerous rocks or sandbars were first used in the Mediterranean. These first lighthouses used torches of blazing pitch to warn sailors of hazards.

Greek poet Lesches of Mytilene described the first known lighthouse at Sigeum (now Cape Inchisari, Turkey), built *c.*650BC. The Pharos of **Alexandria** in Egypt, built in 280BC, was one of the tallest structures of its time at 440ft *135m.*

AD 1

Navigating by depth

Coastal navigation can also be aided with **soundings** to ascertain the depth of water. Taking soundings not only guards against the vessel going aground but can, when combined with knowledge of undersea topography, give some idea of its whereabouts.

The **Vikings** (8th to 11th century) used a lead weight on a rope to take soundings. The rope was measured against the leadsman's outstretched arms and told off in fathoms (Norse *fathmr,* armspan). The lead had a hollow in the base which was filled with tallow and this could pick up sand or mud from the seabed which could also give some indications of the vessel's location.

AD 1000

First compass

Rudimentary magnetic **compasses** were first used by Mediterranean seafarers *c.*1150. The magnetic needle was floated in a bowl of water so that it could swing freely.

The earliest reference to the **cross-staff**, an instrument for establishing the angle of altitude of heavenly bodies, was *c.*1514. It took the shape of a long staff with a short upright crosspiece. The navigator lined the staff up with the horizon and used the scale on the crosspiece to read off the altitude of the heavenly body. Because the height of the Sun or a star above the horizon changes with latitude the angle it made with the horizon could be used to work out the ship's location.

Later devices for the same purpose included the **backstaff**, invented by John Davys (Eng) (*c.*1550–1605), and the reflecting **quadrant**, invented in 1731 by John Hadley (Eng) (1682–1744).

In 1569, a major breakthrough in chart-making came with the invention by Gerardus **Mercator** (Flemish) (1512–94) of the projection

The captain of a cruise ship checks his course on a marine chart. The British Admiralty initiated the first charts in 1801 from their own surveys. By the 20th century some 3500 Admiralty charts covered all the world's waters.

Captain and mate have a great array of instruments at their fingertips as they keep a close watch forward. The gyroscopic compass – which always maintains a northerly orientation despite the roll and movements of the ship – was developed in 1907 by Franz Anschütz-Kaempfe (Ger) (1872–1931). It was a great advance as it meant that a course could be steered consistently. It paved the way for later automatic pilots.

which bears his name. He solved the problem of depicting the surface of the globe on a flat sheet of paper by making the meridians (lines of longitude) vertical and by varying the space between the 'parallels' in proportion to their latitude. Thus, a ship's course could be represented by a straight line.

The ship's **log** was a journal of the ship's course and each day an estimate of the distance travelled was entered. The equation of speed against time was at first ascertained with the 'Dutchman's log', simply a log

US Navy cadets practise using sextants. Traditionally a navigator used the sextant to read the angle made by the Sun or a star with the horizon, and so worked out local time. Then he compared this with a chronometer – a very accurate timepiece set at Greenwich Mean Time – and was able to calculate the ship's longitude.

thrown overboard from the bows (front) of the ship and timed on its arrival at the stern (rear).

This system was refined by the English mathematician

and surveyor Richard Norwood (c.1590–1675) who developed the idea of throwing the log over the stern on a line knotted at intervals and timing the paying out of the line with an hourglass. This gave rise to the expression of speed in '**knots**' (1 nautical mile per hour, 1.15mph *1.85km/h*).

In 1730, French engineer Henri Pitot (1695–1771) invented the device which ultimately superseded the patent log. The **pitometer** protrudes through the bottom of a ship's hull and measures the pressure of fluid against openings at the front and at the sides. This crucial device was only perfected in the 19th century.

In areas where the seabed is shifting sandbars and shoals, **lightships** took the place of lighthouses. The first such ship was the *Nore* in the Thames Estuary, off Chatham, Kent, in 1732.

In 1759, the **Eddystone lighthouse** was built on the reef off Plymouth Sound, England. Designed by the English engineer John Smeaton (1724–92), the Eddystone light was the first hyperbolic-shaped lighthouse.

Robert Stevenson (Scot) (1772–1850) invented

flashing and intermittent lights for lighthouses, thus allowing them to be distinguished by their signals.

Compasses in ships have to be 'swung' each time the ship sets off on a voyage. Whatever deviation the compass gives from magnetic north is tabulated against a set series of bearings. One difficulty was that any iron in the ship itself would affect the compass. Matthew Flinders (Eng) (1774–1814) invented the **Flinders' bar**, an iron bar in the compass case which could be adjusted to offset the effect of accidental deviation.

The British Admiralty compiled its Regulations for the Prevention of Collisions at Sea in 1862, with its standard codes of **signals and lights**. It was accepted internationally in 1889.

The mechanical method of depth sounding was superseded by the **echo sounder**, invented in 1912 by Alexander Behm (Ger). This computes the depth by timing a pulse of sound bounced off the sea bed.

AD 2000

Space-age navigation

Radio navigation uses signals given out by two or more radio transmitters to fix a position. This, in turn, in the 1970s began to be superseded by **satellite navigation**.

The **Navstar** Global Positioning System (GPS) collates signals from three or more satellites, using the time the signal takes to reach the ship to obtain a position accurate to a few metres. By the early 21st century, the Navstar system will have 18 satellites in operation.

Moving by land

BEFORE AD 1

Two feet, not four

About 4 million years ago, early humans' upright mode of **walking** distinguished them from the great apes of Africa. This is demonstrated by a string of footprints made by *Australopithecus africanus* that was preserved in volcanic ash for *c*.3.68 million years at Laetoli, Tanzania.

With the building of the first crude **toboggans** in Scandinavia, probably before *c*.7000BC, humans first moved on icy slopes faster than they could run on the flat.

The domestication of **draught animals** revolutionized transport. They were used first to drag loads, to act as pack animals and to carry mounted humans. Oxen were harnessed for their traction power in Mesopotamia as early as *c*.6000BC. The first evidence of horses being ridden comes from 4570BC at Dereivka in the Ukraine.

Trackways between water sources and hunting grounds left few traces. The earliest known example is the Neolithic timber section of 6000ft *1800m* of the Sweet track in the Somerset Levels, England, which has been precisely dated by tree-rings to 3806BC.

The development of the **wheel** dates from 3550–3400BC in Mesopotamia (modern Iraq/Iran). The earliest evidence is a pictographic character showing a sledge on four solid wheels found on an early Sumerian account tablet in Uruk (Biblical Erech, modern Warka) in present-day southern Iraq.

Two-wheeled **chariots** – used for raiding and warring – appeared *c*.2000BC. Their solid wheels were quickly followed by the invention of spoked wheels in east-central Anatolia, Turkey, by *c*.1900BC.

AD 1

Roman roads

Moving by land was slow and difficult until the Roman Empire constructed its vast network of **military roads**. At its peak under Emperor Trajan (AD52–117), the international Roman road system covered an estimated 53,000 miles *85,000km*.

The **Silk Road** was forged as early as 130BC. At the height of Chinese and Indian trading in AD200, it ran 4000 miles *6400km* from Shanghai and Xian in China to the Levant, and via the sea to Cadiz (then Gades) in southern Spain.

Roads were wholly neglected from the fall of the Roman Empire until the time of **Charlemagne** (742–814), the Germanic leader who became Holy Roman Emperor. He saw the need to improve roads to promote commerce.

In the 8th–9th centuries the **Vikings** established a long trade route, the Varangian road, linking the Baltic with the Middle East via Russia.

AD 1000

Mountain roadway

Perhaps the most awe-inspiring early road system was established in South America by the Incas (1200–1532). They had no wheeled vehicles but engineered tracks to be followed by people and pack animals – such as llamas. The network ran 3400 miles *5470km,* the length of the Andes as far south as Santiago in Chile. The track had rock steps cut in mountainsides and suspension bridges over streams.

In the 18th century, John Metcalf (1717–1810) pioneered the renaissance of road-building in 1765–92 in England. He ran a stagecoach between York and Knaresborough and was responsible for the construction of 185 miles *298km* of road in Lancashire and Yorkshire.

Pierre-Marie-Jérôme Trésaguet (Fr) (1716–96) led

This stone track at Macchu Picchu, the ruined Inca city high in the Peruvian Andes, was part of a vast network of roads created by Inca roadbuilders between the 13th and 16th centuries. Macchu Picchu was never found by the Spanish conquistadors; it was abandoned by the Incas after the conquest and remained a 'lost city' until discovered by Hiram Bingham (US) (1875–1956) in 1911.

the way in improved road building methods that provided a smoother surface. He made workers dig out a 10in *25cm* foundation in which they laid larger flat stones that were then covered with a layer of smaller stones. Thomas Telford (Scot)

(1757–1834), emphasized the need for gentle gradients of not more than 1:30. He built more than 1000 miles *1600km* of road.

Telford's contemporary and fellow Scot John Loudon McAdam (1756–1836) also revolutionized road-building when he realised that Trésaguet's system of cutting a trench to lay the road foundations inevitably led to flooding. Instead, McAdam elevated his roads above the level of the land.

The first modern road to be layered with bituminous material was Vauxhall Bridge Road, London, in 1835. **Asphalt**, a mixture of bitumen and stone, was first used in Rue Saint-Honoré, Paris in 1858 – and from then on, with the development of public transport systems and enormous increase in traffic with the motor car, road and highway development was never-ending.

Road safety, too, became important. The world's first **traffic light** was installed in 1868 for the benefit of Members of Parliament at Bridge Street and Palace Yard, London. It was a cast-iron column 22ft *6.7m* tall and gas-lit with a green (caution) and red (stop) light.

Electric traffic lights were first installed at Euclid Street and 105th Street, Cleveland, Ohio, in 1914.

A new concept in road design, the **parkway**, was pioneered in the USA by William Niles White who masterminded the Bronx River Parkway between 1916 and 1925. This was 15 miles *24km* of four-lane carriageway with parkland on either side.

The parkway was followed by the **freeway** or **motorway**. Italy built the first autostrada from Milan to Varese (53 miles *85km*) in 1924. It was privately financed and paid for with tolls.

Germany followed with a freeway or **autobahn** between Bonn and Cologne, built between 1929 and 1932. During the 1930s and early 1940s, a national network of 4000 miles *6400km* of Reichsautobahnen (state motorways) was created.

In the USA, the spread of the freeway was facilitated by **tolls**. The Pennsylvania turnpike, completed in 1940, ran 327 miles *526km* from the Ohio border to Philadelphia, and was one of the first to have roadside restaurants and filling stations. France introduced tolls – *péage* – on their first **autoroutes** or motorways in 1955.

AD 2000

Long roads, low speeds

The US Congress allocated $25,000 million in 1956 for the National Inter-State Highway system which was eventually to be 44,000 miles *70,000km*. Meanwhile, Italy completed the 500 mile *800km* Autostrade del Sole from Milan to Naples in 1964.

The growing politicization of petroleum supply led to the 1973–4 oil crisis, when major oil-exporting countries inflated oil prices. The USA imposed a Federal **speed limit** of 55mph *88.5km/h* to save fuel. It was repealed in 1995 when nine states allowed 75mph *120.7km/h* on Interstate Highways.

The freeway or motorway was designed to create bands of fast-moving traffic uninterrupted by access from either side. Monster intersections between motorways became increasingly common in the last three decades of the century.

Railways

At 6am on 10 January 1863, the world's first underground railway – later referred to as the Metropolitan tube line – opened to take passengers between Farringdon Street and Paddington in London. It had seven stations and was 4 miles 6.4km long.

BEFORE AD1

Tracks in Babylon

The **Babylonians** were probably the first to run wheeled vehicles on tracks. Parallel lines of grooved stone blocks have been found in Babylon (modern Iraq) and dated to *c.*2250BC. The gauge was *c.*4ft 11in *1500mm*.

The Ancient **Greeks** also left evidence of grooved stone wagonways, which ran 5.5 miles *8.8km* between the city of Athens and the seaport of Piraeus, where the Athenian Navy (established 470BC) was based. The tracks formed part of the fortifications known as the Long Walls, which were built in 461–456BC, but destroyed by an attacking force of Spartans in 404BC.

AD 1000

Mediaeval wagons

The earliest pictorial evidence of **wagonways** dates from *c.*1350 and depicts a miner pushing a square vehicle in a stained glass window of the Minster at Freibert-im-Breisgau, in the area of the Schauninsland mines of Germany. *Chariots sur rail* or **rail**

chariots moved by human muscle power were used in local mines in Leberthal, Alsace, in 1550.

A 16th-century mine wagon and some wooden track with a 18.72in *480mm* gauge survive – together with a single-bladed switch point – from a Transylvanian gold mine (now Siebenbürgen, Romania). The find may be the earliest evidence of rail's characteristic flanged (wooden) wheels and points.

The word **railway** was first used in 1681. It was applied to a section of track 2.5 miles *4km* north-east of Stourbridge, England. On 9 June 1758, the first railway operation to be authorized by the Parliament of Great Britain was a colliery 'wagonway', established and run by Charles Brandling (1758–1826). It linked Middleton to Leeds, Yorkshire.

A first standardization of rail **gauges** – albeit for wooden rails – was established in 1764–5 on a track running from Willington Quay to Killingworth Moor Collieries, Tyneside, England. The track measured 4ft 8.5in *1.435m* and covered a distance of 3 miles *4.8km*.

The world's earliest railed automotive **engine** to be built was designed by Cornish-born English engineer Richard Trevithick (1771–1833) in 1803. His steam-powered, coal-fired locomotive *New Castle* had a single horizontal cylinder and weighed some 5 tons without water on board.

It first ran on 21 February 1804 on unflanged wheels on a pre-existing mining wagonway laid on a bed of L-section cast iron plate rails. The wagonway was built to haul wagons of South Wales iron ore from the Pen-y-Darren Ironworks near Merthyr Tydfil to the Abercynon Glamorganshire Canal wharf – a distance of 9.5 miles *15km*.

On the following day Trevithick's engine proved itself to be capable of hauling a load of 10 tons of iron bars with 70 uninvited passengers at a speed of 4mph *6.4km/h*. However, the track soon proved itself

In 1881 American sleeping car entrepreneur George Mortimer Pullman built a town in Illinois– called Pullman City – for his employees. It is now part of Chicago. In the early days all Pullman porters were African Americans; they were paid no wages and had to survive on passengers' tips.

to be unequal to its gross train weight of 25 tons. All four wheels were driven by external cog gearing. The *New Castle* was said by its ebullient designer to be 'completely manageable by only one man'.

A London, Midland and Scottish Railway diesel-electric locomotive awaits a signal at Derby, England. The first demonstration of a locomotive powered by diesel fuel came in 1898. The subsequent success of diesel (and diesel-electric) engines was due to the earlier invention in 1886–90 of compression ignition by H. Stuart Ackroyd (GB) (1864–1927).

The Trevithick principle was used in 1805 by John Steel (*c*.1780–*c*.1825) for a locomotive with flanged wheels, built by John Whinfield. However, like the *New Castle* it also proved to be too heavy for the then existing wagonways.

The third Trevithick locomotive was the *Catch me who can*, constructed by John Urpeth Rastrick (1780–1856). This ran as a novelty on a circular track in London in July and August 1808, and attracted considerable crowds willing to pay the fare of one shilling per ride.

In 1816–27 Trevithick moved to South America, where his steam engines were put to use in the silver mines.

The era of steam-powered propulsion lasted 178 years. By 1982 only one railway works in the world was still building steam locomotives – at Datong, 170 miles *275km* west of Beijing in Shanxi Province, China.

LANDMARKS IN RAILWAYS

1840 Paddington, London: Daniel **Gooch** (GB) (1816–89) built the first *Firefly* for the Great Western Railway (7ft *2.13m* gauge). It could attain 50mph *80km/h*.

1842 Glasgow–Edinburgh line, Scotland: Robert Davidson (Scot) (1804–94) ran his pioneer **electric freight locomotive** at 3.75mph *6km/h*. Luddite railway workers, fearful for their livelihood, destroyed the engine in Perth.

1846 London: The **Gauge Act**, 1846, fixed the distance between rails at 4ft 8.5in *1.4531m*. This measure was adopted throughout continental Europe, except for in Spain and Russia.

1847 Fairfield, Bow, east London: The *Fairfield* was the first rail-car with a capacity for **48 passengers**. It had six wheels and a vertical steam boiler and could achieve a steady 40mph *65km/h*. It went into service in 1848 on the Tiverton branch of the Bristol and Exeter Railway.

1847 London: William Bridge Adams (1797–1872) patented the **fish plate** for joining lengths of rail.

1853 Troy, New York: The Hudson River Railroad Co. first introduced **corridor carriages**. These coaches – 45ft *13.71m* in length – were built by Messrs Eaton and Gilbert.

1854 Austria and northern Italy: Karl von Ghega (1802–60) completed the construction of the first **trans-Alpine railway**. The line ran between Vienna, Austria, and Trieste.

1854 USA: **Air conditioning** was first installed on a train. It was fitted in carriages on the New York and Erie railroad.

1856 Chicago, Illinois: **Sleeping state rooms** were introduced by the Illinois Central Railroad Co. on their 'Gothic' rolling stock.

1857 Derby Station, England: The Midland Railway laid the first **steel rails**.

1859 Bloomington, Illinois: George **Pullman** (US) (1831–97) ran his first converted sleeping car on the Chicago and Alton Railroad. Bunks were provided – but without bedding – on the Cumberland Valley Railroad in Pennsylvania, as early as 1836.

1863 Philadelphia, Pennsylvania: Philadelphia, Wilmington and Baltimore Railroad trains put the first **dining cars** into service. They offered a selection from self-service buffets.

1867 Canada: Regular **dining cars** were introduced on the Great Western Railroad by Pullman (see 1859).

1869 Canada: The **Trans-Canada railroad** opened, linking the Atlantic seaboard with the Pacific.

1877 Paris: Joseph Monier (Fr) (1823–1906) patented reinforced **concrete ties** for use in place of wooden rail track sleepers.

1879 Berlin: The world's first **electric passenger railway** was built by Werner von Siemens (Ger) (1816–82) for use in Berlin. The oval test track was of 39.33in *1m* gauge and *c*.328 yards *300m* in length, for trains carrying 30 passengers in 3 carriages.

The electric motor delivered 3hp, picking up current and 150 volts from a central 'third' rail, and reaching a top speed of 4mph *6.5km/h*.

1881 Berlin: Werner von Siemens' first electric general **passenger**-carrying service opened in the Berlin suburb of Lichterfelde.

1882 Zaucheroda, Saxony: Siemens and Halske first electrified an underground **mine** hauling rail line.

1883 Chicago, Illinois: The 15hp electric locomotive *The Judge* hauled the train on the first **elevated railroad**. It was at the Chicago Railway Exposition on a 1550ft *473m* long track.

1886 Pittsburgh, Pennsylvania: George Westinghouse (US) (1846–1914) introduced the first automatic **air brakes**.

1886 Berne, Switzerland: The Second International Berne Conference fixed maximum rail **gauges** at 4ft 9.6in/4ft 8.496in *1.463/1.435m*.

1888 Richmond, Virginia: Frank J. Sprague (US) (1857–1934) ran the earliest **electric tramway**, over a 12 mile *19.3km* track.

1888 Ireland: The earliest **monorail** was set up by Charles Lavigne on a 9.25 mile *14.9km* track from Listowel to Ballybunnion, County Kerry.

1890 London: The City and South London Railway was the first electric **underground passenger railway**. It linked the Monument in the City of London to the southern suburb of Stockwell, passing in a deep tunnel beneath the River Thames.

1903 Germany: An electrically powered Siemens and Halske 12-wheeled railcar reached 126.1mph *203km/h* between Marienfeld and Berlin on 6 October. One powered with an AEG motor reached 130.6mph *210.2km/h* on 23 October.

1904 Siberia: The **Trans-Siberian railway** was completed, linking Moscow with Vladivostok. Work had begun in 1891.

1931 Germany: A propeller-driven Krackenberg petrol railcar reached 142.9mph *230km/h* over a 6.2 mile *10km* stretch between Karstädt and Dergenthin.

1938 Hertfordshire, England: The LNER (London and North-Eastern Railway) 'A4' class Mallard reached 126mph *202.7km/h* – an **all-time speed record for steam traction –** on Stoke Bank, near Essendine, while pulling seven coaches. The driver was Joseph Duddington.

1953 France: The French national railway SNCF's 4300hp 106-ton CoCo electric locomotive No. 7121 reached 150.9mph *248.8km/h* while pulling three coaches between Dijon and Beaune in eastern France.

1955 France: SNCF's CoCo No. 7107 reached 205.6mph *330.9km/h* between Facture and Morceaux on the Bordeaux line.

1965 Tokyo–Osaka, Japan: The world's first scheduled rail service to travel at **more than 100mph** *160.93km/h* was inaugurated on the Tokaido line. It travelled 320.6 miles *516km* between Tokyo and Osaka in 3 hours 10 minutes to average 101.3mph *163.02km/h*.

1974 Colorado, USA: The US Linear Induction Motor reached 243mph *391km/h* in tests at Pueblo, Colorado.

1994 France–England: The 31 mile *49.9km* **Channel Tunnel** between England and France was completed; 23.6 miles *38km* ran beneath the seabed. It was officially opened on 6 May. The first Eurostar service ran in November between Waterloo, London, and the Gare du Nord, Paris, in 3 hours.

1997 Yamanashi, Japan: An unmanned **maglev** (magnetic levitation) vehicle reached 341.7 mph *550km/h* in tests.

1998 Argentina–Chile: Feasibility studies begin for a 15.5 mile *25km* tunnel through the Andes.

The nose of the French TGV (Train à Grande Vitesse) is aerodynamically sleek for greater speed. In 1990 the TGV hit 320mph *515km/h* between Courtalain (Eure et Loire) and Tours (Indre et Loire).

Bicycles

The early bicycle or velocipede was put into production by the Parisian coachmakers and wheelwrights Pierre (1813–83) and Ernest (1842–82) Michaud, probably in 1863. In 1866 Pierre Lallemont (Fr) of Paris took out a US patent for an iron-wheeled, rotary-cranked bicycle – known as a 'bone shaker' – based on the Michaud invention on which he had worked.

Off-road sports cycling attracted many devotees from the 1970s on. The BMX (bicycle motocross) is a low-gear, heavy-frame 'scrambling' bike.

The **forerunner of the bicycle** was the *laufmaschine* ('running machine') invented in 1817 by Freiherr Karl Drais von Sauerbronn (Ger) (1785–1851). The rider

propelled himself over the ground with his feet.

The earliest **self-propelled bicycle** with swinging crank pedals was built in Scotland by Kirkpatrick McMillan (1810–78) in c.1840.

On 10 December 1845 the Scot Robert William Thomson (1822–73) took out a patent for the first **pneumatic tyre** called an 'Improvement in Carriage Wheels which is also applicable to other rolling bodies'. However, his unvulcanized rubber became soft and tacky unless the weather was cold.

The **first bicycle race** is usually identified as having taken place in Parc de St Cloud, Paris, in May 1868. In fact there were five provincial races staged before this date. Dr James Moore (GB) (1847–1935) won the

race at St Cloud over 0.7 miles *1km* from a field of five in 2 minutes 35 seconds.

E. Meyer (Fr) patented his **tension wheel** in 1869. He won prizes at the Pré-Catalan Exhibition in Paris of November 1–5 that year, so stimulating the development of the suspension wheel in both France and Britain.

In 1870, James Starley (GB) (1831–81) developed his prototype 'Ordinary' configuration, with its large diameter driving wheel under the rider and a trailing, much smaller, rear wheel. From 1891 this was referred to as a **penny farthing**. In 1877 Starley invented the differential gear for his Coventry Salvo tricycle – the first fully successful chain driven machine.

In 1885 John Kemp Starley (GB) (1854–1901) first exhibited his successful and race-winning Rover Safety Bicycle with a diamond shaped frame. Its geometry allowed the rider to adjust his

height and position of his seat and the handlebars.

John Boyd **Dunlop** (Scot) (1840–1921) re-invented the pneumatic bicycle tyre in 1888. Though Thomson had patented the idea in 1845, Dunlop produced the first commercially available vulcanized rubber tyres. His company became the Dunlop Rubber Company in 1889.

H. Sturmey and J. Archer developed the **Sturmey-Archer gear** c.1901, with three gears inside the rear wheel hub. The cycle company **Raleigh** bought the rights to them in 1902.

Alexander Moulton (GB) (b.1920) introduced in 1962 the first departure from the 1893 diamond frame, with his small 16in *40cm* cross frame and patent rubberized suspension. But cycles were shortly to break away from the norm altogether. The **Chopper** with its high handlebars and banana-shaped seat, was the first of the 'action bicycles'. Launched in the USA in 1969, the design sold 750,000 in the next ten years.

Cycling took on another dimension with the spread of the **mountain bike** in the 1970s and 1980s. Mountain bikes first appeared in California, USA, from around 1973 when cyclists made lightweight cycle frames with up to 21 gears and developed wider stronger wheels and deep-tread tyres for cycling in the mountains of Marin County. Adventure cycling became a popular new sport and the bikes spread worldwide. In 1989 900,000 mountain bikes were sold.

The automobile

The motor car is probably the invention that has changed life on Earth most radically in the 20th century. Cars increase people's freedom to move around, and at the end of the century their popularity in countries across the world shows no sign of falling away.

But the freedom comes at a price, not least that **road-building swallows land** at great public expense. In 1996, China was increasing its road network at a rate of 8078 miles *13,000km* per year. The longest new road project in the late 1990s was Pakistan's Indus Valley Highway – 745 miles *1200km* at a projected $200 million cost.

Road accidents claim thousands of lives a year. In 1999, China had the most road deaths of any country in the world, with a total of 83 million. The World Health Organisation reports the worst road safety records in developing countries, with 150 deaths per 10,000 vehicles in Ethiopia in 1994. Moreover, air pollution comes largely from vehicle emissions. In 1998, the World Bank's Green Top 10 Plan

reported that carbon dioxide emissions had increased by 25% since the 1992 Rio environmental summit.

The history of the car began with the steam-powered gun carriage built by the French military engineer Nicolas-Joseph **Cugnot** (1725–1804) in 1769. The carriage was designed for the transport of artillery and progressed at a stately 3mph *5km/h*. Steam power was the norm for the next 100 years. In 1801, Cornish mining engineer Richard **Trevithick** (1771–1833) achieved around 9mph *14.5km/h* with a steam carriage on a stretch of road at Camborne, Cornwall.

The first patent for an internal combustion gas engine was posted in 1859 by Jean Etienne **Lenoir** (1822–1900), a Belgian inventor, and in 1860 he built a vehicle for the engine. These early vehicles caused such **alarm** that in Britain the 'Red Flag' Act was passed in 1865, requiring a man

carrying a red warning flag to precede every vehicle. The Locomotives on Highways Act imposed a 4mph *6.4km/h* speed limit in 'open country' and half that in towns. The 1896 Amendment (or Emancipation) Act dispensed with the flag man for 'light locomotives' – those of less than 3 tons.

The first petrol-driven internal combustion engine was built by the German engineers Gottlieb **Daimler** (1834–1900) and Karl **Benz** (1844–1929) in 1885.

In the USA, the first **petrol-driven motorcar** was built by the brothers Charles and Frank Duryea in 1892. In the same year Alexander T. Brown (US) (1854–1929) and George F. Stillmen (US) (1858–1906) took out a patent for the first removable pneumatic tyres. By 1895, there were 300 car manufacturers in the USA.

At first, cars were built along the same lines as horse-drawn carriages but with engines. The first cars which looked recognizably like cars were the **Panhard** built by René Panhard (Fr) (1841– 1908) in 1891 with its engine mounted on a wooden chassis, a front radiator and a sliding pinion gearbox, and Daimler's **Mercedes**, built in 1901, which had a pressed steel chassis and an in-line four-cylinder engine. The Mercedes was capable of 53mph *86km/h* – so in 15 years, the speed of the car had risen by *c.*50mph *81km/h*.

Traffic grinds to a halt on the Periferico Norte in Mexico City. Congestion on city roads worsens air pollution and gives rise to the very modern phenomenon of 'road rage'.

HOW CAR USE HAS GROWN

Year	Number of vehicles*
1930	35 million
1940	45 million
1950	63 million
1960	119 million
1980	399 million
1990	548 million
1995	632 million
1997	665.7 million

* World totals

VEHICLE USE BY COUNTRY

Country	No. of vehicles per 1000 people*
USA	816
Italy	575
Canada	557
Japan	539
Germany	536
France	536
UK	478
Belgium	469
Spain	451
Sweden	449
China	8
India	6
World	**114.3**

* 1997

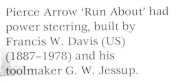
Pierce Arrow 'Run About' had power steering, built by Francis W. Davis (US) (1887–1978) and his toolmaker G. W. Jessup.

1934 Streamlined production car: *US* The Chrysler Air Flow Coupé had flush-mounted headlights and bold re-styling. The term coupé, meaning a short, closed car with two seats was used for automobiles from 1908.

1934 Front-wheel drive: *Paris, France* Pierre Fenaille (1888–1967) launched his Traction Avant (front-wheel drive) 4 door **Citroen** model.

1936 Diesel-engined cars: *Germany* The earliest series production was the 1936 Mercedes 260D.

1938 Indicators: *US* The first car with front and rear flashers was a Buick.

1940 Jeep: *Butler, Pennsylvania* The first jeep was designed in 18 hours by Karl K. Probst (US) (1884–1963) for American Bantam Car Co. The US Army's 40hp, 4 wheel drive, 1840lb *834kg* Light Command and Reconnaissance Car was known as Bantam, Blitz-Buggy, Gnat, Jeep and Peep but the name Jeep stuck.

1951 Fully automated plant: *Cleveland, Ohio* The first fully automated automobile plant went into production making Fords with 42 machines along a 545ft *175m* line.

1954 Fuel injection: *Germany* The 1954 Mercedes-Benz 300SL became the first road-going model using this mechanism.

1954 Rotary engine: *Germany* Felix Wankel (1902–88) of Lindau, Bavaria, demonstrated his rotary

British motor manufacturer Vauxhall first made a name for itself with the racy 3-litre 'Prince Henry' model capable of 75mph *120km/h*, which was on sale from 1911. This elegant traveller, the Vintage, was built in 1931 – a time when luxurious motor cruises were in fashion.

MILESTONES IN AUTO MANUFACTURE

1901 Mass production: *Detroit, Michigan* The earliest model to be constructed at a rate of more than ten cars per week was the $650, 20mph *32km/h* Curved Dash Olds. Production of Olds was 425 in 1901, 3750 in 1902 and rose to 5460 in 1904.

1901 Pre-selected gear: *Sparkbrook, Birmingham, England* F. W. Lanchester mounted the first pre-selector gearbox. This gearbox was first fitted to Armstrong-Siddeleys in Britain and to Talbots in France.

1908 Mass production: *Detroit* US industrialist Henry Ford (1863–1947) started the mass production of his famous Model T Ford. Continuous conveyor belts were installed in 1912 at Ford's new Highland Park factory in Detroit. A Model T cost $260 in 1925.

1911 Self-starter: *Detroit* Charles Kettering (US) (1876–1958) perfected his Delco (derived from Dayton Engineering Laboratories Co.) starter for the Cadillac Motor Car Co.

1919 Mechanical windscreen wipers: *Buffalo, New York* The Trico Corporation marketed vacuum-operated compressed air wipers, devised by William Folberth (US) of Cleveland, Ohio.

1923 Diesel-engined vehicles: *Germany* Benz produced diesel-powered lorries.

1923 Colour choice: *Bordeaux, France* The Ford plant in France first offered a choice of colours.

1926 Power steering: *Waltham, Massachusetts* The

Henry Ford, with his pioneering use of mass production, brought affordable motoring to the American public. The Ford Model T sold 15 million in 1908–27. Its successor, the Model A, was released on 2 December 1927.

piston engine.

1958 Head restraints: *USA* Introduced on US 1959 models in an attempt to prevent whiplash injuries.

1959 Transverse engine: *England* Alex Issigonis (1906–88) designed the 988cc Morris Mini for the British Motor Corporation (BMC).

1968 Anti-lock brakes: *US* Ford introduced rear wheel anti-lock brakes in 1969 Thunderbirds and Lincolns while Chrysler installed 4-wheel anti-lock brakes in 1971 models.

1970 Unleaded fuel: *USA* From 1970 all US engines were designed to run on unleaded fuel by Federal Order.

1970 Ceramic engines: *Solihull, England* The use of non-metallic materials was pioneered at the Lucas Research Centre with the ceramic Sialon invented by Kenneth H. Jack (*b*.1918) and Y. Oyama of Tokyo.

1973 Air cushion or bag: *USA* 'Instantly' inflating anti-shock air-bags were first produced by General Motors in Detroit.

1982 Solar-powered car: *Australia* Hans Tholstrup and Larry Perkins ran their experimental Solar Trek I

2537 miles *4084km* across South Australia in 172 running hours, averaging 14.71mph *23.7km/h*.

1983 Four-wheel drive: *Germany* The first mass-produced 4 wheel drive saloon model was the Audi 80 Quattro in 1983.

1985 Lean burn engines: *England* The Ford Motor Co. research station at Dunton, Essex, announced 'variable inlet geometry' to achieve fuel economy.

1986 Four-wheel steering (4WS): *Japan* Nissan's Skyline became the first 4WS commercial model.

1986 Electronic suspension: *Sweden* Volvo introduced their CCS system by which a microprocessor can transmit adjustments to each wheel 3000 times/sec.

1989 Electronic gear box: *England* Gear ratios changeable by a forefinger pressing on a tab were fitted by John Barnard (GB) (*b*.1946) to the 1989 Ferrari Formula 1 cars.

1990 Collapsible steering wheel: *Germany* First fitted to Audi's 1991 models, the Procon Ten was activated in front-end collisions to jerk or retract the steering wheel into the dashboard.

1990 Twin-engined car: *Germany* The Audi Duo combined a petrol or diesel engine for the front wheels with an electric engine for the rear wheels.

1990 Solar car: *Japan* Kyocera's SCU-O, with 640 solar cells, gave a top speed of 37mph *60km/h*.

1992 Self-parking car: *Germany* The Volkswagen Futura used laser sensors to park automatically in a pre-selected parking space.

1997 Zero-Level Emission engine: *Tokyo, Japan* Honda developed an engine capable of cutting emissions to 10% of the minimum emissions level.

1999 Fuel cell technology car: *US* DaimlerChrysler's NECAR 4 had up to three times the range of a battery-powered vehicle.

The cheap, well-sprung Citroen 2CV – named deux chevaux (two horses) because of its 2hp engine – was released in Paris in 1948 and remained in production for 42 years. It was aimed at French farmers but became a classic of no-nonsense urban style. The year 1948 also saw the release of the first Land Rovers and Morris Minors.

Progressive speed records

Humans are very **slow movers** compared with the spine-tailed swift (219.5mph *353km/h*), the cheetah (84mph *135km/h*) or the kangaroo (45mph *72km/h*). Thanks to their erect, two-legged structure, high centre of gravity and lack of a tail, ancient humans – even if being chased for their lives – would have found it hard to achieve even short bursts of 25mph *40km/h*. The **fastest modern sprinter** is Carl Lewis (US), who touched a speed of 26.95mph *43.37km/h* in the 100 metres race on 24 September 1988 during the Olympic Games in Seoul, South Korea.

This speed was probably first exceeded before 3000BC in southern Fenno-Scandia. Travelling on ice in **snow sledges** and, later, on primitive **wooden skis**, people would have reached speeds of about 35mph *55km/h*. A similar speed would have been reached by early **horse riders**, probably in Anatolia, Turkey, *c.*1400BC.

These peak speeds remained unsurpassed for three millennia – until AD1600, when the first **ice-yachts** were built for use on the frozen canals of the Netherlands. The Dutch ice yachts were capable of speeds of 50mph *80km/h* when swept along by gusting winds.

With the invention of the man-carrying **balloon** by the Montgolfier brothers in Paris (1783) and of **railways** in Pen-y-Darren, Glamorgan, Wales (1804), came the means of moving far faster.

Carl Lewis leads the field in his record-breaking 1988 Olympic bid. Lewis, the fastest runner on Earth and a spectacular long jumper, also holds the record for the most World Championship gold medals (eight) and the most Olympic medals (10).

The Grand Junction railway 2-2-2 engine *Lucifer* was the first vehicle to outspeed the ice-yacht, reaching 56.75mph *91.3km/h* at Madeley Banks, Staffordshire, England, on 13 November 1839.

In 1844, a student, Frank Ebrington, was caught in an uncoupled carriage that was dispatched down the Kingstown-Dalkey atmospheric railway, near Dublin, Ireland. They became the world's **fastest humans** by accident at an average speed of 84mph *135km/h*.

There are several ill-documented speed records claimed by out-of-control **balloons** caught in gales. One sustainable claim is that of the balloon *Atlantic* which reached *c.*90mph *145km/h* while crossing Lake Ontario on the Canada/US borders, on 2 July 1859, during its 809 mile *1301km* flight from St Louis, Missouri, to near Henderson, New York. On board were the Americans John Wise (1808–79), O. A. Gager, John L. Mountain and William Hyde.

The first humans undeniably to surpass 100mph *160.9km/h* were the crews testing the **Siemens und Halske electric engine** on the Marienfeld–Zossen track near Berlin in 1901. Two years later, on 6 October 1903, they reached a speed of 124.89mph *201km/h*; four days after that they raised the speed record again, reaching 130.61mph *210.2km/h*.

On 26 January 1907, Frederick H Marriott (US), driving the steam-powered *Wogglebug* on Ormond Beach, Florida, is believed to have

A Dutch ice-yacht similar to those that proved to be the fastest unpowered land vehicles in the 17th century. For travelling on frozen lakes and canals, wooden rails replace the sea-going hull.

touched 150mph *257.5km/h* – curiously, the only automobile ever to set an absolute speed record, albeit an unofficial one.

Aircraft now took over from steam engines, with World War I fighters such as the Martynside F.4 and the Nieuport Nighthawk known to have attained speeds of *c*.210mph *338km/h* in dives.

A string of 21 official speed records was set between the two World Wars. British pilot George Stainforth reached 415.2mph *668.2km/h* in a Supermarine S6B off Lee-on-Solent, UK, on 29 September 1931 while competing for the Schneider Cup, the international maritime aviation trophy. Fritz **Wendel** (Ger) achieved 469.22 mph *755km/h* in a Messerschmitt Me209 near Augsburg, Germany, on 26 April 1939.

On 6 July 1944, Rudolf Opitz attained 702mph *1130km/h* in an Me163V-18 Komet rocket plane over Peenemünde, Germany. Measured over land, this was a faster speed than Charles 'Chuck' Yeager's **first supersonic flight** over the Mojave Desert, California. On 14 October 1947, in the Bell X-1 *Glamorous Glennis*, Yeager reached Mach 1.105, 670mph *1078km/h*, at an altitude of 42,000ft *12,800m*.

Yeager (*b*.1923) went on to achieve 967mph *1556km/h* in the same aircraft, and then 1612mph *2594km/h* in a Bell X-1A on 12 December 1953. This record was surpassed on 7 March 1961 by Robert M. White, who attained Mach 4.43, 2905mph *4675.1km/h*, in a North American X-15 research aeroplane.

Just 36 days after White's triumph, on 12 April 1961, came the news that Yuri Gagarin (USSR) (1934–68) in Vostok I had become the first human to orbit the Earth. To attain the speed necessary for a 108-minute orbit, Gagarin's capsule was accelerated by a Soviet SL4 rocket to a speed of 17,560mph *28,260km/h* after taking off from the Cosmodrome at Tyuratam, Kazakhstan.

Gagarin's speed record was marginally overtaken by the Soviet spacecraft Voskhod 1 (1965) and Voskhod 2 (1966), but it was shattered by the US Apollo 8 mission on 21 December 1968. Frank Borman (*b*. 1928), James Lovell (*b*. 1928) and William Anders (*b*. 1933) reached 24,226mph *38,988km/h* on their return from the Moon.

The absolute speed record at the end of the 2nd millennium is 24,790mph *39,897km/h*, attained by Americans Eugene Cernan, John Watts and Thomas P. Stafford on 26 May 1969 at the re-entry of US Apollo 10 into the Earth's atmosphere after orbiting the Moon.

Chuck Yeager (US) emerges from *Glamorous Glennis*, the first of a series of record-breaking Bell X-1 rocket aircraft. He named the X-1 after his wife – just like the P-51 Mustang he flew in Europe during World War II.

Ballooning

On 21 November 1783 in Paris Frenchmen Jean Pilâtre de Rozier (1756–85) and the Marquis d'Arlandes (1746–1809) made history's first untethered balloon flight. They were aloft for 22.5 minutes and covered 6.1 miles *9.9km*.

They flew in the richly decorated 72,562ft³ *2055m³* *Montgolfière* balloon, designed and made by the French **Montgolfier brothers**, Joseph Michel (1740–1810) and Etienne Jacques (1745–99). During the flight the passengers had to beat back flames that were scorching the fabric around the balloon's neck.

The first manned hydrogen balloon flight was made in *Le Globe Aerostatique* by French physicist **Jacques Charles** (1746–1823) and Noel Roberts, one of the brothers who had made the balloon, on 1 December 1783. They took off from Paris and flew for 2 hours, reaching a maximum altitude of 1640ft *500m* and covering 22.3 miles *36km*. Charles then made a solo and alarmingly rapid ascent to nearly 9850ft *3000m*, covering a further 3 miles *4.8km* in a flight of some 35 minutes.

On 7 January 1785 Jean-Pierre Blanchard (Fr) (1753–1809) and Dr John Jeffries (US) (1744–1809) flew from the cliffs of Dover to Guisnes, France, becoming the first **balloonists to cross the English Channel**.

French scientist Joseph Louis **Gay-Lussac** (1778–1850) made two ascents in hydrogen-filled balloons to study the Earth's magnetic

The *Montgolfière* balloon that made the world's first manned untethered flight in November 1783 was 66ft *20.1m* tall – the height of a seven-storey building. Its creators, the Montgolfier brothers, were papermakers from Lyon, France.

intensity. On his second ascent, in a Meudon war balloon on 15 September 1804, he claimed to have reached 23,000ft *7000m*.

Windham William Sadler (GB) (1796–1824), with a Mr Burchan, set the **first speed record** on 7 October 1811 by covering 112 miles *180km* from Birmingham to Heckingham, Lincolnshire, England, in a gale, averaging 84mph *135km/h*.

Malcolm D. Ross (USA) (*b.*1919) and Victor A. Prather (USA) (1926–61) set the ballooning **altitude record** of 113,740ft *34,668m* on 4 May 1961 in an ascent from the US Aircraft Carrier *Antietam* in the Gulf of Mexico.

On 1 February 1966 Nicholas **Piantanida** (US) (1933–66) reached 123,800ft *37,750m* above Sioux Falls, South Dakota. He landed in Iowa but did not survive.

The unmanned Winzen Research Inc. balloon of 47.8 million ft³ *1.35 million m³* attained an altitude of 170,000ft *51,800m* over Chico, California, USA, on 27 October 1972.

American adventurer Ben L. **Abruzzo** (1930–85) made the first transatlantic balloon flight in the helium-filled *Double Eagle II*, in 1978.

The first Atlantic crossing in a hot-air balloon was made in 31 hours 41 minutes on 2–3 July 1987 by **Richard Branson** (GB) (*b.*1950) with **Per Lindstrand** (Swe) (*b.*1948) from Maine to Northern Ireland. The distance covered was a total of 3074 miles *4947km*.

The *Breitling Orbiter III* in which Bertrand Piccard and Brian Jones achieved the first balloon circumnavigation of the world had a double skin containing both helium and hot air. It used solar power to heat the helium during daylight hours and propane burners to heat the air by night.

Ben Abruzzo made the first **transpacific** crossing in the helium-filled *Double Eagle V* with three crew, from Japan, to California on 9–12 November 1981. He covered a total of 5768 miles *9244km* in 84 hours 31 minutes.

On 15–17 January 1991 Branson and Lindstrand made the first Pacific crossing in a **hot-air balloon** in 46 hours in the 2.6 million ft³ *73,600m³* *Virgin Otsuka Pacific Flyer*. They covered 4768 miles *7671.9km* from the southern tip of Japan to Lac la Matre, Yukon, Canada.

The first **circumnavigation of the world** in a balloon was completed from 1–20 March 1999 by Bertrand Piccard (Swiss) (*b.*1958) and Brian Jones (GB) (*b.*1948). In the *Breitling Orbiter III* they broke every distance and duration record with a flight of 26,602 miles *42,811km*.

Aviation

The earliest aeronautical devices were arrows, boomerangs and kites. Bows and **arrows** were used by hunters of the northern African Arterian culture possibly before 50,000BC. The oldest **boomerang** was found at Oblazow, southern Poland, and dates to c.21,000BC.

Kite-flying probably originated in China during the Zhou Dynasty c.1000BC. By c.200BC General Han Hsin is recorded to have used kites to estimate distances for military purposes.

In c.1490 Italian artist Leonardo da Vinci (1452–1519) first used the term **helicopter** (from Gk. *helix*, spiral, *pteron*, wing). He was fascinated with the idea of human flight and produced 500 sketches of possible designs for flying machines.

Emmanuel Swedenborg (then Svedbert) (1688–1772) drafted **the first design** for a powered aircraft in 1714. However, no suitable light powerful engine existed for another 185 years.

The first man-carrying free flight took place in late summer 1853. A glider built by Englishman **Sir George Cayley** (GB) (1773–1857) carried his coachman –

probably John Appleby (*b.*1833) – for 1500ft *450m*.

Several aviation pioneers built heavy, **steam-powered** machines. Frenchman Félix du Temple Rivallon de la Croix (1823–90) produced a steam-powered monoplane that made a short hop in 1874. In 1884 another steam-powered design by Aleksandr F. Mozhaiski (Rus) (1825–90) was briefly airborne. Then on 9 October 1890 French inventor **Clément Ader** (Fr) (1841–1925) took off from a ramp and flew his steam-powered, bat-winged *Eole I* for c.165ft *50m* at an altitude of c.8in *20cm*.

Others concentrated on developing ultra-light gliders. On October 10 and 22 1898 Augustus M. Herring (US) (1867–1926) made two uncontrolled hops of 50ft *15m* and 73ft *22m* over a sand beach at St Joseph, Michigan, in his compressed air-engined biplane **hang glider**. It weighed only 88lb *39.8kg*, and had a wing span of 18ft *5.84m*. English aviation pioneer **Percy Pilcher** (1866–99) died on 2 October 1899 from injuries sustained when his fourth powered glider, *Hawk*, collapsed at c.30ft *9m* altitude at Stanford Hall, Leicestershire, on 30 September 1899.

The 18 August 1901 issue of the US *Bridgeport Sunday Herald* published an eye-witness report by Richard Howell that the German-born Gustave Whitehead (1874–1927) had at 2am on 14 August 'soared through the air for fully half a mile' in his Model No. 21 bat-wing monoplane, at Fairfield Beach, near Bridgeport, Connecticut. The plane was 16ft *4.87m* long with a 20lb *9kg* air-cooled motor.

Controversy later raged over whether Whitehead was the first to realize the dream of controlled, powered flight in a heavier-than-air machine. History usually accords that honour to the Americans Wilbur (1867–1912) and Orville (1871–1948) **Wright**. After tests with gliders from 1900 near Kitty Hawk, North Carolina, the brothers succeeded on 17 December 1903 in coaxing their *Flyer* biplane, powered by a 179lb *81.2kg* engine, into the air.

After this triumph, the Wright Brothers progress was swift. At Huffman's Prairie, Dayton,

Igor Sikorsky (Rus/US) (1889–1972) was inspired to create a helicopter by boyhood study of helicopter-like designs by the Italian Leonardo da Vinci. Sikorsky made the first tethered flight of his helicopter prototype the VS-300 on 14 September 1939 at Stratford, Connecticut. A German model developed by Heinrich Focke had flown earlier, on 26 June 1936, and was the first practical helicopter.

At 10.35am on 17 December 1903 American Orville Wright became the first man proven to make a powered, sustained and controlled flight in a heavier-than-air flying machine. His brother Wilbur watched as the *Flyer*, a 12.29m *40ft 4in* wingspan biplane they had built together, took off from the sands at Kitty Hawk, North Carolina, and remained airborne for 12 long seconds.

Ohio, on 20 September 1904 Wilbur piloted the brothers' improved 16hp *Flyer II* on history's first circular flight. It took 96 seconds and was one of 105 flights that year. On 5 October 1905 Wilbur took *Flyer III*, on a flight of 24.2 miles *38.9km* in 38 minutes 3 seconds. The **first sustained aeroplane flight in Europe** was made by Brazilian-born Frenchman Alberto Santos-Dumont (1873–1932) on 23 October 1906 in Paris. He flew the *No14-bis* 197ft *59.1m* at *c*.10ft *3m* height.

The first man to be raised by a helicopter was Louis Bréguet (Fr) (1880–1955) in the tethered Bréguet-Richet No. 1 on 19 September 1907. The first free flight was made on 13 November that year by Paul Cornu (Fr) (1881–1944) in his own machine powered by a 24hp Antoinette engine. He reached a height of 6ft *1.80m* in a 20 second flight.

The first prototype of the British–French Concorde made its maiden flight on 2 March 1969 in Toulouse, France. The Soviet Union, however, won the race to produce the world's first supersonic airliner. Its Tupolev Tu144 first flew in Moscow on 31 December 1968.

Chuck Yeager, on 14 October 1947 the first man to fly faster than the speed of sound, was a World War II 'double ace' who downed 13 enemy aircraft while flying fighter escorts for heavy bombers over Germany. In the 1960s he trained test pilots for the US space programme.

On 25 July 1909 Louis Blériot (Fr) (1872–1936) became the first aviator to **fly the English Channel**, crossing from Les Baraques near Calais, France, to Dover Castle, Kent, England, in his No. XI monoplane, powered by a 25hp Anzani engine. He covered 23.5 miles *38.5km* in 36 minutes 30 seconds.

Henri Fabre (Fr) (1883–1984) achieved the first **take-off from water** in his 50hp Gnome-engined Canard Hydravion near Marseilles on 28 March 1910. **Eugene B. Ely** (US) (1886–1911), made the first take-off from a ship's deck – the US Cruiser *Birmingham* in Hampton Roads, Virginia, on 14 November 1910.

The world's first **scheduled airline service** was opened on 30 August 1914 by the American P. E. Fansler between St Petersburg and Tampa, Florida, with a Benoist flying boat, piloted by Anthony Jannus (US) (1889–1916) for the 22 mile *35.4km* route.

The **first aerial combat** occurred on 5 October 1914 – the 62nd day of World War I – when a German Aviatik was shot down in flames by a French Voisin piloted by Joseph Frantz (1890–1979).

The **first all-metal aeroplane** was the Junkers J1 built by Hugo Junkers (Ger) (1859–1935). It first flew on 12 December 1915.

On 15 June 1919 John Alcock (1892–1919) and Arthur Whitten Brown (1886–1948) completed the **first nonstop flight across the Atlantic** – 1890 miles *3024km* in a Vickers Vimy.

In 1920 the first **retractable undercarriage** was fitted – to the American Dayton-Wright RB Racer. In 1922 Wallace R. Turnbull (Can) (1870–1954) first demonstrated **variable pitch propellers** for the American Propeller Co.

On 3 May 1923 Americans Oakley Kelly and John MacReady made the first nonstop flight **across the USA** – 2650 miles *4240km* from Long Island, New York, to San Diego, California, in 26 hours 50 minutes in a Fokker T-2.

The **first in-flight refuelling** was demonstrated by two US Army Air Service de Havilland 4Bs over Rockwell Field, Coronado, California on

27–28 August 1923 with Lowell H. Smith (US) (1892–1945) in command.

In Madrid on 9 January 1923 Alejandro Gomez Spencer (1896–1984) flew the C4 **autogiro** designed by Juan de la Cierva (1895–1936) more than 2.5 miles *4km* at an altitude of 80ft *24m*. This first autogiro relied on a conventional propeller for forward propulsion and a single free-spinning rotor with hinged blades for lift. On 18 September 1928 Cierva, with Henri Bouché (Fr), flew the English Channel in another autogiro, the C8, crossing from London to Paris in 66 minutes.

Chicago and *New Orleans*, two Douglas World Cruisers (DWC) of the US Army Air Service, completed the first **round-the-world flight**, when they landed in Seattle, Washington State, on 28 September 1924. Four DWCs had set out from Seattle on 19 March but two had dropped out on the way.

Charles **Lindbergh** (US) (1902–74) completed the first nonstop solo transatlantic flight at Paris on 21 May 1927. He flew the 3614 miles *5782km* from New York in his Ryan aeroplane *Spirit of St Louis* in 33 hours 30 minutes and 29.8 seconds.

On 22 February 1928 Bert Hinkler (Aus) (1892–1933) completed the first solo flight from England to Australia when he landed in Darwin in his Avro Avian. The same year Australia's Flying Doctor Service took to the air in Queensland with Dr St Vincent Welch (1885–1961) in a De Havilland DH50.

Australians Sir Charles Kingsford-Smith (1897–1935) and Charles Ulm landed in Brisbane on 9 June 1928 at the end of the **first flight across the Pacific** (7300 miles *11,770km*). In their Fokker F-VII *Southern Cross* they had left San Francisco on 9 May.

The **first in-flight movie** was shown aboard a Trans-continental Air Transport (later part of TWA) Ford Transport plane on 9 October 1929. Nurse Ellen Church (US) (1905–65) became the world's **first airline stewardess** in a Boeing Air Transport on the 0800hrs Oakland, California, to Chicago flight of 15 May 1930. The Boeing Stratoliner of 1938 was the first **pressurized airliner**.

Frank Whittle (GB) (1907–96) pioneered the jet engine, which began trials in April 1937 in England. The German Heinkel He178 was the first **jet-powered aircraft** to fly, on 27 August 1939. It used an engine developed by Hans von Ohain (Ger).

The speed of sound, Mach 1, was first exceeded on 14 October 1947 by **Charles E. Yeager** (US) (*b.*1923) in a rocket-propelled Bell XS-1 over the Mojave Desert, California. The XS–1 was launched from a converted bomber to gain extra speed.

The first **nonstop round-the-world flight** was completed on 2 March 1949 by James Gallacher (US). Four in-flight refuellings kept his Boeing B-50A *Lucky Lady* airborne to cover the 23,453 miles *37,743km* in 94 hours.

The first **jet-to-jet combat** was over North Korea, when a Chinese Mig-15 was shot down by Russell J. Brown Jr. of the US Air Force in a Lockheed F-80C on 8 November 1950.

The world's first **scheduled jet service** began between London and Johannesburg, South Africa, on 2 May 1952. A British Overseas Airways Corporation (BOAC) De Havilland DH106 Comet I, *Yoke Peter*, covered the 6680 miles *10,750km* in a time of 17 hours 6 minutes, including refuelling stops.

The era of mass travel by jet aircraft began when the giant Boeing 747 **jumbo jet** with 340 seats first entered transatlantic service between New York and London on 21 January 1970.

The European-produced Airbus Industrie A300 widebody airliner entered service – with Air France on its Paris–London route – on 23 May 1974. Airbus's mammoth four-engined **double-decker** aircraft is scheduled to enter service in 2003 as the world's first to carry 1,000 passengers.

On 14–23 December 1986 Americans Dick Rutan (b.1938) and Jeana Yeager (b.1952), made the first unrefuelled non-stop round the world flight. In the lightweight Rutan Voyager they covered 24,986.6 miles *40,212.1km* in 9 days 3 minutes 44 seconds, averaging 115.8mph *186.3km/h*. The take-off required 2.65 miles *4.26km* of runway.

Moving in space

AD 1000

A big bang

The pre-history of rocketry began with the discovery in China of **gunpowder**, first described in AD808. This explosive mixture was used to propel fireworks, leading to the first use of rockets as signals in warfare.

The earliest evidence of **military rockets** (*Huo chien*) dates from 1245 when there was a display of military and naval exercises on the Chhien-thang estuary, near Hangchow, China.

The use of rockets in a military context spread to Europe, where they were used by Arabs and Italians in the 13th century. In India, the Raja Haidar Ali (1728–82) used rockets in the Mysore Wars 1780–99 against the troops of the East India Company.

In 1806 the British Royal Navy unleashed more than 2000 32lb *14kg* incendiary Congreve rockets with a

range of 1.6 miles *2.7km* on Boulogne, France, setting fire to the town within 10 minutes.

Early calculations on the forces needed to send rockets into **Earth orbit** were made by Gustave-Gaspard Coriolus (Fr) (1792–1843) in 1835. Then in 1895 Konstantin Eduardovich Tsiolkovsky (Rus) (1857–1935) carried out the first study of the speeds necessary to reach orbital height and then to escape orbit into space.

Robert H. Goddard (US) (1882–1945) invented the **tube-launched rocket** – later known as the bazooka – in 1918. In early 1921, he proposed the use of retro-rockets to act as brakes or thrusters for altering a rocket's course.

In 1926 Goddard launched the first **liquid-propelled rocket**. It had 9lb *4kg* thrust and contained liquid oxygen and ethanol ignited with a blow lamp on the end of a pole. It travelled 184ft *55m* and attained an altitude of 41ft *12.5m* in a flight that lasted just 2.5 seconds before it exhausted its fuel.

In Breslau, Germany (now Wroclaw, Poland) in 1927, Johannes Winkler (Ger) (1897–1947) founded the German **Verein für Raumschiffahrt** (Society for Space Travel). In 1930, the world's first **rocket test site** was established for the society at Berlin-Reinickendorf. Winkler's 2ft *60cm* methane and liquid-oxygen powered rocket reached an altitude of 1800ft *540m* on 14 March 1931 at Dessau, Germany. It was the first flight of a liquid-fuelled rocket in Europe.

Another German rocket pioneer, Wernher **von Braun** (1912–77), won Nazi backing for a rocket research centre at Peenemünde on the Baltic coast of northeastern Germany. At Peenemünde, the German A4 rocket made its first successful test launch on 3 October 1942.

The A4, later rechristened **V2**, stood 46ft *14m* tall and its speed at burnout was 3598mph *5790km/h*, giving a range of up to 200 miles *322km*. It reached space – internationally defined as regions of more than 62.13 miles *100km* above the Earth's surface – in 1944. In a vertical test-firing from the Heidelager Health Camp at Blizna, Poland, it climbed to a height of *c.*85 miles *136km*.

After the war, Wernher von Braun left Germany for the USA with his entire team. In 1947, at White Sands Proving Grounds, New Mexico, von Braun and Frank J. Malina (US) (1912–81) fired a 16ft *4.87m* long WAC Corporal rocket to an altitude of 244 miles *392.6km*, mounted on top of a captured V2.

American physicist Robert Goddard, pioneer of the first liquid-fuelled rocket, argued even in the 1920s that it would eventually be possible to send a rocket to the Moon. In 1926 his first rocket took off from a field on his aunt's farm in Auburn, Massachusetts.

The first man in space, the Soviet Union's Yuri Gagarin, was dubbed a 'new Columbus' by Soviet Premier Khrushchev. Beating the USA in this leg of the space race was a great triumph for the Russians and Gagarin was made a Hero of the Soviet Union.

On 3 August 1957 the USSR fired the world's first **Intercontinental Ballistic Missile** (ICBM) launcher rocket SS-6 (code-named Sapwood) with a range of 5280 miles *8500km*. It was powered by five liquid oxygen-kerosene engines.

Sputnik I ('fellow traveller') – a sphere weighing 184.3lb *83.6kg* and 22.8in *58cm* in diameter, designed by Sergey Pavlovich Korolyov (USSR) (1906–66) – was launched on 4 October 1957 from Tyuratam, Kazakhstan, into Earth orbit. It had a tiny radio transmitter on board, and was the **first artificial satellite** – that is, the first man-made object able to orbit the Earth.

The first **impact on the Moon** was made by the Soviet space probe *Luna II* on 14 September 1959. The first images of the Moon's hidden or 'dark' side were collected by its successor, *Luna III*, on 7 October 1959.

Manned space flight was the great breakthrough. The Soviet *Vostok I* took off from the Baikonur cosmodrome, Kazakhstan, carrying Yuri Gagarin (1934–68) on 12 April 1961. He reached a maximum altitude of 203.2 miles *327km*, making a single orbit of the Earth in 89 minutes 20.4 seconds – a speed of 17,560mph *28,260km/h*. The **first American in space** was John Glenn (*b*.1921) aboard *Friendship 7* on 20 February 1962. Glenn made a three-orbit flight of 4 hours 55 minutes.

On 18 March 1965 Alexei Leonov (*b*.1934) of the USSR made the first **space walk**, outside the capsule of Voskhod 2. Later that year, on 3 June, US astronaut Ed White made the first American space walk outside Gemini 4.

On 17 March 1966 Neil Armstrong (*b*.1930) and David Scott (*b*.1932) achieved the first **docking** in space, between Gemini 8 and an Agena rocket.

The US Apollo 8 six-day, three-hour mission in December 1968, led by Frank Borman (*b*.1928), made 10 manned **orbits of the Moon**. In May 1969 US Apollo 10 mission's lunar module *Snoopy* went within 8.7 miles *14km* of the lunar surface.

The **first Moon landing** was achieved on 21 July 1969 from US Apollo 11 commanded by Neil Armstrong with Edwin Eugene ('Buzz') Aldrin (*b*.1930). Armstrong first set foot on the Moon in the Sea of Tranquillity at 02.56 GMT.

In December 1970 the USSR achieved the **first landing on Venus** with the probe *Venera 7*. The first images from Venus were received in 1975 from the Venera 9 and 10. On 19 April 1971 the **first space station**, the Soviet *Salyut 1*, was launched.

On 14 May 1973, the USA launched its own **space station**, *Skylab*. It orbited the Earth at an altitude of 310 miles *500km* for six years and the astronauts sent down thousands of photographs of the Earth and the Sun.

Meanwhile, US probes were investigating other planets: *Mariner* 10 got to within 620 miles *1000km* of Mercury in March 1974; *Pioneer 10* and 11 flew past Jupiter and Saturn in 1973 and 1974, and *Voyager 1* and *Voyager 2* – both launched in 1977 – passed close to Jupiter and Saturn before continuing past Uranus and Neptune and also out of the solar system.

AD 2000

Round trip to space

The NASA space shuttle is the **first reusable space vehicle**. It is launched vertically like a rocket but is able to return to Earth and land on a runway. The first space shuttle, *Columbia*, was launched on 12 April 1981 on

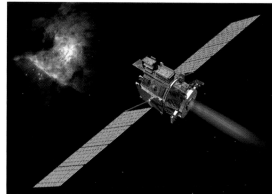

NASA's Deep Space 1 craft, launched in 1998, employs an ion engine – solar panels accelerate charged particles of propellant (the gaseous element xenon) that create thrust as they leave the engine. The unmanned craft is only 5ft *1.5m* high and weighs less than 1100lb *500kg*.

TRANSPORT

The US space shuttle *Atlantis* docked with the Russian space station *Mir* in Earth orbit for five days in 1995 and afterwards took this picture of *Mir*. The shuttle delivered two Russian cosmonauts and picked up a US astronaut to return him to Earth.

a 37-orbit, 54-hour mission from Cape Canaveral, Florida, piloted by John W. Young (*b*.1930).

In December 1988, Vladimir Titov (*b*.1935) and Musa Manarov (*b*.1951) became the first cosmonauts to spend a **year in space**. They worked aboard the USSR Space Station *Mir* ('peace'), which had been placed in Earth orbit in February 1986.

In December 1995, NASA's **Galileo** spacecraft went into orbit around Jupiter and sent back to Earth pictures of Jupiter's moons. For the first time, scientists could see that the ice-covered surface of one of them, Europa, was puckered and blotchy. Scientists believe that the ice covers a huge liquid ocean.

Sergei Avdeyev (Rus) returned to Earth on 28 Aug 1999 aboard the Soyuz spacecraft at the end of his third mission on the Space Station *Mir*. He had lived a **world record 742 days in space**.

NASA's **Deep Space 1** craft, launched on 24 Oct 1998, is testing new technologies in distant regions of space. In May 1999 its onboard computer package, called 'Remote Agent', flew the craft automatically for three days without any input from NASA technicians. In May 2000 the craft was 181 million miles *290 million km* from Earth – 760 times further away than the Moon.

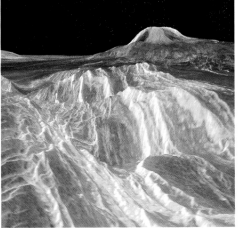

In 1990–94, NASA's *Magellan* spacecraft mapped the surface of Venus with radar. This image taken by Magellan's probe shows twin volcanoes Gula Mons and Sif Mons.

ROCKET ALTITUDE – PROGRESSIVE RECORDS

Miles	Km	Spacecraft	Launch location	Date
0.37	0.603	2in *5cm* rocket by Benjamin Roberts (Eng) (1707–51)	London	12 Oct 1748
0.71	1.14	3in *7.5cm* rocket by Samuel da Costa	London	late Apr 1750
*c.*1.20	*c.*2	5ft *1.5m* long, solid propellant rocket by Reinold Tiling (Ger) (1893–1933)[1]	Osnabruck, Germany	Apr 1931
3.02	4.87	USSR Gird-10	Nakhabino, Russia	25 Nov 1933
>6.20	>10	USSR ORM-52 rocket by Mikhail K. Tikhonravov (1900–74)	Nakhabino, Russia	1935
c. 52	*c.*84.5	German A-4 (Aggregat 4) (or V2) (powered by ethyl alcohol and liquid oxygen)	Peenemünde, Germany	3 Oct 1942
c. 85	*c.*136	German A-4 (Aggregat 4) (or V2) (vertical test)	Heidelager, Blizna, southern Poland	early 1944
118	190	German A-4 (Aggregat 4) (or V2)	Greifswalder Oie (island), Germany	mid-1944
244	392.6	US V.2/WAC Corporal Bumper No. 5 (2 stage)	White Sands, New Mexico	24 Feb 1949
318	512	USSR SS3 'Shyster' (68.9ft *21m* tall)	Tyuratam, Kazakhstan	1954-55
682	1097	US Jupiter C (Composite re-entry test vehicle) (68.2ft *20.8m*)	Cape Canaveral, Florida, USA	20 Sept 1956
>807	>1300	USSR ICBM test flight - SS-6 (Sapwood), 95ft *29m* tall, with 4 lox-kerosene boosters.	Tyuratam, Kazakhstan	27 Aug 1957
70,000	113,770	US Pioneer 1B Lunar Probe	Cape Canaveral, Florida, USA	11 Oct 1958
215.3 million	346.4 million	USSR Luna I or Mechta	Tyuratam, Kazakhstan	2 Jan 1959
242 million	389.4 million	USSR Mars I	Tyuratam, Kazakhstan	1 Nov 1962
6,390 million	10,283 million	US Pioneer 10 – attained 32,114mph *52,682km/h* cosmic escape velocity.[2]	Cape Canaveral, Florida, USA	2 Mar 1972

1. An altitude of 5.9 miles *9.5km* reported by him from Wangerooge, East Friesian Islands. All contemporary independent records are however lost.

2. On 17 Oct 1986, after 14 years 229 days in flight, Pioneer 10 crossed the mean orbit of Pluto at 3670 million miles *5910 million km*, so leaving the Solar System. During AD2000 its altitude should be surpassed by the faster moving US Voyager I (launched 5 Sept 1977).

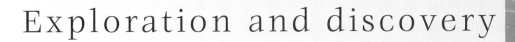

Exploration and discovery

BEFORE AD 1

Might of Persia

One of the earliest documented explorers was **Scylax of Caryanda**. In 515BC Darius I (c.558–486BC), king of Persia (modern Iran), sent him to explore the Indus river, the far point of Persia's wide conquests. Scylax returned by sea some two and a half years later and landed in the Isthmus of Heroönpolis (Suez).

In the 2nd century BC Eudoxus of Cyzicus in Phrygia made the first known **attempt to sail round Africa** from the Mediterranean. He had earlier made two voyages from the Red Sea to India for the ruler of Egypt. He then fitted out three ships in present-day Cadiz in southern Spain and set out down the west coast of Africa but was never heard of again.

AD 1

Rome looks east

At the height of the Roman Empire, traders explored eastward in search of exotic goods. During the reign of the emperor **Hadrian** (117–138), European merchants reached Thailand, Cambodia, Sumatra and Java and may have turned north along the coast of China. In 161, Chinese records assert that Romans sent by **Marcus Aurelius** (r.161–180) reached the emperor Hsiaó-huan-ti.

In the early 5th century, as the Roman Empire was besieged on all sides by the barbarian tribes of central Europe, European knowledge of the east was lost for centuries. The eastern trade was taken over by **Arab seafarers**, who became intimate with the entire eastern coast of Africa and the Indian Ocean.

On the Atlantic seaboard, **Christian missionaries** were the next explorers. Irish abbot St Brendan (484–578) sailed to the Hebrides, Wales and Brittany. *The Voyage of Brendan*, c.1050, records **an Atlantic voyage** to islands which may have been the Canaries or the Azores.

At the same time the **Vikings** of Scandinavia were roaming the northern Atlantic in search of plunder. Iceland was first discovered by Vikings from Norway in 874 and records have preserved the names of the island's first settlers: Ingólfr Amarson and his wife, Hallveig Fródóttir.

Greenland was discovered in 985 by Erik the Red (Eirik Thorvaldsson) (c.950–c.1010) of Norway. The second of his three sons, Leif Eiriksson (pron. Layf) (c.970–c.1020), is believed to have discovered Helluland (Baffin Island), Markland (prob. Labrador) and Vinland (Newfoundland) in c.1001.

AD 1000

Portugal leads the way

During the next centuries, **Portugal** provided the impetus for major discoveries under the aegis of Prince Henry the Navigator (1394–1460). Prince Henry was the third son of King João I and became governor of the Algarve in southern Portugal. There, at Cabo de São Vicente, in the extreme southwest corner of the country, he established an observatory and a school of navigation and sent out several expeditions of discovery.

The islands of Madeira and Porto Santo were discovered by João Gonçalves Zarco and Tristão Vaz in 1418. The Azores in the mid-Atlantic were discovered in 1427 and Prince Henry sent out **Portuguese settlers** to both island groups.

Voyages of exploration continued after Prince Henry's death, with navigators edging down the coast of **West Africa**. In 1482, Diogo Cão (Port) (c.1445–86) erected a stone at the mouth of the Congo River and in 1488

In their sleek oak long boats, the Vikings were masters of the northern seas. When the wind failed, the crew reefed (rolled) the central sail and rowed. The Vikings' reputation as intrepid explorers inspired NASA to name its 1976 unmanned mission to Mars the Viking project.

Bartolomeu Diaz (Port) (c.1450–1500) rounded the **Cape of Good Hope** in a violent storm, opening the way for exploration of the coast of south-eastern Africa and the route to the east. This was followed up by Vasco da Gama (Port) (1469–1525), who rounded the Cape in 1497 and reached Calicut in south-west India in May 1498. On his next expedition, in 1502, he founded colonies in Mozambique.

Christopher Columbus (Genoa) (1451–1506) conceived the idea of reaching India by sailing west. After years of trying to interest sponsors, he persuaded Ferdinand and Isabella, King and Queen of Castile, to back him.

Columbus set sail on 3 August 1492 with three ships, the 117ft *35.5m Santa Maria* and the 50ft *15m* caravels *Pinta* and *Niña*. At 2am on 12 October 1492 he made a landfall on the Bahamian island of Guanahaní – which he renamed San Salvador. On 28 October he reached Cuba, first experiencing tobacco in the form of cigars.

Columbus was slow to realize that he had not landed in the East Indies as expected but had rather discovered the New World. In time cartographers were forced to redraw the map, and Spanish and Portuguese explorers filled in the picture of the Americas and West Indies.

Venetian Marco Polo arrives in China with his father Niccolo and uncle Maffeo in 1275 after their four-year overland voyage. For more than 500 years western readers drew much of their knowledge of the Orient from Polo's account of China, dictated following his return when he was imprisoned after being captured while fighting for Venice against Genoa.

Christopher Columbus, son of a wool weaver from Genoa, began his life of adventure at sea aged just 14. His plan to find a westward sea route to Asia was turned down by Portuguese, French and English monarchs before he found backers in Castile.

Brazil was discovered by the Spanish Vincente Yañez Pinzon (1460–1523) and the Portuguese Pedro Alvarez Cabral (c.1467–c.1520) in the same year, 1500. Both claimed it for their respective monarchs. Pinzon was created governor of Brazil by Ferdinand and Isabella but in fact the Treaty of Tordesillas, ratified by the Pope in 1494, gave Brazil to Portugal.

Portuguese navigators continued to explore the south Atlantic and east Africa, discovering **Madagascar** (1500), St Helena and the Seychelles (1502), Mauritius, Malaysia and **Singapore** (1511).

The interior of Africa was so inhospitable that it remained unexplored, and only offshore islands or coastal enclaves were settled to provide watering and victualling points on the journey east. The Spaniards, however, overran Central and South America, conquering and destroying the Aztec and Inca civilizations in search of gold and silver.

The **Pacific Ocean** was first sighted by a European on 25 September 1513, when Spanish conquistador Vasco Núñez de Balboa (Sp) (1475–1519) reached the ocean after exploring Panama. He called it El Mar de Sur ('The Southern Sea').

In 1516, Juan Diaz de Solis (Sp) (c.1450–1516) reached Rio de Plata in Argentina. In 1519 Hernán **Cortés** (Sp) (1485–1547) reached the Aztec emperor Montezuma II (r.1502–20)'s capital of Tenochtitlán (present-day Mexico City) and plundered the king's treasure house, called Teucalco.

COLUMBUS'S VOYAGES

	Discoveries	Date	Original name
1st Voyage 1492-3	Bahamas	12 Oct 1492	
	Cuba	28 Oct 1492	
	Haiti	24 Dec 1492	Hispaniola
2nd Voyage 1493-6	Dominica	3 Nov 1493	
	Guadeloupe	4 Nov 1493	
	Antigua	1493	Santa Maria de Antigua
	Montserrat	1493	
	St Croix (US Virgin Islands)	1493	Santa Cruz (native: Liamuiga)
	St Kitts Nevis	1493	
	Virgin Islands (British)	1493	
	Puerto Rico	22 Nov 1493	
	Jamaica	5 May 1494	Santiago
3rd Voyage 1498-1500	Trinidad	31 July 1498	
	Venezuela	5 Aug 1498	New Grenada
	(Also sighted Grenada and St. Vincent)		
4th Voyage 1502-4	Martinique	15 June 1502	Matininó
	St Lucia	15 June 1502	
	Costa Rica	18 Sept 1502	
	Cayman Islands	10 May 1503	
	Panama	13 May 1503	

Ferdinand **Magellan** (Port) (*c*.1480–1521) sailed as captain-general of a Spanish fleet of five ships westward from Seville in September 1519 and discovered what became known as the Magellan Strait in southern Chile on 21 October 1520. He and three ships emerged into calm waters on 26 November; he renamed El Mar de Sur the Pacific Ocean, because the waters were tranquil.

After 59 days of extreme privation they reached the Tuamotu Archipelago on 24 January 1521 and Guam on 6 March 1521. Cebu in the **Philippines** was reached on 16 March 1521.

Magellan was killed on 27 April on the Philippine island of Mactan and only the *Vittoria* – under **Juan del Cano** (*c*.1476–1526) – succceeded in rounding the Cape of Good Hope to complete the circumnavigation and return to Spain with 31 men.

Exploration of the **interior of Africa** by Europeans had to wait largely until the 19th century and was driven by the interests of empire-building and missionary activity. The first

explorations were focused on the Sahara in the north, the sources of the great rivers and the watershed of the central highlands which revealed the chain of East African lakes.

The source of the **Blue Nile**, the chief tributary of the main river, the White Nile, was discovered in 1770 by James Bruce (Scot) (1730–94) at Lake Tana, Ethiopia.

James Kingston Tuckey (1776–1816), an Irish officer in the British Navy, was despatched to explore the headwaters of the **Congo** (modern Zaire) in 1815. At the time, geographers thought there might be a connection between the headwaters of the Congo and those of the Niger. Tuckey only penetrated 300 miles *480km* up the 2800 mile *4500km* river before dying of fever in 1816 but sent back valuable notes on his finds.

Meanwhile, Hugh Clapperton (Scot) (1788–1827) and Dixon Denham (Eng) (1786–1828) had been sent to discover the **source of the Niger**.

CIRCUMNAVIGATIONS

Date	Captain	Ships	Nationality
1519–1522	Ferdinand Magellan/ Juan del Cano	*Vittoria*	Portuguese
1577–1580	Francis Drake	*Golden Hind*	English
1768–1771	Capt James Cook	*Endeavour*	English
1895–1898	Joshua Slocum	*Spray*	Canadian
1966–1967	Francis Chichester	*Gypsy Moth*	English
1979–1982	Sir Ranulph Fiennes Charles Burton	On foot	English

They crossed the Sahara from the north and discovered Lake Chad in 1823. Clapperton made a further expedition to find the source of the Niger starting from the Bight of Benin in 1825 but died in Sokoto (Nigeria).

The Niger's source was found by the Scot Alexander Gordon Laing (1793–1826), who crossed the Sahara to reach

Every explorer knows that the voyage might end in a lonely death far from home. In 1610 Englishman Henry Hudson – seeking the North-West Passage – was trapped in the ice in what is now called Hudson Bay (north of Ontario). When the ice broke up in the summer, his mutinous crew cast him and his 12-year-old son adrift in a small boat.

Beginning in the 1890s, American Matthew Henson (1866–1955) made seven expeditions to the Arctic as trusted manservant of US naval officer Robert Peary (1856–1920). On 6 April 1909 they believed they had realized their long-held dream of reaching the North Pole – but later explorers have cast doubt on Peary's measurements.

Englishman Ernest Shackleton sailed the ship *Endurance* on an expedition across the Antarctic in 1914–16. When it became trapped in the ice, Shackleton led five other men in a remarkable 800 mile *1300km* rescue journey to fetch help for the crew.

Timbuktu in 1826 but was killed soon after. German missionary Johannes Rebmann (1820–76) first sighted Mount Kilimanjaro in 1848 and Mount Kenya was first seen by Johann Krapf (Ger) (1810–81) in 1849.

Scottish missionary **David Livingstone** (1813–73) discovered the Victoria Falls on the River Zambesi in 1856 and was commissioned in 1858 by the British government to explore the Zambesi further. He went on to discover Lake Nyasa.

In 1856 the British government sponsored Richard Burton (1821–90) and John Hanning Speke (1827–64) to explore the East African lakes, which led to the discovery of Lake Tanganyika in 1858. Speke went on to discover Lake Victoria and returned in 1860 with James Grant (1827–92) to explore the

lake and to establish that the Ripon Falls that exit from the lake were in fact **the source of the Nile**.

On a further expedition in 1866 Livingstone discovered the River Lualaba. He fell ill and was not heard from for some months, during which several expeditions were mounted to discover his whereabouts.

On 23 October 1871 he was found in the village of Ujiji, on the east shore of Lake Tanganyika, by Henry Morton **Stanley** (Wales/US) (1841–1904) – who had been dispatched by the *New York Herald*. Stanley returned to Africa in 1874, followed the Lualaba to its junction with the Congo and descended the Congo to the sea.

In 1873 an English expedition to find Livingstone was mounted by Verney Lovett Cameron (1844–94). He was in time to discover the corpse of the famous explorer, who had died in Old Chitambo (modern Zambia), being carried by his native companions to the coast.

Cameron went on to Lake Tanganyika and continued west, hoping to descend the Lualaba. He was prevented by native hostility and instead continued overland, reaching Benguela in 1875 and becoming the **first European to cross Africa** from coast to coast.

The Ruwenzori mountains – first seen by Stanley who realized that they were the 'mountains of the moon' that had been described by the Egyptian geographer Ptolemy (82–150) – were first climbed in the following century by the Italian Luigi, Duke of Abruzzi, in 1906.

NORTHERN PASSAGES

East and West

In the northern hemisphere, an early obsession of a series of expeditions was to find a way from the North Atlantic to the North Pacific: the **North-East Passage** was sought from the north of Finland and Russia to Asia and the **North-West Passage** from the north of Canada to the Alaskan coast.

Hugh Willoughby (Eng) (*c*.1500–54) led three ships to find the North-East Passage across northern Asia in 1553–54. The crews of two ships died of scurvy wintering at Arzina Reca in Lapland. The third, Richard Chancellor's (*d*.1556) ship, reached the White Sea in northern Russia; he returned overland via Moscow.

Dutch navigator Willem **Barents** (*c*.1550–79) made three expeditions in search of the North-East Passage. He died off the island of Novaya Zemlya in the Kara Sea but his journal survived, to be found in 1875.

The **passage eastward across the entire north coast of Russia** – and hence the first circumnavigation of Eurasia – was achieved by Nils Adolf Erik Nordenskjöld (Fin/Swe) (1832–1901) in the *Vega*, captained by Adolf Arnold Louis Palander (Swe) (1842–1920). The *Vega* left Norway in July 1878 and reached Kolyutschin Bay, short of the Bering Strait, on 28 September that year.

The North-West Passage was first attempted by John **Cabot** (Genoa/Eng) (1424–*c*.1500), who sighted what was probably Cape Breton Island, Nova Scotia, in 1497. Martin Frobisher (Eng) (c.1535–94) made three expeditions in 1576–78 and visited Labrador, Frobisher Bay and Baffin Island but had to turn back.

In 1819, William Parry (1790–1855) found the entrance to the passage at Bounty Cape in Lat. 74°44'20"N, Long. 110°W. Exploration went on for 409 years until the passage (east-west) was finally travelled by a crew led by Norwegian Roald **Amundsen** (1872–1928) in 1903–06.

THE POLES

North and South

Ever since people began to navigate using compasses showing magnetic north, the poles of the Earth have exercised enormous fascination. For reasons then not wholly understood, the magnetic poles to which compasses align themselves 'wander'. When the magnetic south pole was reached in 1908 it was at 72° 25' S in Victoria Land, Antarctica, but it has migrated 550 miles *885km* since then and at the end of the 20th century is in Adélie Land.

The first recorded **crossing of the Antarctic Circle** was by James Cook (Eng) (1728–79) in 1774. Antarctica was first sighted by Edward Bransfield (c.1783–1852) in the brig *Williams* on 20 January 1820.

The Norwegian Carsten Borchgrevink (1864–1934) was a member of the first party to land on the Antarctic continent in 1894 and then in 1898–99 of the first group to overwinter there. The **race**

for the South Pole was on. In 1901–04, Robert **Scott** (UK) (1869–1912) explored the Ross Sea and discovered what became known as King Edward VII Land. In 1908, the magnetic south pole was first reached by Douglas **Mawson** (Aust) (1882–1958) in an expedition led by Sir Ernest Shackleton (Ire/Eng) (1874–1922).

The Norwegian Roald Amundsen was **first to the South Pole** on 14 December 1911, beating Scott by a month. Scott's expedition members all died on the return journey.

In 1928–29, Richard **Byrd** flew to the South Pole and Lincoln Ellsworth (US) (1880–1951) flew across the Antarctic continent in 1935.

Between 1979 and 1982, English adventurer Sir Ranulph **Fiennes** (1945–) led the Transglobe expedition, which visited both poles following the Greenwich meridian in a circumnavigation of the earth N-S-N.

In the north between 1893 and 1896 Norwegian explorer Fridtjof **Nansen** (1861–1930) deliberately let his ship, the *Fram*, get iced in north of Siberia. The *Fram* drifted with the ocean current beneath the pack ice toward Greenland until, at 84° 4' N, Nansen left the ship and reached as far as 86° 14' N, the furthest then achieved.

This expedition showed that there was no Arctic continent but that the Arctic was a vast frozen ocean. The **magnetic North Pole was first located** by James Clark Ross (Scot) (1800–62) in 1831 on the west side of the Boothia Peninsula, northern Canada.

In 1926, US aviator Richard **Byrd** (1888–1957) and Floyd **Bennett** (1890–1928) made the first aeroplane flight near to the North Pole. In 1958, the US submarine *Nautilus* crossed the North Pole beneath the ice cap.

Their goal achieved, Norwegian Roald Amundsen and his crew savour the triumph of being the first to sail the North-West Passage. They began the journey in the fishing boat *Gjøa* on 16 June 1903 and arrived in Nome, Alaska, on 31 August 1906.

Mapping the world

BEFORE AD 1

Flat Earth

The Babylonians produced the **first known world map** in the 6th century BC – a clay tablet that depicts the Earth as a circular disc. In the centre is Babylon and her neighbours; beyond, an ocean with only fictitious islands.

The Ancient Greek philosopher **Aristotle** (384–322BC) was the first to realize that the Earth must be a sphere. He observed the way ships appear and disappear on the horizon, and concluded that the Earth's surface was actually curved.

The first scientific measure of the Earth's size was the work of Ancient Greek mathematician **Eratosthenes** (*c.*276–194BC), who was head of the library at Alexandria in Egypt. He used observations of the sun in two different towns to calculate the Earth's circumference to be 250,000 stadia (28,584 miles *46,000km*), achieving a remarkable accuracy of about 85 per cent.

Claudius **Ptolemy** (Gk) (*c.*AD90–168), who also worked in the library at Alexandria, drew a world map with lines of latitude and longitude. His 21st parallel at 63°N ran through the Shetland Islands, then the most northerly known lands. When the great library of Alexandria was burned down

In Mesopotamia, early maps were drawn on clay tablets. This one depicts the military campaigns of King Sargon of Akkad (*c.*2371–2315BC).

in AD391, scientific geography ceased for over a millennium.

The picture of the Earth given by Spanish theologian Isidore of Seville (*c.*560–636) was derived from **Biblical geography** and was a flat square with Jerusalem at the centre and Paradise in the Far East, separated from the rest of the world by a wall of flame; to the north, another wall held back the rabble described in the Book of Ezekiel as the 'hordes of Gog and Magog'.

AD 1000

Mariners' charts

Marine charts drawn up from sea captains' descriptions of their voyages were known as 'portolan' charts from the Italian *portolani* ('pilot

books'). They were the first maps to be oriented with north at the top because of the use of magnetic north by mariners.

In 1375, cartographer Abraham Cresques completed his 'Catalan Atlas' with reasonably accurate representations of the coastlines of Africa, India, parts of China and northern Europe. The extent of the **Pacific Ocean** was known after the round-the-world voyage beginning in 1519, during which Ferdinand Magellan (Port) (1480–1521) renamed the ocean previously known as 'the Southern Sea' (see page 185).

In 1492 German Martin Behaim made the first terrestrial globe since the time of the Ancient Greeks. It marks the equator, the tropics and the Arctic and Antarctic circles – as well as mermaids, elephants and saints.

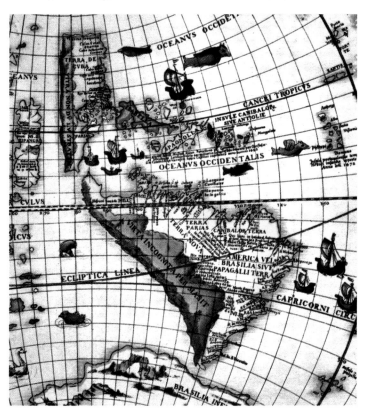

Flemish cartographer Gerardus **Mercator** (1512–94) devised a system of projection – since named in his honour – for representing the globe's curved lines of longitude and latitude in two dimensions, as parallel lines on a flat map.

Surveying on land was refined following the 1551 invention of the **theodolite** – an instrument for measuring horizontal and vertical angles – by English mathematician Leonard Digges (*c*.1520–59).

France was the first country to have a complete **topographical survey**. The work was begun under Giovanni Domenico Cassini (It) (1625–1712) in 1673 and took more than 100 years. It was finally published by Cassini's great-grandson in 1793 in 182 sheets.

Maritime tradition dating back to the Ancient Greeks said that there was a great continent filling the southern waters known as *Terra Australis*. The true proportions of the southern oceans were established by James Cook (Eng) (1728–79). Cook surveyed the coast of New Zealand and the east coast of Australia and sailed as far south as latitude 71°10′, proving that the southern continent did exist, but was smaller than imagined.

In North America the first surveys were mainly concerned with establishing state borders. In 1761, the states of Pennsylvania and Maryland asked England's Astronomer Royal to help settle the disputed boundary between them. He sent Englishmen Charles Mason (1730–87) and Jeremiah Dixon (*d*.1777) to carry out what was to become a celebrated survey.

The **Mason-Dixon line**, drawn in 1763–7, became a symbolic frontier between northern and southern US states that took on great significance in the American Civil War (1861–5).

The great Trigonometrical **Survey of India** began in 1802. William Lambton (Eng) (1756-1823) started at Cape Comorin at the southern tip of the continent, intending to cover 1802 miles 2900km before reaching the mountains of Kashmir in the extreme north. However, he died of tuberculosis and the survey was finished by his assistant George Everest (Eng) (1790–1866) in 1843.

AD 2000

Bird's eye view

The success of military reconnaissance planes in World War I (1914–18) led to the use of **aerial photography** in surveying.

At around the same time, the technology became available to begin **surveying the ocean floor**. Prior to the 20th century, surveys had to rely on soundings taken with the lead – a weight on a fathom line – and beyond a certain depth, this was impracticable.

Following the invention of the **echo-sounder** in 1912, deep sea surveys could begin. Pioneers of this work in the 1940s and 1950s were Bruce C. Heezen and Marie Tharp of Columbia University. Heezen and Tharp mapped the **Mid-Atlantic Ridge** in the Atlantic Ocean and discovered a 6562ft *2000m* canyon in its middle.

The **Amazon Basin** was largely unmapped before the Brazilian government began

building the Trans-Amazonian highway in 1970. Aerial photography over the basin was dogged by persistent cloud problems, so the authorities adopted the

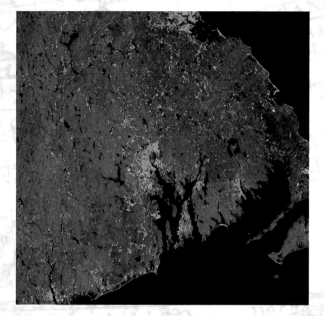

technique of **Side-Looking Airborne Radar** (SLAR). An aircraft fitted with an antenna flew two runs a day each day for a year. As it passed over the terrain, it bounced a series of microwave pulses off the ground beneath; from the resulting readings the SLAR equipment imaged the terrain. Because SLAR uses microwave energy it can work at night or through cloud cover.

Satellite photography transformed cartography. Beginning in 1972, NASA launched Landsat spacecraft carrying TV cameras, multispectral scanners and radio equipment. In 2000, computers are used to process information provided in satellite pictures. Mapmakers use this technology to survey the land, and also to track other phenomena such as changes in weather patterns and the Earth's vegetation cover.

A computer-enhanced satellite image shows the Boston and Cape Cod region on the east coast of the USA. The dominant red colour indicates vegetation and the blue, built-up areas.

WAR

- **Swords and armour**

- **Bombs, grenades and missiles**

- **Pistols and guns**

- **Military strategy**

- **Killing power records**

- **The atomic bomb**

- **Biological and chemical warfare**

- **Major battles**

A Renaissance illumination depicts the bloody conquest of Antioch by the Crusaders during the First Crusade. Although the tools for making war have changed dramatically throughout history, the use of armed aggression to solve disputes and conquer new territories has not.

Swords and armour

BEFORE AD 1

Tools and spears

Early stone tools such as palm-held hand axes could have been used as weapons as well as for hunting. The earliest find of remnants of what may be a wooden **spear** was at Boxgrove, West Sussex, England, on a living site of *Homo heidelbergensis* dated to *c.*500,000BC. A wooden thrusting spear found at Clacton-on-Sea, Essex, has been dated to *c.*425,000BC.

No shield is known earlier than those depicted on Egyptian pre-dynastic wall paintings dated to the Amratian period *c.*4000BC. A metal helmet of electrum – gold and silver alloy – was found in the Sumerian city of Ur (modern Iraq) dated to *c.*2500BC; helmets of copper or later of bronze would have been worn by common soldiers in the ranks.

The khopesti sword, made in one piece with a long grip but comparatively short blade, first appeared in Egypt *c.*1850BC. Scale-armour, ranging from around 700 to 1035 attached pieces or scales of hide or fabric, is known in Egypt from the 17th century BC. Its use survived in China and India more than 3.5 millennia until the 19th century AD.

Mycenaean nobleman warriors from Dendra, southern Greece *c.*1420BC dressed in full **bronze armour**, which included a cuirass (breast and back plate joined) and greaves to protect the calves and shins.

Roman footsoldiers carried a short stabbing sword, the *gladius*, about 2ft *60cm* long, which was designed for hand-to-hand fighting on foot. The iron of these early swords was of poor quality: in the battle of Aquae Sextiae in 102BC Roman soldiers were described as having to straighten their swords with their feet from time to time as they fought against the Teutones and Ambrones.

AD 1

Longer swords

When the Romans encountered mounted warriors in the latter days of the empire, they adopted the longer sword used by their enemies. The Roman foot soldier wore a bronze or iron helmet, a cuirass of overlapping strips of iron on leather and a leather kilt with vertical iron strips.

The Celts wore winged helmets to increase their fierce appearance and the chiefs had finely decorated bronze shields. Ordinary soldiers' shields were of leather or wood.

Straight-blade swords with elaborate hilts first appeared among the Saxons *c.*450 and were adopted *c.*770 by Vikings. The Saxon soldiers of the 11th century wore a knee-length *byrnie* or **chain-mail shirt** with long sleeves and a quilted leather jacket underneath to absorb the shock of blows. The byrnie was adopted by the Normans who called it a hauberk and split its skirt for riding on horseback.

AD 1000

Jousters and fencers

The earliest Japanese swords were the symbol of the **samurai**, the warrior caste of feudal Japan from the middle of the 12th century until 1869, when the feudal system was abolished. Only the samurai were allowed to carry a pair (*daisho*) of swords – the long *katana* and the short *wakizushi*.

Moveable vizors began appearing about 1300, while **plate armour** with small plates let into mail garments was of Persian and Turkish origin, dating to *c.*1450, closely followed in Japan. In

These Chinese bronze daggers date from the 14th century BC. The earliest known Chinese two-edged swords, also made of bronze and up to 10.6in *27cm* in length, were found in tombs in Lingtai, Gansu province, and date from *c.*950BC.

Europe, plate armour became heavier and heavier and, with the spread of jousting in the 15th century, was also developed for the horses.

The manufacture of armour and swords reached a peak in the 13th and 14th centuries and the design of swords changed – becoming more slender and pointed to enable a swordsman to pierce his opponent's mail. They were also made longer, reaching 50–60in *125–150cm* with longer hilts for a two-handed grip. Swords were at first forged by repeated firing and hammering, producing a sort of steel by the introduction of a small amount of carbon.

The earliest mention of the **rapier** – a thin double-edged sword – was in 1474 in France. By 1530 the wearing of 'civilian' rapier-like swords

became general in the courts of European countries.

The Hungarian cavalry adopted the **sabre** from the Turks who invaded the southern half of Hungary in 1526. Its long, curved blade was designed for slashing at the enemy from horseback.

Guns were invented during the 13th century but for a long time were so unreliable that swords continued in use alongside them. The wearing of ever heavier full armour was virtually discarded by 1650, leaving only the helmet and the cuirass. **Rapier-style swords** were then designed to thrust effectively at the relatively unprotected body and the **basket hilt** which protected the swordsman's hand was developed in the 17th century.

The Gaelic great sword known as *claidheamh-mor* or **claymore** became

widespread in the Scottish Highlands *c.*1680. Large, with straight blades and a very long grip, claymores were fitted with straight cross-pieces.

The introduction of guns with repeater action finally made swords obsolete in the 19th century. They became almost entirely ceremonial. When duelling was outlawed, **fencing** became an Olympic sport from the outset of the Games' revival in Athens in April 1896, with both the foil and the sabre.

The **bayonet** was a short stabbing blade mounted on the end of a firearm, used for hand-to-hand encounters by infantrymen. The name derives from the town of Bayonne in France. The bayonet was first used in the French army in 1647 and last used in World War II.

AD 2000

Nylon comes to the fore

Armour survived as the **tin hat** used throughout both World Wars by many armies. **Body armour** was used in World War I as a protection against shrapnel and in World War II the **flak jacket** was made of overlapping plates of steel or aluminium within a nylon jacket. These offered some protection against shrapnel and were fairly flexible but were not proof against bullets.

In the 1960s it was discovered that steel could be dispensed with; composite layers of thick nylon would distort a bullet and absorb its energy. The **bullet-proof vest** used by police and anti-riot troops consists of 16 to 24 layers of nylon cloth.

In conflict a Japanese samurai wore a *mempo* (faceguard) and a *kabuto* (battle helmet), as well as body armour. This warrior, or samurai, presents his *katana*, or long sword.

The modern descendant of the suit of armour is the bullet- and shrapnel-proof vest and helmet, worn by police, anti-riot and bomb teams. This bomb disposal expert wears a protective helmet of Kevlar, a super-strong fabric developed in the 1960s, originally for use in reinforced car tyres.

Bombs, grenades and missiles

BEFORE AD 1000

War machines

The Romans used several **siege weapons**: the onager, catapult and ballista all worked by suddenly releasing tension stored in a twisted rope. The largest could throw missiles, usually rocks, weighing up to 60lb *27kg*.

The eastern Greeks of Byzantium defended their city against Islamic besiegers in 717 with **Greek fire**, a mixture of sulphur, naphtha and quicklime. It was either poured directly on to the soldiers below from the city walls or projected in 'flamethrowers'.

Chinese alchemists were the first to discover the qualities of what became the first known explosive – **black (later gun) powder**, which

they called *huo phao*. This was described in 808 by Chao Nai-An. The formula called for locally available saltpetre (potassium nitrate) and sulphur to be mixed with the dried herb Aristolochia, or *ma tou ling*.

AD 1000

Death from the sky

The Chinese also developed the first military rockets – *huo chien* – which were fuelled by black powder (see page 158). The proportion of saltpetre in the mix was gradually and cautiously increased until detonations were produced. This stage was attained by 1044, the year of publication of *Wu Chang Tsung Yao* ('Collection of Most Important Military Techniques'), edited by Tsing Kung-Liang.

Bombards, or siege guns, were first used in the 1346

siege of Calais, France, during the Hundred Years' War between England and France. Later bombards had barrels of 23.6in *60cm* diameter and ammunition of stone balls bound with iron hoops.

The **hand grenade** – *la grenade* – was first recorded in use by the French in 1585. The first grenades were hollow spheres filled with gunpowder and ignited via a length of fuse. Before the match became common, soldiers handling grenades would have had to keep a slow match burning in battle – neither easy nor safe.

William Bickford (Eng) (1774–1834) invented the **safety fuse** – a length of flax thread impregnated with gunpowder – in 1831 for use in mines, where premature explosions cost many lives. It was adopted for military use.

Samuel **Colt** (US) (1814–62) tested the use of a **mine detonated by electric battery** in New York City harbour in 1842. He later blew up a 500 ton vessel in the River Potomac, Washington D.C., at 5 miles *8km* range.

Gun-cotton was discovered in 1846 by Christian Schönbein (Ger) (1799–1868) (see page 84). **Cellulose nitrate** was later used in explosives.

Ascanio Sobrero (It) (1812–88) first produced **nitro-glycerine** in Turin in 1847. Trinitro-toluene (**TNT**) – a yellow crystalline solid – was first produced in 1863 by

The Christian Crusades against the Muslims from 1095–1270 stimulated the development of siege engines. The trebuchet or mangonel is first mentioned in mediaeval accounts in 1147. Its 50ft *15m* long arm and 10 ton counterweight could hurl a 300lb *136kg* projectile 300yds *274m*.

Bombs, grenades and missiles

World War I saw the birth of the aerial bomb. At first they were merely small missiles dropped from an aircraft, but by the time of World War II (1939-45) mass bomber raids like this could flatten a city.

J. Wilbrand (Ger). It was not adopted as a military explosive until 1904.

In 1864, J. F. E. Schultz (Ger) introduced **smokeless powder**. It was found to be effective for hand grenades and for shotguns and meant, too, that the smoke from gunfire need no longer give away a position to the enemy.

Alfred Bernhard Nobel (Swe) (1833–96) invented a safer form of nitroglycerine called **dynamite** in 1866. In 1875 he produced **gelignite**, a jelly-like mixture of nitroglycerine and cellulose nitrate in a base of potassium or sodium nitrate and wood pulp.

AD 2000

Sophisticated weapons

In 1889, Frederick Abel (1827–1902) and James Dewar (Scot) (1842–1923) succeeded in combining nitroglycerine and nitrocellulose with petroleum jelly into a gelatinous form which could be extracted into cords that could be precisely measured.

In World War I, grenades were widely used in the trenches as they could be thrown into an enemy trench

without the thrower exposing himself. One model, Hale's percussion grenade, was stick-shaped with streamers which unfurled to ensure that the grenade hit the ground point first to detonate the fuse.

Molotov Cocktails, petroleum-filled anti-tank incendiary missiles, were first used by the Republican Army in the Spanish Civil War in 1938, then improved by Finns fighting the Russian Red Army in Karelia in 1940. They devised the name as a taunt to the then Soviet Foreign Minister, Vyacheslav Molotov (1890–1986).

In World War II, **incendiary bombing** was practised on enemy cities on a wide scale. Rocket-type missiles were also used in the form of **anti-tank bazookas** armed with HEAT (High Explosive Anti-Tank) warheads. The bazooka was developed by the Mohaupt brothers in Switzerland.

During the 1991 Gulf War, US bombers in Operation Desert Storm were able to deliver **laser-guided precision bombs** accurate to inches over Iraq. Smart missiles – which can be programmed to hit a target and can turn corners – were developed in the early 1990s. The Stinger POST (Passive Optical Seeker Technology) used by the US Army is guided by a microprocessor and 'locks on' to its target, following every change of direction until it has caught it.

The first **air-to-air missiles** were unguided rockets invented in 1915 by Y. P. G. Le Prieur (1885–1963) and carried in French aircraft in

World War I. They were used against slow-moving observation balloons and zeppelins. Among modern versions, the US AIM-9 Sidewinder (1956), had a range of 5 miles *8km*. The US AA-9 Amos (1969) could cover 62 miles *100km*.

Surface-to-surface missiles are also known as battlefield missiles. The Soviet Scud (1957) has a range of 174 miles *280km* and a 1 tonne warhead. It was used in the 1973 Arab–Israeli war, by the Soviets against Afghan rebels in 1980–1 and also by Iraq against Israel and Saudi Arabia in 1991.

Surface-to-air missiles include the British Sea Wolf (1973), which can fly at twice the speed of sound, with a range of 4 miles *6.5km*. The US Patriot anti-missile missile (1991) knocked Iraqi Scuds out of the sky in 1991.

Anti-ship missiles include the French Exocet, which the Argentinian navy aircraft used to sink the British cruiser HMS *Sheffield* in May 1982. **Anti-submarine** missiles include the US Subroc, with a 5 kiloton warhead and a range of 35 miles *56km*.

Anti-tank missiles began to undermine the supremacy of the tank with the US Tow missile, which entered service in 1970. The US/Swiss Air Defence Anti-Tank System has a 26lb *12kg* warhead and can penetrate armour more than 35in *900mm* thick.

In March 1983, the destroyer USS *Merrill* launches a Tomahawk cruise missile. The Tomahawk has a range of 1730 miles *2780km* and a 271lb *123kg* warhead. It was used in the 1990–91 Gulf War, in 1998 in United Nations attacks on Iraq and by NATO in the 1999 Kosovan conflict.

Pistols and guns

The **Chinese** were able to develop the first guns after their discovery of gunpowder in AD808. In the 14th century gunpowder was introduced via the Arabs to the West – after which the development of firearms was swift.

The earliest guns were simple **bronze tubes** with one closed end, loaded at the mouth with gunpowder and shot. The powder was ignited via a hole at the side. The arquebus adopted by the Spanish army *c*.1495 was about 4ft *1.2m* long, weighed 9lb *4kg* and fired lead balls of about 1oz *28g* in weight that were loaded through the muzzle.

The **musket**, which followed in the early 16th century, was another muzzle-loader. It was about 6ft *1.8m* long and weighed *c*.20lb *9kg*. It fired a lead ball twice as heavy as that used by the arquebus but it took at least two men to fire it. Both musket and arquebus were inaccurate and slow to reload.

The **wheel-lock** dispensed with the need for the soldier to manipulate a lighted fuse. Its invention is attributed to Johann Kiefuss of Nuremberg *c*.1517. The mechanism worked by a piece of iron pyrites striking a spark off a small wheel rotating on the stock of the gun, the whole action being activated by the trigger.

In 1520, August Kotter (Ger) introduced **rifling** in the gun barrel – that is, the cutting of grooves to enhance the range and accuracy of the bullet's flight. But the rifled musket was much too expensive to be generally available for another 200 years. The **flint-lock** improved on the wheel-lock by using a flint to strike

In 1862, Richard Gatling (US) brought out the Gatling machine gun, in which several barrels could be loaded and fired in quick succession. The Gatling had ten manually rotated barrels and could fire 250 rounds per minute from a gravity-fed drum.

the spark against a strike plate. It was invented by a Frenchman, Marin le Bourgeoys, in 1610.

The **paper cartridge** was introduced into the Swedish army *c*.1630 by Gustavus Adolphus (1594–1632). This new kind of ammunition, a package containing both powder and ball, was a great advance on the existing method of measuring out the powder each time and funnelling it into the gun.

James Puckle (UK) (*c*.1667–1724) patented a hand-cranked, six-chambered **revolving gun** or *mitrailleuse* in 1718. It was first manufactured in 1721 with little success, but the idea of a revolving chamber was taken up for the hand-gun in 1814 when James Thomson (Eng) patented a flint-lock pistol with a revolving nine-chambered feed

The irregular troops fighting against the British during the American Revolution used their drab-coloured clothing to hide among dense forest cover. By skilled use of long-barrelled hunting guns, these men could inflict heavy casualties on the more formally trained British, before melting away into the forests.

SOME FIREARMS AND THEIR NAMESAKES

Name	Weapon	Date invented
BROWNING John Moses (US) (1855–1926)	Gas-operated automatic pistol. Also a machine gun (1917)	1911
COLT Samuel (US) (1814–62)	Revolver ('six shooter')	1835
DERINGER Henry (US) (1786–1868)	Derringer or Deringer pistol	1852
GATLING Richard Jordan (US) (1818–1903)	Hand-cranked, 10 parallel-barrelled machine gun (1200 shots/min). Slang term 'gat' derives from him	1861–62
HOTCHKISS Benjamin Berkeley (US) (1825–85)	Revolving barrel machine gun	1893
KALASHNIKOV Mikhail Timoteyevich (USSR) (*b.* 1919)	$^1/_3$ in *7.62mm* AK-47 assault rifle	1959
LEWIS Col. Isaac Norton (US) (1858–1931)	Light machine gun	*c.*1910
LUGER Georg (Ger) (1849–1923)	Forerunner of the short-barrelled parabellum	1897
MAUSER Peter Paul von (Ger) (1838–1914)	Five chamber, breech-loading, magazine rifle	1889
MAXIM Sir Hiram (US/UK) (1840–1916)	Automatic belt machine gun	1884
MILLS Sir William (Eng) (1856–1932)	Hand grenade, termed a Mills' bomb	1915
MINIE Col. Claude-Etienne (Fr) (1804–79)	Internationally-adopted conical-pointed , cylindrical rifle bullet	1849
MOLOTOV Vyacheslav Mikhailovich (né Schriabin) (USSR) (1890–1986)	Hand-thrown anti-tank 'cocktail' of inflammable liquid with a slow fuse, devised by Finns defending themselves from the Soviet invasion ordered by Foreign Minister Molotov	1938
PURDEY James (Eng) (1784–1863)	Highest quality sporting guns, London	1830
SHRAPNEL Gen. Henry (Eng) (1761–1842)	Explosive laced with ball shot – first used in Surinam	1804
SMITH Horace (US) (1808–93)	Smith and Wesson guns – made in Springfield, Massachusetts	1857
THOMPSON Gen. John Taliaferro (US) (1860–1940)	.45 calibre sub-machine (Tommy) gun, adopted by US Army and by Chicago gangsters	1920
VICKERS Thomas Edward (Eng) (1833–1915)	Aviation machine guns first used with Constantinesco synchronizer (firm founded 1867)	1917
WESSON Daniel Baird (US) (1825–1906)	Repeating mechanism (see Smith, Horace)	1854
WINCHESTER Oliver Fisher (US) (1810–80)	Repeating rifle	1862

mechanism. In the USA, Samuel **Colt** (1814–62) introduced his 'six-shooter' revolver in 1835.

G. V. Fosberry (UK) in 1895 gave the revolver **automatic action**. He used the recoil action from one firing to re-cock the gun and to turn the cylinder to the next cartridge.

Soldiers went into World War I equipped with the bolt-action **repeating rifle**, with a range of a 1000 yards *900m*; the **Maxim gun**, a machine gun which could fire 400 rounds a minute, invented by the American Hiram Stevens Maxim (1840–1916); and the German **Luger** automatic pistol developed by George Luger (1848–1922).

The increasing mobility of warfare meant that developments after

World War I concentrated on tanks, destroyers and aircraft all armed with appropriate guns. A major development in the hand-held gun was the **assault rifle**, combining the accuracy and range of the rifle with the capacity to fire in bursts like a machine gun – using gas power as the force.

Modern versions of this deadly weapon include the Kalashnikov AK-47, the US AR-15, widely used in Vietnam, and the US M16 A2, issued to the Marines in 1985.

In 1996, the US Army developed the **Land Warrior** gun, equipped with an infrared rangefinder and a thermal camera that enables the user to see thermal images of the enemy's body heat while remaining under cover.

The celebrated Kalashnikov AK-47 assault rifle was based on an earlier German model, the Sturmgewehr 44 of 1944. This youthful Libyan cadet presents his Kalashnikov with pride.

Military strategy

BEFORE AD 1

Egyptian invasion

The first armed conflict of which details survive is the **Battle of Kadesh** on the Orontes river in Syria in 1275BC. The Egyptian pharaoh, Ramses II (r.1295 –1213BC) invaded Syria at the head of four divisions of 20,000 men. His infantry was divided into spearmen and archers and each division also had war chariots. The opposing Hittites had 2500 war chariots, each carrying three soldiers armed with spears. The Egyptians were victorious and Ramses celebrated his triumph in monumental carvings.

The Assyrian army of the 1st millennium BC was the first to study siege craft – and used the battering ram, siege tower, tunnels and scaling ladders. These Assyrian soldiers swing catapults loaded with rocks during the siege of the Jewish town of Lachish in 701BC. They are depicted in a relief from the palace of the Assyrian king Sennacherib (d.681BC) in Nineveh.

With the development of **iron** c.1200BC, weapons – previously made of softer bronze – became much more effective. The Hittites may have been the first to use iron weapons, introducing the long iron sword to replace the battle axe.

The Assyrian kingdom was the dominant power in the Middle East c.1000BC and made its capital at Nineveh, east of the Tigris River in modern Iraq. The Assyrian army was the first in the Middle East to use **cavalry** and that, combined with the iron sword, gave them great shock potential.

Galleys were developed by both the Phoenicians and Egyptians but were only reliably manoeuvred by oar. Before 1000BC, sea battles were limited to an exchange of missiles, followed by grappling and boarding. The Athenian navy c.500BC began to use an iron ram fitted to the bows of a galley.

In China – where the development of iron weapons was slow – armies were still largely equipped with bronze in 600BC. The **first known treatise on warfare**, the Art of War by Sun Tzu, was written in c.500BC. It describes the provisioning of armies and how an invading army can live off the land.

The Greek city states (500–300BC) had **universal male conscription** to supply their armies. Spartan boys were sent to barracks at the age of seven to begin military training.

The importance of the choice (or accident) of ground was seen in two of the most famous battles in the 5th century BC Persian Wars. At **Marathon** in 490BC, 10,000 Greeks trapped a much larger Persian army with its back to the sea and in a rapid onslaught swept the invaders before them so that only a lucky few Persians managed to escape to their ships.

Ten years later, the Persians returned under Xerxes (c.519–465BC) with some 200,000 troops. The Greek city states had united in the Hellenic League but were vastly outnumbered. Yet their

The foundation of the Greek army was the hoplite soldier, an infantryman with a round shield, armour, a sword and a spear. The hoplites massed in formations or phalanxes six or eight deep with interlocking shields. Their large wood and leather shields protected them from the neck to the knees.

strategy was almost successful. They met the Persians in the mountain pass of **Thermopylae**, 80 miles 129km north of Athens, and for three days 7000 Greeks held off the entire Persian army. It was only when the Persians found out that there was a secret path around the back of the Greeks that the invaders finally triumphed.

This was an era when armies lived by pillaging the land or on provisions carried in baggage trains of mules or camels. The **Macedonians** under Philip the Great (382–336BC) and his son Alexander (356–323BC) were the first to realise that their army could move faster if each soldier was expected to carried his own weapons and much of his food and water. Only one pack animal was allowed for every 50 soldiers. At the head of this very mobile army, Alexander conquered the Middle East and parts of India.

The greatest revolution in military organization came with the **Roman legions**. In its early days the Roman army was based on the Greek model but, during the Great Samnite War in central Italy in 326–304BC, the legions were increased in strength to *c*.6000 men, of which *c*.4200 was infantry.

Each legion was divided into 'maniples' of *c*.120 men. In battle, each maniple was drawn up in three lines – *hastati*, *principes* and *triarii* – with gaps between. The maniples then arranged themselves into blocks of troops in a powerful chequerboard pattern.

If they were hard-pushed the legions would present an unbroken face – the first lines fell back into the gaps between maniples or the rear lines moved forward into place beside the front ranks. The legions became the most formidable fighting force ever known to that time.

AD 1

Horse fighting

A major reason why cavalry were not used effectively by early Western civilizations is that the **stirrup** was not invented until *c*.200BC in China. Without stirrups, a horseman was easily unseated and was unable to use any weapons to effect.

The **saddle** with stirrups entered Europe from the East by the 6th century and the Celts invented the **horseshoe** in the 4th century. These advances enabled the horsemen of the European tribes that demolished the Roman Empire to harass the hitherto impregnable legions on all sides.

AD 1000

Men at arms

In mediaeval Europe, the **feudal system** meant that each lord armed his own band of followers. The basis of the army was the mounted man-at-arms in plate armour. The kingdom of Frankish leader Charlemagne (747–814) could mobilize 35,000 mounted troops.

In the **Crusades**, fought between 1095–1270 by the Christian European powers against Muslims in the Middle East, heavily armed Christian knights and their mounted troops were often at the mercy of Muslim light cavalry armed with scimitars and bows. After England's King **Richard** I (the Lionheart) (1157–99) dismounted many of his men and deployed English archers in the front line, the Christian forces began to make headway.

The **Hundred Years' War** (1337–1453) between France and England saw the longbow at the peak of its power, but also the first successful use of bombards – siege guns powered by gunpowder – at Calais in 1346–47.

The advent of **artillery** gradually changed the face of war and transformed the mediaeval army into a modern one. France's King Charles VIII (1470–98) developed the field gun, mounting it on a gun carriage drawn by horses.

In the mid-15th century armies began to use firearms extensively. The Spanish army under Ferdinand and Isabella had companies of **arquebusiers and musketeers**. The first firearms were inaccurate, slow and unwieldy but steady fire from a company could stop a charge.

Gustavus Adolphus of Sweden (1594–1632) improved the fire-power of his army by providing his musketeers with paper cartridges (see page 172), and introduced the **simultaneous volley**. The first ranks of

A prisoner is taken at the Battle of Agincourt, northern France, on 25 October 1415. English victory at Agincourt was largely due to the English longbowmen. The longbow – *c*.6ft 1.8m long and made of flexible yew – developed in the 12th century. It was much easier to load and fire than the far older, heavier crossbow – which often had to be wound back with a ratchet.

WAR

musketeers would fire, then retire behind the rear ranks to reload. Small manoeuvrable field guns called four-pounders were also introduced.

Naval strategy had been slow to change. In the 16th century, naval tactics were still aimed at grappling and boarding with subsequent hand-to-hand fighting. The first big guns were mounted in 'castles' in the bows and stern, but in England under Queen Elizabeth I (r.1558–1603) ships began to be designed with the ability to fire **broadsides** from big guns lining the sides of the ships. It was essential for such ships to manoeuvre swiftly side-on to the enemy.

The 17th century saw the birth of the **ship of the line**, with two or three gundecks capable of carrying 80 or more guns. But these giants paid the price of greater firepower by being difficult to manoeuvre. The **line-ahead** strategy was developed in the English fleet in 1653. It meant that the ships sailed into battle abreast, separated by perhaps 900ft *270m* between ships and stretching over several miles. Seizing the 'weather gauge' or upwind position was the decisive factor in battle.

In the 18th century, armies were largely based on infantry armed with **muskets and bayonets**. Relatively small improvements in firing

power were critical in establishing superiority.

The 186,000-strong army of **Frederick the Great** of Prussia (1712–86) took on the combined might of Austria, France and Russia in the Seven Years' War of 1756–63. Frederick's musketeers were supplied with iron ramrods instead of wooden ones and with funnel-shaped touch holes assisting the powder to enter the priming-pan.

They could fire three or four volleys to the enemy's two. At the same time, the Prussian infantry adopted the **quickstep** – 120 paces a minute – which meant that they could manoeuvre on the field of battle more quickly.

The **Napoleonic Wars** (1792–1815) contrasted the opposing field strategies of French general Napoleon and England's Duke of Wellington. French officers had begun to criticize the 'linear tactic' that deployed men over a long, thin line, so allowing as many men to fire at once as possible. Such long lines were unwieldy to manoeuvre and the French developed the idea of the **column**. Colonel Jacques de Guibert devised a drill for marching the men almost up to the enemy in columns and then quickly spreading into a firing line.

Wellington retained the thin line but held off the French columns with his exploitation of terrain. He drew his troops up for preference behind the crest of a ridge.

For almost 40 years after the Battle of Waterloo (1815) there were no major wars in Europe. Most armies returned to nuclei of professional soldiers, except in Prussia where the army

created a **General Staff** responsible for training and preparing contingency war plans.

Helmuth von Moltke (1800–91) was chief of General Staff from 1857–88. Under him Prussia adopted the soubriquet of the Nation-in-Arms, with every male doing three years' military service. Moltke also understood that the day of confrontational battles was over and developed tactics of **encirclement** or *Kesselschlacht*. This was demonstrated in the Franco-Prussian War of 1870–71, when Prussian forces out-manoeuvred the French in a series of swift moves and laid siege to Paris.

In the early years of the 20th century France, Italy and Russia adopted the Nation-in-Arms policy. By 1914, Germany could mobilize some 1.8 million troops and France around 1.6 million. Communications and transport still lagged behind, however. Once past the railhead, supplies and artillery had to be moved by horses – and telephones and telegraphs could have their land-based wires cut by opposing sides.

After World War I the 1919 **Treaty of Versailles** tried to stem rearmament but the rise of fascism in the 1920s led to the rejection of all the peace-keeping agreements. The German army rose once more to be the most efficient in Europe. At the same time the Japanese army was modernizing. When Japan invaded Chinese Manchuria in 1931 it was the real start of World War II in the East.

World War II demonstrated amazing advances in **mobility** in just 25 years since the previous global conflict. Aircraft had been used as reconnaissance planes in World War I but became a formidable element in the bombers of World War II. The Germans used the Luftwaffe to provide air support for their fast-moving Panzer divisions of tanks.

German leader Adolf Hitler (1889–1945) was eventually defeated largely because he overreached himself in too many theatres of war. In February 1941 he sent General Rommel to support the invasion of North Africa by the Italian Mussolini (1883–1945) and then in June

Speed was the key to the success of the German blitzkrieg ('lightning war') in World War II. Bombers went first, hitting ground defences. Paratroops followed, air-dropping to seize key locations. Then the ground troops motored in to mop up.

of the same year invaded Russia with a massive force. Hitler predicted that Moscow would fall within a month but, like many before him, he had failed to take in the logistic problems involved.

The German forces were still approaching Moscow as winter set in. They were running out of draught animals and lack of anti-freeze immobilized their vehicles. The Allied forces were able to rally.

AD 2000

Nuclear stand-off

The dawn of **nuclear power** in 1945 brought about a total re-evaluation of military and naval strategy. Such was the impact of this ultimate weapon that a new vocabulary had to be created – for example, **first strike** capability (the ability to wipe

out the enemy's resistance in a single, devastating attack) and **deterrence**, the prevention of conflict by the threatened counter-use of nuclear weapons.

The USA's world monopoly of nuclear power ended in 1949 when the USSR succeeded in detonating a *c.*20 kiloton plutonium bomb. The act signalled the beginning of the nuclear **arms race**. It soon became evident that the race could only be sustained at enormous cost; both sides had a financial interest in **disarmament** and there were intensive efforts to broker limits on testing and stock-piling warheads.

The denouement came with the 'High Frontier' strategy of US President **Reagan** (in power 1981–9) – in which anti-missile weaponry would be developed at a cost that was beyond the economic capacity of the USSR. In 1987, USSR President Mikhail **Gorbachev** (in power 1985–91) signed an Intermediate Nuclear Force (INF) Abolition Treaty.

Since the disintegration of the Soviet bloc in 1991, theatres of war have been largely in countries without nuclear potential and strategies have often been of **slow attrition**. Wars have been continuous between various African countries and within them. Conflict has erupted several times in the Balkans since 1991.

A significant factor in these wars is the **peace-keeping** attempts by United Nations forces. Propaganda is of great importance to smaller nations trying to persuade the USA, Britain, France or NATO to back a particular race or leader in a conflict.

In 1999 NATO used hi-tech reconnaissance aircraft to seek precise information on bombing targets in its campaign against Yugoslavia. Air reconnaissance images of the army barracks in Prizren, southern Kosovo, show the installations before a military strike (top) and afterwards (above). NATO used the latest B-2 stealth bombers, laser-guided missiles and air-launched cruise missiles in the conflict.

Killing power

Humans' ability to kill each other has progressed as technology has developed. The earliest weapons were stones or branches, used as clubs. Herbal poisons and sharp-edged or pointed stone weapons appeared in the Middle Palaeolithic times (*c*.250,000–45,000BC). Next came **bows and arrows** – arrowheads found in Tunisia in northern Africa date from before 25,000BC and possibly even earlier than 45,000BC.

Early peoples were driven to war by hunger, the desire for vengeance or the need to defend their territory. At some point, **race** became a motivation: the first set battles between identifiable races were fought in the 4th millennium BC.

Urbanism and imperialism generated **the first standing armies** and punitive expeditions. The Egyptian campaign against Palestine in *c*.2300BC is chronicled as having required 'tens of thousands of conscripts'.

The lethal capabilities of simple weapons could be awesome. In 216BC the Carthaginian general **Hannibal** (247–*c*.182BC) surrounded a Roman army at Cannae and slaughtered them all. Hannibal's troops killed over 80,000 Romans in a few hours of fighting.

The greatest single advance in killing power came in the early 14th century with **pistols and muskets**. At first guns were less efficient than bows and arrows, but they had one crucial advantage: a man had to be physically strong with years of training to be an archer, but even a small man could be trained to fire a gun in a few hours.

The last century of the 2nd millennium saw intense research in **chemical and biological warfare**. The Germans first used the poisonous gas chlorine at the Battle of Ypres on 22 April 1915 (5000 killed and 15,000 gassed). They had tested it on 3 January 1915 against the Russians in Poland at Bolimov, but with less effect. They followed it on 12 July 1917 with '**mustard gas**', a blistering agent.

In 1937 I. G. Farben of Germany discovered poisonous neurotoxic organophosphates, which were used to kill 5000 Kurds in the 1983–87 Iran–Iraq war. On 15 January 1999, after 21 years of negotiation, an international ban on their use was finally agreed.

In 1945 a new dimension entered warfare with the development of **atomic weapons** (see pages 180–2). It became necessary only to drop a single bomb in approximately the right place to inflict total devastation. About 155,000 people died in and around Hiroshima as a result of the first atomic blast on 6 August 1945.

By 1954 it was possible to load an atomic weapon on to a missile capable of striking with precision at a range of thousands of miles. The 'killing zone' had grown from a few feet in the days of hand-to-hand fighting to cover the entire planet. But these missiles have never been used: the threat of retaliation in similar form has proved a sufficient deterrent.

One of the great advances in killing power came when chemical energy, in the form of gunpowder, was put to use in weapons. This drawing from *c*.1390 shows a European soldier about to fire a gun mounted on a tilting swivel. Such early guns fired stone balls or lumps of iron to ranges of about 500 ft *150m*.

THE LARGEST MASS KILLINGS OF ALL TIME

Death Toll	Event	Date
26.3 million	Chinese leader Mao Zedong's (1893–1976) suppression of counter-revolutionaries.	1949 to May 1969
c.20 million	*T'ai-p'ing T'ien Kuo* (Heavenly Kingdom of Great Peace) rebellion against the Chinese Manchu Government, led by Hung Hsiu-ch'uan, who proclaimed himself to be the younger brother of Christ. The death roll in the sack of Nanking on 19–21 July 1864 alone exceeded 100,000.	1851–64
19 million	Deaths in USSR slave labour camps under Lenin (1870–1924), Stalin (1879–1953) and Khrushchev (1894–1971), comprising starvation, hypothermia, torture and execution. Administered by the GULAG (*Glavnoe upravlenie ispravitel'no-trudovykh lagereï*), the Chief Administration for Corrective Labour Camps.	1921–60
c.8 million	Stalin's Great Purge or *Yezhovshchina*, named after the Commissar Nikolai I. Yezhov (1895–1939), who was shot by his successor Lavrentiy P. Beria (1899–1953).	1936–38
7 million	Induced famine under Stalin's First Five Year Plan to break the resistance of the peasantry against the collectivization of agriculture in the Ukraine, Northern Caucasus, the Volga region and in Kazakhstan.	1931–32
6.3 million	Revolution, civil war fighting and post civil war famine in the Soviet Union under Lenin.	1917–21
c.5.7 million	*Endlösung* ('final solution') – liquidation of European Jewry in German-occupied areas by agencies of the Nazi Party.	April 1941–May 1945
3.05 million	Death roll of Red Army and Soviet civilian prisoners in Germany, Poland and occupied USSR. Another estimate is 4.65 million.	1941–45

PROGRESSIVE KILLING POWER RECORDS

Date	Maximum toll	Range	Weapon	Location
pre 2,700,000BP	One at a time	Close combat	Manual. Throttling and cudgelling	Great Rift Valley, East Africa
c.500,000BP	One at a time	Pike's length	Unhafted stone weapons and wooden spears	Africa and Europe
c.60,000BP	2 +	c.120ft 40m	Wooden javelins with sharpened points	North-west Europe
c.45,000BP	2 +	330ft 100m	Bow and arrow	Aterians, north-west Africa
c.25,000BC	One at a time	180ft 60m	Slings	Franco-Iberia
21,000BC	One at a time	330ft 100m	Boomerang or throwing sticks	Oblazow, southern Poland
c.20,000BC	One at a time	Close quarters	Hafted stone axes and pikes	Northern Australia
c.15,000BC	2 +	Close quarters	Man traps – camouflaged pits	Franco-Iberia
pre 3500BC	Two at a time	100ft 30m	Bolos and lasso (entanglement)	All regions
c.3000BC	One at a time	Close quarters	Swords, now differentiated from daggers	Middle East
pre-2000BC	One at a time	165ft 50m	Blow guns (poisoned darts)	Amazonia
c.1850BC	c.10	Close quarters	Sword blades attached to horse chariot wheel hubs by Hittites	Anatolia, Turkey
c.750BC	2 +	Close combat	Samurai long sword (*katana*)	Japan
399BC	Chance	c.1500ft 450m	Arrow-shooting artillery of Dionysus I	Syracuse, Sicily
c.340BC	c.4	1150ft 350m	Torsion catapults invented by Polydius, Greece	Greece
AD674	whole crew	c.330ft 100m	'Greek Fire' (gasoline, resins, saltpetre, sulphur), catapulted or squirted at sea. Invented by Callinicus.	Byzantium (modern Istanbul)
c.1265	2 +	c.33ft 10m	Earliest hand gun (*huo thung*)	Ta-tsu, Szechuan, China
1245	Unknown	Unknown	Military rocket (*huo chien*). Two stage rocket (*huo lung chhu shui*) followed c.1330	Chhien-Hang estuary, near Hangzhou, China
1324	c.4	c.330ft 100m	Cannons: stone cannon balls of c.40lb 18kg	Metz, France
1376	High potential	990ft 300m	Trebuchet (from *trebucher*, to overturn) with counterpoise 12cwt 600kg missiles, Genoese v. Cypriots. Use ceased c.1480	Cyprus
c.1200	2	825ft 250m	Longbow. Record range 1020ft 308m. Compare Turkish bow record of 2513ft 766m by Sultan Selim at Ok Meydam, Constantinople	Wales
1520	Unknown	Unknown	Rifled gun barrels: devised by August Kotter (Ger)	Germany
1585	Unknown	Unknown	Dutch-built fire-ship first used	Antwerp
1586	High potential	Varied	Cannon: largest made, 35in 890mm calibre, 30 tons	Kremlin, Moscow
1792	No estimate	7500ft 2285m	Tipu Saahib (Ind) (1749–92) deployed 30lb 13.6kg rockets against the British. Military use of solid-fuelled rockets ceased in 1881	Seringapatem, India
1884	High potential	645ft 200m	Belt-loaded, single-barrelled machine gun, invented by Hiram Maxim	London
31 Jan 1915	17,700 war death roll	Shell range	Poison gas: first used by Germans v. Russians. Permanently or temporarily incapacitated c.531,000 (1915–18)	Bolimov, Poland
1 July 1916	60,000	985ft 300m	German machine guns (supported by other weapons) v. French and British. Toll includes missing and wounded on a 15 mile 25km front on first day of the Battle of the Somme	Northern France
9 Nov 1918	c.5	1300ft c.400m	Bazooka liquid-fuelled rocket, devised by Robert Goddard (US) (1882–1945), as first demonstrated by US Army	Virginia, USA
29 Mar 1918	91	76 miles 122km	German 8.66in 200mm gun *Kaiser Wilhelm Geschutz*	St Gervais Church, Paris
1942	-	29 miles 46.4km	German 31.5in 800m siege guns, *Dora* and *Gustav*, firing 7.1 tonne projectiles from 94ft 8in 28.47m barrels	Sevastopol
1944–45	Single hit: 476	160 miles 260km	German V2 (*Vergeltungswaffe Zwei*) (Vengeance Weapon No. 2), formerly A4 (Aggregat 4)	Rex Cinema, Antwerp, Belgium
1944–45	5500	163 miles 260km	V1 (*Vergeltungswaffe Ein*) (Vengeance Weapon No. 1); 6725 fired at Britain. Range later reached 250 miles 400km	Europe
6 Aug 1945	155,000	1702 miles 2740km (from Tinian, Marianas)	4.4 ton atom bomb (uranium) dropped by US B-29 bomber *Enola Gay*, commanded by Col. Paul W. Tibbets	Hiroshima, Honshu, Japan
1954	Extreme potential	Missile range	Lithium$_6$ Deuteride 18–22 megaton thermonuclear warhead mounted on Intercontinental Ballistic Missile	Pacific
27 Jan 1967	Extreme potential	7450 miles 12,000km	First trial of Soviet SS-9 missile (model 3), 111ft 6in 34m tall, carrying a Fractional Orbital Bombardment Satellite (FOBS). Developed for hemispherical range up to 12,560 miles 20,215km	Baikonur cosmodrome, Kazakhstan, USSR

The atomic bomb

Vienna-born scientist Lise Meitner, working with the German Otto Hahn, discovered the radioactive element protactinium in 1917. Meitner's nephew was Otto Frisch, who also played a significant role in the development of the atomic bomb.

Atomic explosions derive their power from the **instability of matter**. When atoms or sub-atomic particles disintegrate, the result is a gigantic release of energy.

The realization that matter and energy were interchangeable was largely the work of the German-born scientist **Albert Einstein** (1879–1955). His famous equation $E = mc^2$ states that, at the square of the speed of light (c), energy and matter become indistinguishable.

In 1934, the Italian physicist **Enrico Fermi** (1901–54) bombarded the nuclei of uranium atoms with uncharged particles named neutrons to split them and produce a new element. He was mainly interested in controlling the release of energy that accompanied the reaction, so that the energy could be harnessed to generate power (see page 155).

In the same year Hungarian-born Leo **Szilard** (1898–1964) filed a British patent for the process of **nuclear fission**, in which the splitting of atoms produces energy. Szilard recognized that the process had implications for explosions as well as for energy production. In Dahlem, Germany, Otto

Hahn (Ger) (1879–1968) and Fritz Strassman (Ger) (1902–80) achieved nuclear fission with uranium on 17 December 1938. They found there was a **chain reaction**, in which, when the uranium nucleus split under bombardment by neutrons, it released new neutrons that could split another nucleus (see page 155).

Einstein and Fermi, both Jews, had fled European fascism to the USA; Szilard, who had moved from Nazi Germany to England in 1933, went on to the USA in 1938. The scientific émigrés in the USA understood the potential of German nuclear research. On 2 August 1939 Einstein wrote to warn President Franklin D. Roosevelt (1882–1945) of this potential.

The scientists knew that only a small amount of energy was needed to split the first uranium nucleus and so start the chain reaction. Given enough uranium, a vast amount of energy could be released. They set out to calculate the amount of uranium needed to sustain the chain reaction. This quantity was called the '**critical mass**'.

A major problem was that only one very rare kind of uranium known as **uranium-235** (U-235) supported nuclear fission. Just 0.7% of naturally occurring uranium was U-235. It seemed impossibly difficult to produce enough U-235 to make a bomb.

But in 1940 Austrian Otto Frisch (1904–79) and German-born Rudolf Peierls (1907–95), working in Britain,

calculated that a bomb could be made with just a few kilograms of U-235 – an achievable amount.

At the same time, scientists sought nuclear elements other than uranium. In 1940 **plutonium** was first obtained from uranium by Glenn Seaborg (US) (b.1912). Researchers found that plutonium gave off more neutrons than uranium during fission. It could be made from another much more widespread form of uranium – known as **uranium-238** (U-238).

Roosevelt formed the **Manhattan Project** to create a US atomic bomb in 1941. It was headed by US General Leslie Richard Groves (1896–1970) and physics professor Robert Oppenheimer (US) (1904–67). Oppenheimer assembled a team of distinguished scientists, including Fermi, Szilard, Frisch and Niels Bohr (Den) (1885–1962). Fermi and colleagues built the world's **first atomic pile** in 1942 (see page 155).

The task of accumulating a sufficient amount of U-235 was tackled at the Oak Ridge site in Eastern Tennessee. After three years, 88lb *40kg* of 80% pure U-235 was ready.

The principle of making the bomb was simple: two sub-critical masses of U-235 were assembled in separate compartments. To trigger the bomb, one mass would be fired into the other by means of a normal explosive charge and the resultant mass would be critical. The finished bomb, code-named **Little Boy**, was 10ft *3.05m* long with

```
                              Albert Einstein
                              Old Grove Rd.
                              Nassau Point
                              Peconic, Long Island
                                   August 2nd, 1939

F.D. Roosevelt,
President of the United States,
White House
Washington, D.C.

Sir:

      Some recent work by E.Fermi and L. Szilard, which has been com-
municated to me in manuscript, leads me to expect that the element uran-
ium may be turned into a new and important source of energy in the im-
mediate future. Certain aspects of the situation which has arisen seem
to call for watchfulness and, if necessary, quick action on the part
of the Administration. I believe therefore that it is my duty to bring
to your attention the following facts and recommendations:

      In the course of the last four months it has been made probable -
through the work of Joliot in France as well as Fermi and Szilard in
America - that it may become possible to set up a nuclear chain reaction
in a large mass of uranium,by which vast amounts of power and large quant-
ities of new radium-like elements would be generated. Now it appears
almost certain that this could be achieved in the immediate future.

      This new phenomenon would also lead to the construction of bombs,
and it is conceivable - though much less certain - that extremely power-
ful bombs of a new type may thus be constructed. A single bomb of this
type, carried by boat and exploded in a port, might very well destroy
the whole port together with some of the surrounding territory. However,
such bombs might very well prove to be too heavy for transportation by
air.
```

Albert Einstein's letter to Franklin Roosevelt warned the US President that German scientists were making progress in nuclear science and might soon be in a position to make a devastatingly powerful bomb. It led to creation of the US atomic program.

a diameter of 2ft 6in *0.76m* and weighed about 4 tonnes.

It was dropped from an American B-29 bomber over the Japanese port of **Hiroshima** on 6 August 1945. The flash reached 3000°C *5400°F*. The bomb obliterated more than 4 sq miles *10km²* and killed *c*.155,000 people.

By 1945, scientists at Columbia River, Washington State, had accumulated enough plutonium for two bombs. The plutonium bomb, code-named 'Fat Man' from its spherical shape, was dropped on the port of **Nagasaki** on 9 August 1945. Of the town's 212,000

population, 73,884 were killed. The Japanese surrender was offered the same month, ending World War II.

In the USA Hungarian Edward Teller (*b*.1908), conceived of the idea of a bomb which worked by the **fusion** of small atoms rather than the fission of large ones. Normally, such fusion only occurs at extremely high temperatures, for instance in the Sun. But Fermi and Teller saw that such temperatures could be produced in a fission reaction. German émigré Klaus Fuchs (1911–88), who was working in the USA as a spy for the USSR, passed on details of the fusion bomb concept. The result was quickly seen in the Soviet Union's explosion of a *c*.20 tonne **plutonium fusion bomb** in Kazakhstan on 29 August 1949.

The 'Cold War', a tense standoff between the USSR and the USA, had begun. The USA developed the fusion bomb, called the **H-bomb** because it used isotopes of hydrogen, deuterium (^{2}H) and tritium (^{3}H)and tested it in 1952 at Eniwetok Atoll in the Marshall Islands of the Pacific Ocean.

Arsenals of nuclear weapons proliferated, with competition between the USA and the Soviet bloc. The USA invented the **neutron bomb** in 1958. This device is a small hydrogen bomb with high radiation but reduced blast.

The Cold War came to an end after the accession to power in the USSR of Mikhail Gorbachev (*b*.1931) in 1985 and the dismantling of the Berlin Wall in 1989.

By this time, **other countries had nuclear potential**. In 2000, seven countries were known to have nuclear weapons (see box), but others, such as Brazil and South Africa, were known to have developed weapons under cover of nuclear energy programmes.

During the Cold War, nations developed missiles with nuclear warheads. The 1979 SALT II arms limitation treaty committed the USA and the USSR to a limit of 2250 strategic nuclear weapons each by 1981. Missiles in excess of this figure were destroyed with the silos (underground shelters) in which they had been stored, leaving craters that could be verified by satellite surveillance.

THE SEVEN DECLARED NUCLEAR POWERS

Country	First fission (A bomb)	Test site	First fusion (H bomb)	Test site
USA	16 July 1945	Alamogordo, New Mexico	1 Nov 1952	Eniwetok, Marshall Is.
USSR	29 Aug 1949	Semipalatinsk, Kazakhstan	12 Aug 1953	Pacific
UK	3 Oct 1952	Montebello Islands, Western Australia	15 May 1957	Christmas Islands, Pacific
France	13 Feb 1960	Reggane, Algeria	24 Aug 1968	Reggane, Algeria
China	15 Oct 1964	Lop Nor, Sin Kiang	17 June 1967	Lop Nor, Sin Kiang
India	18 May 1974	Thar Chagni		
Pakistan	28 May 1998	Baluchistan Desert		

Biological and chemical warfare

The 20th century saw both the initiation of large-scale chemical warfare and successful international efforts to eliminate poison gas and biological weapons.

The **first use of poison gas** was by the German Army against the Imperial Russian Army at Bolimov, Poland, on 3 January 1915. On 22 April that year at Ypres, France, the Germans used chlorine gas on a larger scale against Canadian and French-Algerian forces, killing an estimated 5000 and injuring a further 15,000. Non-fatal effects included lung damage and severe skin blistering.

Gas marks were provided for riders and their mounts on the battlefields of World War 1. Germany, in 1915 the first country to release disabling gases in warfare, had been a signatory to the 1899 Hague Convention that outlawed their use.

The Germans then switched to the choking gas phosgene or carbonyl chloride ($COCl_2$). On 12 July 1917 at Ypres, they used the vesicant (blistering) agent **mustard gas** or dichlorodiethyl sulfide.

The total **World War I death toll from gas warfare** used by both sides has been put at 85,000. A further 1.3 million suffered injury.

On 17 June 1925, leading nations signed a protocol prohibiting the use of asphyxiating and poisonous gases in warfare. The international ban broke down, however, when Japan used gas against the Chinese in Manchuria in 1931. Five years later the Italian army employed gas to kill 15,000 Ethiopians during the Abyssinian campaign.

In 1937 IG Farben in Germany discovered the deadly neurotoxic properties of organophosphates. Farben also manufactured the Zyklon B gas that was used in Nazi extermination camps, where c.5.7 million Jews were put to death in 1941–45.

In the Vietnam war of 1964–73 US forces used the **chemical defoliant** Agent Orange to combat guerrilla resistance by the Viet-Cong.

Both sides in the **Iran-Iraq war** of 1980–88 used chemical weapons, and Iraq is also believed to have used them against dissidents at home. On 16 March 1988, c.5000 Iraqi Kurds were killed at Halabja, Iraq, after being attacked with mustard gas, nerve gas and cyanide. Survivors said it was one of many attacks by the Iraqi authorities in the 1980s on those seeking the creation of an autonomous Kurdish state in the region.

In 1993 more than 120 countries signed an international ban on chemical and biological Warfare, and agreed to establish an independent body to check compliance. By this time chemists had created far more lethal **nerve gases** such as Sarin and Tabun, followed by VX, CB and CH. Wholesale destruction of stocks of the biological and chemical weapons ensued.

In the 1990s certain US and British veterans of the 1991 Gulf War (provoked by Iraq's August 1990 annexation of Kuwait) suffered from a medical condition dubbed Gulf War Syndrome (GWS). Some veterans alleged that the symptoms of GWS – headaches, muscle and joint pains, vomiting and sleep difficulties – were caused by prolonged low-level exposure to Iraqi chemical and biological weapons.

The exposure, they said, might have been the result of an Iraqi attack or of US bombing of Iraqi weapons production sites that released the agents into the atmosphere. Official US and British explanations, however, tended to describe GWS as a form of post-traumatic stress disorder.

Major battles

PRE AD 1

An empire won

The Macedonian general Alexander the Great (356–323BC) won a great victory over the Persian monarch Darius III at **Gaugamela** – near Nineveh (modern Iraq) – in 331BC. It gave him control of the vast Persian Empire, with its majestic capital of Persepolis and also opened the gate to the east. After defeating the last vestiges of Persian resistance in the Zagros Mountains, Alexander took and torched Persepolis. He continued to northern India, which he conquered in 326.

The **Battle of Actium**, off the Adriatic coast of Greece was fought in 31BC between Octavian (63BC–AD14) and Mark Antony (*c*.83–30BC), two of the three *triumvirs* who controlled the Republic of Rome after the murder of Julius Caesar.

Octavian had 400 *liburnae* (manoeuvrable triremes, galleys with three tiers of oars) whereas Antony's 360 vessels were heavier war galleys. The two fleets fought with missiles and fire darts.

Antony was persuaded by his lover Cleopatra, Queen of Egypt, to desert the battle and flee with her; 300 of his vessels surrendered to Octavian. Victory left Octavian master of the Roman world and from 27BC as **Augustus**, its emperor.

AD 1000

Saxons humbled

The Norman conquest in 1066 largely transformed the face of England from a Nordic and Saxon country to a French culture. Saxon King Harold (*c*.1020–1066) was defeated and killed by the invading forces of Duke William of Normandy at the **Battle of Hastings**, Sussex.

The Normans introduced French into the English language, thus doubling its lexical resources. Latin was reintroduced as the language of government and Norman architecture introduced a great phase of Church building.

In 1453 **Constantinople**, the capital of the Byzantine empire, seemed all but impregnable. Time after time, during the 1000-year history of the empire, the city had withstood barbarian attacks. Its walls were massively thick and the sea approach up the Golden Horn was blocked by a boom. But that year the city fell finally to the forces of the Ottoman Mehmet II (*r*.1444, 1451–81).

He succeeded through vast superiority of numbers – 100,000 Turks were brought to bear against the city's 7000 defenders – and large cannon, which repeatedly breached the walls. He also pulled off the astounding feat of transporting ships on rollers overland past the boom in the sea approach.

The fall of Constantinople meant the end of the Byzantine empire and the reinforcement of Islam in the Middle East. It came as Christian armies were driving the 'infidels' out of Europe.

In 1521, Hernan **Cortés** (Sp) (1485–1547) inflicted a decisive defeat on the

In 31BC the sea Battle of Actium in the waters off northwestern Greece was the end of the Roman Republic and the beginning of the Roman Empire. The victor, Octavian, became the first Roman Emperor, taking the name Augustus ('Revered One').

English history changed course in 1066 with the Norman invaders' victory over the Saxons at the Battle of Hastings. Horse power was crucial in the battle – mounted Norman knights overpowered the Saxon King Harold's army of foot soldiers.

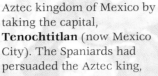

Aztec kingdom of Mexico by taking the capital, **Tenochtitlan** (now Mexico City). The Spaniards had persuaded the Aztec king, Montezuma II (1466-1520), to become a Spanish vassal, but the Aztecs rebelled.

Cortés utterly destroyed Tenochtitlan and Spain gained control of a large tract

French Emperor Napoleon's retreat from Moscow in winter 1812 left only 30,000 survivors of the 675,000 men he had taken into Russia the previous summer. It inspired his enemies in Europe to attack and he suffered a major defeat at Leipzig the following year. Forced to abdicate in April 1814, he was exiled to the Mediterranean island of Elba.

of Central America from which to continue its exploratory invasion of the South American continent.

The downfall of the French Emperor Napoleon I (1769-1821) began in Russia in 1812. In fact, Napoleon had triumphed at the Battle of Borodino 70 miles *110km* west of Moscow and occupied Moscow on 14 September 1812, but the next day fire broke out and destroyed a great part of the city. A month later, Napoleon began his disastrous **retreat from Moscow**.

The French army was decimated by the rigours of the Russian winter and the Russians' systematic destruction of crops and livestock in the countryside. The disaster cost Napoleon

his reputation for indestructibility and destroyed the hitherto blind hero-worship of the French soldiers and nation for their leader.

In 1863 during the American Civil War, the forces of the Union (North) were enabled to take the initiative after the defeat of Confederate General Lee (1807-70) at **Gettysburg**, Pennsylvania. Lee had successfully prevented the Union army from making an advance on the Confederate capital of Richmond, Virginia, and was advancing his rebel army north up the Shenandoah and Cumberland valleys. The Union army was manoeuvring to get between Lee and Washington, D.C.

The two armies had temporarily lost each other, each thinking the other was hundreds of miles away when scouts reported that instead they were within 25 miles *40km*. Lee's defeat was by no means crushing: he lost 28,000 men while the Union commander, George Meade (1815-72), lost 23,000. However, Lee was forced into retreat

and the Confederacy forces never regained the offensive.

The First **Battle of the Somme**, France, in World War I was fought between 24 June and 18 November 1916. The British and French allies launched the offensive hoping to break through the German lines. One and a half million shells were fired at the German positions in a seven-day bombardment before the troops were ordered 'over the top' of their trenches on 1 July.

By November, 6 miles *10km* of ground had been gained at a cost of 614,105 Allied casualties and approximately the same number of Germans.

This was the first battle to use **tanks**, developed in England by Winston Churchill (1874-1965) and Ernest Swinton (1868-1951) but the armoured vehicles were still too cumbersome to achieve more than an initial shock. Tanks first made a decisive

For centuries, generals have deliberately damaged the environment as a war weapon. In the 1991 Gulf War, Iraqi leader Saddam Hussein wreaked havoc in Kuwait's oilfields. After flooding the Persian Gulf with crude oil, his retreating troops set fire to the oil wells themselves. This satellite photo shows the resulting plumes of smoke, hundreds of miles long.

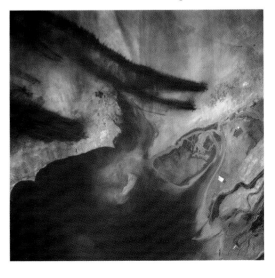

impact at Cambrai on 20 November 1917.

The unparalleled casualties of the Battle of the Somme achieved very little. They did underline the fact that trench warfare, with its high cost in lives per foot of gain, was not a sound strategy.

The worst war in more than five millennia of military history was **World War II** (1939–45). It was fought in or by all six continents and in every ocean, by close to 100 million combatants, for only two weeks short of six years.

The total of military personnel killed and missing was more than 15 million and the civilian dead more than double that figure. One estimate puts the total loss of life at 54.8 million, including 7.8 million Chinese civilians. The country suffering worst was Poland with just over 6 million (22.2 per cent of her population) killed.

One of the turning points of World War II was the **Battle of Britain** fought in the skies over southern England from 10 July to 31 October 1940. German leader Adolf Hitler (1889–1945) used airfields in the Netherlands, Belgium and France to launch air raids over England preparatory to invasion across the English Channel – a plan code-named Operation Sea Lion. The Royal Air Force held the German Luftwaffe at bay, leading Hitler to call off his plans to invade England and turn his attention to **Russia** instead – a strategy that was to prove as fatal for him as it had been for Napoleon 128 years earlier.

The USA became embroiled in the **Vietnam War** in 1964 after the Communist Vietcong in South Vietnam

attempted a coup with the support of North Vietnam and China. The USA made many blunders: they ultimately lost some 56,000 soldiers and it is estimated that one-fifth of these were killed by their own side; troops massacred 109 civilians at the village of My Lai; and they destroyed 50 per cent of Vietnam's forest cover in an attempt to expose guerilla fighters.

When the North Vietnamese army and the Vietcong launched the **Tet Offensive** against a series of South Vietnamese targets including Saigon in 1968, they were unsuccessful. The US and South Vietnamese troops expelled all the Communists, but paid a terrible cost in civilian lives.

The USA began a gradual withdrawal from Vietnam in 1969. South Vietnam was annexed by the north in 1976 and the united country was renamed the Socialist Republic of Vietnam.

AD 2000

The desert war

The 1991 **Gulf War** between an alliance of 28 nations and Iraq was a demonstration of a short effective offensive. Iraq invaded Kuwait on 2 August 1990 with an army of 200,000. **Operation Desert Storm** under US General Norman Schwarzkopf (*b.*1934) deployed some 762,000 men and launched a massive air bombardment of Baghdad.

It is estimated that over 90,000 tonnes of ordnance were dropped on Iraq and occupied Kuwait in the space of six weeks, killing between 100,000 and 200,000 civilians.

Anti-Communist fervour drove the USA into the war in Vietnam, but when the conflict ended in 1975 – two years after American troops had been withdrawn – the Communist North Vietnamese were victorious. Defeat came as a severe shock to the Americans. In the USA a strong anti-war movement had developed, thanks largely to television reporting that brought the stark realities of the conflict into people's living rooms.

COMMUNICATIONS
& MEDIA

- **Writing**

- **Postal services**

- **Personal communication**

- **Printing and publishing**

- **Photography**

- **Cinematography**

- **Recorded sound**

- **Popular music**

- **Radio**

- **Television**

- **Computing**

Cinema represents an essentially 20th-century
form of communication that today can be
produced by anyone with a video camera.
Whereas writing systems can be dated as far
back as 4000BC and early woodblock printing
presses to the 7th and 8th centuries, it has
been the 20th century that has seen the most
complete realization of communications and
media to make planet Earth a global village.

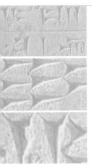

Writing

BEFORE AD 1

A tool of commerce

Civilization rests on the invention of writing. Communication, records of history and sophisticated trade all depend on the ability to pass on or note down information. Because the exchange of property in trade is one of the earliest activities of man, simple **records of numbers** are the oldest prototypes of writing.

The **earliest known writing system** may date from c.4000BC. Fragments of pottery from the 5th millennium BC Yangshao culture – known since 1921 – were excavated at Banpo, near Xian City, China in 1954–57, and have marks which are probably numbers.

The next development was **pictograms** – simplified pictures of objects – in c.3300BC. The **hieroglyphic language** of Egypt and the ideogram script of China (in which every thing has its own symbol) are both based on this system, which entails having many thousands of symbols. The earliest known pictograms, impressed on soft clay with a

The first written scripts were developed for keeping records of trade and tax accounts. This tablet (c.2350BC) from Tello in southern Mesopotamia is a tally of goats and sheep. Among the cuneiform writing and pictographic symbols are figures recognizable as four-legged animals.

stylus in Uruk, Mesopotamia, appear to be numeric and pictographic. They reflect the increasing economic complexity of the earliest city states in this area. Numerals and the sign for barley – six chevrons, looking like an ear of barley on its side – have been deciphered.

Cuneiform writing (from Lat. *cuneus*, a wedge, *forma*, a shape) was in use from c.3300BC until AD75. It began in the Sumerian civilization in Mesopotamia and was used by many of the civilizations of the Middle East, including the Hittites and the Persians. The script was formed by pressing a wedge-shaped stylus into clay. Cuneiform uses a combination of ideograms and phonetic word symbols – that is, symbols representing the sounds of language.

Two scripts have been found from the Bronze age **Minoan civilization** in Crete c.2000–1500BC. The script called **Linear A** syllabic script – where a symbol stands for a spoken syllable, as in modern Japanese – remains very largely undeciphered, but is not Greek. **Linear B**, which replaced Linear A, was deciphered by Michael Ventris (Eng) (1922–56) and is an early form of Greek.

Excavations at Boghazköy, Anatolia, Turkey revealed a royal archive of 10,000 cuneiform tablets dating to 1350–1300BC. This was confirmed to be the site of the ancient Hittite capital of Hattusas. By 1933 most of the

Cuneiform writing developed over millennia, becoming a complex and subtle script. This 6th-century BC inscription in stone is from the magnificent palace of Persian ruler Darius – self-styled 'King of Kings' – at Persepolis in southern Iran.

Sumero-Babylonian syllabary borrowed or adopted by the Hittites had been deciphered.

In c.1050BC the **Phoenicians** developed the alphabetic concept, with 22 letters. The first three signs were the glottal stop *aleph* (an ox), *beth* (a house) and *gimel* (throwing stick). This script, stabilizing by 800BC, lasted for more than 1000 years around the eastern Mediterranean. It was first read from right to left.

The Modern **European alphabet**, now of 26 letters, derives from Euboean Greek, which was adopted in Italy by the Etruscans c.750BC. It was inherited by the Romans and spread throughout the Roman Empire as **classical Latin** script. The Romans invented the letter G, and the letters J and V only came into general use after AD1630.

In India during the reign of Asoka (Ashokavardhana), (272–231BC) the earliest **alphabetic Indian writing** appeared on stone inscriptions. The Brahmi writing system contained both consonants and vowels.

It was the root of the Devangari script, employed in recording Sanskrit and later Hindi, and is believed to be of Phoenician origin.

The early **Chinese Shang script** of some 4500 characters was replaced by a simplified small seal script in the unified empire of Qin Huang Di (r. 221–210BC). Despite this reform, the number of characters grew to more than 9500.

The discovery of the Rosetta Stone in August 1799 was the key to the **deciphering of Egyptian hieroglyphs**. Hieroglyphs were used in Egypt from the mid-4th millennium BC to the 3rd century AD. The Rosetta Stone dates from 197BC and has the same inscription written in three scripts – hieroglyphs, Greek and 'demotic' (that is, a simplified form of hieroglyph).

AD 1

A northern script

From *c.*AD100 to 1200, the Nordic, 24-letter **Runic script** was widespread from Greenland to present-day Poland. Runes are combinations of straight lines which developed from being carved on sticks, probably by traders. The Runic alphabet is known as the 'futhark' after the order of the first six letters – f, u, th, a, r, and k.

Paper was invented by the Chinese *c.*AD105. The invention was attributed to Cai Lun (Tsai Lun) (*c.*57–*c.*121). The paper-making process did not reach the Islamic world until *c.*750.

In 150 the **first dictionary** arranged 9353 Chinese characters in 540 groups according to their meaning.

Arabic writing, like that of **Hebrew**, developed from the Phoenician alphabet. The earliest Arabic inscriptions appeared *c.*512.

PUNCTUATION MARKS AND ACCENTS

*c.*400 BC Colon	:	Plato (*c.*428–*c.*348BC) introduced a double point (:) or modern colon to indicate the end of a section. Used from *c.*1480 to separate a general statement from an explanatory statement or example. In mathematics used to express a ratio.
*c.*360 BC Paragraph	¶	Aristotle (Gk) (384–322BC) first indicated a break of sense or the beginning of a new topic by placing a short horizontal stroke under the start of a new line. The present-day practice of indenting new paragraphs dates from the 17th century. Derived from the Greek *paragraphos*, side writing.
*c.*195BC Accenting	´ `	Introduced by Aristophanes of Byzantium (Gk) (*c.*257–180BC) in the recitation of classical Greek. Derived from the Latin prefix *ac* indicating intensification + *cantus*, song.
*c.*195BC Asterisk	*	Introduced by Aristophanes in the Alexandrian library to indicate ambiguity. Re-introduced into English text in Arcadia by Sir Philip Sidney (1554–86) in 1587. Derived from the Greek *asteriskos*, little star.
*c.*195BC Circumflex	∧	Introduced by Aristophanes to indicate rising-falling tone in verse recitals. Adopted by French typographers to indicate the dropping of a consonant.
*c.*765 Full Stop	.	Introduced to end long sections of writing by the European scholar Alcuin (735–804). It was later known as the 'period' from the Greek *periodos*.
*c.*1510 Apostrophe	'	Originally used to denote the omission of letters (e.g. can't). It was by *c.*1720 extended in English to all possessives. Late Latin for turn away, from Greek *apo*, away; *strepho*, turn.
1534 Comma	,	The earliest appearance in English was in *A Devout Treatyse called the Tree and XII Fruites of the Holy Goost*. Latin, from Greek *komma*, a clause or separated piece.
1553 Exclamation mark	!	Derived by Renaissance typographers from the Latin *io*, an exclamation of joy. At first written as an i over an o, the exclamation mark proper (known to printers as a shriek) first appears in the English *Catechism of Edward VI* in 1553.
1587 Question mark	?	The original Latin *quaesto*, a seeking, written at the end of a sentence which contained a query, was abbreviated in turn to Qo, then the Q was written above the o and this evolved in the curved mark above a dot, to give the sign '?'. It was used in this final (modern) form by Sir Philip Sidney (1554–86) in his *Arcadia*.
*c.*1610 Acute and Grave	é è	As with the circumflex (rising-falling) so the acute (rising) and the grave (falling) accents were first employed by Aristophanes (see *c.*195BC) to indicate voice inflections in Greek verse-speaking. Introduced in France to distinguish vowel lengths. Acute is derived from the Latin *acutus*, sharp; grave from the Latin *graves*, heavy – originally indicating a falling or low pitch.
1599 Cedilla	ç	Originally written as a small subscript letter 'z' under a 'c' to indicate a soft pronunciation, first in Spanish and later in French and Portuguese. Spanish *cedilla*, diminutive of *zeda* from Gk. *zeta*, letter 'z'.
1750 Square brackets	[ ]	Introduced as crochets. Now generally confined to mathematical texts.
1837 Ampersand	&	A corruption of 'and per se - and', tacked on to the early Victorian classroom recitation of the alphabetic order for the sign &.
Parentheses	( )	Round brackets used for the insertion or isolation of incidental material. *Parenthesis* is Latin, derived from the Greek for 'place in beside'.

Three scripts – Hebrew, Arabic and Roman – share space on a Jerusalem wall. Diverse written scripts are an indelible mark of difference at a time of increasing cultural homogenization. People continue to feel a fierce love for their own language, and this would appear to doom any attempt (such as the universal language Esperanto, invented in 1887) to create a single tongue for all peoples.

AD 1000

New letters for the Slavs

In 863–69 the Slavic-speaking people of the Eastern Orthodox faith started to use a 43-letter alphabet based on the Greek and Hebrew scripts. It was named after St Cyril (Gk) (*c*.827–869) and his brother, St. Methodius (*c*.825–884), who translated the Bible into Old Church Slavonic (akin to modern Bulgarian) using what became known as Cyrillic script. The **Cyrillic alphabet** is used in Bulgaria, Russia, Serbia and the Ukraine.

The South American **Inca civilization** of Peru, conquered by the Spanish in 1532, possessed no script. *Quipucamayocs*, or **knot keepers**, kept track of trade and bureaucratic requirements. The quipu system was decimal, with the absence of a knot denoting a zero. Some quipu bunches had as many as 75 knotted strings. The **Mayan civilization** from Yucatan, Central America, had a script which proved to be syllabic. In *c*.1570 Fray Diego de Landu (Sp) (1524–79) wrote his *Relación de las Cosas de Yucatán* containing the first attempt to decipher Mayan.

Thomas Shelton (GB) (1601–*c*.1650) invented a **shorthand** script in the 1620s and published it in his *Tachygraphy* in 1638. It was used by the diarist Samuel Pepys (Eng) (1633–1703).

Sir Isaac **Pitman** (GB) (1813–97) invented in 1837 the most widely used of the more than 400 shorthand systems for writing the world's most widespread language – English. His **phonetic** system, initially called Stenographic Sound-Hand, had 49 consonants and 16 vowel sounds, comprising 65 'letters' in all.

In 1847 Sir Henry Rawlinson (GB) (1810–95), aided by a 'wild Kurdish boy', completed the copying of the Behistun trilingual inscription (comprising texts in Old Persian, Elamite and Babylonian) on a mountainside in the Zagros Mountains of western Iran. His papier mâché casts and drawings of the inscription enabled linguists finally to decipher the mysterious cuneiform script.

AD 2000

Alphabets, politics and the force of big business

In the 20th century, written script has become a political tool as rulers attempt to align their countries with ideologies or with the developed world. In 1928 Kemal **Atatürk** (Tur) (1881–1938) decreed that Turkey should abandon her Arabic script and adopt the Roman (western) script. In 1940 Adolf **Hitler** (Aus/Ger) (1889–1945) banned German Gothic or black-letter script because he believed it to be of 'Jewish' origin.

In 1948 **Hebrew**, the language of the Old Testament and other Jewish scriptures, was declared the national language and script of Israel.

First **typewriters** and then **word processors** had a deep effect on languages with symbolic scripts. In China, Mao Zedong (1893–1976) introduced a westernized Chinese script known as Pinyin (spell-sound) in 1958. The system soon proved essential for inputting Chinese into word processors and computers.

In 1981 the western (or Roman) alphabet made its first appearance in Japan via advertising, and established itself as 'Romanjii' – a third system, alongside the existing Kanji and Kana scripts.

International trade has led to many **symbols** becoming **international** – in road signs, on dashboards or on remote controls. In the 1990s, communication by email has produced a spate of symbols which can be created on a keyboard, such as the **smiley** :-).

Postal services

BEFORE AD 1

Royal messengers

The earliest postal system of which there is any firm knowledge is that of Ancient Egypt. The Egyptian pharaohs had a **royal courier system** for relaying messages across their territories from as early as 2850BC. The letters bore the message 'In the name of the living King – speed'.

The **Ancient Greeks** used homing pigeons for reporting the results of Olympic contests c.450BC. The Greeks also developed semaphore (from the Greek words *sema*, sign and *phores*, bearing), for military uses in c.140BC.

AD 1

Imperial order

The **Roman** Emperor Augustus (r.27BC–AD14) refined an existing mounted postal system – the *cursus publicus* – so that speeds of 170 miles *270km* a day were attainable. In the East, the Roman postal system was absorbed under Arab rule and its centre was transferred from

The world's first adhesive postage stamp was Britain's Penny Black, which went on sale on 1 May 1840, followed a week later by the Twopenny Blue.

Constantinople (modern Istanbul) to Baghdad.

American civilizations, such as the Mayans (c.AD250–900) of southern Mexico and the Inca (c.AD1300–1550) of the Andes, evolved a system of **relay runners** along fixed routes.

AD 1000

First private post

Private postal systems sprang up in Europe in the early Middle Ages. Both the Church and groups of merchants maintained messenger systems from c.1150, and the early European universities soon followed suit.

The Counts of Thurn and Taxis, in Germany, developed a highly profitable postal network after 1447. It covered Europe from Poland to Spain and employed more than 15,000 couriers.

State-run postal systems appeared in Europe with Louis XI's *Ecurie du Roi* in France in 1477 and the appointment of Sir Brian Tuke (d.1545) in 1516 as Master of the Post in London. Houses were first numbered in 1463 in Paris on the Pônt Notre-Dame, which aided delivery.

Postal charges for non-official mail between Paris and other major French cities were begun in 1627. The world's **first post boxes** were set up in Paris in 1653, but were soon vandalized and scrapped. In 1672 the post was made a state monopoly in France and private services were banned.

The first public postal service in America was set up in

Boston on 5 November 1639 with the appointment of Richard Fairbanks as the Postmaster of the Massachusetts Bay Colony.

In late 18th-century England road-building made it practicable to utilize **stage coaches** for moving mail. The coaches could travel more than 120 miles *195km* in about 12 hours.

Railways were first used to carry mail on 11 November 1830 between Liverpool and Manchester, England. **Transatlantic mail** was first carried by steam power aboard the SS *Royal William* from Quebec to Cowes, Isle of Wight, on 4–29 August 1833.

The world's first official **air mail** by powered aircraft was between the cities of Allahabad and Naini, India, on 18 February 1911.

AD 2000

Addressing by numbers

Post codes were introduced by the German government in 1942. The system was adopted by other countries after World War II, with Britain being the first to have an alphanumerical system in 1959.

At the end of the 2nd millennium, email and facsimile machines offer a swift and reliable alternative to postal services. These could pose a threat to the post, yet postal services are thriving. In mid-1998, the US Postal Service (in the country with the widest computer ownership) had 858,066 staff, higher by far than that of any other US independent agency.

In 1860, the Pony Express postal service was established across the American West from St Louis, Missouri, to California. A team of riders on relays of horses could cover the distance in just 10 days. The system was short-lived, being superseded by the telegraph in 1861. This rider is taking part in a re-creation of the Pony Express route in 1988.

Personal communication

BEFORE AD 1

Before language

Ancestors of modern humans such as Australopithecines in East Africa 4.4 million years BP communicated by **touching**, **gesture**, **grunting** and **screaming**. Other forms of early communication included **tree-blazing** by cutting bark (beginning *c.*2.7 million years BP), **log drumming** (*c.*1.9 million years BP), **smoke signalling** (*c.*1.5 million years BP) and **whistle-blowing** (*c.*60,000BC).

People in Anatolia, Turkey, were signalling using **hill-top beacons** before 6000BC. The first mirrors – of polished

Claude Chappe, pioneer of semaphore visual signalling, demonstrated his new system in 1793. It took two minutes to send a message 144 miles *231km* from Paris to Lille using a network of 15 stations equipped with signalling arms.

copper or bronze – were made *c.*2950BC and may have been used to send signals by reflecting sunlight.

AD 1000

A distant voice

Speaking tubes and ear trumpets were known in the late 15th century: Leonardo da Vinci (It) (1452–1519) was familiar with their use in the palace of the Duke of Milano.

In 1667 Robert Hooke (Eng) (1635–1703), Curator of Experiments at London's Royal Society, reported of **string telephones**: 'Tis not impossible to hear a whisper a furlong's distance.' (A furlong is 220 yards *201m.*)

The invention of the **telescope** in 1609 (see pages 90–91) made long-

distance visual signalling more practicable. The semaphore (Gk. *sema*, sign; *phoros*, bearing) method was pioneered by Claude Chappe (Fr) (1763–1805) on 2 March 1791 when he sent signals by means of pivoted beams with moveable arms on the end of each a distance of 15km *9.3 miles* between stations in Paris and Château de Brûlon.

Such methods were superseded by the invention of the electric telegraph, which sent electric signals along a wire, in the mid-19th century. In 1835 Professor Moncke of Heidelberg demonstrated the earliest electromagnetic telegraph,, which took advantage of the fact that the electric current produces a magnetic effect, to Baron Schilling von Canstadt (Ger) (1786–1837).

Moncke used a copy of this instrument in a March 1836 lecture attended by William Fothergill Cooke (Eng) (1806–79), and in July 1837 Cooke performed trials of a system that he, together with Charles Wheatstone (Eng) (1802–75), had patented a month earlier. The trial was between Euston and Camden Town, London, a distance of more than 1 mile *1.6 km.*

In the USA Samuel Finley Breese Morse (US) (1791–1872) independently devised a telegraph system *c.*1835. His assistant Alfred Vail (US) (1807–59) in 1838 re-designed Morse's crude system, creating the dot-dash

Morse code. With a US government grant, Morse was able to complete his first line over 37 miles *60km* from Baltimore to Washington, D.C. It was first used on 24 May 1844.

The possibility of translating sound waves into electrical

Scottish-born telephone inventor Alexander Graham Bell made the first long-distance call on 3 Apr 1877, from New York City to Thomas Watson in Boston on telegraph lines across 292 miles *470km*.

impulses and transmitting them along wires occurred to several 19th-century inventors. Antonio **Meucci** (It) (1807–89) is honoured in his birthplace, Florence, as the inventor of the **telephone**. When working as an electro-plater in Cuba in 1835–44, he added to his income by applying wires to patients as an electrotherapist. He heard the voices of patients over one of these when 82ft *25m* distant. He developed a working telephone but after moving to the USA in 1850 was unable to raise the $250 necessary to take out a final patent on his invention.

Scottish-born **Alexander Graham Bell** (US) (1847–1922) independently conceived of the idea of transmitting speech telegraphically in July 1874; he concluded that it should

be possible to 'make a current of electricity vary in intensity precisely as the air (voice) varies in density during the production of sound'. Bell filed his basic telephonic patent on 14 February 1876.

The first telephone call was made on 10 March 1876 in Boston. Bell addressed his assistant Thomas Augustus Watson (1854–1934) via his mouthpiece. It was variously recorded as 'Mr. Watson (please) – come here – I want (to see) you'. The **first sustained telephone conversation** took place between Bell in Boston and Watson in Cambridgeport, Massachusetts – 2 miles *3.2km* – on 9 October 1876.

The first **permanent domestic telephone** was installed between 27 March and 4 April 1877 at the home of Charles William Williams Jr. (*c.*1840–1910) in Somerville, Massachusetts.

The **first telephone numbers** were assigned to 200 subscribers at Lowell, Massachusetts, in 1879. Previously, names only had been used when calling via the exchange.

The first **radio telephone** was developed by Reginald Aubrey Fessenden (Can) (1868–1932) and first demonstrated at Cob Point, Maryland, over 1 mile *1.6km* in December 1900.

The first **outdoor telephone kiosk** was installed in High

Holborn, London, in May 1903. The traditional British glazed red telephone boxes date from 1921.

AD 2000

The mobile age

International direct dialling became possible in 1962. Bell Telephones introduced **push-button** – touch-tone – telephones between Carnegie and Greensburg, Pennsylvania, on 18 November 1963.

The first telephone service **via satellite** was introduced using the 'Early Bird' satellite on 28 June 1965 between the USA, the UK, Germany, France, Switzerland and Italy.

Cellular radio telephones were developed in Japan in 1979. They were introduced on a large scale in 1983, by AT&T. In the first year, they had 200,000 subscribers; by 1988, 2 million.

The first mobile phones to offer **email and internet access** (see pages 246–7) were introduced by Motorola in 1996. By 2000, over 500 million mobile phones were in use around the world.

WAP phones, introduced in 2000, enable users to access news, weather, traffic reports and other information via the Internet. Subscribers can also use the phones to send and collect email messages. WAP stands for Wireless Application Protocol.

Printing and publishing

Johannes Gutenberg pioneered printing using moveable metal type in Mainz, Germany. In 1460 he lost his press because he failed to pay back a loan to business partner Johann Fust, who thus seized it.

BEFORE AD 1

Reed paper

The Ancient Egyptians first made a writing material *c.*3000BC from the reed *cyperus papyrus*, found in the Nile valley. The Chinese had books as early as 1300BC but these were made of **wood or bamboo** strips bound together with cords.

The Library at **Alexandria** in Egypt was founded by Ptolemy II (308–246BC), who ruled Egypt from 283BC until his death. The library was the most famous centre of learning of the ancient world. It had between 200,000 and 700,000 scrolls up to 100ft *30.5m* long.

The Ancient Greeks wrote books in scroll form also. Their scrolls were shorter, up to 35ft *10.5m* long. Rolled up, they stood about 9in *23cm* high and were 1–1.5in *2.5–3.8cm* in diameter.

Parchment, named after Pergamum in Asia Minor (modern Turkey), was made from calf, goat, sheep, gazelle and even ostrich skin. It began to break the Egyptian monopoly of papyrus *c.*150BC. **Vellum**, from Old French *velin*, a calf, was leather made from the skins of calves. The use of sharpened goose quills as pens became practicable.

The Romans produced **books on a commercial scale** in *scriptoria* or writing-rooms. The book was dictated by a *lector* (reader) and copied by several scribes at once.

AD 1

Hand-written manuscripts

In AD100–150 books began to be bound in **codex** form – that is, as folded sheets of vellum bound together and then cut along their edges, rather than as rolls or scrolls.

In the early Christian era, scribes were employed to copy the **scriptures**. In abbeys and monasteries scribes copied, illuminated and bound manuscripts. The *Book of Kells* is one such, produced in the 8th century in the monastery of Kells in Co Meath, Ireland. The *Book of Kells* is written on vellum, which continued in use for centuries after the Arabs brought paper to Europe.

AD 1000

Printed Bible

The **earliest known book on European paper** is the Silos missal from Burgos, Spain, dating from *c.*1010.

In 1455 Johannes **Gutenberg** (Ger) (*c.*1400–68) printed the first book using moveable type. Only 31 perfect copies and 18 imperfect copies of his Latin Bible survive. A copy was auctioned at New York in 1987 for $5.39 million.

William **Caxton** (Eng) (*c.*1422–91) introduced printing to England, having learned his trade in Germany. His first press was set up in Belgium where he produced the first book printed in English, the *Recuyell of the Historyes of Troye* (1474). The first book printed in England was *Dictes or Sayengis of the Philosophres* in 1477. Caxton printed about 100 books in total, including a French–English dictionary.

In 1605, Abraham Verhoeven in Antwerp produced the first regular **newspaper**, the *Nieuwe Tijdinghen*. The first daily paper was in Leipzig, Germany, produced by Thimotheus Ritzch in 1650.

Cloth binding for books was introduced instead of the more expensive calf in 1820. With the advent of the cheaper material, publishing houses began to bind books themselves; previously, the

The English word paper is derived from the Latin name for the reed used to make writing material in Ancient Egypt. The Egyptians chopped the pith of the papyrus reed into pieces of equal length then beat them into smooth, flat sheets. This papyrus is from the Book of the Dead, a collection of religious texts often buried in tombs with the deceased.

leather binding had been done by the bookseller or the bookbuyer himself.

Cheaper methods of production and a rising middle class encouraged book production. In Britain, for example, 600 new titles were published in 1825, compared with barely 100 a year in the previous century. In the USA, publishers would wait at the quay for ships to bring new books over from Europe.

At this time, authors had no protection from copying. As soon as a book appeared, it could be pirated. Denmark imposed the first measures towards international **copyright** in 1828.

In the 1850s, publishers began to produce cheap **reprint** collections. One of the largest at 1060 volumes was George Routledge's (1812–88) *Railway Library*. The books were sold on railway station stalls at 1 shilling (5p) each.

The **Berne convention** established a uniform international system of copyright in 1885. Authors' work belonged to them or their heirs during their lifetime and for 50 years after their death.

In 1887, Germany became the first country to adopt a **net price agreement** between publishers and booksellers, instigated by Reich Publishers. The publisher agreed to give booksellers a discount provided that the bookseller did not undercut a fixed price.

In Britain, this was instituted as the Net Book Agreement in 1901, but the USA only adopted the system to a limited extent.

The first **mass-market paperbacks** were produced by Sir Allen Lane (1902–70) of Penguin in 1935, priced at 6d (2.5p).

Penguin's best-selling reprint was *Lady Chatterley's Lover* by English novelist D. H. Lawrence (1885–1930), which sold 3.5 million copies. The book had become notorious after it was prosecuted on the grounds of obscenity. A jury in the Old Bailey, London, declared it not to be obscene on 2 November 1960.

AD 2000

The electronic age

Publishers began to issue books as **CD-Roms** in 1994. By 1995, most encyclopaedias were made in that format.

The Net Book Agreement in the UK, which fixed book prices between publishers and bookshops, collapsed in January 1997. This meant that bookshops were able to introduce discounts and became more reliant on high volumes of low-priced titles. The late 1990s saw large bookshops open in Britain after the pattern of Barnes and Noble's New York store, which has 64,584 sq ft *6,000m²* floor space.

Publishing became increasingly competitive, with books – like pop albums – plugged for the **best-seller** list when they came out but soon forgotten. Spectacular **advances** to authors included a $21 million three-book deal for Jeffrey **Archer** (Eng) (*b*.1940) from HarperCollins in 1995 and $600,000 paid to Tom **Wolfe** (US) (*b*.1931) in 1998 for the magazine serialization of *A Man in Full*.

KEY DATES IN PRINTING

AD600 The use of **wooden blocks** for printing was practised in China.

1040–48 The Chinese used **moveable type** made of earthenware set in an iron frame. This invention is attributed to Pi Sheng (*c*.990–1051).

1430s Johannes Gutenberg began to experiment with **metal** moveable type, basing his idea on the Chinese wood blocks.

English novelist Charles Dickens spoke out in favour of international copyright while on a visit to the USA in 1842 – at the same time calling on Americans to abolish slavery. He began his prolific writing career as a parliamentary reporter but made his name as an author aged 24 with *The Pickwick Papers*. He was working on a novel, *The Mystery of Edwin Drood*, when he died on 9 June 1870.

THE WORLD'S LEADING COPYRIGHT BESTSELLERS

	Title	First published	Description	Author/Editor	Published number (millions)
1	*Guinness Book of Records*	Oct 1955	Compilation of superlatives in, on and beyond the Earth, in 36 languages	Norris and Ross (1925–75) McWhirter (twins), until 1986	83
2	*World Almanac and Book of Facts*	1868	Fact book of world-wide scope, 'Compendium of universal knowledge'. Annually from 1868 except in 1876–86.	New York World newspaperman (name not recorded). First named editor was Robert Hunt Lyman in 1923–37	72
3	*The Common Sense Book of Baby and Child Care*	1946	Parental advice on infant care by a paediatrician	Dr Benjamin McLane Spock (US) (1903–98)	51
4	*A Message to Garcia*	1899	Pro employer polemic on US labour relations	Elbert Hubbard	*c.*45
5 =	*Gone With the Wind*	1936	Romantic novel of the American South	Margaret Mitchell (US) (1900–49)	30
5 =	*To Kill a Mockingbird*	1960	Novel of childhood in American South	Harper Lee (US) (1926–)	30
5 =	*The Valley of the Dolls*	1966	Novel on sex, drugs and violence.	Jacqueline Susann (US) (1921–74)	30
8	*In His Steps*	1896	Religious book on moral crises	Rev. Charles Sheldon (US) (1857–1946)	28.6

Note: The Holy Bible *was first printed in Latin in Mainz, Germany by Johann Gutenberg (Ger) (c.1400–1468) in 1455. Attempts to estimate the total printings suggest that the number distributed by Bible Societies and Christian missionary organizations and churches since the early 19th century may be close to 6,000 million copies or part copies.*

The two staple pre-copyright educational manuals, The American Spelling Book *by Noah Webster (1758–1843) and* The McGuffey Readers *by William Holmes McGuffey, were respectively first published in 1783 and 1853. Aggregated printings have now been estimated at 100 million and 60 million copies respectively.*

Possession of *The Quotations of Chairman Mao,* known as the 'Little Red Book', was virtually compulsory in China in the years 1966–71 when printings reached 800 million.

1798 Aloys Senefelder (Ger) (1771–1834) invented **lithography**. The writing or drawing was done with a greasy crayon on an absorbent stone surface. The stone was wetted and inked. The wet stone did not absorb the ink but the greasy marks did and so could be printed.

1812 The German F. Koenig developed the first **steam-driven** flat-bed press. This machine, first used by *The Times* newspaper in London in 1814, could print 1100 sheets an hour. The first rotary press was patented by Richard Hoe (US) (1812–86) in 1845. In this press, not only the platen (the plate holding the paper), but also the typeface itself was cylindrical.

1822 Nicéphore Niepce (Fr) (1765–1833) invented the **photogravure** method, in which an image was photographically transferred to a plate which was prepared for printing by being etched.

1886 **Linotype** printing – so called because it produced each line of type separately in one piece of hot metal – was invented by Ottmar Mergenthaler (Ger/US) (1854–99). Linotype was widely used until the 1980s.

1889 American Tolbert Lanston (1844–1913) developed **monotype** – in which individual letters were moveable separately.

1960s **Offset** printing was developed – a flat plate of hard rubber had print set on it via a photographic method and then this was treated as in lithography. It had been invented using zinc sheets by W. Rubel (US) in 1904.

1960s **Electronic typesetting** eliminated the job of compositor, who previously had had to adjust the type with tweezers.

1990s Computerised typesetting and the computer-controlled **digital printer** became common.

Photography

Photography relies on two strands of technology. **Optics** are used to focus an image and import it into a camera via a lens; **photochemistry** is used to record the image on a light-sensitive medium. These technologies were developed separately at first and it was not until they were brought together that photography was born.

The principle of the **camera obscura** (Latin for 'dark chamber') is said to have been discovered by the 11th-century Arabian scholar Alhazen (c.965–1039). Light rays from an external illuminated object passed through an aperture in a side wall of the box and were focused on the opposite whitened wall, where an image appeared upside-down, enabling eclipses or sun-spots to be viewed without damage to the eyes.

The Italian Renaissance interest in perspective led to various experiments with the camera obscura. The device was described by **Leonardo Da Vinci** (It) (1452–1519) in his *Codex Atlanticus*.

Daniele Barbaro (It) (1513–70) inserted a **lens** into a camera obscura to provide a better image. Giovanni Baptista della Porta (It) (1543–1615) also described the usefulness to the artist of the 'pinhole camera' in his *Magiae naturalis* of 1589. These single biconvex lenses would distort the image – straight lines were seen as curves, for instance.

Photography (Gk. *photos*, light; *graphia*, writing) in a literal sense of 'writing by light' was discovered in 1727 by the German Johann Heinrich Schulze (1687–1744) at the University of Altdorf, near Nuremberg. He discovered the **photosensitivity of silver salts** when he found that silver nitrate turned dark on exposure to light.

Schulze inscribed words and whole sentences on silver sediments which turned, as he reported, 'deep red, inclining to violet blue' on exposure to sunlight. He called the light-sensitive, silver-impregnated mixtures in Latin *scotophorus* or in German *dunkelheitsträger*, meaning 'carrier of darkness'.

In 1790, Thomas **Wedgwood** (GB) (1771–1805) – son of the celebrated English potter Josiah – began to experiment with using silver nitrate or silver chloride paper to 'copy paintings upon glass and make profiles'. Wedgwood was described by a biographer as 'the first photographer in the world', but he was unable to fix his ephemeral images, so they disappeared when exposed to light. His work was lost for many years, but rediscovered in 1839.

The inventor of photography in the camera was French chemist Joseph Nicéphore **Niépce** (1765–1833), working from his family's country house at Gras, Saint-Loup-de-Varennes, central France, from 1801. In May 1816 he used paper sensitized with silver chloride, but his images could not be 'fixed' with the dilute nitric acid that he used.

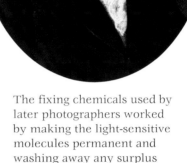

Frenchman Joseph Nicéphore Niépce had a prominent role in the government of Nice at the end of the 18th century, but in 1801 withdrew to dedicate his time to photographic research. He worked for a quarter of a century before he produced the world's first photograph c.1826.

The fixing chemicals used by later photographers worked by making the light-sensitive molecules permanent and washing away any surplus not affected by exposure.

Niépce experimented with various methods before in 1822 he hit on using a **pitch** that turns white and hardens on being exposed to light. This could be used as a kind of negative and in 1826 he first produced a positive image in a camera obscura after eight hours' exposure.

This **first photograph from nature** was taken from the upper-floor workroom window at Gras. Niépce's

English physicist and photographic researcher William Henry Fox Talbot took this picture, entitled 'The Open Door', in March 1843. Fox Talbot's was the first photographic process to use negatives and positives. He called his negatives calotypes (Gk, meaning 'beautiful impression').

camera, invented by Jacques Louis Vincent Chevalier (1770–1841) and his son Charles Louis (1804–59), was fitted with a *prisme ménisque* – a lens concave on one side and convex on the other. After exposure the image was developed by being washed over with a solution of white spirit (from petroleum) mixed with oil of lavender. This dissolved off such parts of the bitumen as were unhardened by the long exposure, leaving a permanent positive picture.

This historic photograph measures 7.8 x 6.3in *20 x 16cm* and was given by

Stereographs – views taken with a twin-lens camera – gave a three-dimensional image when seen through a special viewer and were very popular from the mid-19th century. The viewer was invented by David Brewster (Scot) (1781–1868) and first exhibited at the Great Exhibition in London in 1851.

Niépce to the naturalist Francis Bauer (GB), when visiting his dying brother in Kew, west London, in December 1827. Lost in 1898, it was rediscovered in 1952 in a trunk in an English country house. It was presented in 1964 to the University of Texas, Austin, and is preserved in a container in helium gas – the world's oldest photograph, dated to 1826 or 1827.

Niépce entered into a partnership with Louis Jacques Mandé Daguerre (Fr) (1787–1851), originally a scene-painter in the opera. In 1835, Daguerre invented a new chemical process to capture images using a

copper plate coated with silver sensitized to light with iodine. These first **daguerreotypes** were reversed left to right but became very popular.

The next development was the work of the English physicist William Henry **Fox Talbot** (1800–77) who had, as a mere sideline to his parliamentary, mathematical and other scientific interests, discovered that silver iodized paper could be further sensitized with trihydroxy-benzoic acid. After an exposure of one to five minutes, he used potassium bromide to fix his images.

Talbot's earliest surviving photographic negative is of a leaded oriel window of some 200 panes, taken from the inside of the south gallery of his family's Lacock Abbey, Wiltshire, in August 1835. He also reintroduced the use of sodium thiosulphate (known as 'hypo') as a most effective fixing agent.

This substance's capacity to dissolve silver salts had been discovered in 1819 by John Herschel (Eng) (1792–1871) and was rediscovered by Joseph Bancroft Reade (Eng) (1801–70) in 1838. Herschel – son of William Herschel, the discoverer of the planet Uranus in 1781 – also first introduced the terms 'positive' and 'negative' in relation to photography in the Proceedings of the Royal Society in 1840.

Meanwhile the photographic lens had seen several improvements. In Vienna, Josef Max Petzval (Cz) (1807–91) introduced a much wider **portrait lens** with an aperture 16 times the size of Chevalier's. These lenses were made from May 1840 by Peter Wilhelm Friedrich

Voigtländer (Aus) (1812–78) and reduced exposure time to 45–75 seconds.

Colour retouching was practised by Johann Baptist Isenring (1796–1860) of St Gallen, Switzerland, as early as November 1840.

The first successful **daguerreotype of the Moon** was taken on 23 March 1840 by John William Draper (GB) (1811–82) using a 5in *1.5cm* reflector. The exposure time was 20 minutes. However, daguerreotypy was doomed to become a cul-de-sac. Its single positives, which so fired the popular imagination of the era, could not be duplicated by any economic method and had to be kept under glass.

Longman, Brown, Green and Longman of London published, in parts from 1844–46, the world's first **photographically illustrated book** – *The Pencil of Nature* by Fox Talbot. He revealed in it that it was in the autumn of 1833 on honeymoon at Lake Como, Italy, that it first occurred to him 'how charming it would be if it were possible to cause these natural images to imprint themselves … and remain fixed upon the paper'.

A further refinement came in 1851 with the development of the **wet-collodion process**. It was invented by Englishman Frederick Scott Archer (1813–57) and used gun-cotton (nitro-cellulose) dissolved in ether to sensitize the plate. Archer's new process produced a much higher quality of image.

The first **aerial photographs** were taken in 1858 from a balloon by the French journalist and portraitist Nadar (real name Gaspard-

George Eastman's affordable box camera (1888) brought photography within reach of the masses. By 1900 Eastman's leatherette-covered cardboard box camera, the Brownie, cost only $1. They were produced until 1968.

Félix Tournachon, 1820–1910) over Petit Bicêtre. In 1859, Nadar took photographs underground lit by battery-powered arc lights. Ever the pioneer, he went on to perform the first photo-interview on record in 1886.

The collodion process was vindicated in July 1860 by Englishman Warren de la Rue (1815–89), who took a photo-heliograph during a total eclipse of the sun that was visible over Spain. His image demonstrated that the prominences around the moon's disc were a solar and not a lunar phenomenon.

Two Frenchmen working independently came up with the basis of modern **colour photography** in the same year. In 1869, Charles Cros (1842–88) discovered the 'subtractive principle', in which different coloured filters absorb different wavelengths of light. By subtracting one colour from white light, another colour is produced. Louis Ducos du Hauron (1837–1920) proposed the same principle in his *Les couleurs en photographie, solution du problème*, published in 1869.

In 1871 English doctor Richard Leach Maddox (1816–1902) suggested that silver bromide could be suspended in gelatin as a substitute for the wet collodion process, which had the disadvantage of not being storable. The **dry plate** was introduced in 1878 and revolutionized photography.

Maddox's gelatin plate was about 60 times more sensitive than collodion. This meant that a photograph's exposure time could be much less, paving the way for 'instant' cameras.

The white light produced by burning magnesium had been known for some time but in 1887 two Germans, Adolf Mietke and Johannes Gaedicke, produced **flash powder** – a mix of magnesium, potassium chlorate and antimony sulphate. Photographers began to use it for indoor illumination.

In 1888 George Eastman (US) (1854–1932) introduced the **box camera** and stimulated popular photography with his 25oz *708g* Kodak roll film camera. It measured only 6.5 x 3.75 x 3.25in *16.5 x 9.5 x 8.2cm* and cost $25. The cameras were mass-produced at the Eastman Dry Plate and Film Co., Rochester, New York. The Kodak motto for 'snapshots' was 'You press the button – We Do the Rest', since the entire camera, with 100 exposures, had to be sent to the factory for processing.

Thomas Rudolphus Dallmeyer (Ger/Eng) (1859–1906) introduced the first **telephoto lens** to produce an enlarged image of its subject into standard practice. Dallmeyer patented his device in 1891.

In 1893 the Belgian-born US chemist Leo H. **Baekeland** (1863–1944) – inventor of the first commercial plastic, Bakelite – revolutionized the print-making process with his

American Ansel Adams wanted photography to have the same status as painting and other fine arts and in 1937 established the world's first museum-held photograph collection – in the Museum of Modern Art, New York. A campaigner for the protection of the American wilderness, he took breathtakingly beautiful photographs of California's Yosemite National Park, which he visited every year for 67 years after his first trip in 1916.

American inventor Edwin Land demonstrates the almost instant image produced by his 1948 Polaroid Land camera. The 5lb *2.25kg* camera cost $95 and could print its own pictures within one minute of taking them.

The Box Brownie's late 20th-century equivalent was introduced by Japanese firm Fuji in 1986. Disposable cameras typically take around 24 pictures and then the whole camera is sent to the laboratory for processing.

Velox photographic paper. It was sufficiently sensitive to print in artificial light.

In 1914 Oskar Barnack (Ger) (1879–1936) designed the first camera to use 35mm film for the Ernest Leitz Company of Wetzlar, Germany. World War I intervened and the **Leica** camera was not launched until 1924. It was the first precision miniature camera to be available commercially and became the favoured tool of journalists because of its compactness and reliability.

Flash photography was rendered more reliable by Paul Vierkotter who in 1925 patented the principle of enclosing the inflammable mixture in a bulb, which was 'flashed' by means of an electric current. The **flash bulb** was further developed by the German Ostermeier, who in 1929 created the first silent and smoke-free bulb – the Vacublitz.

In 1928 the **Rolleiflex** was introduced by the German company Franke & Heidecke. It was a twin-lens reflex camera in which one lens transmitted the image to the film, while the other served both as a viewfinder and a focusing device.

Kodak introduced **Kodachrome** transparency film in 1935. The process, using colour dyes embedded in three layers of emulsion, had first been developed by a Herr Siegrist (Ger) (*d.*1914) and Rudolph Fischer (Ger) (1881–1957) in 1912. The German company Agfa produced their first colour film in 1936. The **Agfacolor** positive/negative film came in 1939 and the **Kodacolor** negative film in 1942.

In 1940 Edwin Herbert Land (US) (1909–91) designed a film that included a sealed pocket of processing chemicals in a paste, which could process the film dry inside the camera. In 1948 Land launched the Land **Polaroid Model 95**, at the Jordan Marsh Store, Boston, Massachusetts.

Instant-print colour film, Polacolor, was introduced in 1963, developed by Elkan R. Blout (US) (*b.*1919) and Howard G. Rogers (US) (*b.*1915). The pocket-sized Polaroid SX70 of 1972 was able to deliver 'instant' dry colour photographs in under 60 seconds.

The SX70 was a **single-lens reflex** (SLR) camera. The single-lens reflex allows the viewer to see the image being projected on to the film through a mirror up to the moment of pressing the shutter, when the mirror is moved to allow the picture to be taken.

The first compact **auto-focus** camera was the Japanese Konica, produced in 1976. Automatic focusing means that the focus is selected by the camera itself according to light conditions.

In 1989, Canon introduced the Ion **magnetic camera** into the market. It uses a floppy disk to record images and therefore does away with chemicals and film. The first magnetic camera was a 1981 Sony video camera.

PhotoCD was introduced by Kodak in 1990. Normal 35mm format photographs are converted into digital form on a CD so that they can be viewed on television.

The world photographic industry market **turnover** in 1996 was estimated to be £27,200 million, with market shares of 45% by Eastman-Kodak, 25% for Fuji, 15% for Agfa-Gevaert and 15% others.

In 1996, a new film cassette jointly developed by Kodak, Fuji, Canon, Nikon and Minolta was launched. The **Advanced Photo System** (APS) integrates the camera, 24mm film and the photofinishing process. The cassette is much smaller than the standard 35mm one, so the camera can be smaller. The film can be loaded into the camera without being touched and it offers the choice of three print formats – standard, wide-angle or panoramic.

Digital cameras, which store images as binary computer code, entered the mass market in 1996/7. The cheaper cameras for popular use have a low resolution at *c.*150,000 pixels compared with the multi-million pixel resolution of costly professional models.

Cinematography

In the production of a cinema film a continuous light-sensitive ribbon – the film – is exposed at standard intervals of time. The human eye's capacity for **persistence of vision** enables the retina to retain briefly an impression of each image after it has actually disappeared. This phenomenon was first recorded by the Egyptian astronomer Ptolemy (82–150) as early as *c*.130AD.

There were various forerunners of film proper. The screen, for example, has been used for the projection of **shadow puppets** in Asia for centuries.

In the Netherlands *c*.1650, after lenses had been developed, the **Magic Lantern** was used to give picture shows. The early Magic Lantern was simply a box with a strong light source, a series of images and a lens. The Belgian Etienne-Gaspard Robert (1763–1837) put on a show called the *Fantasmagorie*. It premièred in Paris in 1798 and toured various European countries.

In the 19th century various **toys** took advantage of persistence of vision to produce in the viewer the sensation of seeing continuous movement. The Thaumatrope (1826), the Phenakistoscope (1830) and the Zoetrope (1860s) all used a strip of drawings like modern animated frames. The drawings were spun and viewed through a slot.

Emile **Reynaud** (Fr) (1844–1918) invented one of these toys, the Praxinoscope, in the 1870s but then combined the principle of the strip of moving pictures with the lens and screen used for the Magic Lantern. His Théatre Optique opened in Paris in 1892 using stories made up of as many as 700 separate drawings on strips pulled through the apparatus, each show lasting 15 minutes.

Reynaud's invention was the forerunner of animation. But it was when the infant art of **photography** was coupled with projection that cinema was born. Still photography had been invented in the 1830s (see pages 195–98). What had to be developed was the ability to take a **sufficiently rapid series of photographs** to produce the illusion of continuity.

English photographer Eadweard **Muybridge** (1830–1904) first solved this problem by recording a horse's trotting with 12 separate cameras, each one taking a single shot. The shutters were activated by the breaking of threads by the horse's legs.

A French scientist, Etienne-Jules **Marey** (1830–1903) developed Muybridge's work further to record the movements of small animals, birds and insects. Rather than using several cameras triggered by the subject itself, however, he invented a rotating photographic plate which could hold up to 12 images. He refined the shutter of the camera until he had achieved an exposure time of 1/25,000 second.

George **Eastman** (US) (1854–1932) invented light-sensitive paper film in 1885. Marey adapted his camera to move the film through in a series of exposures.

The **first motion picture film** was shot some time before Wednesday 24 October 1888, , by the French-born Augustin Le Prince (1842–90). He took film at 10–12 frames per second on a 2⅛in *53.9cm* wide sensitized paper roll in the garden of his wife's father, Joseph Whitley (Eng) (1818–91) at Roundhay, Leeds, Yorkshire. Part of this film survives. Fragments also survive of Le Prince's film of traffic on Leeds Bridge, taken at 20 frames per second, later in October 1888.

On 16 September 1890 Le Prince boarded a Paris-bound train at Dijon with his equipment. Neither he nor

Magic lanterns were the first slide projectors but could be used by travelling showmen to create the illusion of moving pictures. A wide slide moved slowly through a lantern had a similar effect to the film-makers' later 'pan' – a sweeping shot across a group or landscape.

French film pioneer Etienne-Jules Marey entertained the members of the Paris Academy of Science with a film of a falling cat on 22 October 1894. He also developed an early projector and in May 1899 in Paris he patented the device it used for moving the film.

Japanese director Akira Kurosawa's 1954 film *The Seven Samurai (Shiichinin no samurai)* transplanted the themes of the Hollywood western to 17th-century Japan. US director John Sturges (1911–92) repaid the compliment, basing his 1960 hit *The Magnificent Seven* on Kurosawa's stirring film.

Perhaps cinema's most celebrated couple, Richard Burton (1925–84) and Elizabeth Taylor (b.1932) began their love affair while making *Cleopatra* (1963). They were married from 1964 to 1974 and again from1975 to1976. *Cleopatra* made Taylor the first actress to be paid $1 million for a single film.

Sheikh (Valentino, 1921) and *The Thief of Baghdad* (Fairbanks, 1924).

Early Soviet cinema was made to serve the state in creating propaganda films or up-beat news reels. Sergei **Eisenstein** (1898–1948) managed to transcend his political remit to produce genuine dramatic masterpieces in such films as *The Battleship Potemkin* (1925) and *Alexander Nevsky* (1938).

In Weimar Germany, Leni **Riefenstahl** was commissioned by Adolf Hitler to record the Nazi Party's Nuremberg rally in *Triumph of the Will* (1936) and Germany's triumph hosting the 1936 Berlin Games in *Olympia* (1938). The two films were tainted by their pro-Nazi stance but include superb footage, for example of the men's diving events at the Games.

Meanwhile **Walt Disney** (1901–66) had produced the first feature-length coloured cartoon in *Snow White and the Seven Dwarfs* (1937). Disney established his Hollywood studio in 1923. **Mickey Mouse** first saw the light of day in 1928 and the first cartoon with synchronized sound featured Mickey Mouse in the short movie *Steamboat Willie* in 1928.

French cinema in the 1930s was more experimental and artistically ambitious than the standard Hollywood production. Jean **Vigo** (1905–34) produced an anarchic vision of freedom in *Zéro de conduite* ('Zero for conduct') (1933) and *L'Atalante* (1934) and Jean **Renoir** (1894–1979) combined committed social critique with experimental film technique in *Le Crime de M Lange* ('The Crime of Mr Lange') (1935) and *La Règle du Jeu* ('The Rules of the Game') (1939).

The only country to rival the output of the USA in the 1930s was **Japan** with an average 500 features a year, but these pictures were only seen in the domestic market. The two central directors were Kenji **Mizoguchi** (1898–1956) and Yasujiro **Ozu** (1903–1963), whose films often dealt with themes from Japan's uneven social development – the position of women and class differences.

After World War II (1939–45), remarkable cinematic talents arose in Japan, producing films that gained worldwide recognition. Akira **Kurosawa**'s *Rashomon* (1950) was the breakthrough, winning the Grand Prize at the Venice film festival in 1951. Kurosawa (b.1910) used effects from traditional Japanese Noh theatre and themes from Japan's feudal past in films such as *The Seven Samurai* (1954).

During the late 1950s and 1960s competition from television caused cinema audiences to fall. Some studios responded by turning to **big-budget** extravaganzas. Twentieth Century Fox's *The Sound of Music* (1965) was a runaway success, but *Cleopatra* (1963) had lost the same studio $10 million.

In France the *Nouvelle Vague* (**New Wave**) broke in 1959. Young directors well grounded in Hollywood's history set out to make films that challenged narrative and stylistic convention. Jean Luc Godard's (*b*.1930) *A Bout de Souffle* ('Breathless') and Francois Truffaut's (1932–84) *400 Coups* ('400 Blows') were in the vanguard of a movement that had great influence on many later Hollywood directors.

In the late 1960s, **violence** began its steady escalation in American cinema, with scenes too brutal to be shown on the television of the day. Arthur **Penn**'s *Bonnie and Clyde* (1967) was criticized for romanticizing violence and alienation, while Sam **Peckinpah**'s *The Wild Bunch* (1969) was a portrayal Texas–Mexico border warfare.

Science fiction, too, could create effects beyond the resources of television. *2001: A Space Odyssey* (1968) directed by US-born Stanley **Kubrick** (1928–99) cost $11 million and is a classic of the science fiction genre.

European cinema in the 1970s remained rather more subtle than Hollywood with films such as *The Discreet Charm of the Bourgeoisie* (1972), directed by Luis **Buñuel** (Sp) (1900–83) and *Novecento* ('1900') (1976), an epic sweep through Italian history directed by Bernardo **Bertolucci** (It) (*b*.1940).

German cinema enjoyed a resurgence through a group called Young German Film. Their star was Rainer Werner **Fassbinder** (1946–1982). The themes running through his prolific output mostly dealt with sexual desire and its manipulation. *The Marriage of Maria Braun* (1978) and many of Fassbinder's later films focused on women's lives in post-war Germany.

The far-reaching influence of Hollywood was certainly felt by European directors, and some, like the German Wim **Wenders** (*b*.1945), actually went to Hollywood to work. Nevertheless, Wenders' most telling films, like *Alice in the Cities* (1973), were made in Germany and are explorations of how German and American culture meet and clash.

In the 1980s a new threat arose for the cinema. **Video recorders** meant that people could record films from TV's growing number of channels or rent them from hire shops. Mainstream cinema went the way of the **blockbuster** – immense-budget films advertised with the maximum of hype and the sale of lucrative licensed products.

Steven Spielberg's *Jaws* (1975) was one of the earliest, followed by George Lucas' *Star Wars* (1977), which was even more successful. Spielberg followed with *ET: The Extra-Terrestrial* (1982) and *Jurassic Park* (1993), then demonstrated his ability to make more serious films with *Schindler's List* (1993).

However, independent directors showed that films did not have to be blockbusters to attract an audience. Spike Lee's (b. 1957) *Do the Right Thing* (1989) and *Jungle Fever* (1991) probed the racial tensions existing between New York's black and Italian-American communities.

One of those New York Italians, Martin **Scorsese** (*b*.1942), had earlier made his name with *Mean Streets* (1973) and gone on to produce a varied and acclaimed output

including *Taxi Driver* (1976) and *Raging Bull* (1980). David **Lynch** (US) (*b*.1946) won a devoted cult following with the surreal *Eraserhead* (1978), and followed it with a mainstream success in *Blue Velvet* (1986).

Quentin **Tarantino** (US) (*b*.1963)'s gangster film *Reservoir Dogs* (1993) was the first of a group of sophisticated – often violent – Hollywood films full of knowing references to cinematic history and to popular culture.

Chinese film-making at last threw off some of its restraints in the late 1980s and 1990s

US-born British director Stanley Kubrick lines up a shot for his anti-war comedy *Dr Strangelove* (1964). He was master of many styles, producing the historical epic *Spartacus* (1960), war film *Full Metal Jacket* (1987) and special effects bonanza *2001: A Space Odyssey* (1968). When he died on 7 March 1999 he had just finished work on an erotic thriller, *Eyes Wide Shut*.

with some visually stunning films by young directors. Zhang **Yimou**'s *Red Sorghum* (1987) and *Raise the Red Lantern* (1991) became box-office successes in the West.

The independent director Zhang **Yuan**, however, suffered from a ban on his employment and the withdrawal of his passport for his more outspoken films, including *East Palace, West Palace* (1998), the first Chinese film to depict homosexuality.

The compact digital recording format **MiniDisc** (MD) was developed by Sony in 1992. MiniDiscs look like mini computer discs (measuring 2^1/$_2$in *64 mm* in diameter), but work like CDs, recording up to 80 minutes of sound.

Editing facilities include re-recording and deleting or changing the running order of recorded tracks. One of the smallest MiniDisc players is the Sony MZ-R90, weighing a mere 3.6oz *105g*.

Designed as an alternative to the 30-year-old compact cassette, the MiniDisc had a difficult launch on the market. However, by 1998–99 sales had quadrupled and it was on its way to replacing the cassette Walkman.

In 2000 Casio marketed a portable MP-3 player small and light enough to to be worn on the wrist like a watch. MP3 equipment uses compression technology to squash audio files so that they can be stored in minimal disk space and quickly retrieved.

In 1994, Pioneer and Philips launched **CD-Recordable** (CD-R) technology. CD-R discs can only be recorded once. At first the machines and the discs were so expensive that they were only available in professional recording studios, but by 1998 prices had dropped dramatically and a choice of CD-R recorders was available

to the public. There are also CD-RW discs which can be recorded over and over again like the old-fashioned tapes.

As cassettes were gradually phased out of production in the early 21st century, it remained to be seen whether MiniDisc or CD-RW would become the preferred medium of recorded sound. The launch of **DVD** (digital video or versatile disc) in 1997 pointed a way forward for the compact disc. DVD offered picture and audio quality superior to that of video cassettes and added bonuses such as multi-channel surround sound, subtitles, alternate endings to movies, stills and computer games. It uses data compression to store the billions of bits (see page 245) that make up a film's moving images (see also page 242).

DVD players can also play ordinary CDs. In 1999, Icelandic pop singer Björk (Björk Gudmundsdóttir, *b.*1966) was one of the first artists to embrace the format, releasing the first DVD-V single, *All is Full of Love.*

Major manufacturers stated their intent to replace all CD-based products with DVD equivalents by 2007.

MP3 is the abbreviated term for a method of compressing digital sound files by a factor of 12. It was introduced as an agreed standard in 1997 to help download music in digital form from the Internet to a personal computer or a dedicated MP3 player.

The first portable MP3 player was the palm-sized Diamond Rio PMP300, released in 1998; it could store 60 minutes of stereo music (or 16 hours of mono) and came with 32MB built-in memory. Weighing

only 2.5oz *70g*, the Rio had no moving parts. Because the music is stored on a microchip, the old problems of 'skipping' – familiar to portable CD and tape users – were eliminated.

Enthusiasts converted music to MP3-format files on a PC using special software and made them available to other music lovers free, causing alarm in the record industry. Future CD players will be able to record and play MP3-downloaded music.

MP3 technology was launched at a time when music sales over the Internet were forecasted to explode 20-fold and websites offering downloadable music were mushrooming.

Shortage of bandwidth (the network's capacity to transfer data) was the only cloud on the horizon. In 2000, Toshiba announced the launch of Asymmetric Digital Subscriber Line (ADSL) chipsets, which could turn standard copper telephone lines into high-speed connections, allowing smooth download of multi-channel CD-quality music.

Objections raised by the music industry – that the new technology allows easier recording of pirated music – were dealt with by the incorporation of the Serial Copyright Management System (SCMS) into MP3 and MiniDisc player designs, preventing second-generation copying of digital audio recordings.

Super Audio CD (SACD) was developed by Sony and Philips in response to DVD. Launched in June 2000, it was primarily targeted at the more expensive end of the hi-fi market.

Popular music

At one time, pieces of music could be sung or performed by anyone who had a good enough ear to 'steal' them by listening. Even with written scores, a composer's music was available to anyone until **copyright laws** were enacted. Copyright in Britain first became enforceable under the Copyright Act 1709, but it was very ineffective. In the 1911 Copyright Act the performing right – that is, the right to give a public performance – was integrated into copyright.

Copyright in the USA began with Acts in Connecticut and in Massachusetts in 1783, but there was no Congressional Act until 108 years later, in 1891 (revised 1909). The earliest of all **performing rights societies** is the French SACEM (Societé des auteurs, compositeurs et éditeurs de musique), formed in 1851.

Three pieces of non-copyrighted sheet music are known to have exceeded sales of 20 million before they were submerged by mechanical sound reproduction and recording. They are: *Old Folks at Home* (1851) by Stephen Collins Foster (US) (1826–64), published under the name of Edwin P. Christy; *Listen to the Mocking Bird* (1854) by Septimus Winner (US) (1827–1902), written under the name of Alice Hawthorne; and the *Blue Danube* waltz (1867) by Johann Strauss (the Younger) (Austrian) (1825–99), with lyrics by Joseph Weyl. The *Blue Danube*'s German title is *An der Schönen, blauen Donau* ('On the beautiful blue Danube').

Of later pieces that were under copyright, two attained sheet sales of 6 million: *Let Me Call You Sweetheart* (1910) by Whitson and Friedmann and *Till We Meet Again* (1918) by Richard A. Whiting (US) (1891–1938) and Ray Egan.

The **earliest jazz** ever recorded was *Indiana* and *The Dark Town Strutters' Ball* in January 1917, for the Columbia label in New York City, by the 'Original Dixieland Jass Band' of Chicago, led by Dominick James 'Nick' La Rocca (US) (1889–1961) on cornet. The Dixieland Jass Band's first actual record release was, however, on the Victor label on 7 March. The tracks *Livery Stable Blues* and *Original Dixieland One-Step* were recorded at Victor's New York Studios on 26 February 1917.

The **first Big Band recording** was made by Art Hickman and his Orchestra in September 1919 from St Francis Hotel, San Francisco, for Columbia. The first dance band to sell **over a million records** was that of Paul Whiteman (US) (1890–1967) of San Francisco, playing *The Japanese Sandman* and *Whispering*, issued in November 1920 by Victor. By 1925 the recording had achieved sales of 1.3 million in the USA alone.

The **first instrumental blues** were recorded c.1913. W.C. Handy (US) (1873–1958) published his popular *Memphis Blues* in 1912 and *St. Louis Blues* in 1914. The first vocal blues song, *Crazy Blues*, composed by Perry Bradford and sung by Mamie Smith (US) (1883–1946), was

Operatic tenor Enrico Caruso (1873–1921), the first international recording star, made his stage debut in his native Naples aged 21. British talent scout Fred Gaisberg persuaded Caruso to record a set of discs in 1902 after hearing him perform at Milan's La Scala opera house. Caruso's fee was £100; the records made £15,000.

American crooner Bing Crosby first sang 'White Christmas' on screen in *Holiday Inn* (1942). He returned to it in *White Christmas* (1954) – the first film shot in Paramount's widescreen Vistavision format. Crosby (left) starred with (left to right) Rosemary Clooney, Vera Ellen and Danny Kaye.

recorded on the Okeh Records label on 10 August 1920. It is said to have sold 75,000 copies in the first month, convincing record companies at a stroke of the viability of the new form. In 1928, 'Pinetop' Smith had the first boogie beat hit with, *Pinetop's Boogie Woogie*.

On 18 October 1926 Harry Lillis 'Bing' **Crosby** (US) (1903–77) recorded the first of his 2725 recordings, with *I've Got the Girl*. He recorded *White Christmas*, written by Irving Berlin (Rus/US) (1888–1919), on 29 May 1942. It has had the greatest sales of any song by one singer – with more than 50 million.

In 1939, Charlie Christian (US) (1916–42) introduced the

The King of rock 'n' roll, Elvis Presley, had 192 chart entries – more than any other performer. They included 18 No. 1 singles and nine No. 1 albums on the US charts. Born in Tupelo, Mississippi, he first became a star in the southern USA before rocketing to national attention in 1956 with hits such as 'Hound Dog' and 'Heartbreak Hotel'.

electric guitar sound to blues music, when he first played with Benny Goodman's Band, at the Victor Hugo restaurant in Beverly Hills.

Singles charts were first published by *Billboard* magazine on 20 July 1940. Its **album chart** first appeared on 15 March 1945. Film music composer Bernard Herrman (US) (1911–75) first used the **overdub**

technique of building up the sound of several separate soundtracks in the film *All That Money Can Buy* in 1941.

The first **golden disc** was sprayed by RCA Victor for the US band leader, Alton 'Glenn' Miller (1904–44) and presented to him on 10 February 1942 for *Chattanooga Choo Choo*.

Lata **Mangeshkar** (India) (*b*.1928) began her career in 1948. By the mid-1970s, she had recorded *c*.25,000 chorus, duet and solo songs in 20 Indian languages. She also 'backed' 1800 films.

Rock'n'roll music took off after Bill Haley and the Comets' *Rock Around the Clock* went straight to No.1 in the US pop charts of 1955.

The **first rock'n'roll record** came earlier – most likely contenders are *Rocket 88*, released in 1951 by Ike **Turner** (US) (*b*.1931) or *Ida Red* as performed by Chuck **Berry** (US) (*b*.1926) at the Cosmopolitan Club, St Louis, Missouri, in 1952 and then released as *Maybelline*.

On 10 January 1956, Elvis Aaron Presley (US) (1935–77) recorded his single *Heartbreak Hotel* at the RCA studios in Nashville, Tennessee. It stayed as No. 1 in the US Charts for eight weeks and launched him on the road to unique **lifetime solo sales**, believed to exceed 1,000 million. On 9 September 1956 Presley first appeared on *The Ed Sullivan Show*, a variety show on US TV, and attracted a record audience of 50 million.

The **Tamla Motown** label, based in Detroit, Michigan and run by Berry Gordy (US) (*b*.1929), produced a string of hit records throughout the

1960s. Tamla promoted a heavily produced sound, combining rhythm and blues with elements of soul and gospel. It launched the careers of a wide range of artists, including the Temptations, the Supremes, Stevie Wonder (US) (b.Steveland Judkins Morris, 1950), Marvin Gaye (US) (1939–84) and Smokey Robinson (b.William Robinson, 1940).

British group the Beatles – George Harrison (*b*.1943), John Lennon (1940–80), Paul McCartney (*b*.1942) and Ringo Starr (*b*. Richard Starkey, 1940) – were probably **the most successful group in rock history**, selling about one billion records and cassettes worldwide during and after a performing career which ran from 1956 to 1970.

Rap or hip-hop emerged in 1970s New York from the break-beat performances of disc jockeys (DJs) who mixed together records as they played them on twin turntables and sang or rhymed over the top. Kool Herc (Jamaica) (*b*.Clive Campbell) pioneered the style, which he developed from that of DJs in Jamaica who would 'toast' – sing or rhyme – when introducing reggae records in dancehalls. The first hit rap record came in 1979 with *Rapper's Delight* by The Sugar Hill Gang.

In 1982, Michael Joseph Jackson (US) (*b*.1958) released the album *Thriller* which, by 1999, had achieved a **world album record** with 46 million in sales. In 1984, he won a record eight Grammy awards. He accumulated 13 No. 1 singles and four No. 1 albums in the US charts. The remarkable sales of *Thriller* established a

Gangsta rap artist Snoop Doggy Dog (b.Calvin Broadus, 1972) first came to rap fans' attention when he performed on the 1992 album *The Chronic* by Dr Dre (b.Andre Young, 1965), a founder member of *N.W.A.* Snoop's solo debut album *Doggystyle* was an immediate hit when released the following year.

The Temptations formed in Detroit in 1961 and signed for the city's Motown label in the same year. Their first big hit came three years later with *The Way You Do the Things You Do*.

pattern record companies came to rely on: a few huge hits to generate their profits.

In 1987, Lionel Richie (US) (b.1949) achieved a record **10th consecutive year** with a No. 1 hit in the USA.

In 1988 rap group N.W.A. of Los Angeles released their album *N.W.A. And The Posse*, followed in 1989 by the hit *Straight Outta Compton*. With a confrontational account of violent relations between Los Angeles gang members and police officers, it was one of the pioneers of a new rap style: **gangsta rap**.

Gangsta rap acts included Snoop Doggy Dogg, who was charged with and cleared of an August 1993 murder at the same time that his *Murder Was the Case* was being promoted and sold, and Tupac Shakur, whose *Me Against the World* (1995) was a hit before he

was murdered in a drive-by shooting in September 1996.

In 1998 in the USA, rap music outsold country and western, which had previously been the biggest grossing US musical form. Rap artists sold 81 million CDs, cassettes and records compared to country's 72 million.

Candle In The Wind, composed by Elton John (Eng) (b. Reginald Kenneth Dwight, 1947) and Bernie Taupin in 1973 about Hollywood actress Marilyn Monroe (US) (1926–62), was re-written and re-recorded in 1997 by Elton John in tribute to Diana, Princess of Wales (1961–97). By 19 December 1997 it had sold 33 million copies worldwide and was declared **the biggest selling single of all time**.

Two songs have received more than **7 million plays on US radio** – *Yesterday*, written by Lennon and McCartney; and *You've Lost that Lovin' Feelin'*, written by Phil Spector (US) (b.1940), Barry Mann and Cynthia Weill.

In 2000 Madonna Louise Veronica Ciccone (US) (b.1958), better known as Madonna, was the world's **best-selling female artist**, with total album sales of more than 100 million. Originally trained as a disco dancer, she enjoyed her first success with *Madonna* (1983), which included five US top ten singles. In the USA and the UK, she has had 11 and 13 Top 10 albums respectively, including *Like a Virgin* (1983), *Erotica* (1992) and *Ray of Light* (1998).

Frank **Sinatra** (US) (1915–98) holds the record for **the longest span of Top 20 albums** in the USA and UK, covering almost 40 years. His first US chart entry was *In the Wee Small Hours*, which entered the charts in May 1955, and his most recent was *Duets II*, which exited the Top 20 in December 1994. In the UK, he first entered the charts in November 1958 with *Come Fly with Me*, and the compilation *My Way – The Best of Frank Sinatra*, finally dropped out of the Top 20 in June 1998.

Radio

The basis of radio is the conversion of sound waves into electromagnetic waves which are broadcast through the air, then turned back into sound waves for the listener. The sound waves are turned into electromagnetic waves by a microphone, broadcast by a radio transmitter and aerial, picked up by a radio receiver and converted back into sound by a loudspeaker.

It was James Clerk Maxwell (GB) (1831–74) who first laid the **theoretical basis for radio**. He realized that light-waves, soundwaves, magnetism and electricity could all be reduced to a simple set of mathematical descriptions. In *A Dynamical Theory of the Electromagnetic Field,* published in 1864, Maxwell maintained that electromagnetic waves travelled at the speed of light, about 186,000 miles per second *300,000km/sec*, and that they could be made in a laboratory.

Electromagnetic waves were first made by the German physicist Heinrich Rudolf Hertz (1857–94), who built a transmitter, which he called a resonator. This created electromagnetic waves which could be detected some distance away. Hertz was honoured for his work in 1924, when his name was given to the unit of frequency,

The Italian radio pioneer, Guglielmo Marconi photographed on 21 December 1901, just days after his historic first wireless signal across the Atlantic Ocean.

measured in cycles per second.

In 1894, the English physicist Oliver Lodge (1851–1940) succeeded in sending a **radio signal** 180 ft *55m* at a meeting of the British Association in Oxford. It was Lodge who first realized the necessity of tuning the receiving apparatus to the same wavelength as the broadcasting equipment, a process he called the 'syntony of circuits'.

The great pioneer of radio transmission was the Italian-born Marchese **Guglielmo Marconi** (1874–1937) who, in 1895 achieved a transmission over 1.5 miles *2.4km* in the grounds of his father's house, Villa Griffone, in Pontecchio, near Bologna, Italy.

In July 1897 Marconi, not yet 21, formed his Wireless Telegraph and Signal Co. Ltd in Britain. In November of that year he built the world's **first permanent radio station** at The Needles, a headland on the Isle of Wight. On 26 August 1898 Marconi established, for Lloyds of London, the first commercial station for **ship-to-shore messages** at Rathlin Island lighthouse, off Northern Ireland.

On 12 December 1901 at a receiver in the Old Fever Hospital, St. John's, Newfoundland, Marconi picked up the Morse code letter S transmitted from the

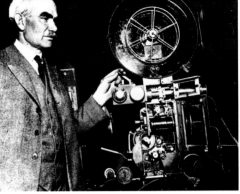

American electrical engineer Lee De Forest shows off his thermionic amplifier, or Audion. De Forest's vacuum tube, or valve, became the key technology that made the spread of radio and television possible.

10kW spark-transmitting station at Poldhu, Cornwall. The **first transatlantic signal** had travelled 2175 miles *3500km*, but because it was not recorded, reports of the transmission met with widespread disbelief.

Marconi proved his case on 25 February 1902, when signals from Poldhu were picked up *and* recorded aboard the American liner SS *Philadelphia* at a range of more than 1551 miles *2496km* at night.

In 1904, Sir Ambrose Fleming (1849–1945) a professor of electrical engineering who worked with Marconi, patented the **diode valve** (in the US known as a tube), for converting alternating current (AC) radio signals into direct current (DC) signals for reproduction by a receiver. The valve works by allowing current to pass through in one direction only.

Charles Samuel Franklin (1879–1964), an inventive member of Marconi's staff, patented his horizontal **directional aerial** in 1905. This was later superseded by the Marconi–Franklin short-wave beam system.

In November 1906, Professor Reginald Fessenden (Can) (1868–1932) transmitted the **first broadcasts** from the 429ft *131m* mast of the National Electric Signalling Company at Brant Rock, Massachusetts, USA. The message transmitted fish prices on the Boston market to a small fishing schooner of the south shore fleet of Plymouth catching fish in Massachusetts Bay.

In New York City Lee De Forest (1873–1961), the pioneer of radio in the USA, developed Fleming's diode valve into the **triode valve** by adding a third electrode in December 1906. He called his device the Audion. This controlled the flow of electrons much more accurately and made possible the broadcasting and receiving of voices and music rather than merely signals.

By 1910, **ship-to-shore** radio messages were commonplace and the first air-to-ground signal was sent from an aircraft that year.

World War I put an end to private experiments in Europe but stimulated the development of radio for **military purposes**. This had begun in 1911 when the Marconi Company developed the first portable radio pack for short-range use by the British Army.

Between 1916 and 1920, C. S. Franklin (GB) developed the first beamed **short-wave** system, with a spark transmitter operating in compressed air and his rotating parabolic reflector station at Inchkeith, Firth of Forth, Scotland, on a wavelength of six metres. This system showed a practical use as a radio beacon for navigation.

The ability to tune a radio receiver into a signal by twisting a single knob instead of having to push numerous buttons came in 1917 when Lucienne Levy (Fr) (1892–1965) patented the variable frequency superheterodyne receiver.

Ready-made receivers were first sold in September 1920, by Westinghouse at East Springfield, Massachusetts. In June 1921, Westinghouse marketed the first popular radio set at $25 – the Aeriola Junior. It measured 6x6x7in *15x15x17.8cm*, and had a range of about 12–15 miles *19–24km*. Marconi's first ready-made models were first marketed in Britain in 1922.

In 1927, H. S. Block (US) (1898–1983), at Bell Laboratories, discovered that by feeding part of the amplifiers' output back into the input, signal distortion was largely eliminated. This **negative feedback** was the basis of the Pentode valve, developed in 1928 by Dutchmen Dr Gilles Holst (1886–1968) and Bernard Tellegren (1900–90) of Philips at Eindhoven. The pentode valve had five electrodes and allowed even greater clarity of sound.

In 1933, Edwin H. Armstrong (USA) developed **frequency modulation (FM)**, varying the frequency of a transmission to match variations in the sound. The first FM transmitter was installed in Schenectady, New York in 1938. FM was adopted by the American police force in 1939.

CB (Citizens' Band) radio is the term for two-way, short waveband communication between private citizens. A waveband was set aside for CB in the USA in 1948, but other countries have been slow to follow suit.

The transistor was invented in 1948 by John Bardeen, Walter Brattain and William Shockley, Bell Laboratory scientists in the USA. The transistor replaced the fragile tube or valve and made receivers more portable. The **first transistor radio** was sold by Sony (Japan) in 1952.

In 1945, Arthur C. Clarke (GB) (*b.*1917) had the idea of **geo-stationary satellites** placed at an altitude of 22,236 miles *35,786km* above the Earth to relay radio signals around the globe. In

1958, the world's first communications satellite, the US Atlas-Score, relayed a worldwide Christmas message from US President Eisenhower.

Broadcasting of radio shows to the public developed along different lines in different countries. The large size of the USA encouraged local

A student wireless telegraph operator being trained on a 1 kilowatt transceiver set at Marconi House, London in March 1913. The first radios could not transmit complex signals, such as speech, and were used for transmitting the simple clicks of Morse code. It took many hours of training to learn to use one effectively.

mechanically scanned low-definition pictures, three times weekly for 30 minutes.

On 3 July 1928 Baird achieved the **first colour TV** images in his new studio at 133 Long Acre, London, and in July the Davan Corporation of Newark, USA, marketed the **world's first TV sets**. These retailed for $75 and were adjustable to 24, 36 or 48-line reception. On 10 August 1928, Baird first demonstrated stereoscopic TV in his Long Acre studio.

Closed circuit television (CCTV) was first introduced in 1931 to transmit share prices in the Stock Exchange in Chicago, Illinois. On 8 May of that year Baird mounted the first

Russian-born US physicist Vladimir Zworykin holds the cathode-ray tube he developed for television display in 1929. Zworykin worked for the US Radio Corporation. Later in the century he contributed to the development of the first colour television.

American television pioneer Philo Taylor Farnsworth, who on 1 September 1928 demonstrated his set in Green Street, San Francisco. His test transmission showed an image of his brother-in-law Clifford Gardner smoking a cigarette.

outside broadcast of street scenes in Covent Garden, London. In October Vladimir Zworykin (US) (1889–1982) first demonstrated his all-electronic iconoscope transmitter, the forerunner of the cathode ray tube in every television, on which he had been working since 1927.

On 22 August 1932, the British Broadcasting Corporation (BBC) instituted four-times-a-week 30-minute transmissions on 30 lines from Broadcasting House, London. A total of 4000 sets were sold in 1932–35.

TV **programming** began in Germany in 1935 by the Reichs Rundfunkgesellschaft (State Broadcasting Co.) with the sending of 180-line transmissions of mechanically scanned films to 13 viewing rooms in Berlin and Potsdam.

The 1936 Berlin Olympic Games were televised by the Reich

Rundfunkgesellschaft using Vladimir Zworykin's Ikonoskop-Kamera to 29 viewing salons in five German cities. The world's first **high definition** (405 lines at 25 frames/sec) public TV service was launched by the BBC for home TV sets on 2 November 1936 from Studio A, Alexandra Palace, Haringey, north London.

On 13 February 1937, after 104 days of alternating between the Marconi-EMI electronic system and Baird's mechanical tele-cine system, the BBC opted for the former. But this service closed down on 1 September 1939 for the duration of the Second World War.

The USA's first **public service television** was the National Broadcasting Co. (NBC)'s 525-line outside broadcast of the New York World Fair on 30 April 1939. There were an estimated 5000 viewers.

On 1 June CBS's New York City station WNBT inaugurated the world's **first colour TV service** on 375 lines. However, it was not fully electronic, being in part mechanical. A month later, on 1 July, the NBC New York station WNBT became the first **commercial** TV station. The first advertiser was Bulova Watches, with a 20-second spot which cost $9 and which reached an estimated 4700 viewers.

In Britain, broadcasting remained non-commercial and was funded exclusively from **licence fees** until the advent of commercial television in 1954. A combined TV and radio licence was introduced in 1946 at £2. The number of sets then estimated at 7500, rose to 1 million by 1951 and to 10 million by 1959.

The world's first **pay TV** system was launched on 1 January 1951 by the Zenith Radio Corp in Chicago, Illinois on station KS2KBS. The signal for the film *April Showers*, sent to 300 selected households, could only be 'unscrambled' by viewers who paid for a key signal.

Also in 1951, CBS in New York City first transmitted colour TV on the NTSC (National Television System Committee) system with 525 lines and with 30 frames per second. The total number of TV sets operating in the USA jumped from the 1950 figure of 1.5 million to 15 million in 1951. This total grew to 140 million by 1998.

On 14 April 1956 commercial **video tape** recording was first demonstrated by the Ampex Corporation of Redwood City, California.

In 1959 the Japanese launched the first **transistorized** TV set, the 8in *20 centimetre* screened Sony TV-8-301. The Sony

5V-201 transistorized **video recorder** followed on 21 January 1961. A miniaturized transistor TV set was first marketed in Japan from 1965.

On 10 July 1962 the first active communications **satellite**, Telstar I, was launched. Satellites make it possible to to relay signals from high above the earth.

In 1974, Samuel Fedida (Egypt/UK) (*b.*1918) of the Post Office Research Centre, UK, devised the combination of computers, telephony and TV with key pad controls to produce the Prestel system of **teletext**. The Ceefax service followed in Britain on 23 September 1974.

The first **flat screen** pocket TV was patented by Matsushita Electric Co. of Japan in 1979. The pocket-sized Sony Watchman® personal TV was the world's **smallest, flattest and lightest set** when it was launched in 1982.

Sony launched the **Betamax** videocassette recorder and player in 1975, but soon had a

rival in the **VHS** (Video Home System) cassette and player launched by JVC (Victor Company of Japan) on 9 September 1976.

The VHS system was invented by Yuma Shiraishi (*b.*1929) and Shizuo Takano (1923–92). In the 1970s and early 1980s Betamax and VHS competed directly for a share of the video market; Betamax was technically superior, although the higher quality could not readily be seen on domestic-standard TVs.

VHS eventually triumphed because it could make longer recordings – two hours as against a single hour for Betamax. As Betamax fell behind there were fewer prerecorded tapes available in that format. In 1988 even Sony began to manufacture VHS-format video recorders, although in 2000 the company continued to sell some Beta-format models in the USA.

In 1998 there were **150 million VHS-format machines globally**. However, in 2000 the TV

Broadcasting House, the headquarters of the British Broadcasting Corporation, dominates London's Great Portland Street. The BBC was the world's first regular television broadcaster.

On 11 July 1962 US Vice-President Lyndon Johnson (1908–73) views television pictures that have been broadcast from France to the USA via the Telstar satellite, launched into Earth orbit on the previous day. The French broadcast featured singer and actor Yves Montand.

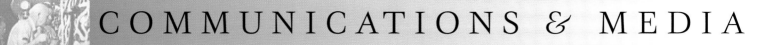

industry makes wide use of the professional-quality version of Betamax, **Betacam**.

CDV (Compact Disc Video) was developed in 1989, along with DVI (Digital Video Interactive). In this system, a computer broke down each image into 250,000 pixels (individual picture elements), storing as data *only* the changes between frames.

A technician checks components for a high-definition TV (HDTV) set. HDTV technology provides greater image clarity, transmitting pictures of 1000 or more lines in comparison to the 625-line picture traditionally used in the UK and the 525-line picture used in the USA and Japan.

High-definition television (HDTV) was developed in Japan in 1990. To enable viewers to take advantage of its clearer pictures, TV companies searched for ways of building wide, bright screens that were not as bulky as the conventional set based on the cathode ray tube.

In 1989, Sharp of Japan launched a development programme to replace bulky cathode-ray tubes with LCD (**liquid crystal display**) panels.

Another candidate was the **plasma display panel** (PDP), or gas discharge display. Prototype screens were built 50in *1270mm* corner to corner, and were thin enough to be hung on the wall like a framed photograph or painting. The plasma display unit is filled with a mixture of helium and xenon gas, which is ionized by electric current. The ionized gas emits ultraviolet light, which stimulates phosphors in the panel to produce visible light.

Digital Video Discs (**DVDs**) were first marketed in 1997 in the USA. Taking advantage of the latest compression technology, these compact discs could carry up to 133 minutes of video and up to eight soundtracks, and offered much higher definition pictures and sound quality than the videotape cassettes they were intended to replace. They could be played on a DVD player plugged into a conventional TV set, or on a personal computer (see also page 232).

Digital broadcasting was introduced in the USA and the UK in 1998. The picture signal is converted into digits before transmission and re-converted on reception into signals that can be interpreted by a television in the home.

The technology produced sharper pictures and improved sound quality, and because many digitized signals could be transmitted on a single frequency, there was a great increase in the number of available TV channels.

The US TV network ABC made the **world's first digital TV broadcast** on 1 November 1998, with a showing of Disney's *101 Dalmatians*.

Digital and analogue systems are set to continue side-by-side until 2006, when the analogue system is to be phased out.

Interactive television technology enabled viewers to use suitably equipped TVs to access banking and home shopping services and send and receive electronic mail messages. It also enabled viewers to download additional information about a programme and, for sports events, to select their own camera angles and action replays.

A number of broadcasters offered limited interactive services before March 1998, when Hong Kong Telecom launched iTV, billed as the **world's first truly interactive TV service**; it offered home shopping at four 'cybermalls' and pay-per-view videos, horse racing and music on demand.

In the UK, the **first nationwide interactive TV service** was launched in 1999. Earlier, Sky Sports had launched an interactive option on its live **football broadcasts**.

In 2000 the record for the **largest global audience for a TV programme** was the estimated 2.5 billion who watched coverage of the funeral of Diana, Princess of Wales, on 6 September 1997.

Computing

BEFORE AD 1000

Counting with beads

The **abacus** was used to aid arithmetical calculation as early as *c.*1850BC in Babylonia and may well have been in use a millennium earlier. The early Chinese used a *hsüan-pan* or a computing tray and, later, bamboo rods in place of beads. The Roman version used grooves for pebbles (Latin for pebble is *calculus*, hence the word calculation).

The Ancient Greeks devised complex mechanical devices to calculate the calendar. A specimen dating from *c.*80BC of an epicyclic, differentially geared **calendrical computer** was found off the island of Antikythera in 1900.

AD 1000

Heyday of the abacus

The abacus – in its familiar form, with counters strung on wires – reached its zenith in Europe *c.*1550. It still survives at the start of the 3rd millennium in some parts of the Middle East – and also in Japan, where it is known as the *soroban* and was adopted early in the 16th century.

John **Napier** (Scot) (1550–1617) announced his discovery of logarithms – a system of expressing numbers as powers of a base number, which makes complex calculations simple – in 1614. He called logarithms 'proportionate numbers'. In 1617 Henry Biggs (Eng) (1581–1630) worked out the logarithms for

all numbers from 1 to 1000. In 1624 he completed 2000 to 29,000 and 90,000 to 100,000.

William Oughtred (Eng) (1574–1660) invented the **slide rule** in 1622 and the multiplication sign (*x*) in 1631. Oughtred devised the first rectilinear slide rule, with a sliding stock between two slats, in 1633.

A six-dialled calculating machine was invented in 1623 by Wilhelm Schickard (Ger) (1592–1635). He anticipated by 19 years the six-dialled and cogged 'Pascaline', developed in 1642 by Blaise **Pascal** (Fr) (1623–62). Pascal devised his machine to ease the tedium of adding and subtracting, to which his father – Etienne (1588–1651), a tax collector – had long been subjected.

Charles **Babbage** (GB) (1792–1871) planned an accurately cogged calculating machine in 1812 as an undergraduate at Cambridge University. On 3 July 1822 Babbage won British government funding to build a Difference Engine. After 20 years, he had not perfected it; by then, he had moved on to the Analytical Engine, the first designs for which were dated 26 December 1836. He put this, too, aside.

Augusta Ada, Countess of Lovelace (1815–52), only child of the English poet Lord Byron, first met Babbage on 5 June 1833 and later became his assistant. In 1842 she published her *Observations on*

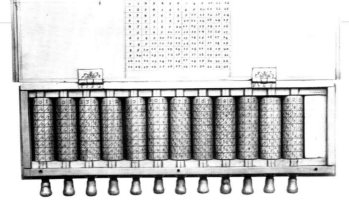

John Napier devised a calculating machine that contained rods and was later nicknamed 'Napier's Bones'. He explained how to use it in his book *Rabdologiae*, published in 1617.

Mr. Babbage's Analytical Engine. In the last 15 years of his life (1856–71) Babbage resumed work on his analytical engine, making 300 engineering drawings and 6500 pages of notes.

The mathematical work of most significance for the development of the electronic computer came in 1854 with George **Boole**'s (GB) (1815–64) publication of *An Investigation of the Laws of Thought*, which uses mathematical symbols to express logical elements – a system that became known as 'Boolean algebra' and proved to be basic to the design of binary computers.

The breakthrough into electro-mechanical computing was in 1906 when Lee De Forest (US) (1873–1961) patented his triode vacuum valve (tube) or Audion in New York City. It paved the way for binary logic circuits. In 1919, William Henry Eccles (GB) (1875–1966), with F.W. Jordan (GB), devised the bistaple or 'flip-flop' (on or off) circuit, which was to enable high-speed electronic counting.

The 19th-century English mathematician Charles Babbage left his calculating machine unfinished. His design for an analytical engine anticipated modern computers by proposing that a mechanical device could make calculations on the basis of a 'program' of instructions punched into cards. The engine was finally built at the London Science Museum in 1988–91.

The vast ENIAC (Electronic Numerical Integrator and Computer) built at the University of Pennsylvania in 1943–45 contained 17,468 vacuum tubes and consumed 174kW of power. But size brought power – in a single second it could carry out 5000 calculations.

Vannevar Bush (US) (1890–1974) built a semi-automatic **analogue calculator** Product Integraph at Massachusetts Institute of Technology in 1925. Such machines use varying voltages or rods of varying length to represent numbers proportionately (the word analogue is from the Greek *analogos*, proportionate).

Charles Eyrl Wynn-Williams (GB) (1903–79) built the first **electronic high-speed counter** in 1931 in Cambridge, England. He used thyratrons (gas-filled electronic valves). In 1936–38 Konrad Zuse (Ger) (1910–95) built a pioneer binary mechanical computer, later termed the Z1, which had a memory.

The world's first **electronic computer** was completed on an unrecorded date in late October or early November 1939. It was built at Iowa State College, Ames, Iowa, USA, by John Vincent Atanasoff (US) (1904–95) and his assistant Clifford Edward Berry (US) (1918–63). It could solve simultaneous equations, though its internal clock set at 60 pulses per second meant that it required a full second to add two 50-digit numbers.

In June 1941, an electro-magnetic relay machine, known as BOMBE, began operating in Hut 8 of the British cipher-breaking HQ at Bletchley Park in Buckinghamshire. It was designed by Alan **Turing** (GB) (1912–54) and Gordon **Welchman** (GB) (1906–85) to process the 9×10^{20} combinations necessary to crack the ENIGMA code, devised by Artur Scherbius in the 1920s, and used by the Germans for secret military communications in the war.

After making two prototype machines, German engineer Konrad Zuse produced the **first general-purpose program-controlled computer** to become operational – the Z3 – in December 1941. It had a memory capacity for 64 22-digit numbers, a central pulse clock and 2600 relays. It was used for aerodynamic wind tunnel calculations until it was destroyed in April 1945 by Allied aerial bombardment of Berlin. In 1950 Zuse's next model, the Z4, was installed at the Technical Institute in Zürich, Switzerland.

COLOSSUS, built for cryptanalysis with 1500 valves by Thomas Harold Flowers (GB) (1905–98) and Allen W. M. Coombes (GB) (1911–95), was first run at Bletchley Park in 1943 with five optical punched-tape readers. The COLOSSUS Mark II, with 2400 valves, first ran on 1 June 1944. In one trial, a printer reached 9700 characters per second before breaking down.

In 1944, Konrad Zuse devised his **programming language** Plankalk l (program calculus) in Hinterstein, Germany, where his Z4 had been moved for safety to an Alpine shelter. However, his work was only published in 1972.

In November 1945, the giant 17,468 valve **ENIAC** (Electronic Numerator Integrator and Computer) – commissioned on 5 June 1943 to solve ballistic calculations for the Aberdeen Proving Grounds, Maryland – was completed by John W. Mauchly (US) (1907–80) and J. Presper Eckert Jr (US) (1919–95). The 30-tonne machine cost $500,000 to construct.

John Atanasoff's historic 1939 computer was dismantled in 1948 and only two drums and some photographs survive. Atanasoff had failed to grasp the significance of his achievement, but his place in history was secured by Judge Earl R. Larson on 19 October 1973 when he ruled that the creators of ENIAC, Eckert and Mauchly, 'did not themselves first invent the automatic electronic digital computer, but instead derived that subject from one Dr John Vincent Atanasoff'.

In fact the Atanasoff computer was only semi-automatic, while the ENIAC machine, with its stored

program, represented an enormous advance in power and towards automation.

In 1947 the term **bit** (a single binary digit) was coined by John W. Tukey (US) (*b*.1915). The term **byte** (eight bits) followed in June 1956, first appearing in an IBM development manual.

John Bardeen (US) (1908–91) and Walter H. Brattain (US) (1902–87) invented the **point-contact transistor** in December 1947 at the Bell Laboratories, New Jersey. The tiny device, made of the element germanium, could amplify an electrical signal 100-fold; transistors began to be used in place of bulky, easily broken glass vacuum tubes in electrical circuits. Over time the circuits were made smaller, as were the computers that ran on them.

In June 1948, at Manchester University, Tom Kilburn (GB) (*b*.1921) wrote the world's first **computer program** for the first fully electronic stored-program computer – 'Baby, Mark I'. The 17-step program required 52 minutes to run.

The floppy disk was invented by Yoshiro Nakamatsu (Jap) at the Imperial University, Tokyo, in 1950.

The world's first **commercial computer**, the Ferranti Mark I, was installed for Ferranti Ltd by Manchester University's Electrotechnical Laboratories in February 1951. Priority has been claimed by Remington Rand of Philadelphia on the grounds that their Univac I (Universal Automatic Computer) was inaugurated at the US Bureau of Census on 14 June 1951, while the Ferranti was not inaugurated until 25 days later, on 9 July.

Geoffrey William Arnold Dummer (GB) (*b*.1909) first published his concept of the **integrated chip** in 1952. Within 70 hours Sydney Darlington (US) (*b*.1906) of Bell Laboratories applied for a US patent for a semi-conductor signalling device. The same day, Bernard 'Barney' M. Oliver (US) (*b*.1916), also of Bell, patented the integration of several transistors into a single chip of germanium or silicon.

The world's first **software company** – Computer Usage Co. (CUC) – was formed in March 1955 by John W. Sheldon (US) (*b*.1923) and Elmer C. Kubie (US) (*b*.1926). It filed for bankruptcy in 1986. The term software was first used in the USA in June 1960 and in the USSR in 1963.

The first **computer language**, Fortran (Formula Translation), was launched by John Backus (US) (*b*.1924) and Irving Ziller (US) in 1957. Other computer languages followed: COBOL (Common Business-Oriented Language), launched on 28 May 1959; ALGOL (Algorithmic Language), on 11 January 1960; BASIC (Beginners' All-purpose Symbolic Instruction Code), on 1 May 1964.

Ivan Edward Sutherland (US) (*b*.1938) developed **computer graphics** with his 'Sketchpad Project' from 1960–68. He later developed light pens (1963) and colour graphics (1968).

The **mouse** – a hand-held device that is moved over an adjacent flat surface to command a corresponding movement of a cursor on a VDU (Visual Display Unit) – was invented by Douglas Engelbardt (US) in 1965.

IBM first used the term **word processor** in 1967 to describe

its magnetic-tape electric typewriter. The processes had been invented by the company's German-born employee Ulrich Steinhilper (*b*.1918). In November 1970 Intel introduced a word processor that was able to display text on a screen, where it could be edited before printing.

The **Internet** grew from 1969, when the Advanced Research Projects Agency (ARPA) of the US Department of Defense established an experimental four-computer network. By 1971, 20 other sites (including Harvard University and the Massachusetts Institute of Technology) were linked. By 1974, this had grown to 199.

In 1970 the 'Alto' work station created by Alan Kay (US) (*b*.1940) of Xerox's PARC (Palo Alto Research Station) further developed computer graphics. Xerox PARC also developed WYSIWYG ('what

In contrast to the familiar PCs that sit neatly one to a desk in many modern workplaces, the first office computers were monsters, usually occupying their own rooms. The early computers had their own specialist operatives and were viewed with awe by the majority of the workforce.

Steve Wozniak lays proprietorial hands on the Apple II personal computer he designed in 1977. It was the first really successful PC and propelled Wozniak and Steve Jobs, co-founder of Apple Computer, to multimillionaire status.

Patterns in fractal images are repeated endlessly at ever smaller sizes. Fractals are used in computer graphics to create growing or changing shapes and to help predict natural events such as the gradual creation by accretion or erosion of a coastline.

you see is what you get') screen displays and invented the laser printer – two of the key technologies behind **desk-top publishing**.

AD 2000

Small but powerful

The first personal computer or **PC** was marketed at $750 in 1971 – the 256-byte memory Kenbak-1. In 1972, the first electronic **arcade game**, PONG – devised by Nolan K. Bushnell (US) (*b*.1943) – was marketed. Pong, also known as Tele-Tennis, was sold as the **first home computer game** the following year.

In 1975, William Henry ('Bill') **Gates** (US) (*b*.1955) dropped out of Harvard to write programs, the first of which was a compiler for BASIC. In 1977 he co-founded Microsoft to develop DOS

(disk operated systems). These were first adopted by IBM for PCs in 1981 and then by over 100 other companies under licence.

In June 1977, the **Apple II** PC was launched by Steven Jobs (US) (*b*.1955) and Stephen G. Wozniak (US)

(*b*.1950) at a price of $1195. Incorporated on 3 January 1977, Apple's growth was the fastest of any US company in history – in three years annual revenues topped $100 million. Their Visicalc accounting program was devised by Dan Bricklin (US); Bob Frankstron (US) created the **first spreadsheets**.

Apple introduced the **first disc drive** on a personal computer in 1978; the Lisa, which used a mouse and pull-down menus, in 1983; and the first of its **Macintosh** range of computers in 1984.

The first fully **portable PC** – the 24lb *10.9kg* Osborne I with a 5in *12.7cm* screen, two built-in disc drives and a 64-kilobyte memory – appeared in April 1981. The first **lap-top computer** was the Epson HX-20 in 1982.

Very Large Scale Integrated chips – with five circuit elements miniaturized to 50 nanometres across – were announced in 1983. (One nanometre is 1/1000 millionth of a metre.) In 1986 Seymour Cray (US) (1925–91) launched the Cray 2 with a two gigabyte central memory. (One gigabyte is *c*.1000 million bytes.) In 1989 Intel launched its neuro-chip – able to perform 2 billion calculations per second.

The term **'hacker'** was first used in 1983 to describe someone who breaks into the computer system of a company or government organization to gain access to restricted files. In 1985, a gang of 23 hackers made a concerted assault on the computer system of the Chase Manhattan Bank; since then there have been major

hacking attacks on high-security targets including the Pentagon in Washington, D.C. In the USA, hackers operating for criminal ends are known as 'crackers'.

Early computer games were sold on 5^{1}/4 in floppy discs, but a major breakthrough came with the release of the **first game on a CD-ROM** – 'The Manhole', created by US firm Activision in 1989. Because they have far greater information capacity than floppies, CD-ROMs can carry more complex games with much better graphics. The first CD-ROMs had been marketed by Sony and Philips in 1985 (see also page 231).

CD-ROM games proved phenomenally popular. The fantasy game *Myst*, released by Cyan in 1993 and using three-dimensional animation, sold half a million copies in its first year and went on to become the first CD-ROM game to sell **more than 2 million copies**.

Virtual Reality (VR) was created in 1989 by Scott Fisher (US) (*b*.1962). In modern systems, a 'cybernaut' fitted with fibre-optics, an eye-phone and a 'data glove' can – when cabled to a computer – experience the sensation of walking around a still unbuilt building, aircraft or ship, or of walking in a fantasy world. Virtual reality rides are a popular feature in many amusement arcades.

In 1989 Thomas Bein (US) (*b*.1954) and Chun Guey Wu (Taiwan/US) (*b*.1961) proposed replacing silicon chips with molecular 'wires' of polypyrole, polyanilene or polythiophene in zeolite channels, so miniaturizing components to a nanometric (extremely small) scale.

The Gridpad, the first portable computer able to respond to handwritten commands, was invented and marketed in 1990 by Jeff Hawkins (US).

The first commercial **speech-driven computers** – IBM Speech Server and the DragonDictate – were sold in 1993. They matched digitized speech waveforms against a 'library' of word models specific to the user.

The **World Wide Web** developed in 1992 from the network used by scientists at CERN, the European Organization for Nuclear Research in Geneva, Switzerland. It was to become the main method by which people accessed information on the Internet.

The key technology, called HyperText Transfer Protocol, was invented by Tim Berners-Lee (Eng) (*b*.1955). It was a simple system that enabled anyone to request information from another computer over the Internet without expert knowledge.

In 1993 the National Center for Supercomputing Applications (NCSA) in the US released 'Mosaic', the **first web browser**. This sparked an explosion in public use of the Internet, and in 1993–95 traffic grew at the rate of 341,000 per cent a year.

Enterprising individuals saw the potential of the web, with its easy-to-use method of showing information and pictures, as a means of selling goods. The **first virtual shopping site** was Branch Mall, launched by Jon Zeeff (US) in 1993. It offered the services of two outlets, Grant's Flowers and Calling Cards. In the first month Branch Mall received just 400 visits by members of the online community, but soon the boom in **e-commerce** was under way as consumers started to use websites for shopping online. They could select items for mail order delivery and pay by typing in their credit card number.

Encryption software was developed that scrambled users' financial data while it was in transit, so that it could be deciphered only at the point of sending and of receipt and could not be intercepted and misused by anyone else. The online bookstore **Amazon** opened for business in July 1995 and by May 2000 had served 17 million people in 160 countries.

Investors rushed to buy into the projected future profits of such enterprises and so-called 'dotcom' shares proved so popular that many **Internet business were valued at billions of US dollars** even though their present business operation was unprofitable. In the UK, only 0.25 per cent of all retail sales were transacted on the Internet in 1999, but company flotations could attract vast sums. However, a series of well-publicised failures in 2000 brought greater caution.

The capacity of **computer viruses** to travel swiftly around the world over the Internet and cause websites to shut down or the network to malfunction was demonstrated in 1999-2000. The term computer virus, first used in 1972, describes a hidden sequence of computer code or a programme that can damage computers. In March–April 1999 the viruses known as Melissa, Mad Cow and Papa caused communication problems for the US-led allies in their campaign in the former Yugoslavia.

On 4 May 2000 the Lovebug virus – so called because it spread in an attachment to an email message headed *I Love You* – forced the US Congress and the Houses of Parliament to close down their email systems and disrupted hundreds of computer networks worldwide.

The number of Internet users in the developed world was growing rapidly in 2000. In the first quarter of the year 5 million people in the USA connected to the web, an increase of 26 percent on the same period in 1999.

In March 2000 the **number of people online** was estimated to be 304 million worldwide, with 137 million of these in Canada and the USA, 83 million in Europe. Meanwhile there were just three million users in the entire African continent.

On 11 May 1997, IBM's Deep Blue computer concluded a six-game match in New York City, USA, matching the five-time world chess champion, Gary Kimovich Kasparov (*né* Weinstein) (Azerbaijan) (*b*.1963). Kasparov had beaten the previous Deep Blue in 1996, but in 1997, out of six games, he won one, lost one and drew four. The 1997 Deep Blue could analyse 200 million chess positions a second.

SPORTS

Sweden's Bjorn Borg serves his way towards the men's title in the 100th Wimbledon tennis competition, held in 1977. Today's sophisticated and aggressively competitive tournaments are a relatively new phenomenon, but the sporting qualities of fitness, stamina, quick thinking and nobility – both in victory and defeat – have been prized for centuries.

The origins of sport

The competitive instinct runs strong in humans, and for millennia individuals have felt the urge to test their physical prowess against others. The birth of some sports can be pinpointed exactly. Rugby, for example, traditionally originated on a day in 1823 when a schoolboy picked up a football and ran with it. Others, like skateboarding, have arisen as a result of technological progress. But most have developed so slowly that it is impossible to say where and when they began. In these cases, the date given here refers to the sport's first mention in surviving records.

Sport	Date	Details
Archery	c.AD300	Practised by the Genoese. Society of Kilwinning Archers (Strathclyde, Scotland) first contested their Pa-Pingo shoot, 1488. An Olympic sport since 1900.
Athletics	c.3400BC	Ritual races recorded at Memphis, Egypt, in proto-dynastic period. Ancient Olympic Games. Earliest named sprint or *stade* champion: Coroibos, July 776BC. Earliest national championships by Amateur Athletic Club: Beaufort House, London 23 Mar 1866. Modern Olympic sport since 1896.
Australian rules football	AD1858	Ballarat goldfields, Australia. Founders were Tom Willis (1835–80) and Henry Harrison (1836–1924). First match (7 Aug) at Melbourne with 40 per side and goals 0.5 mile (800 + metres) apart, lasting six or more hours. Rules codified on 8 May 1866 in Melbourne.
Badminton	AD1869	Made famous at Badminton House, Gloucestershire, England by Lady Henrietta Somerset (1831–63). First rules codified at Poona, India, 1876. Rules re-codified 1893.
Ballooning	AD1783	First manned free flight (hot-air): Paris, 21 Nov. First hydrogen flight: Paris, 1 Dec 1783. Hot air ballooning revived in USA: 1961. First world championships: New Mexico, USA 10–17 Feb 1973.
Baseball	c.AD1700	English provenance, first played in Maidstone, Kent. Devised from rounders. Rules codified with the diamond layout and home plate, 1845. World Series from 1903.
Basketball	c.AD1520	Aztec two-player game *Ollamaalitzli* with stone hoop and rubber ball and the beheading of the loser, Mexico. Modern game invented by Dr James A. Naismith (Can) (1861–1939) in mid-Dec 1891 and first played 20 Jan 1892, Springfield, Mass., USA.
Boxing	c.3000BC	Boxing depicted on two votive tablets at Nintu Temple, Khafaje, Iraq; known in Greece, c.1520BC. Ancient Olympics: 686BC. First ring rules: 1743, England by Jack Broughton (1704–89). Queensberry Rules first applied in Cincinnati, Ohio on 19 Aug 1885, named after 8th Marquess (1844–1900). Olympic sport since 1904.
Cricket	c.AD1550	Earliest recorded match: Guildford, Surrey, England, c.1550. Eleven-a-side: Sussex, 1697. Formal rules: 1744. Earliest recorded women's match: Gosden Common, Surrey, 26 June 1745. Marylebone Cricket Club (MCC) founded by Thomas Lord (1755–1832) in 1787, and moved to St John's Wood site in North London in 1814.
Cross country	AD1898	Derived from steeplechasing (village church to church). First international contest: England v. France at Ville d'Avray near Paris (20 Mar).
Curling	AD1551	First depicted by Flemish painter Pieter Breughel (c.1520–69). Rules codified by Grand (later Royal) Caledonian Curling Club 1838.
Cycling	AD1868	First international race: 30 or 31 May, Parc de St Cloud, Paris, over 5940ft *1800m*. Olympic track, velodrome and road events since 1896. Tour de France devised by Henri Desgranges (Fr) (1865–1940), 1903, first race on 1 July. *Maillot jaune* (yellow jersey) worn by race leader since 1919.
Equestrianism	c.680BC	Ancient Olympic chariot racing: horses with riders from 648BC. Show jumping: Ireland, AD1766. Modern Olympics Grand Prix since 1900. Dressage and 3 day event since 1912.
Fencing	c.1360BC	Ancient Egyptians used masks and blunted swords. Established as a sport in Germany AD 1383. Hand guard invented c.1510 in Spain; foil 17th century; épée mid-19th century; and sabre in Italy, late 19th century. Olympic sport since 1896. Electronic scoring in épée, 1935.
Football	c.350BC	Chinese ball-kicking game *Tsu-chin* known c.350BC. Earliest reference in England, proclamation by Edward II (1284–1327). First modern rules, Cambridge University, 1846. Eleven-a-side standardized in 1870. The name 'soccer' coined by Charles Wreford Brown (1866–1951) of Oxford University in 1886. Olympic sport since 1900.
Football (American)	AD1880	Rules of the game, which originated at Harvard University and McGill, Montreal (1873–74), codified by Walter Camp (US) (1859–1925). Super Bowl first played in January 1967.
Football (Gaelic or Irish)	AD1712	Meath v. Louth at Slane, Ireland (no time limit, area of play or rules); rules codified at Thurles, Ireland, 1 Nov 1884.
Golf	c.AD1450	Roman game of *panganica* c.150BC, and Chinese *Ch'ui Wan* (hitting, ball) AD943, were ball-hitting games, the latter into large holes. Earliest reference to golf is in a parliamentary prohibition on the game in March 1457, Scotland.

Sport	Date	Details
Gymnastics	c.776BC	Ancient Olympic Games. Modern sport developed in AD1776 by Johann Friedrich Simon in Dassau, Germany.
Hockey	c.2050BC	Depicted at Beni Hasan tomb, Egypt. Played in Lincolnshire, England: AD1277. Modern forms (English Hockey Association rules): 1875. Olympic sport since 1908.
Horse Racing	c.1200BC	Olympic sport since Hittites of Asia Minor staged race in 33rd Ancient Olympic Games, 648BC. Earliest steeplechase: Butterant Church to St Mary's, Doneraile steeple, County Limerick, Ireland, 1752.
Ice Hockey	c.AD1650	On frozen canals, Netherlands (termed Kalv). Played in Kingston, Ontario: 1855. Puck first recorded 1860. Rules devised in Montreal 1879. Winter Olympic sport since 1920.
Ice Skating	c.800BC	Northern Europe, bone skates on wooden soles. Metal blades c.AD1600. Earliest club, Edinburgh 1742. First world figure championships, St Petersburg 1896. Winter Olympic event since 1924 (Chamonix, France).
Lawn Tennis	AD1793	Field tennis, as opposed to court tennis, first recorded in England (29 Sept). Leamington Club founded 1872. Patented as *sphairistike* (Gk. 'ball game') by Major Walter Clopton Wingfield (1883–1912), 23 Feb 1874. All England Croquet and Tennis Club formed 1876. First championships at Worple Road, Wimbledon, 1877.
Motor Racing	AD1894	Earliest competitive race, Paris to Rouen, France, June 22. Indianapolis 500 mile race inaugurated 30 May 1911.
Mountaineering	c.AD806	Fujiyama, Japan, climbed. Earliest recorded rock climb in British Isles: Stac na Biorroch, St Kilda, 1698 by Sir Robert Murray. First major Alpine ascent (Mont Blanc): 1786. Continuous history only since 1854.
Polo	c. 525BC	Known as *pulu* in Persia, but possibly of Indian origin from Manipur (as Sagol Kangjei). Imported to Europe from Bengal, India by 10th Hussars, based in Aldershot, Hampshire, 1869. Olympic sport from 1900 to 1936.
Rodeo	AD1847	Santa Fe, New Mexico, USA. Steer wrestling: 1900.
Rowing	AD1300	Venice regattas. Scheduled Olympic sport since 1896.
Rugby Football	AD1823	Traditionally, invented by William Webb Ellis (c.1807–72) at Rugby School, England. Game formulated at Cambridge, 1839. The Rugby Union founded: 26 Jan 1871. International Rugby Football Board founded: 1886.
Rugby League	AD1895	Professional breakaway from Rugby Union at Huddersfield, Yorkshire. Team reduced from 15 to 13: 12 June 1906. Rapprochement with Rugby Union in Great Britain: 1995.
Shinty (or hurling)	AD1770	Inter-village or clan game, West and Central Highlands of Scotland (Gaelic *Iomain* – driving forward). 'Shinty' is from the Gaelic *sinteag*, a bound. Rules suggested 1879 and adopted in 1893 by the Camanachol Association. Irish Hurling Union formed: 24 Jan 1879.
Shooting	AD1472	Target shooting recorded in Zurich, Switzerland. Game bird shooting, pigeons: England, 1814. Olympic sport since 1896 (free and rapid fire pistol and rifle); trap 1900; live pigeon 1900; small bore 1908. Clay pigeons, Britain 1880.
Skateboarding	AD1963	First 'world' championship in USA: 1966. Upsurge in 1970s from introduction of softer urethane wheels. Motorized boards from 1977.
Ski Jumping	AD1808	Ole (Olaf) Rye (Norway) (1791–1849) reportedly jumped 31ft *9.5m*. Official world records instituted: 1914. Winter Olympic event since 1924.
Skiing	c.2500BC	Earliest ski found at Hoting, Sweden measuring 3ft 7in *1,10m*. First downhill races: Australia, c.1855. Oldest club: Trysil, Norway, 1861. First Olympic Nordic events: 1924; first world Alpine championships: 1931. Ski-bobbing invented by J. C. Stevenson (US), 1892. Slalom introduced by Sir Arnold Lunn (GB) (1888–1974).
Sumo Wrestling	AD1684	Ikazuchi Gondaiyu first proposed rules with a clay ring or *dohyo* for the centuries-old activity. Japanese Sumo Association formed 1889.
Surfing	AD1771	Canoe surfing (*ehorooe*) first recorded by Capt. James Cook (1728–79) in the Hawaiian Islands. Board surfing reported by Lt James King, 1779. Sport revived by 1900 at Waikiki, Honolulu. Plastic boards introduced: 1956.
Swimming	c.36BC	First recorded in Japan. Inter-school contests in Japan by Imperial edict from 1603. Sea-bathing at Scarborough, Yorkshire, by 1660. Earliest bath: Pearless Pool, North London, 1743. Olympic sport from 1896.
Tennis (Royal or Real)	c.AD1050	Originated in French monasteries. *Jeu de paume* banned by the French church, 1245. Earliest surviving court: Paris, France, 1496. First 'world' champion: c.1740.
Volleyball	AD1895	Invented by William G. Morgan (US) (1837–84) at Holyoke, Mass., USA, as Minnonette. Internationalized in 1947. World championships for men 1949 and for women 1952. Olympic sport from 1964.
Weightlifting	776BC	Lifting weights of stone included in Ancient Olympic Games. Introduced to Britain by 'Professor' Szalay (Hungary) founder of the City of London based Amateur Weight-lifting Club. First international contest: 18 Mar 1891, Cafe Monico, London. Olympic sport from 1896.
Wrestling	c.3000BC	Nintu Temple Khafaje, Iraq, depicts wrestling on a votive tablet. Ancient Olympic Games of 708 BC. Graeco-Roman style, France, c.AD1860. Modern Olympic Games: Graeco-Roman style, 1896; freestyle 1904.
Yachting	AD1661	First contest between Greenwich and Gravesend on the River Thames, near London (1 Sept). Earliest club: the Cork Harbour Water Club, Cork, Ireland, 1720. Cowes Regatta: 1826; Americas Cup inaugurated 22 Aug 1851 and internationalized in 1870. Olympic sport since 1900 (0.5 to 20 ton classes and open class). Board-sailing invented: 1958.

Athletics

The great Finnish athlete Paavo Nurmi was known as the Flying Finn. At the Paris Olympics of 1924, Nurmi became the first man to win five gold medals at a single Games, winning the 1500m and 5000m within an hour of each other.

Athletics is the simplest of sporting activities and probably the oldest. Running, jumping and throwing are natural activities. The generally accepted classes of athletics are: running events – from 100m sprints to marathons; jumping events – high jump, pole vault, long jump, triple jump; and throwing events – shot, discus, hammer and javelin.

Running events are held not only against the other athletes in the field, but also against the clock. At first, times were measured by stop watches, operated by hand by track-side officials. Because of the inevitable inaccuracies of such a system, times were rounded up to the nearest tenth of a second. Even when more accurate **electronic timing** became available the times were still rounded up, which could cause disputes.

At the Olympic Games in Paris in 1924, Harold Abrahams' winning 100m run was electronically timed as 10.53 secs but rounded up to 10.6 secs, equalling the record first set in the first round of the 1912 Games by Donald Lippincott (US) and again in the 1924 quarter- and same-year's semi-finals by Abrahams himself.

Automatic timing to one-hundredth of a second became mandatory under the rules of the International Amateur Athletic Federation (IAAF) only in 1977.

The first record time for the **100m sprint** recognized by the IAAF was 10.8 sec by Luther Cary (US) on 4 July 1891. The 10.5 sec mark was first achieved by two Germans: Emil Ketterer on 9 July 1911 and Richard Rau on 13 August, but neither was recognized by the IAAF. On 18 June 1921, America's reigning Olympic champion, the Texan, Charles William Paddock (1900–1943) running in Pasadena, California, recorded 10.2 secs over 110 yards (330 feet). The meeting officials did not claim the time as a world's 100m record because the distance, at 100.58m, was too long.

The man for whom the IAAF first ratified 10.2 sec for a 100m record was the Alabaman, **James Cleveland 'Jesse' Owens** (1913–1980) who ran this time three times in Berlin during the 1936

The British runner Roger Bannister breasts the tape to break the four minute mile with a time of 3minutes 59.4 secs on 6 May 1954 at Iffley, Oxford, England. At the time Bannister was a medical student in London and could train for only one hour a day due to his studies.

Olympic Games. Owens also held the record for the slightly shorter 100 yards at 9.4 secs, which he ran for the fourth time at Ann Arbor, Michigan, in the Big Ten Championships on 25 May 1935. That was the day on which, in the space of 46 minutes, he made six new world records – 100 yards; long jump; 220 yards; and 200 metres; 220 yards low hurdles; and 200m hurdles.

The first sprinter to have a 10.0 sec 100m ratified was the Saarlander Armin Hary (b.1937) at Zurich on 21 June 1960. He won in a hand-timed 10.0 sec, but the starter had failed to recall the field after an 'anticipatory' start by Hary. The event was re-run with Hary returning a hand-timed 10.0 secs again (only 10.25 secs on the automatic timer) which the IAAF ratified. At the Mexico City Olympics in 1968, held at 7400ft 2250m above sea level, James (Jim) Hines (US) broke the **10 second barrier** when he finished in 9.95 secs to take gold.

At the Los Angeles Olympics in 1984 (Frederick) **Carlton Lewis** (US) put in a winning burst over the last 20 metres which carried him from second behind Sam Graddy (US) to an 8ft *2.4m* margin of victory during which he must have exceeded 27mph *43.45km/h*. Lewis went on to take a second gold in the 200m (with an Olympic record of 19.80 secs); a third gold in the long jump and a fourth in the 4x100m relay, won by the USA in a world record 37.83 secs. His flying anchor stage was timed at 8.94 secs giving a speed of 25.02mph *40.26km/h*.

The next Olympic 100m final at Seoul on 24 September 1988 was won by Jamaican-born Benjamin Sinclair Johnson Jr. (*b.*1961), who was running for Canada. Johnson's time was a record-shattering 9.79 secs. However, Johnson had been using anabolic steroids and the record was disallowed.

On 25 August 1991 the world record was lowered to 9.86 secs by Carl Lewis and again by two hundredths of a second in the 1996 Atlanta Olympics by Donovan Bailey (Can), with his winning time of 9.84 secs. On 16 June 1999 **Maurice Greene** (US) also achieved 9.79 secs, matching Johnson's disallowed record.

The Marathon was created in honour of the Greek Pheidippides, who ran from Athens to Sparta with the news of the Persian invasion of Greece in 490BC. It was inaugurated in 1896 as the culminating event of the first modern revival of the Olympics. The race was won by Spiridon Louis (Gk) (1873–1940). Welcomed at the stadium with joy by tens of thousands of Athenians, Louis was the host country's sole victor at the eleventh hour on the last day. But for his triumph, the frail revival of the Games – which depended on the goodwill of

PROGRESSIVE RECORDS FOR ONE MILE

Time min:sec	Athlete	Location	Date
*4:17.25	William Lang (GB) William Richards (GB)	Manchester, England	1865
4:12.75	Walter George (GB)	London, England	23 Aug 1885
4:12.6	Norman Taber (US)	Cambridge, USA	16 July 1915
4:10.4	Paavo Nurmi (Fin)	Stockholm, Sweden	23 Aug 1923
4:09.2	Jules Ladoumègue (Fr)	Paris, France	4 Oct 1931
4:07.6	Jack Lovelock (NZ)	Princeton, USA	15 July 1933
4:06.7	Glenn Cunningham (US)	Princeton, USA	16 June 1934
4:06.4	Sydney Wooderson (GB)	London, England	28 Aug 1937
4:06.2	Gundar Hägg (Swe)	Göteborg, Sweden	1 July 1942
4:06.2	Arne Andersson (Swe)	Stockholm, Sweden	10 July 1942
4:04.6	Gundar Hägg (Swe)	Stockholm, Sweden	4 Sept 1942
4:02.6	Arne Andersson (Swe)	Göteborg, Sweden	1 July 1943
4:01.6	Arne Andersson (Swe)	Malmö, Sweden	18 July 1944
4:01.3	Gundar Hägg (Swe)	Malmö, Sweden	17 July 1945
3.59.4	Sir Roger Bannister (GB)	Oxford, England	6 May 1954
3:57.9	John Landy (Aust)	Turku, Finland	21 June 1954
3:57.2	Derek Ibbotson (GB)	London, England	19 July 1957
3:54.5	Herb Elliott (Aust)	Dublin, Ireland	6 Aug 1958
3:54.4	Peter Snell (NZ)	Wanganui, New Zealand	27 Jan 1962
3:54.1	Peter Snell (NZ)	Auckland, New Zealand	1964
3:53.6	Michel Jazy (Fr)	Rennes, France	9 June 1965
3:51.3	Jim Ryun (US)	Berkeley, USA	17 July 1966
3:51.1	Jim Ryun (US)	Bakersfield, USA	23 June 1967
3:51.0	Filbert Bayi (Tanz)	Kingston, Jamaica	17 May 1975
3:49.4	John Walker (NZ)	Göteborg, Sweden	12 Aug 1975
3:49.0	Sebastian Coe (GB)	Oslo, Norway	17 July 1979
3:48.8	Steve Ovett (GB)	Oslo, Norway	1 July 1980
3:48.53	Sebastian Coe (GB)	Zurich, Switzerland	19 Aug 1981
3:48.40	Steve Ovett (GB)	Koblenz, West Germany	26 Aug 1981
3:47.33	Sebastian Coe (GB)	Brussels, Belgium	28 Aug 1981
3:46.31	Steve Cram (GB)	Oslo, Norway	27 July 1985
3:44.39	Noureddine Morceli (Alg)	Rieti, Italy	5 Sept 1993
3:43.13	Hicham El Guerrouj (Mor)	Rome, Italy	7 July 1999

*Dead heat – professional race

the Greeks – may well have faltered at the very moment of their rebirth.

In 1964, a witness confided to Harold Abrahams (then an Olympic historian) that the only way that Louis could have overtaken the leader, Edwin Flack (Aust) was by 'hitching a lift' for part of the way on a horse.

The distance of the 1896 Marathon was 24 miles 1500 yards *40km*. At the Paris Olympic Games of 1900 the course was 25 miles *40.26km*, and in the London Olympic Marathon of July 1908, it was 26 miles 385 yards *42.195km* –

the length at which it was standardized. The 1969 **Boston Marathon** was the first to attract a field of more than 1000.

Marathon courses vary in the severity of slopes and types of surface. Because it is not possible to compare like with like, marathon times are not strictly 'records' but rather 'fastests on record'.

The British runner Sebastian Coe competing at the 1984 Los Angeles Olympic Games. Coe broke the world record for the mile on 18 August 1981, lost it to Steve Ovett (GB), on 26 August, then won it back again two days later.

MARATHON RECORDS (WOMEN)

Time hr:min:sec	Athlete	Place	Date
3:40:22	Violet Piercy (GB)	London, England	3 Oct 1926
3:27:45	Dale Grieg (GB)	Isle of Wight, England	23 May 1964
3:19:33	Mildred Sampson (NZ)	Auckland, New Zealand	21 July 1964
3:15:22	Maureen Wilton (Can)	Toronto, Canada	6 May 1967
3:07:26	Anni Pede-Erdkamp (W Ger)	Waldniel, Germany	16 Sept 1967
3:02:53	Caroline Walker (USA)	Seaside, USA	28 Feb 1970
3:01:42	Elizabeth Bonner (USA)	Philadelphia, USA	9 May 1971
2:55:22	Elizabeth Bonner (USA)	New York, USA	1971
2:46:30	Adrienne Beames (Aust)	Werribee, Australia	31 Aug 1971
2:46:24	Chantal Langlacé (Fra)	Neuf-Brisach, France	27 Oct 1974
2:42:24	Liane Winter (W Ger)	Boston, USA	21 Apr 1975
2:40:15.8	Christa Vahlensieck (W Ger)	Dolmen, Germany	3 May 1975
2:38:19	Jacqueline Hansen (USA)	Eugene, USA	12 Oct 1975
2:35:15.4	Chantal Langlacé (Fra)	Oyarzun, Spain	1 May 1977
2:34:47.5	Christa Vahlensieck (GFR)	West Berlin, Germany	10 Sept 1977
2:32:29.8	Grete Waitz (Nor)	New York, USA	22 Oct 1978
2:27:32.6	Grete Waitz (Nor)	New York, USA	21 Oct 1979
2:25:41	Grete Waitz (Nor)	New York, USA	26 Oct 1980
2:25:28.8	Allison Roe (NZ)	New York, USA	25 Oct 1981
2:25:28.7	Grete Waitz (Nor)	London, England	17 Apr 1983
2:22:43	Joan Benoit (USA)	Boston, USA	18 Apr 1983
2:21:06	Ingrid Kristiansen (Nor)	London, England	21 Apr 1985
2:20:47	Tegla Loroupe (Ken)	Rotterdam, Netherlands	19 Apr 1998
2:20:43	Tegla Loroupe (Ken)	Berlin, Germany	26 Sept 1999

Tegla Loroupe of Kenya carries her national flag to celebrate winning a bronze medal in the 10,000m event at the World Championships held in the Ullevi Stadium at Gothenburg, Sweden.

MARATHON RECORDS (MEN)

Time hr:min:sec	Athlete	Place	Date
2:55:18.4	John J. Hayes (USA)	London, England	24 July 1908
2:52:45.4	Robert Fowler (USA)	New York, USA	1 Jan 1909
2:46:52.6	James Clark (USA)	New York City, USA	12 Feb 1909
2:46:04.6	Albert Raines (USA)	New York City, USA	8 May 1909
2:42:31	Henry Barrett (GB)	London, England	26 May 1909
2:40:34.2	Thure Johansson (Swe)	Stockholm (track), Sweden	31 Aug 1909
2:38:16.2	Harry Green (GB)	London, England	12 May 1913
2:36:06.6	Alexis Ahlgren (Swe)	London, England	31 May 1913
2:32:35.8 *	Johannes Kolehmainen (Fin)	Antwerp, Belgium	22 Aug 1920
2:29:01.8	Albert Michelsen (USA)	Port Chester, USA	12 Oct 1925
2:27:49	Fusashige Suzuki (Jap)	Tokyo, Japan	31 Mar 1935
2:26:44	Yasuo Ikenaka (Jap)	Tokyo, Japan	3 Apr 1935
2:26:42	Kitei Son (Jap) (b.Kee Chung Sohn (Kor))	Tokyo, Japan	3 Nov 1935
2:25:39	Yun Bok Suh (Kor)	Boston, USA	19 Apr 1947
2:20:42	Jim Peters (GB)	London, England	14 June 1952
2:18:40.2	Jim Peters (GB)	London, England	13 June 1953
2:18:34.8	Jim Peters (GB)	Turku, Finland	4 Oct 1953
2:17:39.4	Jim Peters (GB)	London, England	26 June 1954
2:15:17	Sergey Popov (USSR)	Stockholm, Sweden	24 Aug 1958
2:15:16.2	Abebe Bikila (Eth)	Rome, Italy	10 Sept 1960
2:15:15.8	Toru Terasawa (Jap)	Beppu, Japan	17 Feb 1963
2:14:28	Leonard Edelen (USA)	London, England	15 June 1963
2:13:55	Basil Heatley (GB)	London, England	13 June 1964
2:12:11.2	Abebe Bikila (Eth)	Tokyo, Japan	21 Oct 1964
2:12:00	Morio Shigematsu (Jap)	London, England	12 June 1965
2:09:36.4	Derek Clayton (Aust)	Fukuoka, Japan	3 Dec 1967
2:08:33.6	Derek Clayton (Aust)	Antwerp, Belgium	30 May 1969
2:08:12.7	Alberto Salazar (USA)	New York, USA	25 Oct 1981
2:08:18	Rob de Castello (Aust)	Fukuoka, Japan	6 Dec 1981
2:08:05	Steve Jones (GB)	Chicago, USA	21 Oct 1984
2:07:12	Carlos Lopes (Port)	Rotterdam, Netherlands	20 Apr 1985
2:06:50	Belayneh Dinsamo (Eth)	Rotterdam, Netherlands	17 Apr 1988
2:06:05	Ronaldo da Costa (Braz)	Berlin, Germany	20 Sept 1998
2:05:42	Khalid Khannouchi (Mor)	Chicago, USA	24 Oct 1999

*Course 26 miles 990 yds *42.75km*

Algerian Noureddine Morceli leads the field to take the gold medal in the 1500m at the 1996 Olympics. This made up for his 1992 disappointment when he started as favourite, but was boxed in by the pack and finished seventh.

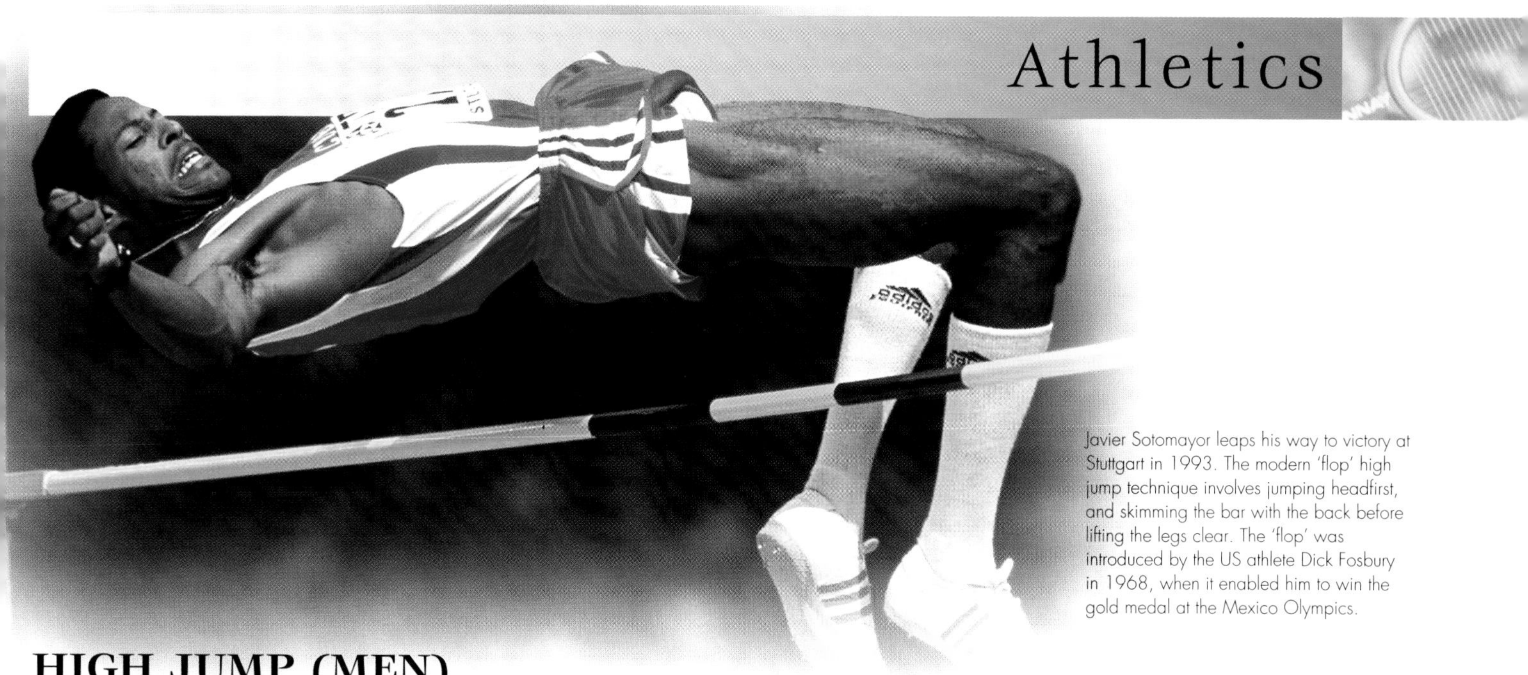

Javier Sotomayor leaps his way to victory at Stuttgart in 1993. The modern 'flop' high jump technique involves jumping headfirst, and skimming the bar with the back before lifting the legs clear. The 'flop' was introduced by the US athlete Dick Fosbury in 1968, when it enabled him to win the gold medal at the Mexico Olympics.

HIGH JUMP (MEN)

Height ft.	metres	Athlete	Place	Date
6ft 1/8 in	1.83	Hon. Marshall James Brooks (GB)	Oxford, England	17 Mar 1876
6ft 2¾ in	1.9	Patrick Davin (Ireland)	Carrick-on-Suir, Ireland	5 July 1881
6ft 4 in	1.93	William Byrd Page (USA)	Philadelphia, USA	7 Oct 1887
6ft 5⅝ in[1]	1.97	George W. Rowden (GB)	Stonebridge, England	6 Aug 1890
6ft 4½ in	1.94	J. M. Ryan (Ireland)	Tipperary, Ireland	19 Aug 1895
6ft 5⅝ in	1.97	M. F. Sweeney (USA)	New York City, USA	21 Sept 1895
6ft 7 in	2.00	George L. Horine (USA)	Stanford, USA	18 May 1912
6ft 7⁵⁄₁₆ in	2.01	Edward Beeson (USA)	Berkeley, USA	2 May 1914
6ft 7⅞ in[2]	2.03	Clinton Larson (USA)	Provo, USA	1 June 1917
6ft 8¼ in	2.04	Harold M. Osborn (USA)	Urbana, USA	27 May 1924
6ft 9⅛ in	2.06	Walter Marty (USA)	Palo Alto, USA	28 Apr 1934
6ft 9¼ in	2.07	Cornelius C. Johnson (USA)	New York City, USA	12 July 1936
6ft 9¾ in	2.07	Dave D. Albritton (USA)	New York City, USA	12 July 1936
6ft 10¼ in	2.089	Mel Walker (USA)	Malmö, Sweden	12 Aug 1937
6ft 10⅜ in	2.092	William Stewart (USA)	Provo, USA	26 Apr 1941
6ft 10¾ in	2.10	Lester Steers (USA)	Seattle, USA	26 Apr 1941
6ft 11 in	2.11	Lester Steers (USA)	Los Angeles, USA	17 June 1941
6ft 11⅝ in	2.12	Walter Davis (USA)	Dayton, USA	27 June 1953
7ft 0⅝ in	2.15	Charles Dumas (USA)	Los Angeles, USA	26 June 1956
7ft 1 in[3]	2.162	Yuriy Styepanov (USSR)	Leningrad, USSR	13 July 1957
7ft 1½ in	2.17	John Curtis Thomas (USA)	Philadelphia, USA	30 April 1960
7ft 3¾ in	2.22	John Curtis Thomas (USA)	Palo Alto, USA	1 July 1960
7ft 4 in	2.236	Valeriy Brumel (USSR)	Moscow, USSR	18 June 1961
7ft 5¾ in	2.28	Valeriy Brumel (USSR)	Moscow, USSR	21 July 1963
7ft 6 in	2.29	Ni Zhinquin (China)	Shang Sha, China	18 Nov 1970
7ft 6 in	2.29	Patrick Matzdorf (USA)	Berkeley, USA	3 July 1971
7ft 7¼ in	2.32	Dwight Stones (USA)	Philadelphia, USA	4 Aug 1976
7ft 8⅛ in	2.33	Vladimir Yashchenko (USSR)	Tblisi, Georgia	16 June 1978
7ft 8½ in	2.35	Jacek Wszola (Pol)	Ebberstadt, Germany	25 May 1980
7ft 8⅞ in	2.36	Gerd Wessig (Ger)	Moscow, USSR	1 Aug 1980
7ft 10 in	2.39	Zhu Jianhua (China)	Ebberstadt, Germany	10 June 1984
7ft 10¾ in	2.40	Rudolf Povarnitzyn (USSR)	Donyetsk, USSR	11 Aug 1985
7ft 10⅞ in	2.41	Igor Paklin (USSR)	Kobe, Japan	4 Sept 1985
7ft 11¼ in	2.42	Carlo Thränahardt (Ger)	Berlin, Germany	26 Feb 1988
7ft 11⅝ in	2.43	Javier Sotomayor (Cuba)	Salamanca, Spain	8 Sept 1988
8ft ¼ in	2.45	Javier Sotomayor (Cuba)	Salamanca, Spain	27 July 1993

Notes:

[1] Disallowed because of sloping ground.

[2] In an unsanctioned meeting reputedly cleared 2.07m 6ft 9.5in.

[3] Made with a 'built-up' (or orthopaedic) shoe. After 1958 the IAAF stipulated 13mm as a maximum thickness.

The Olympic Games

The Olympic Games are named after **Olympia**, the main sanctuary of the god Zeus in Elis, Greece. Scholars cannot agree on the date of the Games' origin, but it is certain that there was a quadrennial event from at least July 776BC, as a list of champions from then until AD217 was drawn up by Julius Africanus in AD221 and preserved by Eusebius of Caesarea's (c.AD260–340) *Chronicle*.

The Games included athletics, throwing events such as javelin and discus, chariot-racing and wrestling. The last of the ancient Games was

In the first games of the modern era, in Athens (1896), the sprinters in the 100m race await the starter's gun. Winner was Thomas Burke (US) in 12.0 seconds from Fritz Hoffman (Ger). Alajos Szokolyi of Hungary came in third.

terminated by decree of the Emperor **Theodosius** I (c.346–395) of Rome in 394.

The revival of the Olympic Games in modern times was the inspiration of the French educationalist, Pierre de Fredi, **Baron Coubertin** (1863–1937). After conceiving of the idea in 1887, he spent seven years persuading national sporting bodies to participate. Coubertin was an early advocate of physical education and believed that the Games would promote international amity.

The first celebration of the modern era was opened in the Averoff Stadium, **Athens**, on 6 April 1896. The XXVIIth Games open in **Sydney**, Australia, on 15 September 2000. Though there were ice-skating events in 1908 and 1920, with ice hockey also in 1920, the **Winter Games** were not inaugurated until 1924.

American Jesse Owens (1913–80) won four golds – including the 100m and 200m – at the 1936 Berlin Games. Nazi propaganda minister Josef Goebbels had expected a triumph for blond-haired, blue-eyed athletes.

The Olympic flame symbolizes the Games' pure ideals, but big money and politics have increasingly left their impression in the last three decades of the millennium. US TV rights for the 1996 Atlanta Games fetched $456 million; the contests of 1976, 1980 and 1984 were all struck by political boycotts.

100 YEARS OF SPORTING GLORY – THE MODERN OLYMPICS

No. (summer)	No. (winter)	Dates	Location	Nations	Participants
I		1896 6–15Apr	Athens, Greece	13	311
II		1900 20 May–28 Oct	Paris, France	22	1330
III		1904 1 July–23 Nov	St Louis, USA	13	625
		1906 22 Apr–2 May	Athens, Greece	20	884
IV		1908 27 Apr–31 Oct	London, England	22	2056
V		1912 5 May–22 July	Stockholm, Sweden	28	2546
VI (not held)		1916 cancelled (war)	Berlin, Germany	-	-
VII		1920 20 Apr–12 Sept	Antwerp, Belgium	29	2692
	I	1924 25 Jan–4 Feb	Chamonix, France	16	294
VIII		1924 4 May–27 July	Paris, France	44	3092
	II	1928 11 Feb–19 Feb	St Moritz, Switzerland	25	495
IX		1928 17 May–12 Aug	Amsterdam, Netherlands	46	3014
	III	1932 4 Feb–15 Feb	Lake Placid, NY, USA	17	306
X		1932 30 July–14 Aug	Los Angeles, California, USA	37	1408
	IV	1936 6 Feb–16 Feb	Garmisch-Partenkirchen, Germany	28	756
XI		1936 1 Aug–16 Aug	Berlin, Germany	49	4066
	V (not held)	1940 cancelled (war)	Sapporo, Japan, then St Moritz	–	–
XII (not held)		1940 cancelled (war)	Tokyo, Japan then Helsinki, Finland	–	–
	V (not held)	1944 cancelled (war)	Cortina d'Ampezzo, Italy	–	–
XIII (not held)		1944 cancelled (war)	London, England	–	–
	V	1948 30 Jan–8 Feb	St. Moritz, Switzerland	28	713
XIV		1948 29 July–14 Aug	London, England	59	4099
	VI	1952 14–25 Feb	Oslo, Norway	30	694
XV		1952 19 July–14 Aug	Helsinki, Finland	69	4925
	VII	1956 26 Jan–5 Feb	Cortina d'Ampezzo, Italy	32	820
XVI		1956 22 Nov–8 Dec	Melbourne, Australia*	67	3184
	VIII	1960 18–28 Feb	Squaw Valley, California, USA	30	665
XVII		1960 25 Aug–11 Sept	Rome, Italy	83	5346
	IX	1964 29 Jan–9 Feb	Innsbruck, Austria	36	1091
XVIII		1964 10 Oct–24 Oct	Tokyo, Japan	93	5140
	X	1968 6–18 Feb	Grenoble, France	37	1158
XIX		1968 12 Oct–27 Oct	Mexico City, Mexico	112	5530
	XI	1972 3–13 Feb	Sapporo, Japan	35	1006
XX		1972 26 Aug–10 Sept	Munich, West Germany	121	7123
	XII	1976 4–15 Feb	Innsbruck, Austria	37	1123
XXI		1976 17 July–1 Aug	Montreal, Canada	92	6028
	XIII	1980 13–24 Feb	Lake Placid, NY, USA	37	1073
XXII		1980 19 July–3 Aug	Moscow, Russia (USSR)	80	5217
	XIV	1984 8–19 Feb	Sarajevo, Yugoslavia	49	1274
XXIII		1984 28 July–12 Aug	Los Angeles, California, USA	140	6797
	XV	1988 13–28 Feb	Calgary, Canada	57	1423
XXIV		1988 17 Sept–2 Oct	Seoul, South Korea	159	8465
	XVI	1992 8–23 Feb	Albertville, France	64	1801
XXV		1992 25 July–9Aug	Barcelona, Spain	169	9364
	XVII	1994 12–27 Feb	Lillehammer, Norway	67	1737
XXVI		1996 19 July–4 Aug	Atlanta, Georgia, USA	197	10,310
	XVIII	1998 7–22 Feb	Nagano, Japan	72	2,176
XXVII		2000 15 Sept–1 Oct	Sydney, Australia		
	XIX	2002 9–24 Feb	Salt Lake City, Utah, USA		
XXVIII		2004 July–Aug	Athens, Greece		
	XX	2006	Turin, Italy		

*Equestrian events held in Stockholm, Sweden, because of Australian veterinary regulations.

Alpine sports

SKIING

The oldest surviving ski (Old Norse *skith*, snow-shoe) was found at Hoting, Sweden, and dated to *c*.2500BC. The **first downhill ski-race** was recorded in Australia in 1855, although *langlauf* (cross-country) competitions are known from 1843 in Tromsø, northern Norway. Ski races at Mount Hotham, Victoria, Australia, were held three years before the earliest in Scandinavia at Iverslökka, Norway, in 1866.

Skiing as a sport is split into **Alpine skiing** for speed on prepared slopes and **Nordic skiing** over undulating cross-country courses of up to 31 miles 120 yards *50km*. Competitors in Alpine skiing **slalom** events aim for speed but must pass through a succession of gates (pairs of poles) set out on the course. **Ski jumping** is regarded as a Nordic event.

Nordic events (Men's 15km and 50km cross country and ski jumping) were included in the first Winter Olympic Games, held 25 January–4 February 1924 at Chamonix, France. Alpine events were not included until the first Winter Games after World War II at St. Moritz,

Switzerland, on 30 January–8 February 1948.

Skiing's **downhill speed record** is 150.028mph *421.448km/h*, set by Jeffrey Hamilton (US) at Vars, France, on 14 April 1995. The **fastest woman downhill skier** is Karine Dubouchet (Fr), timed at 140.864mph *226.700km/h* at Les Arcs, France, on 20 April 1996.

In Alpine skiing there have been three **triple Olympic gold medal winners**. Toni Sailer (Austria) (b.1935) won the downhill, slalom and giant slalom in 1956, Jean-Claude Killy (Fr) (b.1943) won the same three events in 1968 and Alberto Tomba (It) (b.1966) won the slalom and giant slalom in 1988 and the giant slalom in 1992. In Nordic skiing, Norway's Bjørn Dæhlie (b.1967) won seven golds in the Winter Games of 1992, 1994 and 1998.

The **longest recorded ski-jump** is 669ft *204m* by Andreas Goldberger (Austria) at Harrachov, Czech Republic, on 9 March 1996.

Frenchman Jean-Luc Cretier is holder of the record for highest average speed in an Olympic downhill event: 66.64mph *107.24km/h* at the Winter Games in Nagano, Japan, on 15 February 1998.

BOBSLEIGH

There are three classes of race down steep, ice-bound tracks: **bobsleighing** (or bobsledding) for two-man or four-man crews; **tobogganing**, for solo riders on a 'skeleton' sledge and **lugeing** for singles and two-seaters, in a sitting position.

Toboggan racing dates back at least as far as the 16th century in Austria. Four-man bobsleighing was one of 13 events at the first Winter Olympic Games in 1924. Two-man bobsleighing came in at Lake Placid, New York at the third Winter Games on 4–15 February 1932. Three lugeing events (Men's Singles and Doubles and Women's Singles) were introduced at the ninth Winter Games at Innsbruck, Austria on 29 January–9 February 1964.

Speeds of more than 85mph *136.8km/h* have been photo-timed even on skeleton sledges, where the competitor's face is only 8in *20cm* above the ice.

The *France II* sleigh hurtles down the track in the four-man bob at the Winter Olympics in Albertville, France, in 1992. Home advantage did not help the French: the winners were the crew of *Austria I* with a time of 3 minutes 53.90 seconds, just 0.02 secs ahead of the men in *Germany I*. It was the event's smallest ever margin of victory.

Baseball

References to 'base ball' as a variant of cricket, rounders and trap ball in England date back to 1700. The American game seems to have been devised in 1839 at Cooperstown, New York, by **Abner Doubleday** (1819–93), a cadet at West Point military academy.

The rules of the modern game were codified by Alexander Joy Cartwright Jr (1820–92) in 1845. The first match played under them was on 19 June 1846 when the **New York Nine** beat the New York Knickerbockers 23–1 in four innings at the Elysian Fields, Hoboken, New Jersey. The **first fully professional team** were the Cincinnati Red Stockings, who were unbeaten in 64 games in 1869.

There are two baseball leagues in the USA: the National League (NL) (formed 1876) and the American League (AL) (formed 1901). In October 1903 a play-off between the champions of the two leagues was inaugurated as the **World Series**. The first result was a 5-3 win for the Boston Red Sox (AL) over the Pittsburgh Pirates (NL). The 100th World Series will be in October 2004 (there were no contests in 1904 and 1994).

ALL-TIME RECORDS

Peak achievements

The New York Yankees (AL) hold the record for the **most World Series wins** with 24 victories in 35 appearances. The **most successful NL team** has been the St Louis Cardinals with nine wins in 15 appearances.

The record for **most individual appearances** in the World Series is held by Lawrence Peter 'Yogi' Berra (New York Yankees) (*b*.1925) who made 14 between 1947 and 1962. He was on the winning team a record 10 times and also set a record of 259 at bats and 71 base hits. **Mickey Charles Mantle** (*b*.1931) (New York Yankees) hit a record 18 home runs in the world series of 1951–53, 1955–58, 1960–64.

George Herman 'Babe' Ruth (1895–1948) shares the record for **most home runs** in a game of the World Series with Reginald Martinez Jackson (*b*.1946). Ruth hit three for the New York Yankees against the St Louis Cardinals on 6 October 1926 and Jackson matched his feat for the Yankees against the Los Angeles Dodgers on 18 October 1977.

The World Series record for **most strikeouts** is 94 and is held by Edward Charles 'Whitey' Ford (*b*.1928) (New York AL) who achieved it in 12 matches.

Don James Larsen (*b*.1929) is the only pitcher to have achieved a perfect pitch – when no opposing runner reaches à base – in a world series game. He did so on 8 October 1956 for the New York Yankees against the Brooklyn Dodgers.

The New York Yankees have won the most **American League titles** with 35 victories 1901–98. The New York Giants hold the equivalent record for the National League, with 17 triumphs since 1876.

Henry Louis 'Hank' Aaron (*b*.1934) hit a record 755 home runs in his career 1954–76. In April 1973 he broke Babe Ruth's existing career record of 714 – and afterwards was the target of much hate mail.

On 27 September 1998 Mark McGwire of the St Louis Cardinals wound up a triumphant summer in which he had set a new record for **most home runs** scored in a season – 70 from 155 games. In 1927 Babe Ruth had hit 60 from 151 games played and he had been overtaken in 1961 by Roger Maris with 61 from 161 games.

Tyrus Raymond **'Ty' Cobb** (1886–1961) scored a record 2245 runs in his career with the Detroit Tigers (AL) 1905–26 and the Philadelphia Athletics (AL) 1927–8.

Walter Perry Johnson (1887–1946) of the Washington Senators holds the career record for **most shutouts** – 113 in 1907–27.

Lynn Nolan Ryan (*b*.1947) achieved a record 5714 **strikeouts** in 1966–93. In 1974 his fast pitch – the 'Ryan Express' – was measured at 100.9mph *162.3km/h*.

'Babe' Ruth began his career as a pitcher but went on to set a host of records as a big hitter. After helping the Boston Red Sox win three World Series (1915–18) he transferred to the New York Yankees for a record $125,000 in 1920. The next year he hit 59 home runs.

Basketball

Members of the 1992 US 'Dream Team' savour victory over Croatia to take Gold in the 1992 Olympic Games in Barcelona, Spain. The Dream Team averaged a remarkable 117.25 points per game.

WORLD CHAMPIONS

The World Championship was inaugurated for men in Buenos Aires in 1950 and was first held for women in 1953.

Men	Women
1950 Argentina	1953 USA
1954 USA	1957 USA
1959 Brazil	1959 USSR
1963 Brazil	1964 USSR
1967 USSR	1967 USSR
1970 Yugoslavia	1971 USSR
1974 USSR	1975 USSR
1978 Yugoslavia	1979 USA
1982 USSR	1983 USSR
1986 USA	1986 USA
1990 Yugoslavia	1990 USA
1994 USA	1994 Brazil
1998 Yugoslavia	1998 USA

Basketball was invented in 1891 by Canadian-born James A. Naismith (1861–1939) in Springfield, Massachusetts. Naismith laid down 13 rules for his new team sport, of which 12 are still in place, but the rules did not become standardized until 1934. At first there were seven players on each side, but the number soon changed to nine and then eight. Today the game is played by five players on each side.

The National Basketball League (NBL) was formed in 1898 with Pennsylvania, New Jersey and New York as founding teams. The NBL faded in 1900 but was refounded in 1937. In 1949, the **National Basketball Association (NBA)** was formed when the League merged with the Basketball Association of America.

Major scandals erupted in 1934 and 1951, when professional gamblers fixed important matches by bribing the players. More than 30 were arrested in 1951 and 49 fixed matches uncovered.

The sport's best known team were the **Harlem Globetrotters**, formed by Abe Saperstein in January 1927. In 1951 they played for a record crowd of 75,000 in the Olympic Stadium in Berlin. Team stars included Reece 'Goose' Tatum with a unique 84in *213cm* arm span, Meadowlark Lemon and Wilt Chamberlain.

Basketball became an **Olympic sport** at Berlin in 1936. The USA won the first seven tournaments (1936–1968) before, in 1972 at Munich, after 62 wins and no

losses in Olympic matches, they lost to the USSR in a highly charged and controversial final 51–50. Sergey Aleksandrovich Belov (1944–1976) scored the winning basket in the very last second of the game.

The USA then won the Olympic titles of 1976, 1984, 1992 and 1996, to make 11 out of the 12 for which they had competed to that date. The US team boycotted the 1980 Moscow Games in protest at the 1979 Soviet invasion of Afghanistan. The gold medals were taken by Yugoslavia, who beat Italy. The 1992 US Olympic team was the first to include NBA players and was dubbed 'The Dream Team'. Captained by Larry Joe Bird (*b.*1957), it also included Earvin 'Magic' Johnson (*b.*1959) and Michael 'Air' Jordan (*b.*1963).

The first **women's Olympic basketball** tournament took place in the 1976 Games at Montreal, Canada. The first title was won by the USSR, who fielded the formidable 7ft 1in *2.16m* tall, 285lb *129kg* Latvian, Uljana Larionovna Semjonova (*b.*1962). She averaged more than 19 points and 12 rebounds per game, despite spending half the time sitting out on the bench.

In the absence of the USA, the Soviet women won again in 1980. The USSR retaliated for the 1980 boycott by withdrawing from the 1984 Los Angeles Games and the USA beat Korea in the final. The Americans retained their title at Seoul in 1988, but in the 1992 final the Soviets won again but the title was taken back by the USA at Atlanta, Georgia, in 1996.

NBA WINNERS

The US National Basketball Association (NBA) championships began in 1947. Winners were:

Date	Champion
1947	Philadelphia Warriors
1948	Baltimore Bullets
1949	Minneapolis Lakers
1950	Minneapolis Lakers
1951	Rochester Royals
1952	Minneapolis Lakers
1953	Minneapolis Lakers
1954	Minneapolis Lakers
1955	Syracuse Nationals
1956	Philadelphia Warriors
1957	Boston Celtics
1958	St Louis Hawks
1959	Boston Celtics
1960	Boston Celtics
1961	Boston Celtics
1962	Boston Celtics
1963	Boston Celtics
1964	Boston Celtics
1965	Boston Celtics
1966	Boston Celtics
1967	Philadelphia 76ers
1968	Boston Celtics
1969	Boston Celtics
1970	New York Knicks
1971	Milwaukee Bucks
1972	Los Angeles Lakers
1973	New York Knicks
1974	Boston Celtics
1975	Golden State Warriors
1976	Boston Celtics
1977	Portland Trail Blazers
1978	Washington Bullets
1979	Seattle Supersonics
1980	Los Angeles Lakers
1981	Boston Celtics
1982	Los Angeles Lakers
1983	Philadelphia 76ers
1984	Boston Celtics
1985	Los Angeles Lakers
1986	Boston Celtics
1987	Lost Angeles Lakers
1988	Los Angeles Lakers
1989	Detroit Pistons
1990	Detroit Pistons
1991	Chicago Bulls
1992	Chicago Bulls
1993	Chicago Bulls
1994	Houston Rockets
1995	Houston Rockets
1996	Chicago Bulls
1997	Chicago Bulls
1998	Chicago Bulls
1999	San Antonio Spurs

Most wins:	
16	Boston Celtics
6	Los Angeles Lakers
6	Chicago Bulls

Boxing

The earliest significant **international bout** was a 'World Title' fight between John Heenan (US) and Tom Sayers (Eng) on Farnborough Common, Hampshire, England, on 17 April 1860. In the 37th round the police intervened and the result recorded was a draw.

John (Jack) Broughton (Eng) (1705–89) drew up the sport's first set of **rules** in August 1743. His rules held sway for 95 years until in 1838 the British Pugilists' Protective Association introduced their London Prize Ring Rules.

These in turn were widely superseded when in about 1865 the British Marquess of **Queensberry** (1844–1900) drew up his 12 rules of boxing. Queensberry rules were used internationally and introduced the three-minute round and the one-minute interval between rounds.

Boxing has long been beset by rival bodies claiming to be the World Governing Body. The World Boxing Association (WBA) was formed in 1962. The World Boxing Council (WBC) was created in Mexico in 1963. In 1983 the International Boxing Federation (IBF) (formerly the US Boxing Association International (USBAI)) was set up in the USA to end the WBA and the WBC duopoly, but failed. In 1988 the World Boxing Organization (WBO) was established.

Jack Dempsey (left), world heavyweight champion from 1919 to 1926, takes on Tom Gibbons in 1923. Dempsey took his fighting pseudomym from the Irishman who won the first World Title under the Queensberry Rules on 30 July 1884.

WBC heavyweight champion Lennox Lewis took on his IBF counterpart Evander Holyfield in New York on 13 March 1999. The pointing of the match as a draw provoked furious controversy.

WORLD HEAVYWEIGHT CHAMPIONS

Date	Champion		Location	Result	Defeated
1892 Sept 7	James John Corbett	(1866–1933) (US)	New Orleans	KO–21	Sullivan
1897 Mar 17	Bob Fitzsimmons	(1863-1917) (GB)	Carson City, Nevada	KO–14	Corbett
1899 June 9	James Jackson Jeffries	(1875–1953) (US)	Coney Island, N.Y.	KO–11	Fitzsimmons
1905 July 3	Marvin Hart	(1876–1931) (US)	Reno, Nevada	Stopped–12	Root
1906 Feb 23	Tommy Burns	(1881–1955) (Can)	Los Angeles	Pts–20	Hart
1908 Dec 16	Jack Johnson	(1878–1946) (US)	Sydney, Australia	Stopped–14	Burns
1915 Apr 5	Jess Willard	(1881–1968) (US)	Havana, Cuba	KO–26	Johnson
1919 July 4	Jack Dempsey	(1895–1983) (US)	Toledo, Ohio	Retired–3	Willard
1926 Sept 23	Gene Tunney	(1897–1978) (US)	Philadelphia	Pts–10	Dempsey
1930 June 12	Max Schmeling	(b. 1905) (Ger)	New York	Disqu–4	Sharkey
1932 June 21	Jack Sharkey	(b. 1902) (US)	Long Island	Pts–15	Schmeling
1933 June 29	Primo Carnera	(1906–67) (It)	Long Island	KO–6	Sharkey
1934 June 14	Max Baer	(1909–59) (US)	Long Island	KO–11	Carnera
1935 June 13	James J. Braddock	(1906–74) US	Long Island	Pts–15	Baer
1937 June 22	Joe Louis	(1914–81) (US)	Chicago	KO–8	Braddock
1950 Sept 27	Ezzard Mack Charles	(1921–70) (US)	New York City	Pts–15	Louis
1951 July 18	Jersey Joe Walcott	(b. 1914) (US)	Pittsburgh	KO–7	Charles
1952 Sept 23	Rocky Marciano	(1923–69) (US)	Philadelphia	KO–13	Walcott
1956 Nov 30	Floyd Patterson	(b. 1935) (US)	Chicago	KO–5	Moore
1959 June 26	Ingemar Johansson	(b. 1932) (Swe)	New York City	Stopped–3	Patterson
1960 June 20	Floyd Patterson	(b. 1935) (US)	New York City	KO–5	Johansson
1962 Sept 25	Charles 'Sonny' Liston	(1932–70) (US)	Chicago	KO–1	Patterson
1964 Feb 25	Cassius Clay	(b. 1942) (US)	Miami	Retired–6	Liston
1971 Mar 8	Joe Frazier	(b. 1944) (US)	New York City	Pts–15	Clay
1973 Jan 22	George Foreman	(b. 1948) (US)	Kingston, Jamaica	Stopped–2	Frazier
1974 Oct 30	Muhammad Ali	(b. 1942) (US)	Kinshasa, Zaïre	KO–8	Foreman
1978 Feb 15	Leon Spinks	(b. 1953) (US)	Las Vegas	Pts–15	Ali
1988 June 27	Mike Tyson	(b. 1966) (US)	Atlantic City	KO–1	Spinks
1990 Feb 11	James Douglas (WBA)	(b. 1960) (US)	Tokyo	KO–10	Tyson
1990 Oct 25	Evander Holyfield (WBA/IBF)	(b. 1962) (US)	Las Vegas	KO–3	Douglas
1992 Nov 13	Riddick Bowe (WBA/IBF)	(b. 1967) (US)	Las Vegas	Pts–12	Holyfield
1993 Nov 6	Evander Holyfield	(b. 1962) (US)	Las Vegas	Pts–12	Bowe
1994 Apr 22	Michael Moorer	(b. 1968) (US)	Las Vegas	Pts–12	Holyfield
1994 Sept 24	Oliver McCall (WBC)	(b. 1965) (US)	London	Pts–12	Lennox Lewis
1994 Nov 5	George Foreman (WBA/IBF)	(b. 1948) (US)	Las Vegas	Pts–10	Moorer
1995 Apr 8	Bruce Seldon (WBA)	(b. 1967) (US)	Las Vegas	Pts–7	Tony Tucker
1996 Mar 16	Mike Tyson (WBC)	(b. 1966) (US)	Las Vegas	Pts–3	Frank Bruno
1996 June 22	Michael Moorer	(b. 1968) (US)	Dortmund, Germany	Pts–12	Alex Schulz
1996 Sept 7	Mike Tyson	(b. 1966) (US)	Las Vegas	Pts–1	Bruce Sheldon
1996 Nov 9	Evander Holyfield (WBA)	(b. 1962) (US)	Las Vegas	Pts–11	Tyson
1997 Feb 7	Lennox Lewis (WBC)	(b. 1966) (GB)	Las Vegas	Pts–5	McCall
1997 Nov 8	Evander Holyfield	(b. 1962) (US)	Las Vegas	Pts–8	Moorer
1999 Mar 13	Holyfield (WBA-IBF) Lewis (WBC)	(b. 1962) (US) (b. 1966) (GB)	New York	Draw	
1999 Nov 13	Lennox Lewis	(b. 1966) (GB)	Las Vegas	Pts–12	Holyfield

Cricket

CRICKET WORLD CUP WINNERS

Year	Winner	Score	Beat	Margin	Venue
1975	West Indies	291–8	Australia	by 17 runs	Lord's
1979	West Indies	286–9	England	by 92 runs	Lord's
1983	India	183	West Indies	by 43 runs	Lord's
1987	Australia	253–5	England	by 7 runs	Calcutta
1992	Pakistan	249–6	England	by 22 runs	Melbourne
1996	Sri Lanka	243–3	Australia	by 7 wickets	Lahore
1999	Australia	103-1	Pakistan	by 8 wickets	Lord's

The game of cricket evolved from English bat and ball games that date back to the **13th century**. Rules were not drawn up until 1744.

Test matches between countries began with the first Australia *v.* England match on 15–19 March 1877. South Africa entered competition in 1889, but because of sanctions against the country's apartheid system, was barred from tests in the years 1961–92. Other countries joined in as follows: West Indies (1928), New Zealand (1930), India (1932), Pakistan (1952), Sri Lanka (1982) and Zimbabwe (1992).

The **highest test match score** remains the 1981 runs hit by South Africa and England in Durban, South Africa, on 3–14 March 1939. South Africa's two innings ran to 530 and 481 (total 1011); England hit 316 and 654 for five (970). The match was left drawn after 43 hours 16 minutes play, due to the sailing of England's ship.

The **highest score in a five-day test** is 1764. In Adelaide, Australia, on 24–29 January 1969 Australia hit 533 and 339 for nine (872) while the West Indies scored 276 and 616 (892). The match was drawn. The **highest single innings total** is 952 for six, scored by Sri Lanka *v.* India in Colombo on 4–6 August 1997. The **lowest** single innings total is the 26 hit by New Zealand *v.* England in Auckland on 28 March 1955.

Englishman Walter Hammond holds the record for the **fastest test century** (100 runs). On 31 March–1 April 1933 in Auckland during his innings of 336 not out against New Zealand, he took 47 minutes to move from 200 to 300.

In 52 tests for Australia 1928–48, **Don Bradman** (*b.*1908) scored 6996 runs – 99.94 per innings, the highest test average. Bradman made 117 centuries in first-class cricket; 29 were in tests.

Cricket's most successful captain is **Clive Lloyd** (*b.*1944), who led the West Indies to 36 wins 1974–85. **Allan Border** (Aus) holds the records both for most test appearances (156 in 1979–94) and most runs scored – 10,262 (average 51.06).

English bowler James Charles Laker (*b.*1922) holds the record for the **most wickets in a test match**. On 30–31 July 1956 at Old Trafford, Manchester, he took 19 wickets from Australia: nine for 37 runs in the first and 10 for 53 in the second innings. Sir Richard Hadlee of New Zealand took 431 test wickets in 86 tests 1973–90 – the record for most test wickets over a career.

Rodney Marsh (Aus) (*b.*1947) is the best-scoring test wicket keeper. In 96 tests 1970–84 he caught 343 batsmen and stumped 12 more.

Ian Botham (Eng) (*b.*1955) is the most successful all-rounder, with 5200 runs and 383 wickets in 102 tests 1977–92. In 1982 his 200 off 219 balls against India at Lord's was the fastest test double century.

The highest team score in a one-day international is the 363 for seven scored by **England** *v.* Pakistan in Nottingham, on 20 August 1992. **Viv Richards** (*b.*1952) of the West Indies scored the highest one-day individual score – 189 not out *v.* England at Old Trafford, Manchester, on 31 May 1984.

On 6 June 1994 at Edgbaston, Birmingham, Brian Lara hit a world record 501 not out for Warwickshire against Durham in the English County Championship. In April the same year he had set a new record for a test innings – 375 not out for the West Indies against England in Antigua.

Association football

There have been a number of ball games played with the feet. The ball-kicking game of *Tsu-chu* was played in China *c*.300BC and mediaeval Europe saw unruly contests between villages in which goals were miles apart and there were an unlimited number of players.

However, modern football dates from 1846, when a set of rules was drawn up at Cambridge University. The first English football league club, Sheffield Football Club, was founded in 1855. The Football Association evolved from a meeting of clubs in London in 1863.

The **rules and equipment** of association football became standardized fairly quickly. In 1865, goals were made 8ft *2.43m* high, with a tape stretched from pole to pole. In 1866, the off-side rule was introduced and **eleven players per side** became the standard in 1870 with goal-keepers and corner kicks introduced the following year. Cross-bars replaced goal tapes in 1875. Officials, then known as umpires, first used whistles in 1878. Finally, goal nets were introduced in 1890.

The advantages of standard rules were appreciated outside England. In 1872 England sent its first national team to Glasgow where it drew with Scotland 0–0. That same year, the first non-British club was founded in Le Havre.

By 1882 football teams existed in many countries and an International Board was established to control rules and procedures.

As more teams were founded, national football associations were established. By 1900 Denmark, Natal, New Zealand, New South Wales, Wales, Ireland, Scotland, Canada, Argentina, Italy, Germany and Uruguay all had their own Associations.

In that year, amateur football was introduced into the **Olympic Games**. Britain was represented by Upton Park Football Club of Essex and took the gold medals by defeating the France XI.

In 1904, **FIFA** (Fédération Internationale de Football Association) was formed in Paris on 21 May by Belgium, Denmark, France, Spain, Netherlands, Sweden and Switzerland. Other nations soon joined and by the end of the century a total of 191 countries were affiliated.

In 1925, the off-side rule was amended so that only two, instead of three, defenders were required between the attacker and the goal.

The **European Champion Clubs Cup** was first held in 1955 and the **European Nations Cup** in 1960. In 1971–72 the **UEFA Cup** was established by the Union of European Football Associations, formed in 1954.

In 1930 the **World Cup** was inaugurated in Montevideo, Uruguay on 13th July. This competition and trophy was created because the International Olympic Committee's strict adherence to amateurism was excluding the teams of many countries. At the 1928 FIFA Congress in Amsterdam, the FIFA President, **Jules Rimet** (Fr), suggested organizing an 'open' tournament for footballing nations.

The World Cup is held every four years and has become,

The great Pelé (*b.* Edson Arantes do Nascimento, 1940) at a training session in 1963. In a 20 year career from 1957–77, Pelé scored 1281 goals in 1363 first class matches.

Brazil celebrate their knife-edge victory over Italy in the 1994 World Cup final. The match was tied 0–0 at full time, but Brazil won a penalty shoot-out to clinch the match and the championship.

after the Olympic Games, the most popular sporting event in the world. The competition has been staged 16 times since its foundation.

The **first World Cup** was by no means trouble free. Ten boat-loads of Argentine supporters were searched for weapons, and the home team were guarded by Uruguayan troops with fixed bayonets.

The **1934 World Cup** was held in Italy, then under the dictator Benito Mussolini. Such was the fervour that after the 1–1 draw between Italy and Spain in Florence, four injured Italians and seven injured Spaniards were unable to play in the replay. Mussolini watched Italy defeat Czechoslovakia to take the title in Rome on 10 June.

The Argentinian player, Diego Maradona prepares to take on six Belgian defenders during a run on goal during the 1982 World Cup in Spain. Maradona went on to dominate the 1986 World Cup, won by Argentina from West Germany in a controversial 3–2 final.

Perhaps the most extraordinary match in the entire history of the World Cup took place in Strasbourg on 5 June 1938, between Brazil and Poland. Brazil's Léonidas da Silva scored a hat trick in 18, 25 and 44 minutes, followed by a fourth in the 93rd minute. Poland's Ernst Willimowski replied with his own hat trick at 22, 59 and 88 minutes, followed by a fourth goal in the 107th minute. The match was settled in extra time when Romeo snatched the winner for Brazil.

FIFA chose Brazil as the venue for the **fourth World Cup**. India withdrew in protest at the rule that all players must wear boots. The final on 16 July 1950 in Rio de Janeiro's Maracana Stadium saw a crowd of more than 200,000 assembled to watch the home team lose 2–1 to Uruguay in the final.

The **sixth World Cup** was staged in Sweden in 1958. The final, before 49,000 in Stockholm's Räsunda Stadium was between Brazil and the host team. It finished with the South Americans winning 5–2, of which the 17-year-old **Pelé** scored two.

Pelé became the most famous of all footballers and, according to many, is the greatest player of all time. Before retiring from Brazilian football in 1971, he won 111 caps for his country, and scored 97 international goals.

In 1966, four months before the tournament in England in July, the gold **Jules Rimet Trophy was stolen** from a display at an exhibition in London. A week later, a dog named Pickles found it hidden under a bush. The final was between England and Germany at Wembley on 30 July. England won 4–2 with a hat-trick from Hurst.

The **ninth World Cup** in Mexico was the first to be covered on live colour television. In the qualifying tournament, the matches between El Salvador and the Honduran Republic resulted in what was known as the Football War, when more than 2000 people were killed in riots. The final saw Brazil's third victory, giving them permanent possession of the Jules Rimet trophy.

In 1986, Mexico became the **first country to stage the World Cup twice** and 113 nations embarked on the qualification process. Argentina were the winners against West Germany, before a crowd of 114,000 on 29 July 1986.

Italy built two new stadiums to add to the ten already earmarked for the 14th World Cup of 1990 – Italia 90. Both semi-finals were decided by penalty shoot-outs and the final was a repeat of the 1986 clash between Argentina and West Germany. The Germans got a penalty in the final five minutes from which Brehme scored, so winning the title 1–0, for their third win.

The preliminaries of the **15th World Cup**, staged in the USA in 1994, were marred when the entire Zambian team was killed in a plane crash. In the Asian group, Macao played six matches and lost six, scoring no goals, but having 46 goals scored against them.

The US venues included the first indoor arena used in a World Cup – the Pontiac Silverdome, Detroit. On 22 June the USA defeated the highly rated Colombians 2–0 after Andres Escobar scored an own goal. When Escobar returned home, he was gunned down in his native town of Medellin by a man who reportedly shouted 'That's for the own goal'.

The 1994 final between Brazil and Italy in the Pasadena Rose Bowl, proved to be the **first goalless final** ever. In the penalty shoot-out Roberto Baggio (Italy) missed and Brazil won 3–2 on penalties.

In the 16th World Cup, staged in France in 1998, the host nation triumphed over Brazil 3–0. Paris at once erupted into massive celebrations which lasted until the following dawn.

The 17th World Cup in 2002 is due to be staged in two Asian countries – Japan and South Korea.

American football

A descendant of British association football and rugby, American football evolved at 19th-century US universities. The first college match under the Harvard Rules was played by Harvard University against McGill University of Montreal, Canada, in 1874. The **professional game** dates from August 1895 when Latrobe played Jeanette at Latrobe, Pennsylvania.

The greatest college football coach in the game's history was **Knut Rockne** (Nor) (1888–1931). Coaching Notre Dame, New Hampshire, from 1918 to 1930, he had a game-winning percentage of more than 88 per cent which remains unmatched.

Other greats of college football were Howard **'Hopalong' Cassady** (US) (b.1934), who won every honour possible as a running back for Ohio State University, and **Pete Dawkins** (US) (b.1938), who won the 1958 Heisman Trophy for the outstanding college football player when at West Point military academy.

Quarter back **Joe Montana**, (US) (b.1956) won fame both in college football for Notre Dame and from 1979 in the pro game for the San Francisco 49ers. He is celebrated as the hero of Notre Dame's claw-back victory from 11–34 to 35–34 over Houston in the 1979 Cotton Bowl college championship game.

Defensive line man Roosevelt **'Rosey' Grier** (b.1932) was one of the all-time great players for the Los Angeles Rams. Standing 6ft 5in *1.96m* and weighing 21st 6lb *136kg* he was the most imposing of the Rams' **Fearsome Four** – comprising also Deacon Jones, Lamer Lundy and Merlin Olsen.

Bronislaw **'Bronko' Nagurski**, (Can) (1908–90) was one of the most feared tackling full-backs of all. He was central to the three championships won by the Chicago Bears. His massive thighs and barrel chest were crowned by a 19in *48cm* neck. Football legend has it that awe-struck spectators once heard Nagurski's tackle crack his opponent's ribs.

SUPER BOWL

All-American championship

Two rival associations, the NFL (National Football League) and the AFL (American Football League), inaugurated the Super Bowl, a grand play-off between their respective champions in 1966–67. The match is held each January at the end of the football season.

With five wins each, the most successful Super Bowl teams are the Dallas Cowboys (1972/78/93/94/96) and the San Francisco 49ers (1982/85/89/90/95).

SUPER BOWL RESULTS

No.	Year	Teams	Score
1	1967	Green Bay Packers v. Kansas City Chiefs	35–10
2	1968	Green Bay Packers v. Oakland Raiders	33–14
3	1969	New York Jets v. Baltimore Colts	16–7
4	1970	Kansas City Chiefs v. Minnesota Vikings	23–7
5	1971	Baltimore Colts v. Dallas Cowboys	16–13
6	1972	Dallas Cowboys v. Miami Dolphins	24–3
7	1973	Miami Dolphins v. Washington Redskins	14–7
8	1974	Miami Dolphins v. Minnesota Vikings	24–7
9	1975	Pittsburgh Steelers v. Minnesota Vikings	16–6
10	1976	Pittsburgh Steelers v. Dallas Cowboys	21–17
11	1977	Oakland Raiders v. Minnesota Vikings	32–14
12	1978	Dallas Cowboys v. Denver Broncos	27–10
13	1979	Pittsburgh Steelers v. Dallas Cowboys	35–31
14	1980	Pittsburgh Steelers v. Los Angeles Rams	31–19
15	1981	Oakland Raiders v. Philadelphia Eagles	27–10
16	1982	San Francisco 49ers v. Cincinnati Bengals	26–21
17	1983	Washington Redskins v. Miami Dolphins	27–17
18	1984	Los Angeles Raiders v. Washington Redskins	38–9
19	1985	San Francisco 49ers v. Miami Dolphins	38–16
20	1986	Chicago Bears v. New England Patriots	46–10
21	1987	New York Giants v. Denver Broncos	39–20
22	1988	Washington Redskins v. Denver Broncos	42–10
23	1989	San Francisco 49ers v. Cincinnati Bengals	20–16
24	1990	San Francisco 49ers v. Denver Broncos	55–10
25	1991	New York Giants v. Buffalo Bills	20–19
26	1992	Washington Redskins v. Buffalo Bills	37–24
27	1993	Dallas Cowboys v. Buffalo Bills	52–17
28	1994	Dallas Cowboys v. Buffalo Bills	30–13
29	1995	San Francisco 49ers v. San Diego Chargers	49–26
30	1996	Dallas Cowboys v. Pittsburgh Steelers	27–17
31	1997	Green Bay Packers v. New England Patriots	35–21
32	1998	Denver Broncos v. Green Bay Packers	31–24
33	1999	Denver Broncos v. Atlanta Falcons	34–19
34	2000	St Louis Rams v. Tennessee Titans	23–16

Miami Dolphins quarterback Dan Marino has set new standards in his illustrious career. He holds the records for most yards gained – 55,416; most passes leading directly to a touchdown – 385; and most passes completed, that is caught by the player to whom they were thrown – 4,453.

Golf

The invention of golf has been claimed by **China**, where a game called *ch'ui wan* was played in 150BC. The Romans had a similar game they called *paganica*.

In the **Netherlands** the playing of a golf-like game called *colven* was recorded on 26 December 1297. It was played on a four-hole course at Leonen aan de Vecht, now in Belgium. In medieval Dutch, *colf* meant club.

A famous anti-gaming law passed by the **Scottish Parliament** in March 1457 enacted that the game of 'golf be vutterly criyt done and nocht vsyt' (golf be utterly cried down and not used).

The first recorded **Golf Club** is the Honourable Company of Edinburgh Golfers in March 1744.

The earliest golfer known by name was King James IV of Scotland (1473–1513) who played in 1504. His granddaughter, Mary, Queen of Scots (1542–87), played in 1563 and after the death of her husband, Henry Stuart, Lord Darnley (1545–67), in February 1567.

Golf was played at St Andrews, Fife, for some 200 years before the renowned Royal and Ancient Club was founded in 1754.

On 17 October 1860 the sport was truly launched when the **Open Championship** was inaugurated at the Prestwick Club on the coast of Ayrshire, Scotland, overlooking the Firth of Clyde, over 36 holes. It was won by Willie Park Sr, from Musselburgh. Park was to win again in 1863, 1866 and 1875.

The Open was dominated in its early years by 'Old' Tom Morris and his son 'Young' Tom Morris. They each won four times – 'Old' Tom in 1861/62/64/67 and 'Young' Tom in 1868/69/70/72.

Five-time winner James Braid – 1901/05/06/08/10 – scored 291 on his fourth win in 1908. This was equalled in 1926 by Bobby Jones (US) and bettered the following year by him with a 285.

A string of great golfers followed. Gene Sarazen (US) was 1932's winner with a score of 283 that was not bettered for the next 18

years. Henry Cotton (UK) was the first British winner in 11 years in 1934 and won again in 1937.

In 1953 Ben Hogan achieved a remarkable feat when he won the British Open, the US Open and the US Masters. He was the first person to win all three in the same year.

Arnold Palmer (US) first played in the British Open in 1960, its centenary year, and won in the following two years. In 1969, Tony Jacklin pulled off the first British win in the competition for 18 years. Severiano Ballesteros of Spain won in 1979 at the age of 22 – the first win by a professional from continental Europe for 72 years.

Apart from the British Open, three other World Major Championships are held each year in the northern hemisphere. These are the **US Open**, the US Professional Golfers' Association or **PGA** Championship and the **US Masters**.

The US Open was inaugurated in October 1895 at Newport, Rhode Island. It

American Bobby Jones wins his second consecutive British Open at St Andrews on 16 July 1927. To 1999, 19 American golfers have won the British Open a total of 32 times. Tom Watson is the most successful American with five victories over nine years, in 1975, 77, 80, 82 and 83.

American great Arnold Palmer's best period was the early 1960s. Palmer (b.1929) was four-time winner of the US Masters – 1958/60/62/64. He also triumphed in the U.S. Open in 1960 and took two British Opens, 1961/62.

Golf

THE WORLD'S MAJOR GOLF TOURNAMENTS

Year started	Tournament	Venue/notes	First winner
MEN			
1860	British Open	First held at Prestwick, Ayrshire, Scotland	Willie Park, Sr
1895	US Open	First held at Newport, Rhode Island	Horace Rawlins (GB)
1916	US PGA	First held at Siwanoy	Jim Barnes (GB)
1922	Walker Cup	Amateur match between USA and Britain, instituted by George Herbert Walker. First held at the National Golf Links, Long Island	USA
1927	Ryder Cup	Professional match between US and UK, held every two years. Instituted by the businessman Samuel Ryder	USA
1934	US Masters	By invitation only. Played on the Augusta National course, Georgia	Horton Smith
1953	World Cup	The brainchild of American industrialist John Jay Hopkins, and played by two-man national teams. First held at Beaconsfield Golf Club, Montreal, Canada	Argentina
WOMEN			
1893	Ladies British Open Amateur Championship	Held at St Anne's, Lancashire	Lady Margaret Scott, winner of the first three competitions
1895	US Women's Amateur Championship	Held at Meadow Brook	C. S. Brown
1932	Curtis Cup	International match between USA and Britain. Named after Harriet and Margaret Curtis. First held at Wentworth, Surrey, England	USA
1946	US Women's Open	Pro-am competition. First held at Spokane, Washington	Patty Berg
1955	US LPGA Championship	Held at Fort Wayne, Indiana	Beverly Hanson
1976	British Women's Open	First held at Gosford Park, Fulford, Devon	Jennifer Lee Smith

THE RYDER CUP

Year	Winner	Score	Venue
1927	USA	9.5–2.5	Worcester, Massachusetts
1929	GB	7–5	Moortown, Yorkshire
1931	USA	9–3	Scioto, Ohio
1933	GB	6.5–5.5	Southport & Ainsdale, Lancashire
1935	USA	9–3	Ridgewood, New Jersey
1937	USA	8–4	Southport & Ainsdale, Lancashire
1947	USA	11–1	Portland, Oregon
1951	USA	9.5–2.5	Ganton, Yorkshire
1953	USA	6.5–5.5	Wentworth, Surrey
1955	USA	8–4	Thunderbird G &CC, California
1957	GB	7.5–4.5	Lindrick, Yorkshire
1959	USA	8.5–3.5	Eldorado CC, California
1961	USA	14.5–9.5	Royal Lytham, Lancashire
1963	USA	23–9	Atlanta, Georgia
1965	USA	19.5–12.5	Royal Birkdale, Lancashire
1967	USA	18.5–8.5	Houston, Texas
1969	drawn	16–16	Royal Birkdale, Lancashire
1971	USA	18.5–13.5	St Louis, Missouri
1973	USA	19–13	Muirfield, Ohio
1975	USA	21–11	Laurel Valley, Pennsylvania
1977	USA	12.5–7.5	Royal Lytham, Lancashire
1979	USA	17–11	Greenbrier, West Virginia
1981	USA	18.5–9.5	Walton Heath, Surrey
1983	USA	14.5–13.5	PGA National, Florida
1985	Europe	16.5–11.5	The Belfry, Sutton Coldfield
1987	Europe	15–13	Muirfield Village, Ohio
1989	drawn	14–14	The Belfry, Sutton Coldfield
1991	USA	14.5–13.5	Kiawah Island, South Carolina
1993	USA	15–13	The Belfry, Sutton Coldfield
1995	Europe	14.5–13.5	Oak Hill, New York State
1997	Europe	14.5–13.5	Valderrama, Spain
1999	USA	14.5–13.5	Brookline, Massachusetts

started out over 36 holes, with an Englishman, Horace **Rawlins**, winning in 1895, but in 1898 became a 72-hole championship. In 1926, Bobby Jones became the **first man to win the British and US Open** in the same year.

In 1960 Jack Nicklaus recorded the **lowest ever aggregate** (282) by an amateur at the US Open to take second place. He returned in 1962 as a professional and pipped Arnold Palmer to the title.

South African Gary Player was the first US Open winner (1965) to be neither British nor American, and the first non-American since 1920. In 1970, Tony Jacklin became the first British winner since Ted Ray in 1920. Jack Nicklaus broke the record for the lowest aggregate, with 272, when he took the 1980 trophy 18 years after first winning it in 1962.

The PGA tournament was first held in 1916, before the April 1917 entry of the USA into World War I.

The biennial Ryder Cup, named after Samuel Ryder (1858–1936), was launched in 1927, originally as Great Britain against USA (1927–71) with Ireland included from 1973 to 1977 and Europe from 1979.

The by-invitation **US Masters** comprises 72 holes of stroke play at the Augusta National course in Georgia. The competition began when the great Bobby Jones invited some colleagues to an informal match in 1934 to raise money for the club.

Jack Nicklaus has had the most wins of the competition – five, between 1963 and 1975 – and set a record **lowest aggregate score** of 271 in 1965. This was equalled by Raymond Floyd in 1976 but stood until Tiger Woods broke it with 270 in 1997. Woods, aged 22, was the youngest player to win the Masters.

Horse racing and gambling

Red Rum won the Grand National steeplechase at Aintree, Liverpool, a record three times in 1973, 1974 and 1977. Here Barry Ellison, Red Rum's head stable hand, appeals for the right result before the 1975 race, which was won by L'Escargot.

The Ancient Greeks included horse racing in the Olympic Games from 776BC. Philip of Macedon competed and won in the Games with his horse **Cephalus** on the same day in 356BC that Philip's son Alexander was born.

In the Roman Empire great honours were showered on victorious horses, jockeys and trainers. The Emperor **Caligula** (AD12–41) gave 2,000 sesterces (silver coins) to his jockey Eutychus for one race.

The **first public horse races in England** were held at Smithfield, London, during the reign of Henry II (1154–89). By the time of James I of England (1603–25), public races were established at Gartely, Yorks, and at Croydon, near London.

The **first racecourse to be opened in North America** was in 1664 in New York. The first English governor of New York, Richard Nicholl, had a 2-mile 3.2km racecourse laid out on Long Island; it was inaugurated in 1665 with a spring meeting. In 1681, Louis XIV started the first **French race meeting** at St Germain.

In England, Queen Anne (1665–1714) promoted the establishment of the **Royal Ascot** meeting in Berkshire in 1711. The Jockey Club, the governing body of racing, was founded in 1750.

Steeplechasing developed from the training of hunters and was at first practised across natural courses. The first recorded race was in Ireland between a Mr O'Callaghan and Mr Edmund Blake, from Buttevant Church to St Leger Church in 1752.

The first steeplechase held at **Cheltenham**, England, was in 1834. The first **Grand National** steeplechase at Aintree, Liverpool, was in 1839, won by Mr Elmore's Lottery, ridden by Jem Mason.

Many of the 'classic' English flat races were established in the 18th century. The **St Leger** at Doncaster was first run in 1776; the **Oaks** at Epsom in 1779; the **Derby** at Epsom was inaugurated by the Earl of Derby in 1780, and was run annually from 1784.

GAMBLING

The *pari-mutuel* system was devised by a French chemist called Pierre Oller in 1872. The system is based on a pooling of the total amount staked and an equitable distribution of the takings.

The **Tote** or totalizator was first used to operate a *pari-mutuel* betting system in New Zealand in 1880. In 1913, an electronic calculator was introduced and in 1928, the French adopted the *pari-mutuel* system on their racecourses.

The **record accumulator bet** was in 1951 when a man from Coventry, England, won £3000 from what would now be a 50p bet on a four-horse accumulator (in which the winnings from one race are bet on the next). The odds against this were 60,640 to 1.

Orrin A Hickok drives the powerful St Julien, 'the King of the Turf', to victory in an American race c.1880. In the late 19th century, many US jockeys came to England. One of them, Tod Sloan (1874–1933), became Edward, Prince of Wales' jockey in 1897.

Motor racing

Motor racing started on 20 April 1887. Playboy and gambler Count Jules de Dion (Fr) (1856–1946) was the only entrant in a 19.3 mile *31km* race around Paris organized by the journal *Le Vélocipède*. He averaged 37mph *59 km/h* on his steam quadricycle.

The **first race to include petrol-engined cars** was the Paris to Bordeaux round event of 11–13 June 1895, won by Emile Levassor (Fr) (1844–97) in his 3.5 hp 1.2 litre Daimler-engined Panhard et Levassor No 5, in 48hrs 47mins. His average over the 732 miles *1178km* was 15.01mph *24.15km/h*.

The **first closed-circuit race** was held at Narragansett Park, Cranston, Rhode Island, USA, on 7 September 1896 and won by a Riker electric driven by A.H. Whiting. The UK's first track race was held at Crystal Palace, London, on 8 April 1901 and won by Charles Jarrott in a Panhard.

The **first US National Champion driver**, selected by the American Automobile Association (AAA), was George Robertson in 1909.

The **Indianopolis 500** mile event was inaugurated in 1911. The winner was Ray Harroun (US) (1879–1968) in a Marmon single-seater at an average 74.6 mph *120km/h*.

The **Formula One** World Drivers' Championship was launched in 1950. At Silverstone, Northants, England, on 13 May Guiseppe Farina (It) (1906–66) won the inaugural race in an Alpha Romeo Alfetta, averaging 90.95mph *146.39km/h*.

Farina won the 1950 world title with 30pts for the then six Grand Prix events, taking also the Swiss and the Italian Grand Prix. His Alfa Romeo team-mates Juan Manuel Fangio (Arg) (1911–95) and Luigi Fagioli (It) (1898–1952)

Giuseppe Farina (right) savours victory in the European Grand Prix at Silverstone, England, on 13 May 1950 alongside Juan Manuel Fangio (centre) and Alberto Ascari. Farina, first winner of the Drivers' Championship, was to be eclipsed by Fangio who is widely regarded as the sport's best ever driver.

SPORTS

Frenchman Alain Prost, winner of a record 51 Grands Prix, had his first Grand Prix triumph at Dijon-Prenois, France, on 5 July 1982. He also won the Dutch and Italian races that year.

A Courage Porsche C30LM eats up the miles in the Le Mans 24 hour race for sports cars in 1993. The event, started in 1923, was revived in 1949 after a break necessitated by World War II.

came second and third respectively. Fangio went on to win a record five drivers' titles: 1951, 1954, 1955, 1956 and 1957, the last when he was 46 years old.

Having won 24 Grand Prix in only 51 starts, the man dubbed 'the Maestro' because of his consummate driving ability chose to make the French GP at Reims on 6 July 1958 his last race. The crowd was unaware that, from early on, his Maserati had lost its clutch and that even at

8,000rpm he was judging every gear shift purely by ear. He finished fourth behind Englishmen Mike Hawthorn (1929–59) and Stirling Moss (b.1929), who came respectively first and second, and German Wolfgang von Trips (1928–61), who was third. Hawthorn went on to win the 1958 drivers' title.

Competitiveness reached a new level when, in the 1971 Italian GP at Monza, the first four drivers finished the 196.51 mile *316.25km* course within 0.18 secs of one another. Mike Hailwood (Eng) (1940–81) was fourth in his Surtees-Ford 0.09 sec behind Frenchman François Cevert (1944–73); Cevert was 0.08 sec behind the Swede Ronnie Peterson (1944–78), who was 0.01 sec behind the victor, Peter Gethin (Eng) (b.1940) in his British Racing Motors (BRM) car.

The driver with the **most Grand Prix wins** is Alain Prost (Fr) (b.1955) who accumulated 51 between 1981 and 1993. The winner of **the most pole positions** – first on the race's starting grid – is Ayrton Senna (Brazil) (1960–94) with 65 in 1985–94.

The **longest Formula One racing career** was that of Graham Hill (Eng) (1929–75) with 16 years 8 months from 1958 to 1975. Hill won the World Drivers' Championship in a BRM in 1962 and in a Lotus in 1968.

Over 50 years of the Drivers' Championship winners have come from 13 countries:
United Kingdom 8
Brazil 3
Australia 2
Austria 2
Finland 2
Italy 2
USA 2
Argentina 1
Canada 1
France 1
Germany 1
New Zealand 1
South Africa 1

The **most successful constructors** up to 2000 are Williams (UK) with nine world titles in 1980–7 and Ferrari with 119 wins in 1951–98.

The **fastest average speed** attained in the Le Mans 24 hour sports car race is 138.133mph *222.304km/h* by the Porsche driven by Dr Helmut Marko (Austria) and Gils van Lennep (Neths) (b.1942) in 1971. This was the equivalent of driving 3319.92 miles *5342.89km* in a day.

The **most successful cars** at Le Mans are Porsche with nine wins and the **most successful driver** is Jacky Ickx (Belgium) (b.1945) with six wins in 1969–82.

The two **four-time winners** of the Indianapolis 500 race are A. J. Foyt Jr (US) (b.1935) in 1961, 1964, 1967 and 1977 and Al Unser (US) (b.1939) in 1970, 1971, 1978, and – aged 47 – in 1987.

The **fastest average speed** at the Indy 500 is 185.981mph *299.307km/h*, set in 1991 by Arie Layendyk (US) in his Lola-Chevy Indy V8.

Mountaineering

A contemporary view of British mountaineer Edward Whymper on his way to conquering the Matterhorn (14,688ft *4477m*), in the Swiss Alps, on 14 July 1865.

BEFORE AD 1

Sacred peaks

The greatest height above sea level known to have been attained before 1550BC was the summit (22,057ft *6723m*) of the sixth highest peak of the Andes, Llullaiyaco (pronounced Yu-yai-ya-ko) in the Salta Province on the Argentine-Chilean border.

In early times mountain tops were regarded as the **abodes of gods**, dragons or evil spirits. In pre-Columbian times Atacama Indians probably climbed Llullaiyaco to

make sacrifices to their gods. A cache of Bronze Age artefacts *c.*1500 BC has been found on the Riffelhorn in Switzerland (9605ft *2927m*).

AD 2000

Mountaineering as a sport

The King of Aragon, Pedro III (reigned 1276–85), is reputed by his chroniclers to have climbed the East Pyreneean peak, **Mont Canigou** (9140ft *2786m*) solo in *c.*AD1280 and encountered an enormous dragon there.

Alpinism began on 8 August 1786 when Jacques Balmat (1762–1834) and Dr. Michel Paccard made the first ascent of **Mont Blanc**, the highest of the French Alps (15,771ft *4807m*). For 150 years the Alps remained the focus of climbing activity.

In the late 19th century, mountaineers ventured to more remote countries and the **Andes** in South America and the **Himalayas** in central Asia became the challenges of the future. The volcanic Cotopaxi (19,347ft *5897m*), in the Andes south of Quito, Ecuador, was first climbed by W. Reiss and A. M. Escobar on 28 November 1872.

From 1714 to 1810, people believed that **Chimborazo** (20,561ft *6267m*) in Ecuador was the world's highest mountain. The first recorded ascent was made by Edward Whymper with J. A. and L. Carrel on 4 January 1880.

Mount Everest (29,035ft *8849.8m*) in the Himalayas was established as Earth's highest known mountain in 1852 and in 1865 named by the British after Sir George Everest (1790–1866), former Surveyor General of India. It is pronounced 'Eve-rest'.

The 6600ft *2000m* North Face of the Eiger (13,025ft *3970m*) in the Swiss Alps was first climbed on 21–24 July 1938 by Heinrich Harrer and Fritz Kasparek of Austria with Andreas Heckmair and Wiggerl Vörg of Germany.

Kangchenjunga (28,205ft *8597m*) on the Sikkim-Nepal frontier was first climbed by a British/New Zealand expedition on 25 May 1955. George Band and Joe Brown stopped short of the summit as they had promised the Maharajah of Sikkim that they would not tread on it.

Mount Everest (29,035ft *8849.8m*), the world's highest peak and so the mountaineer's greatest challenge. It was first climbed on 29 May 1953 by Sir Edmund (Percival) Hillary (NZ) and the Sherpa Tenzing Norgay (Nepal). It attracts some 700 climbers each year. Reinhold Messner (Italy) (*b.*1944) became the first person to climb it solo on 20 August 1980.

Rugby Union

Rugby football was born in November 1823 during a game of soccer at Rugby School in Warwickshire, England. Schoolboy William Webb-Ellis (c.1807–72) picked up the ball and ran with it, inspiring the creation of the new game.

In 1835 English novelist Thomas Hughes (1822–96) wrote a descriptive account of the embryonic sport in his best-selling novel *Tom Brown's Schooldays* (1857). An ex-Rugby schoolboy, Albert Pell (1820–1907), is credited with spreading word of the new game to Cambridge University. The Cambridge Rules were drawn up in 1848.

Rugby spread to Wales in 1850, to Dublin University, Ireland, in 1854 and also to Scotland. A match between Merchiston School and Edinburgh Academy took place on 11 December 1858, and there was a fixture in Cape Town, South Africa, in August 1862.

In 1864 the game was introduced into Canada at Trinity College, Toronto, and also into Australia at Sydney University. The earliest recorded club match in New Zealand was between Nelson College and Nelson Football Club on 14 May 1870.

The **first international rugby match** was England v Scotland at Raeburn Place, Edinburgh, on 27 March 1871. Scotland won by a goal and a try to England's try.

The number of players was reduced from 20 to 15 in 1875, though this change was not formalized until 1892. **Seven-a-side rugby** was inaugurated at Melrose, Roxburghshire in the Scottish borders in 1883.

In 1889, the **Rugby Football Union** established 1 May to 31 August to be a close season. In 1895, 22 clubs seceded to create the new professional sport of Rugby League (see opposite).

The **Twickenham** ground in west London was opened on 2 October 1909, with a club match: hosts Harlequins v. Richmond. The first England international to be played there was on 15 January 1910, against Wales.

In 1911, Wales won the first 'Grand Slam', triumphing in all four of the season's international matches – against England, Scotland, Ireland and France. England hold the record for the most Grand Slams – 11 – in the International Championship 1884–1999 (known as the Five Nations since 1910). Other countries have won the Grand Slam as follows: Wales (6), France (6), Scotland (3), Ireland (1). Italy join the tournament in the year 2000.

In 1987, the **Rugby Union World Cup** was inaugurated and was won by New Zealand. In 1991 it was won by Australia, and in 1995 by South Africa.

Rugby football has only been included four times in the **Olympic** programme of sports. In 1900 the French side won; in 1908 Australia defeated England 32–3; in 1920 the USA defeated France 8–0 and in 1924 the USA won again, beating France 17–3.

The **highest score** in any full international was at Kuala Lumpur, Malaysia, on 27 October 1994. In a World Cup qualifying match, Hong Kong beat Singapore 164-13 and Ashley Billington (Hong Kong) contributed a record 10 tries for 50 of these points. The biggest score in a club match came on 13 November 1973 in Denmark, when Comet defeated Lindo by 194–0.

Australian David Campese holds the record for the **most tries in international matches**: in 101 internationals 1984–96 he scored 64 tries.

Campese's fellow Australian Michael Patrick Lynagh scored a record 911 points in 72 matches 1984–95. Frenchman Philippe Sella won a world record 111 international caps 1982–95.

New Zealand's Jonah Lomu scored four tries as his country overpowered England 45–29 in the 1995 World Cup semi-final in Cape Town, South Africa. In the final in Johannesburg the New Zealand All Blacks were beaten 15–12 by the host nation, South Africa.

Rugby League

The sport of Rugby League dates from 29 August 1895, when 22 rugby clubs from the northern English counties of Cheshire, Lancashire and Yorkshire seceded from the Rugby Football Union to form the **Northern Rugby Football Union**.

The split was provoked by a quarrel over the Rugby Union's refusal to allow the players in these clubs to receive 'broken time' payments for loss of wages from playing fixtures.

The **first Rugby League fixtures** were played on 7 September 1895, with broken time payments of six shillings (30p) permitted. Professionalism in the form of wages for the players remained unlawful.

In 1897, the League inaugurated the first **Challenge Cup Final**. Batley, Yorkshire, beat St Helens, Lancashire.

Changes in Rugby League rules widened the gulf with the Union game. In 1897 the line-out was abolished; in 1901 the transfer of players was permitted; in 1905 open professionalism was sanctioned; and in 1906 the teams were reduced from 15 to 13 players.

The sport developed internationally with England's tour of New Zealand in 1907–08 and of Australia in 1908–09. The **first international** took place on 20 April 1908 between Wales and England: Wales won 35–18.

The game was introduced to France with an exhibition match between England and Australia at the Pershing Stadium, Paris, on 31 December 1933. In 1948, the **International Rugby League Board** was created at Bordeaux, France.

The **World Cup** was established in 1954 between Australia, France, Great Britain and New Zealand. In 1975, it was replaced by the World Championship, including Wales. In 1995, Papua New Guinea, Samoa, South Africa and Tonga were added to make a ten-nation tournament in three groups.

James (Jim) Sullivan of Wigan (1903–1977) set the world record for **most internationals** with 60 appearances for England and Great Britain. He scored an international record of 160 goals and 329 points.

Michael (Mick) Sullivan (*b*.1934) (Huddersfield, Wigan, St Helens and York), scored a record 45 tries for England and Great Britain between 1954 and 1963.

Australian Brian Beavan (Aust) (1924–91) set the record for league tries, with 796 in his career playing for Warrington and Blackpool Borough 1946–64.

Australian Albert Aaron Rosenfield (1885–1970) held the record for **most goals** scored in a season, with 80. He set it in 1914 playing for Huddersfield.

Rugby League's world record attendance is the 102,569 who packed the Odsal Stadium, Bradford, for the Halifax v Warrington Challenge Cup final replay in 1948. Warrington won 8–4.

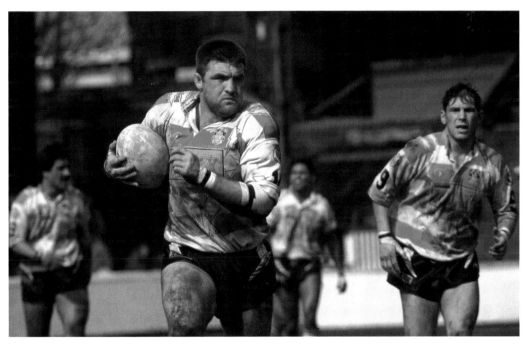

RUGBY LEAGUE WORLD CHAMPIONSHIP WINNERS

Year	Teams	Venue
1954	Great Britain *beat* France	France
1957	Australia *beat* Great Britain	Australia
1960	Great Britain *beat* Australia	England
1968	Australia *beat* France	Australia/NZ
1970	Australia *beat* Great Britain	England
1972	Great Britain *beat* Australia	France
1975	Australia *beat* England	Worldwide
1977	Australia *beat* Great Britain	Australia/NZ
1988	Australia *beat* New Zealand	New Zealand
1992	Australia *beat* Great Britain	England
1995	Australia *beat* England	England

Tennis

Modern tennis is derived from the much earlier sport of **court tennis**, also known as real or royal tennis. Although the oldest surviving tennis court is that built in Paris in 1496, the game was played in French monasteries as long ago as *c*.1050.

King Henry V of England (1387–1422) was an early royal participant. King Henry VIII (1491–1547) was reputedly champion of England in *c*.1530.

Lawn tennis derives from a game played in 1866 by J. B. Perera and Major T. Harry Gem on the lawn at Fairlight, Ampton Road, Edgbaston, Birmingham, England. The game was also called Pelota or Lawn Rackets. Major Gem formed the world's first tennis club, The Leamington Club, Warwickshire, in 1872.

On 23 February 1874, Major Walter Clopton **Wingfield** (1833–1912) entered a patent application for 'A New and Improved Portable Court for Playing the Ancient Game of Tennis' which he marketed under the Greek name *Sphairistike* (ball-playing). Enthusiasm for 'sticky', as it was called, was promoted by Henry Jones (1831–99).

On 24 June 1875 the **All England Club** (for croquet) agreed that the 'MCC (Marylebone Cricket Club) laws of lawn tennis be adopted' for playing on their new tennis court. The MCC became the governing body for court tennis and for rackets as well as cricket.

Such was the game's popularity that the All England Club brought four more courts into use at Worple Road, **Wimbledon**, on 14 April 1877 and formally changed its title to 'The All England Croquet and Lawn Tennis Club'. The first All England Championship, for men's singles only, began at Wimbledon on Monday 9 July 1877 with 22 competitors.

The game's original hour-glass shaped court was soon replaced with a rectangular court 78ft *23.77m* long by 27ft *8.23m* wide, which has remained to this day. The droopy net was to be 5ft *1.52m* high at the posts and 3ft 3ins *0.99m* at the centre.

In 1882 the net was raised to 3ft 6in *1.05m*; the modern game uses a 3ft *0.914m* net.

The winner of the first **Wimbledon championship** – in 1877 – was Spencer William Gore (1850–1906). The following year, with an injured wrist, he lost to Patrick Francis Hadow (1855–1946). At those second championships, A. T. Myers introduced the **overhead service**.

Men's doubles began at Wimbledon in 1884. This year was also the first in which there was a ladies' singles competition. Women's doubles and mixed doubles became full championship events in 1913 to complete the present-day standard championship range of five competitions.

The record for most Wimbledon titles including doubles championships is held by **Billie Jean King** (USA) in the years 1961–79, with 20 – six singles, 10 doubles and four mixed doubles.

The highest number of men's singles victories at Wimbledon is seven – by William Renshaw (champion 1881–86, 1889). In the modern era the Swede Björn Borg (champion 1976–80) has five titles and the American Pete Sampras (champion 1993–95, 1997–99) six.

Martina Navratilova (Cz/US) (née Subert) (*b*.1956) won the greatest number – nine – of ladies' singles at Wimbledon (1978-79, 1982–87 and 1990). In 1985, **Boris Becker** (Ger) became the youngest man to win

Czech-born US superstar Martina Navratilova edges closer to victory over American Chris Evert in the ladies' singles final at Wimbledon on 7 July 1978 – her first Wimbledon win. In her career to 1994 Navratilova won a world record 167 championships.

Wimbledon (17 years 227 days). The youngest woman was **Martina Hingis** (Switz) in the 1996 ladies' doubles at 15 years 282 days.

The **US Championships** was instituted by the US Lawn Tennis Association in 1881. The **Davis Cup** between national teams was first held in 1900. The **Australian Championship** was instituted in 1905. The **Wightman Cup**, for national women's teams, began in 1923 and the **French Open** followed in 1925.

The principle of **seeding** was accepted in the US Championship men's singles in 1922. Seeding was not used at Wimbledon until 1927.

In 1938 John Donald Budge (US) (b.1915), master of the attacking rolled backhand, first won the French, Australian, US and Wimbledon titles in a single year. This feat – known as the **Grand Slam** – was not matched until 1962 by Rodney George Laver (Aust) (b.1938), who then repeated it in 1969.

The first two women to win the Grand Slam were Maureen Catherine Connolly (later Brinker) (US) (1934–69) in 1953 and Margaret Jean Smith (later Court) (Aust) (b.1942) in 1970. In 1983 and 1984 Martina Navratilova matched Laver in twice winning the Grand Slam.

Lawn tennis was an Olympic sport from the outset in 1896 but was dropped in 1928. It was reinstated in 1988. In 1896 in Athens there were only men's singles, with seven nations entering 13 players. In the final the Irishman **John Boland** won 6-3 and 6-1 over the Egyptian Dionysios Kasdaglis.

When tennis reappeared at the Seoul Olympics in 1988 the Czech Miloslav Mecir triumphed. In 1992 in Barcelona Marc Rosset (Switz), ranked only 44th in the world, won the gold medal. In 1996 in Atlanta, Andre Agassi (US) and Lindsay Davenport (US) took the singles titles, while the Australians Mark Woodforde and Todd Woodbridge took the doubles titles.

Tennis's unusual **scoring system** is believed to derive from the fact indoor royal tennis courts often had a clock face at one or both ends. After each rally the clock's hands were moved round a quarter of its face – hence 15, 30, 45 (abbreviated to 40) and 60 to make a complete circuit and finish the game.

The **tie-break** was initiated at the 1970 US Professional Indoor Championship in Philadelphia, USA. The 12-point tie-break was incorporated in the laws to break ties at 6–6 (or by choice at 8–8) in 1975.

Records for **speed of service** before present electronic measurements tended to be crude adaptations from stop watches. In the 1932 Wimbledon men's singles final the match point ace by Henry Ellesworth Vines (US) (1911–94) against 'Bunny' Austen (GB) (b.1906) was said to be 'invisible'. The fastest reliably measured electronic speed by 1999 is 149mph *239.8km/h* by Canadian-born **Greg Rusedski** (GB).

Australian left-hander Rod Laver won the Wimbledon men's singles four times, the Australian Championship three times and the French and US Opens twice. He was an amateur player when he first won the Grand Slam in 1962.

1990s WIMBLEDON CHAMPIONS

Year	Men	Women
1990	Stefan Edberg (Swe) *beat* B. Becker (W. Ger)	Martina Navratilova (USA) *beat* Z. Garrison (USA)
1991	Michael Stich (W. Ger) *beat* B. Becker (W. Ger)	Steffi Graf (Ger) *beat* G. Sabatini (Arg)
1992	Andre Agassi (USA) *beat* G. Ivanisevic (Cro)	Steffi Graf (Ger) *beat* M. Seles (USA)
1993	Pete Sampras (USA) *beat* J. Courier (USA)	Steffi Graf (Ger) *beat* J. Novotna (Czech)
1994	Pete Sampras (USA) *beat* G. Ivanisevic (Cro)	Conchita Martinez (Sp) *beat* M. Navratilova (USA)
1995	Pete Sampras (USA) *beat* B. Becker (W. Ger)	Steffi Graf (Ger) *beat* A. Sanchez Vicario (Sp)
1996	Richard Krajicek (Neth) *beat* M. Washington (USA)	Steffi Graf (Ger) *beat* A. Sanchez Vicario (Sp)
1997	Pete Sampras (USA) *beat* C. Pioline (Fr)	Martina Hingis (Switz) *beat* J. Novotna (Czech)
1998	Pete Sampras (USA) *beat* G. Ivanisevic (Cro)	Jana Novotna (Czech Rep) *beat* N. Tauziat (Fr)
1999	Pete Sampras (USA) *beat* A. Agassi (USA)	Lindsay Davenport (USA) *beat* S. Graf (Ger)

Water sports

SWIMMING

The first records of competitive swimming date from 36BC in Japan during the reign of Emperor Zinmu.

The most historic **long-distance sea swimming trial** is the crossing of the 21 mile *33.8km* wide English Channel which, because of the tides, often involves swimming 35 miles *56km* or more.

The first person to swim the English Channel without a life-jacket was Matthew **Webb** (Eng) (1848–83) in 21 hours 45 minutes from Dover to Calais Sands on 24–25 August 1875. The present record for the crossing is 7 hours 17 minutes by Chad Hundeby (US) in 1994.

The **longest recorded swim** is that of Fred Newton (US) who swam 1,826 miles *2938km* down the Mississippi River, USA, between Ford Dam and New Orleans, Louisiana, from 6 July to 29 December 1930. Newton was in the water, covered with axle grease to keep the cold at bay, for 30 days 22 hours.

The **first indoor swimming-pool** was The Bagnio (43ft *13.1m* in length) in Lemon St, London. It was opened on 28 May 1742.

The **fastest swimming speed** is the 5.24mph *8.44km/h* achieved by Mark Foster (GB) over a 50m course at Sheffield, England, on 13 December 1998.

The record number of individual Olympic gold medals is five, held by Krisztina **Egerszegi** (Hun) (*b.*1974); she won them in 1988 (200m backstroke), 1992 (100m and 200m backstroke and 400m individual relay) and 1996 (200m backstroke).

Mark **Spitz** (US) (*b.*1950) won four individual golds at the Munich Olympics of 1972 (100m and 200m in both freestyle and butterfly) and during his career also won five team relay gold medals, making a record total of nine golds. In 1968, he had won a silver (100m butterfly) and a bronze (100m freestyle), making another record of 11 medals of all kinds – one equalled by Matt Biondi (US) in 1984–92.

ROWING

Competitive rowing has its origins in Ancient Greek and Roman races between oared galleys. Equipped with two or more banks of oars, these galleys were built for speed of manoeuvre in battle.

From the 14th century, Venetian gondoliers raced their long, flat-bottomed gondolas for prestige and trade. The first competitive regatta or gondola race in Venice was held on the Feast of St Paul (January 25) in 1315. Women competed for the first time in 1493 when 48 women rowed a 12-oar craft in honour of Eleonora d'Este and her daughter Beatrice.

Krisztina Egerszegi (Hun) holder of a record five individual Olympic gold swimming medals was aged just 14 years 41 days when she won her first, for the 200m backstroke, at Seoul in 1988.

Venetian-born artist Giovanni Antonio Canal, better known as Canaletto (1697–1768), captured the bustle and excitement of the rowing races in 32ft *10m* flat-bottomed gondolas that were held in Venice lagoon or, as here, on the city's Grand Canal. The word regatta comes from the Venetian dialect word *regata* for gondola race.

In London, the annual Doggett's Coat and Badge race for Thames watermen upriver from London Bridge to Chelsea was first held on 1 August 1716.

The **Oxford v Cambridge university boat race** was first held on 10 June 1829 at Henley-on-Thames and has been staged 147 times (annually since 1839). Oxford have 70 wins and Cambridge 76, while there was a dead heat in 1877. The contest is rowed over 4 miles 1 furlong 180 yards *6.803 km* in the Putney-to-Mortlake reaches of the Thames. The record time of 16 minutes 19 seconds achieved by the Cambridge crew in 1998 represents an average of 15.21mph *25.28km/h*.

The only oarsman ever to have won **four consecutive Olympic gold medals** is Steven Geoffrey Redgrave (UK) (*b.*1962): in 1984 (coxed fours), 1988 (coxless pairs), 1992 (coxed pairs) and 1996 (coxless pairs).

YACHTING

Yachting began in Holland. The word 'yacht' for a light sailing vessel, rigged for racing, is derived from the Dutch *jacht*, to chase. English King Charles II (1630–85) learnt the sport while in exile in Holland and took it back to England when he was restored to the throne in 1660 (see page 160).

Dutch traders introduced yachting to north America in the seventeenth century. The oldest surviving US yacht club is the Detroit Boat Club (established in 1839).

The **world's oldest yacht club** is the Royal Cork Yacht Club (formerly Cork Harbour Water Club) in the Irish Republic, established in 1720. The **America's Cup** was first offered by the New York Yacht Club as a challenge trophy in 1870. It was in honour of the 170 ton schooner *America*, which in 1851 had won a 16-boat race around the Isle of Wight. The first challenge was by the English schooner *Cambria*. She failed in seven races to overcome the US schooner *Magic*. There then followed 23 further successful American defences of the trophy in 1871–1980.

The first time that the cup was won by a **non-American crew** was in 1983 when *Australia II*, skippered by John Bertrand, won against the US boat *Liberty*.

Offshore or ocean racing began in December 1866 with a race from Sandy Hook, USA, to Cowes, Isle of Wight. The $30,000 prize event was contested by three schooners of *c.*105ft *32m*; the *Henrietta*, owned by US newspaper magnate James Gordon Bennett, won in 13 days.

The first **solo transatlantic crossing** was made by Alfred Johnson (US) in 1876 to mark the 100th year of US Independence. The first **solo round-the-world yachtsman** was also a US sailor, Joshua Slocum; he made his circumnavigation in 1898 in the 37ft *11.3m Spray*.

Yachting was first included in the Olympic Games in 1900 in France. The outstanding Olympic yachtsman was the Dane Paul D. Elvström (*b.*1928) who won **four successive gold medals** in the Finn Class of centreboard dinghy in 1948, 1952, 1956 and 1960.

The **Fastnet race**, from Cowes, Isle of Wight, round the Fastnet Rock in SW Ireland covers *c.*605 miles *975km* and was first held in 1925. In 1957, the Fastnet Race was incorporated into the **Admiral's Cup**, set up by the Royal Ocean Racing Club; it is contested by international teams of three yachts in six races.

In 1960, Sir Francis **Chichester** (Eng) (1901–72) won the first solo transatlantic race in *Gipsy Moth III*, having sailed from Plymouth to New York City in 40 days.

In 1966–67, Sir Francis circumnavigated the world alone in his 55ft *16.7m* yacht *Gipsy Moth IV*, sailing in a easterly direction. The 15,517-mile *24,971km* leg from Sydney, Australia, to Plymouth, England, was then the **longest non-stop passage ever made**. The first person to sail solo round the world in a westerly direction was Chay **Blyth** (Scot) (*b.*1940) in 1970–71.

The world's longest yachting race is the quadrennial **Whitbread Round the World Race,** first held in August 1973. Originally over 26,180 nautical miles and, since 1990, over 32,000 n. miles, it starts and finishes off Portsmouth, England, rounding the Cape of Good Hope in S Africa and eastabout round Cape Horn in S America. (One nautical mile is 6706ft *1852m*.) In the fourth race of 1986 Pierre Fehlmann (Swiss) in *UBS Switzerland*, completed his circumnavigation in 117 days 14 hours 32 minutes.

The **world speed record under sail** is 46.52 knots or 53.5mph *86.15km/h* set by Simon McKeon (Australia) in *Yellow Pages Endeavour* in October 1993.

In November 1996–March 1997, Frenchman Christophe Auguin sailed single-handedly non-stop around the globe aboard his yacht *Géodis* in a record 105 days 20 hours 31 minutes.

Pastimes

The oldest known board game in the world was the ancestor of modern **backgammon**. Boards found in the royal tombs of Ur in Sumeria (now southern Iraq) have been dated to *c*.3000BC. Each player had seven pieces and used six pyramidal dice – three white and three blue lapis lazuli dice. Egyptian boards have also been found in tombs dating to 1580BC. In modern backgammon, two players each have 15 pieces and share two dice, and the aim is to be first to move all one's pieces into the inner part of the board.

Lotto, the ancestor of modern **bingo**, was first recorded as a children's game in 1778. It was the first form of gambling permitted in the British armed services. In the USA it became very popular during the economic depression of the 1930s, when prizes of hundreds of dollars in cash or merchandise were offered.

The card game **bridge** was derived from whist and is said to have developed in Plebna, Istanbul, where the first rules were compiled *c*.1885 by John Collinson, an English visitor to Constantinople. By February 1886 it was known as 'biritch' or 'Russian whist'. The first official laws were issued by a joint committee of the Turf and Portland Clubs, London, in July 1895.

Auction bridge is traditionally believed to have been the invention of three Anglo-Indian civilians marooned in a remote Indian hill station in 1902 without the necessary fourth player. In 1906 the rules were regularized by the Bath Club, London, for four players.

Contract bridge was first called 'Saac' – the initials of the four men who devised it in Poona, India, in 1912. Sir Hugh Clayton (1877-1947) published the rules in the *Times of India* on 15 July 1914.

The name 'contract bridge' was introduced by Harold S. Vanderbilt (US) (1884–1970) in 1925 at the Whist Club in New York City and the laws were codified by a Committee of the Portland Club in December 1929. The **first international match** was held on 15 Sept 1930 between Britain and the USA. The USA won the match of 200 deals by 4845 points. The first World Championship was won by USA in Bermuda, on 13–16 Nov 1950.

A board game similar to **chess** evolved in India, almost certainly as early as AD450–550. It was named *chaturanga*, a Sanskrit military term for four divisions. The earliest reference to it is by Subandhu, author of the romance *Vasvadatta*, *c*.620, by which time the game had migrated into Persia (modern Iran). It reached the Christian west via Spain and Muslim northern Africa. Anglo-Saxon

Backgammon, known in Ancient Egypt, was brought to western Europe by soldiers returning from the Crusades, but did not take its present name until the mid-18th century. These players form a detail from a 17th-century Flemish oil painting.

Hungarian chess players exercise their minds over the chequered board as they soothe their bodies in the mineral baths at the spa of Szechenyi in Budapest. The familiar chess pieces have existed in their current form for around 500 years.

chessmen found in Witchampton, Dorset, England have been dated to *c.*AD950–1050.

Darts originated in close-quarters fighting. The pilgrims who sailed to North America aboard the *Mayflower* in 1620 played a shipboard game with 'dartes' to while away the hours during their 66-day journey. The present numbering system, attributed to an English carpenter, Brian Gamlin of Bury, Lancashire, dates from 1896.

Dominoes originated in China in the 16th century AD. Chinese dominoes used dotted cards (with no blank faces) that were designed to represent all possible throws of two dice. The first record of dominoes in Europe is in the mid-18th century in Italy and France. The game was introduced to England by French prisoners toward the end of the 18th century. The name may have derived from the resemblance of a black cloak called a domino to early pieces made with ebony and ivory faces.

Board games similar to **draughts** were played in the Egyptian New Kingdom (*c.*1600BC) and were later mentioned by the poet Homer (possibly 8th century BC) and the philosopher Plato (Gk) (*c.*427–347BC). The game was adapted to the 64-square chessboard in the 12th century.

By the 16th century, the rule of compulsory capture of a piece was incorporated. The first book on the game was published by Antonio de Torquemada of Spain, in 1547. William Payne's *Introduction to the Game of Draughts* appeared in 1756.

Saltwater and freshwater **fishing** in many countries attract more participants than any other sport. The oldest national angling association in the world was formed on 1 July 1880 at Loch Leven in Scotland.

The premier recorder and ratifier of saltwater and freshwater fish by species is the International Game Fishing Association. As at 15 October 1998, the selected species shown in the boxes below constituted official records.

The card game **gin rummy** derived from rummy, first described in 1887 under the name 'coon can', and then in 1897 as 'conquian'. The etymology remains uncertain. It was first played extensively in Mexico and Texas. Rhum or rhummy first appeared in 1905, although the game is not recorded as gin rummy much before 1940 when it became popular among the film stars of Hollywood. The so-called 'Hollywood method' of scoring can accommodate three games being played simultaneously.

The building brick toy Lego was first marketed by Ole Kirk Christiansen (Den) (1891–1958) in 1932. His son Godtfred (1920–95) patented the standard 8-stud bricks that are sold in 120 countries. These giant pieces can be seen at the Legoland theme park in Billund, Denmark.

RECORD CATCHES OF SALTWATER FISH

Species	lb	kg	Location	Date	Caught by
Barracuda, Great	85lb	38.56	Christmas Is., Kiribati	11 Apr 1992	John W. Helfrich
Cod, Atlantic	98lb 12oz	44.79	Isle of Shoals, New Hampshire	8 June 1969	A. J. Bielevich
Halibut, Atlantic	335lb 6oz	152.13	Valevag, Norway	20 Oct 1997	O.A. Gunderstad
Marlin, Atlantic blue	1402lb 2oz	636	Vitoria, Brazil	29 Feb 1992	Paulo Amorim
Sailfish, Pacific	221lb	100.22	Santa Cruz Is., Ecuador	12 Feb 1957	C. W. Stewart
Shark, White	2664lb	1199.3	Ceduna, South Australia	21 Apr 1959	Alfred Dean
Swordfish	1182lb	536	Iquique, Chile	7 May 1953	L. Marron

RECORD CATCHES OF FRESHWATER FISH

Species	lb	kg	Location	Date	Caught by
Carp, common	82lb 3oz	37.28	Lake Roduta, Romania	26 May 1997	C. Baldemair
Salmon, Atlantic	79lb 2oz	35.89	Tana River, Norway	1928	Henrik Henriksen
Salmon, chinook	97lb 4oz	44.11	Kenai River, Alaska	17 May 1985	Les Anderson
Sturgeon, white	468lb	212.28	Benicia, California	9 July 1983	Joey Pallotta
Trout, lake	72lb	32.65	Great Bear Lake, Canada	10 Aug 1995	Lloyd Bull
Trout, rainbow	42lb 2oz	19.11	Bell Island, Alaska	22 June 1970	David R. White

The board game Mah Jong first became popular in China in 1900 and enjoyed a great vogue in Western Europe in the 1930s. It is played with a set of 136 tiles, 128 counters and two dice.

Poker was originally played by two players with a 20-card pack, but was later adapted to the commonly used 52-card pack – partly to accommodate more players. The game's mounting tension attracts both high-stakes gamblers and screenwriters, and it has been the centrepiece of many a tense scene in a Hollywood western.

The board game known as **Go** or **I-go** in Japan, **Wei-chi** in China and **Pa-tok** in Korea is regarded by many as the greatest intellectual game. It originated in China c.1500BC.

The leading exponents are Japanese and professional games can last as long as three days. The board is marked with a grid of 19x19 lines, forming 361 points. Each player has a bowl containing disk-shaped stones – 181 black and 180 white, with the weaker player having the black stones and playing first. The object is to surround and capture the opponent's pieces.

Jig-saw puzzles are so called because the first puzzles were cut from wood using a saw. In France an entrepreneur named Dumas began cutting up maps and selling them as an educational toy in 1762. A year later, one John Spilsbury of London was listed as an 'Engraver and Map Dissector in Wood, in order to facilitate the teaching of geography'. He mounted maps on a thin layer of mahogany and cut them up along the county borders. About 25 years later William Darton (GB) began producing puzzles with portraits of every monarch since William the Conqueror (c.1027–87), which proved to be very popular. **Fully interlocking puzzles** were not introduced until c.1900.

The board game **ludo**, or pachisi, has been called the national game of India. Originally cowrie shells were used instead of dice; the number of spaces moved depended on the number of shell mouths facing upward.

The Mughal Emperors of the 16th–17th centuries laid out courtyards in their palaces as pachisi boards. Brightly attired harem girls moved about the board in response to the throws of the players gathered on a central platform. The game was patented and marketed in the West under the names 'Ludo' and 'Parcheesi'.

Meccano was invented by Frank Hornby (Eng) (1863–1936) of Liverpool. It consisted of metal strips with holes at half-inch intervals, with nuts, screws, rods, wheels and so on for building models and was first patented in 1901, Meccano Ltd being registered in 1908. It became widely used by designers and engineers and scientists for mechanical research. Meccano Ltd also began the manufacture of **Hornby model trains** in 1920 and **Dinky Toys** in 1933.

The board game **Monopoly** was created, developed and patented by Lizzie J. Magie in 1904 as 'The Landlord's Game'. The idea was adapted by Charles Darrow, an unemployed heating engineer, of Germantown, Pennsylvania, in 1934 and launched nationally in the USA as Monopoly in 1935. Although the rules were originally thought to be too complicated to sell well, more than 200 million sets have been sold worldwide.

Patience, or solitaire, is the earliest recorded solo-player card game, with a first reference in 1783. The oldest known compendium of patience games was published in Moscow in 1826 but did not reach England until the second half of the 19th century.

Plasticine was invented in 1897 by William Harbutt (1844–1921), an art teacher from Bath, southern England. He made it for his students as a substitute for clay, which they found more difficult to use.

The **pogo stick** – a pole with a strong spring at the bottom and a raised step on each side – was invented either by a French explorer, who returned to Paris in 1919 with sketches of a stick used by the Dayaks of Borneo in their sacrificial dances, or by George Hansbury (US), who patented it in 1919. It was a craze in Paris in the early 1920s and a few years later spread to the USA.

In 1971 a gas-powered pogo stick was introduced, followed a year later by a battery-powered model, complete with spark plug, carburettor, piston and dual exhausts; it was abandoned in 1975.

The card game **poker** originated in the gambling saloons of New Orleans, Louisiana. The first mention was in 1836 in *Dragoon Campaigns to the Rocky Mountains*. Earlier Englishman Edmund Hoyle (1672–1769) had made reference to a similar game in his compendium of card games.

Quoits – a game in which players try to toss rings (of iron, weighing about 3lb *1.3kg*, rope or rubber) over a stake called the hob – may have been devised by Roman soldiers of the 2nd century AD. Quoits was played in mediaeval times in England when horseshoes were sometimes used instead of the traditional rings.

The **Rubik Cube** puzzle was invented by Erno Rubik (Hungary) (*b*.1944). It consists of a single cube made up of 26 other cubes, in six colours, all of which rotate on vertical and horizontal axes, the aim being to twist the cubes so that the six small cubes on each side form a single block of colour. The lowest number of moves that are needed to unscramble a cube is 22, but the puzzle is capable of being arranged in 43,252,003,274,489,856,000 ways. Rubik used the cube as a tool for teaching algebra to a class at the Budapest Academy of Applied Arts. During a three-year craze in the early 1980s, 150 million were sold.

The word game **Scrabble** was invented by Alfred Mosher Butts (1900–93) of Rhinebeck, New York, in 1931 and originally called 'Criss-Cross'. He estimated the values of the letters by counting the number of times they were used on a single front page of the *New York Times*. It was first sold as 'Lexico' in 1946.

Originally made in Butts's garage in Danbury, Connecticut, the game was mass-produced by Selchow and Righter in 1948, who changed the named to Scrabble. By the time of Butts's death in 1993 over 100 million sets had been sold worldwide. The first Scrabble world championships were held on 30 September 1991 and were won by Peter Morris (US) with a score of 371.

Shuffleboard – or shovelboard, and originally shoveboard – is a game in which disks are shoved by hand or with an implement, so that they come to a stop within a scoring area marked on the board or 'court'. It was first popular with the aristocracy in England in the 15th century. Shove-ha'penny, a later version of shovelboard, is still popular in some English pubs.

Shuffleboard was introduced to the USA *c*.1913.

Snooker was invented by Colonel Sir Neville Chamberlain (1856–1944) in 1875 in the Ootacamund Club, Madras, India. The term 'snooker' was contemporary military slang which referred to a first-year military cadet and reflected his lowly status. It was also used to indicate that someone was playing poorly or of a player who was left unable to hit the target ball by his opponent.

Snooker's ancestor was **billiards**. The first billiard table was built for France's King Louis XI (1423–83) by Henri de Vigne. The first treatise on the game was by Clément Marot (Fr) *c*.1550. Another forerunner of snooker was **pool**, so called because the players pay forfeits into a betting pool.

The **Yo-Yo** is the proprietary name for a toy registered by Donald F. Duncan (US) (1899–1971) in 1929. It is possible that the first examples were used in Ancient Greece since Greek vases show youths playing with spinning discs; however, these could be the forerunner of the frisbee.

The future English King George IV is known to have played with a Yo-Yo (then called a bandalore) in 1791. Heavy wooden Yo-Yos were used in the Philippines as hunting tools. **Yo-Yo mania** gripped depression America in the mid-1930s, largely due to William Randolph Hearst (US) (1863–1951), who promoted the toy in his newspapers and sold over 3 million yo-yos in one month in Pennsylvania alone. Yo-Yos were once again the subject of a renewed craze in 1998–99.

Roulette players place chips to lay bets on which red or black numbered compartment of a revolving wheel will receive a small ball (which is spun in the opposite direction). The odds vary according to whether the bet is on a single number, a range of numbers or one of the colours.

Index of People

A

Aaron, 'Hank' 259
Abraham 41
Abrahams, Harold 252, 253
Abruzzo, Ben L. 176
Achard, Franz Karl 30
Adams, Ansel 223
Ader, Clément 230
Aeschylus 35
Agassi, Andre 275
Agricola, Gnaeus Julius 15
Akihito, emperor of Japan 129
Albee, Edward 69
Alcock, John 178
Aldrin, Edwin Eugene 181
Alexander, 'the Great', king of
    Macedonia 42, 198, 207
Alexanderson, Dr Ernest 239
Alfonso X, king of Spain 90
Alhazen 113, 221
Al-Jazari 94
Al-Khwarizmi, Muhammad
    ibn Musa 83
Alvarez, Luis 60
Ammianus Marcellinus 15
Ampére, André Marie 149
Amundsen, Roald 187
Anaximander 82
Anderson, Carl D. 96
Anderson, Elizabeth Garrett
    39
Anne, queen of England 38
Anschütz-Kaempfe, Franz 164
Antipater 146
Antonius, Marcus (Mark
    Antony) 206
Aquinas, St Thomas 43
Appel, Kenneth 86
Arbeau, Thoinot 70
Archer, Frederick Scott 222
Archer, Jeffrey 219
Archerau, Dr Henri 27
Archilocus of Paros 67
Archimedes 94
Archytas of Tarentum 94, 104
Arcolani, Giovanni 114
Arezzo, Guido d' 64
Aristarchus of Samos 90
Aristotle 38, 42, 188
Arlandes, Marquis d' 176
Armstrong, Edwin H. 237
Armstrong, Louis 66
Armstrong, Neil 153, 181
Arrhenius, Svante August 100
Artaud, Antonin 69
Ascham, Roger 38
Ash, Claudius 114-15
Ashton, Frederick 71
Ashurnasipal II 12, 13
Aspdin, Joseph 138-9
Atahualpa, emperor of the
    Incas 128
Atanasoff, John Vincent 244
Atatürk, Kemal 124
Aubriet, Claude 29
Augustus, emperor of Rome
    14, 206, 214
Augustus, Romulus, 16
Aurillac, Gerbert d' 88
Avdeyev, Sergei 182
Avicenna 16, 94, 110
Avogadro, Amedeo 99

B

Babbage, Charles 243, 244
Bach, Johann Sebastian 66
Bacon, Roger 98, 104
Backus, John 245
Baekeland, Leo Hendrik 100,
    223
Bailey, Donovan 253
Baird, John Logie 239, 240
Bakunin, Mikhail 124
Balanchine, George 71
Ballard, Robert 105
Ballesteros, Severiano 266
Banchieri, Adriano 66
Band, George 271
Bannister, Roger 252
Banting, Frederick Grant 101
Barbaro, Daniele 221
Bardeen, John 237, 245
Barents, Willem 186
Barnack, Oskar 224
Barnard, Christiaan 111
Barnardo, Thomas John 39
Basil II, Emperor 16
Beardsley, Aubrey 78
Beaufort, Sir Francis 56
Beavan, Brian 273
Becker, Boris 274-5
Beckett, Samuel 69
Becquerel, Antoine Henri 54,
    100, 154, 239
Bednorz, Johannes Georg 150
Bégon, Michel 29
Behm, Alexander 164
Bell, Alexander Graham 217,
    230
Bell, Rev. Patrick 30
Bellinger, E. C. 30
Benedict, St 109
Benz, Karl 171
Berlin, Irving 233
Berliner, Emile 230
Berners-Lee, Tim 247
Bernhardt, Sarah 32
Bertillon, Alphonse 44
Bertolucci, Bernardo 229
Best, Charles H. 101
Best, Daniel 30
Bevan, Aneurin 117
Bickford, William 194
Biggs, Henry 243
Bird, Larry Joe 260
Blériot, Louis 178
Bloch, Felix 150
Block, H.S. 237
Blumlein, Alan 231
Bodley, George 24
Bohr, Niels 96, 154, 156
Boland, John 275
Bolden, Charles Joseph
    'Buddy' 66
Boleyn , Anne 37
Boole, George 84, 85, 216, 243
Boot, John 49
Border, Allan 262
Borg, Björn 274
Botham, Ian 262
Boudicca 15
Bougainville, Louis de 29
Boulez, Pierre 66
Boyce, Joseph 30
Boyle, Robert 98, 99
Bradman, Don 262
Braid, James 266

C

Brancusi, Constantin 75
Brand, Hennig 27
Brandling, Charles 167
Branson, Richard 176
Brattain, Walter H. 245
Braun, Wernher von 180
Bréguet, Louis 178
Brendan, St 183
Brezhnev, Leonid 205
Broughton, John (Jack) 261
Brown, Joe 271
Bruce, James 185
Brueghel, Pieter, the Elder 32
Brunel, Isambard Kingdom
    161
Brunel, Mark 143
Brunelleschi, Filippo 73, 137
Buddha, Prince Gautama
    Siddhartha 13, 42
Buñuel, Luis 229
Burbage, James 67
Burke, Thomas 256
Burnell, Dr Jocelyn Bell 93
Burton, Charles 185
Burton, Richard (actor) 228
Burton, Richard (explorer)
    186
Bush, Vannevar 244
Butts, Alfred Mosher 281
Byrd, Richard 187

C

Cabot, John 186-7
Cabral, Pedro Alvares 129
Caesar, Julius 44, 59, 86, 87,
    126
Cage, John 66, 71
Calment, Jeanne Louise 110
Calvin, John 42
Camargo, Maria Anna de 70
Campese, David 272
Cantor, Georg 85, 86
Cão, Diogo 183
Capek, Karel 104
Caro, Heinrich 100-1
Carothers, Wallace H. 33, 35
Carrel, Alexis 110
Carreras, José 233
Carroll, Lewis 39
Carter, Jimmy, 205
Cartwright, Alexander Joy 259
Caruso, Enrico 230, 233, 238
Cassady, 'Hopalong' Howard
    265
Cassini, Giovanni 189
Catherine II, 'the Great',
    empress of Russia 34, 129
Catherine of Aragon 37
Catherine of Medici 70
Cattley, William 29
Caxton, William 218
Cayley, Sir George 177
Cernan, Cdr 19
Chadwick, Edwin 39, 117, 120
Chadwick, James 155
Chain, Ernst 117
Chamberlain, Sir Neville 281
Chamberlain, Wilt 260
Chaplin, Charlie 227
Chares of Lindus 147
Charlemagne, Holy Roman
    Emperor 38, 123, 127, 199
Charles I, king of England 123
Charles II, king of England
    160

C (cont.)

Charles, Jacques 95, 176
Chersiphron 142
Chevalier, Jacques 222
Chichester, Francis 185
Chionis 19
Chippendale, Thomas 76
Christian, Charlie 234
Christiansen, Ole Kirk 279
Christo (Christo Javacheff) 75
Churchill, Winston 208
Clark, William 29
Clarke, Sir Arthur C. 237
Claude, Georges 28
Clegg, Samuel 27
Cleisthenes 122
Cleopatra, queen of Egypt 207
Cobb, 'Ty' 259
Cochran, Josephine G. 25
Cockerel, Christopher 162
Coe, Sebastian 253
Cohen, Paul 86
Collins, Francis S. 112
Collinson, John 278
Colt, Samuel 194
Columbus, Christopher 128,
    133, 184
Colvin, L. O. 30
Confucius 13, 14
Connolly, Maureen 275
Constantine XI, emperor of
    Byzantium 127
Cook, James 185, 187, 189
Cook, Thomas 49
Cooke, James 30
Cooke, William Fothergill 216
Coolidge, William D. 28
Coombes, Alan W. M. 244
Cooper-Hewitt, Peter 28
Copernicus, Nicolaus 90
Copland, Aaron 71
Coriolus, Gustave-Gaspard
    180
Correggio, Antonio 79
Cortés, Hernando 206-7
Cotton, Henry 266
Coubertin, Pierre de Fredi,
    Baron 256
Courbet, Gustave 73
Cram, Steve 252
Cray, Seymour 246
Crick, Francis 101
Croesus, king of Lydia 44
Cros, Charles 223
Crosby, Bing 234
Crosskill, William 30
Cugnot, Nicolas-Joseph 171
Cunningham, Merce 71
Curie, Marie and Pierre 100,
    150, 154
Cuvier, Baron Georges 60
Cyril, St 214
Cyrus II, king of Persia 126

D

Daguerre, Louis 222
Dahl, Anders 29
Daimler, Gottlieb 171
Dalén, Nils Gustav 25
Dallmeyer, Thomas 223
Dalton, John 99
Damadian, Raymond 112
Darius I, king of Persia 126,
    146
Darlington, Sydney 245
Darrow, Charles 280

D (cont.)

Darton, William 280
Darwin, Charles 60
Davenport, Lindsay 275
David, king of Israel 12, 41
Davidson, Robert 168
Da Vinci, Leonardo 73, 79,
    177, 216, 221
Davy, Humphrey 109, 149
Davys, John 163
Dawkins, Pete 265
De Coriolis, Gustave-Gaspard
    56
De La Rue, Warren 27, 223
De Mille, Cecil B. 227
Deere, John 31
Degas, Edgar 74
Deleuil, L. J. 27
Demling, Ludwig 112
Dempsey, Jack 261
Deringer, Henry 197
Desaguliers, John 95
Descartes, René 43, 84
Desgranges, Henri 250
Devol, George C. 105
Diaghilev, Sergei 70
Diaz, Bartolomeu 184
Dickens, Charles 219
Dickson, William 226
Dines, William Henry 56
Diodorus Siculus 146, 147
Dionysius Exiguus 88
Diophantus of Alexandria 83
Dixon, Jeremiah 189
Disney, Walt 228
Dogg, Snoop Doggy 235
Dolby, Ray Milton 231
Domingo, Placido 233
Donatello 75
Doppler, Christian Johann 92
Doubleday, Abner 259
Douglas, David 29
Dowson, Thomas A. 40
Drake, Sir Francis 185
Draper, John William 222
Drebbel, Cornelis Jacobszoon
    van 160-1
Drummond, Thomas 69
Dubouchet, Karine 258
Dummer, Geoffrey Arnold
    245
Dunant, Henri 117
Duncan, Donald F. 281
Dunlop, John Boyd 170
Duryea, Charles & Frank 171

E

Eames, Charles & Ray 77, 78
Eastman, George 223, 225
Ebrington, Frank 174
Eccles, William Henry 243
Eckert, J. Presper 244
Edison, Thomas 27, 230
Edward III, king of England
    48
Edwards, Robert 111
Eiffel, Alexandre Gustave 137
Einstein, Albert 95, 96, 154,
    204, 228
Eisenhower, Dwight David,
    president of the USA 237
Eisenstein, Sergei 228
Eisler, Paul 150
Elizabeth I, queen of England
    128, 129, 200
Ellis, William Webb 251, 272

E (cont.)

Engelbardt, Douglas 245
Engelberger, Joseph F. 105
Engels, Friedrich 124
Erasmus, Desiderius 43
Eratosthenes 188
Ericsson, John 129
Ericsson, Leif 133, 160, 183
Erik the Red 183
Eristratus of Alexandria 114
Escalongen, Ernest 89
Escobar, Andres 264
Espitallier, Georges 137
Euclid 82-3
Euler, Leonhard 84
Eupalinos 142
Euripides 67
Evans, Sir Arthur 133
Everest, George 189, 271
Eyck, Jan van 7965

F

Fabergé, Peter Carl 77, 104
Fabre, Henri 178
Fahrenheit, Gabriel Daniel 56
Fairbanks, Douglas 227-8
Faraday, Michael 95, 149
Farina, Giuseppe 269
Farnsworth, Philo Taylor 240
Fassbinder, Rainer Werner
    229
Fauchard, Pierre 114
Fedida, Samuel 241
Fermat, Pierre de 84, 85, 86
Fermi, Enrico 155, 204
Fessenden, Professor
    Reginald 237
Fibonacci, Leonardo 84
Fick, A. E. 113
Fielding, Henry 44
Fiennes, Sir Ranulph 185, 187
Finlay, James 142
Fisher, Scott 246
Flack, Edwin 253
Fleischer, Max 226
Fleischmann, Martin 97
Fleming, Alexander 117
Fleming, Sir Ambrose 236
Flinders, Matthew 164
Florey, Howard 117
Flowers, Thomas Harold 244
Floyd, Raymond 267
Ford, Henry 172
Forest, Lee de 236, 237, 243
Forlanini, Enrico 161
Forsyth, William 29
Fortnum, William 49
Fosberry, G. V. 195
Foyt Jr, A. J. 270
Franklin, Benjamin 24, 56, 77,
    113, 148
Franklin, Charles Samuel
    236-7
Frederick II, 'the Great', king
    of Prussia 200
Freeman, Dr Leslie G. 40
Friedman, Aleksandr 88
Frisch, Otto 204
Frobisher, Martin 187
Frontinus, Sextus Julius 115
Fuchs, Klaus 205
Fuchs, Leonard 29
Fujita, Dr T. Theodore 56
Fulton, Robert 161
Furth, Harold 97

ABBREVIATIONS

The following abbreviations
have been used in this book:
b. born
BC before christ
BP before the present
c. circa
cm centimetre (0.394 in)
cu cubic
fl. floruit (Latin, he or she
    flourished) active
FRS Fellow of the Royal
    Society
ft foot (0.3048 m)
in inch (2.54 cm)

kg kilogram (2.2046 lb)
km kilometre (0.6214 miles)
km/h kilometres per hour
kW kilowatt
Lat. Latin
lat latitude
long longitude
lb pound (0.4536 kg)
m metre (3.281 ft)
mph miles per hour
mW megawatt
r. reigned
sq square
St saint

COUNTRY ABBREVIATIONS

Alg Algeria
Arg Argentina
Aus Austria
Aust Australia
Belg Belgium
Bul Bulgaria
Can Canada
Croat Croatia
Cz Czechoslovakia, Czech
    republic
Den Denmark

Eng England
Eth Ethiopia
Fin Finland
Flan Flanders
Fr France
GB Great Britain
Ger Germany
Gk Greece, Greek
Hun Hungary
Ire Ireland
It Italy

Jap Japan
Ken Kenya
Neths Netherlands
NZ New Zealand
Pol Poland
Prus Prussia
Rus Russia
S Afr South Africa
Scot Scotland
Sp Spain
Swe Sweden

Switz Switzerland
Tanz Tanzania
Tur Turkey
UK United Kingdom
US United States
USSR Union of Soviet
    Socialist Republics
    (1922-91)
W Ger West Germany
    (1945-90)

General Index

Acknowledgments

Picture Credits

These picture credits refer to
images in the main body of
the text only. Page position is
indicated by the abbreviations
t (top), b (bottom), c (centre),
l (left), and r (right).

All pictures were supplied by
Corbis UK Ltd, except for the
following:

025t Kenwood Limited
055   Guildhall Library,
      Corporation of
      London/Bridgeman
      Art Library
058   Themba Hadebe/
      Associated Press
059br Tim Zielenbach/

      Associated Press
059t NASA - Terra Project
082   Science Photo Library
085   Science Photo Library
086   National Museum of
      Archaeology,
      Naples/AKG - London
087   Bridgeman Art Library
088   SOAS, London/
      Bridgeman Art Library
089c Alexander Tsiaras/
      Science Photo Library
090   Space telescope
      Science Institute/
      Science Photo Library
093   NASA/Zooid Pictures
097t Philippe Plially/
      Eurelios/Science Photo
      Library
097b David Parker/Science
      Photo Library

100t Science Photo Library
104   Honda UK
108t Georges Gobet/
      Associated Press
112r Alfred Pasieka/Science
      Photo Library
113r John Greim/Science
      Photo Library
129   Illustrated London
      News
130t Peter Menzel/Science
      Photo Library
148t Science Photo Library
155b Science Photo Library
176t Rex Features
176b AKG - London
181b NASA/Zooid Pictures
188l British Museum/
      Bridgeman Art Library
198l AKG - London
198   AKG - London

199   AKG - London
200   AKG - London
201t Rex Features
201c Rex Features
220   Rex Features
228t Ronald Grant Archive
235t Michael Ochs
      Archives/Redferns
      Music Picture Library
235b Chi Modu/Redferns
      Music Picture Library
246b Gregory Sams/Science
      Photo Library
247   Adam Nadel/
      Associated Press
248   Tony Duffy/Allsport
      (UK) Ltd.
252t Hulton Deutsch/
      Allsport (UK) Ltd.
254l Clive Mason/Allsport
      (UK) Ltd.

255   Mike Powell/Allsport
      (UK) Ltd.
256t Hulton Getty /Allsport
      (UK) Ltd.
256b Allsport (UK) Ltd.
259   Hulton Deutsch/
      Allsport (UK) Ltd.
261t Hulton Getty/Allsport
      (UK) Ltd.
261b Hulton Deutsch/
      Allsport (UK) Ltd.
262   Ben Radford/Allsport
      (UK) Ltd.
263t Hulton Getty/Allsport
      (UK) Ltd.
263b Mike Hewitt/Allsport
      (UK) Ltd.
264   Steve Powell/Allsport
      (UK) Ltd.
265   Allsport (UK) Ltd.
266t Hulton Getty/Allsport

      (UK) Ltd.
266b David Cannon/
      Allsport (UK) Ltd.
268b Hall of Fame of the
      Trotter, New York,
      USA/Bridgeman Art
      Library
272   Simon Bruty/Allsport
      (UK) Ltd.
274   Tony Duffy/Allsport
      (UK) Ltd.
275   Allsport (UK) Ltd.
277   Kos Picture Source

The 25 Civilisations listed on
page 132 are based on the
work of Professor Arnold
Toynbee.